Introducing Maya® 8: 3D for Beginners

Introducing Maya® 8: 3D for Beginners

DARIUSH DERAKHSHANI

WILEY PUBLISHING, INC.

Acquisitions and Development Editor: Mariann Barsolo
Technical Editor: Keith Reicher
Production Editor: Martine Dardignac
Copy Editor: Judy Flynn
Production Manager: Tim Tate
Vice President and Executive Group Publisher: Richard Swadley
Vice President and Executive Publisher: Joseph B. Wikert
Vice President and Publisher: Dan Brodnitz
Media Development Specialist: Angie Denny
Book Designer: Caryl Gorska
Compositor: Chris Gillespie, Happenstance Type-O-Rama
Proofreader: Nancy Riddiough
Indexer: Ted Laux
Cover Designer: Ryan Sneed
Cover Image: Dariush Derakhshani, Juan Guitierrez, Robert Jauregui, Huyen Dang, and Yoom Thawilvejakul

Dear Reader,

Thank you for choosing *Introducing Maya 8: 3D for Beginners*. This book is part of a family of premium-quality Sybex graphics books, all written by outstanding authors who combine practical experience with a gift for teaching.

Sybex was founded in 1976. Thirty years later, we're still committed to producing consistently exceptional books. With each of our graphics titles we're working hard to set a new standard for the industry. From the the writers and professional artists we work with to the paper we print on, our goal is to bring you the best graphics books available.

I hope you see all that reflected in these pages. I'd be very interested to hear your comments and get your feedback on how we're doing. To let us know what you think about this or any other Sybex book, please send me an email at: sybex_publisher@wiley.com. Please also visit us at www.sybex.com to learn more about the rest of our growing graphics line.

Best regards,

Dan Brodnitz
Vice President and Publisher
Sybex, an Imprint of Wiley

Acknowledgments

As this book goes essentially into its fourth edition, I am thrilled that *Introducing Maya 8: 3D for Beginners* is finding a growing audience. I have always thought that education is the foundation for a happy life, and with that in mind I'd like to thank the outstanding teachers from whom I have had the privilege to learn. It's ultimately important to remember those who have taught you. And of course I want to thank my students, who have taught me as much as they have learned themselves. Juan Gutierrez, Victor J. Garza, Robert Jauregui, and Peter Gend deserve special thanks for helping me complete the models and images for this book.

Thanks to the student artists who contributed to the color insert; of course, thanks to my bosses, colleagues, and friends at work for showing me everything I've learned and making it interesting to be in the effects business; and thanks to Dell for their support and keeping me on the cutting edge of workstations. Thanks kindly to my editors at Wiley and Autodesk for their support and help and for making this process fun. (Mariann, Willem, and Martine: I'm looking in your direction.) And thanks to Danielle Lamothe, Carla Sharkey, and Michael Stamler at Autodesk. My appreciation goes also to an awesome technical editor, Keith Reicher. And special mad single hand blackjack props to my friends Bill, Mark, Frank, Terry, and Brett.

Thank you to my mom and brothers. Thank you for your strength, wisdom, and love throughout.

And a special thank you to my lovely wife, Randi, for putting up with the long nights at the keyboard; the grumpy, sleep-deprived mornings; and the blinking and buzzing of all my machines in our apartment. A better woman is pure fiction.

About the Author

Dariush Derakhshani is a Digital Effects Supervisor, writer, and educator in Los Angeles, California. Previously using Autdoesk's AutoCAD software in his architecture days, Dariush migrated to using 3D programs when his firm's principal architects needed to show their clients design work on the computer. Starting with Alias PowerAnimator version 6 when he enrolled in USC Film School's Animation program, Dariush has been using Alias animation software for the past 11 years. From USC Film School, he received an M.F.A. in Film, Video, and Computer Animation in 1997. Dariush also holds a B.A. in Architecture and Theatre from Lehigh University in Pennsylvania and worked at a New Jersey architecture firm before moving to L.A. for film school. He has worked on feature films, music videos, and countless commercials as a 3D animator, CG supervisor, and sometimes compositor. Dariush also serves as Editor in Chief of *HDRI3d,* a professional CG magazine from DMG Publishing.

CONTENTS AT A GLANCE

Contents

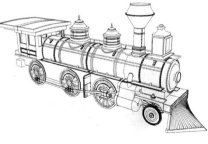

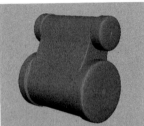

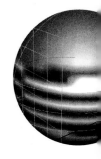

Introduction

Welcome to *Introducing Maya 8: 3D for Beginners* and the world of computer-generated imagery (CGI). Whether you are new to 3D graphics or venturing into Autodesk's powerhouse animation software from another 3D application, you'll find this book a perfect primer. It introduces you to Maya and shows how you can work with Maya to create your art, whether it is animated or static in design.

This book is part of the Maya Press series; a collaboration between Sybex and Autodesk to create books dedicated to teaching artists all over the world how to use Maya.

This book exposes you to all the facets of Maya by introducing and explaining its tools and functions to help you understand how Maya operates. In addition, you'll find hands-on examples and tutorials that give you firsthand experience with the toolsets. Working through these will give you skills as well as knowledge. These tutorials expose you to various ways of accomplishing tasks with this intricate and comprehensive artistic tool.

And, finally, this book explains work flow—not only how specific tasks are accomplished but why—that is, how they fit into the larger process of producing 3D animation. By doing that, these chapters should give you the confidence to venture deeper into Maya's feature set on your own or using any of Maya's other learning tools and books as a guide.

It can be frustrating to learn a powerful tool such as Maya, so it's important to remember to pace yourself. The number one complaint of readers of books like this is a sense that either the pace is too fast or the steps are too complicated or overwhelming. That's a tough nut to crack, to be sure, and no two readers are the same. But what this book offers is a chance to run things at your own pace. The exercises and steps may seem confusing at times, but keep in mind that the more you try, even the more you fail at some attempts, the more you learn how to operate Maya. Experience is key to learning work flows in any software program, and with experience comes failures, and aggravations. But try and try again, and you will see that further attempts will always be easier and more fruitful.

Above all, this book aims to inspire you to use Maya as a creative tool to achieve and explore your own artistic vision.

What You Will Learn from This Book

Introducing Maya 8: 3D for Beginners will show you how Maya works and introduce you to every part of the toolset to give you a glimpse of the possibilities available with Maya.

You'll learn the basic concepts underlying animation and 3D and how to work with the Maya interface. You'll then learn the basic methods of modeling—creating objects and characters that appear to exist in three-dimensional space and that can be animated. You'll also explore shading and texturing, the techniques of applying surfaces to the objects you create, and you'll learn how to create lights and shadows in a scene. Animation is an enormously rich topic, but the practice and theory provided here will give you a solid footing. Then you'll learn how to control the process of rendering, turning your images into files that can be viewed. Perhaps Maya's most dazzling capability is its dynamics engine, software that allows you to make objects behave as if controlled by the real-world laws of physics.

Once you've finished this book and its exercises, you will have some experience in almost everything Maya offers, giving you a solid foundation on which to base the rest of your Maya and CGI experience.

Quite simply, the goal of this book is to get you familiar enough with all the parts of Maya to get you working on your own and to start a long, healthy education in a powerful and flexible tool.

You will, however, have the greatest to learn from yourself.

Who Should Read This Book

Anyone who is curious about learning Maya or who is migrating from another 3D software package can learn something from this book. Even if you are highly experienced in other 3D packages such as Lightwave or XSI, you will find this book helpful in showing you how Maya operates, to start you migrating your existing skill set quickly and efficiently. By being exposed to everything Maya has to offer, you will better understand how you can use its toolset to create or improve on your art and work.

If you already have a cursory or even an intermediate experience with Maya, culled from time spent learning at home, you can fill many holes with the information in this book. Self-education is a powerful tool, and the more you expose yourself to different sources, opinions, and methods, the better educated you will be.

How to Use This Book

Introducing Maya 8: 3D for Beginners approaches the subject in a linear fashion in line with how most animation productions are undertaken. But the book has numerous cross-references to make sure the chapters make sense in any order you might want to tackle them. You may open this book to any chapter and work through the tutorials and examples laid out for the Maya task being covered. Feel free to browse the chapters and jump into anything that strikes your fancy. However, if you are completely new to CG, then perhaps taking the book on chronologically is best.

Although you can learn a lot just by reading the explanations and studying the illustrations, it is best to read this book while you are using Maya 8 (Complete or Unlimited) or Maya Personal Learning Edition so that you can try the exercises for yourself as you read them. This book also includes a CD that contains all the example files and support files you'll need for the tutorials in the text, which is quite valuable as an educational aid. You can use these example files to check the progress of your own work, or you can use them as a starting point if you want to skip ahead within an exercise, which could save the more experienced readers tons of time. You'll also find it valuable to examine these files in depth to see how scenes are set up and how some of the concepts introduced in the book are implemented. Because Maya is a complex, professional software application, the tutorials are both realistically ambitious and simple enough for new users to complete. Take them one step at a time and find your own pace, accepting aggravations and failures as part of the process. Take your time; you're not working on deadline—yet.

How This Book Is Organized

Chapter 1, "Introduction to Computer Graphics and 3D," introduces you to the common computer graphics terms and concepts to give you a basic overview of how CG is facilitated and how Maya relates to the overall process. This chapter explores the basics of CG creation and its core concepts. In addition, it describes the process of CG production and discusses how to establish a commonly used work flow.

Chapter 2, "The Maya Interface," presents the entire Maya interface and shows you how it is used in production. Beginning with a roadmap of the screen, this chapter also explains how Maya defines and organizes objects in a scene.

Chapter 3, "Your First Maya Animation," creates a simple animation to introduce you to Maya work flow and give you a taste of how things work. By animating the planets in our solar system, you will learn basic concepts of creating and animating in Maya and how to use its object structure.

Chapter 4, "Modeling with Polygons," is an introduction to modeling concepts and work flows in general and shows you how to model using polygonal geometry to create various objects, from a human hand to a complex locomotive engine.

Chapter 5, "Modeling with NURBS," will take your lesson in polygonal modeling a step further by showing you how to model with NURBS and patch model by modeling an axe and a part of the locomotive.

Chapter 6, "Further Modeling Topics: Deformers and Subdivision Surfaces," will round out your modeling lessons by showing you how to use lattices to model your objects. In this chapter, you'll learn how to model a starfish and a teakettle using subdivision surfaces.

Chapter 7, "Maya Shading and Texturing," shows how to assign textures and shaders to your models. Using the axe you created in Chapter 5, you'll learn how to texture it to look like a real axe. You'll also learn how to take advantage of Maya 8's ability to work with layered Photoshop files and the basics of working with polygonal UVs.

Chapter 8, "Introduction to Animation," covers the basics of how to animate a bouncing ball using keyframes and moves on to creating more complex animation—throwing an axe and firing a catapult. You will also learn how to import objects into an existing animation and transfer animation from one object to another. In addition, you'll learn how to use the Graph Editor to edit and finesse your animation as well as animate objects along paths.

Chapter 9, "Further Animation Practices," expands on Chapter 8 to show you how to use Maya's skeleton and kinematics system to create a walk cycle. Also covered is how to animate objects by using relationships between them. A thrilling exercise shows you how to rig your locomotive model from Chapter 4 for automated animation, one of Maya's most productive uses.

Chapter 10, "Maya Lighting," begins by showing you how to light a 3D scene and shows you how to use the tools to create and edit Maya lights for illumination, shadows, and special lighting effects. mental ray for Maya's Global Illumination is explored in this chapter as an introduction to some sophisticated techniques for mental ray lighting.

Chapter 11, "Maya Rendering," explains how to create image files from your Maya scene and how to achieve the best look for your animation by using proper cameras and rendering settings. You'll also learn about the Maya renderer, the Vector renderer, and Final Gather using mental ray for Maya, as well as raytracing and motion blur.

Chapter 12, "Maya Dynamics," introduces you to Maya's powerful dynamics animation system. You will animate pool balls colliding with each other using rigid body dynamics, and using particle animation, you will create steam to add to your locomotive scene from Chapter 4. This chapter also introduces you to Maya's amazing Paint Effects module and shows how to use Paint Effects to create animated flowers and grass within minutes.

Hardware and Software Considerations

Because computer hardware is a quickly moving target, and Maya now runs on three distinct operating systems (Windows 2000/XP, Linux, and Mac OS X), specifying which particular hardware components will work with Maya is something of a challenge. Fortunately, Autodesk has a "qualified hardware" page on its website that describes the latest hardware to be qualified to work with Maya for each operating system. Go to this URL:

`http://usa.autodesk.com/adsk/servlet/index?siteID=123112&id=6904894`

Although you can find specific hardware recommendations on these web pages, some general statements can be made about what constitutes a good platform on which to run Maya. First, be sure to get a fast processor; Maya eats through CPU cycles like crazy, so a fast processor is important. Second, you need lots of RAM (memory) to run Maya; 512MB is a minimum, but 1 or even 2GB is a good amount to have, especially if you are working with large scene files. Third, if you expect to interact well with your Maya scenes, a powerful video card is a must; although Maya will putt along with a poor graphics card, screen redraws will be slow with complex scenes, which gets frustrating quickly. You might want to consider a "workstation graphics card" as opposed to a consumer-grade gaming video card for the best compatibility. Several companies make entry-level through top-performing workstation cards to fit any budget. A large hard disk is also important, but most computers these days come with huge drives anyway. Some suggested setups might be as follows (current at the time of writing):

- Windows or Linux
  - AMD Athlon XP 2400+, 2GB RAM, ATI FireGL V5000, 250GB hard disk
  - Intel Pentium 4 3.4GHz, 2GB RAM, nVidia Quadro FX1400, 250GB 7200rpm hard disk
- Mac OS X
  - PowerMac G5 dual 2.3GHz, 1GB RAM, ATI Radeon X850XT, 250GB hard disk, third-party three-button mouse

Fortunately, computer hardware is so fast these days that even laptop computers can now run Maya well. Additionally, even hardware that is not officially supported by Autodesk can often run Maya—just remember that you will not be able to get technical support if your system does not meet their qualifications chart.

The Book's CD

The CD in the back of this book provides all the sample images, movies, and files that you need to work through the projects in *Introducing Maya 8: 3D for Beginners*, as well as Maya Personal Learning Edition.

The CD is organized into project folders. Each folder contains all the scene and support files for that project. The folders are arranged as Maya projects, so you can copy them to your hard drive and then work directly from them.

Maya Personal Learning Edition

If you don't already have a version of Maya, you might want to install the Maya Personal Learning Edition (Maya PLE) software, which you can find on the CD at the back of this book or for download at Autodesk's website. Maya PLE is a special version of Maya that gives you free access to Maya Complete for noncommercial use. Maya PLE works on Windows 2000/XP Professional and Mac OS X.

Contact the Author

You can contact the author at koosh3d.com.

The Next Step

By the time you finish *Introducing Maya 8: 3D for Beginners*, you'll have some solid skills for using Maya. When you're ready to move on to another level, be sure to check out other Maya titles from Sybex at www.sybex.com.

CHAPTER 1

Introduction to Computer Graphics and 3D

This book is to introduce you to the workings of 3D animation (called computer graphics, or CG) with one of the most popular programs on the market, Autodesk's Maya. It will introduce you to a lot of the features and capabilities with the hopes of energizing you to further study. The best way to study for almost anything is to practice, so prepare yourself to go through exercises in this book, but also to think of exercises and projects that can take you further in the learning process. A book or class or video can take you only so far; the rest is up to you. Imagination and exploration will serve you well.

Throughout this book you'll learn how to work with Maya tools and techniques. This chapter will prepare you for the hands-on study that follows by introducing the most important CG concepts and the roles they will play in your Maya work. You'll begin with the most important concept that learning how to work with Maya is a process of learning how you work as an artist. Topics include:

- **Embrace the Art**
- **Computer Graphics**
- **The Stages of Production**
- **The CG Production Work Flow**
- **Core Concepts**
- **Basic Film Concepts**

Embrace the Art

Art, in many instances, requires transcendence of its medium; it speaks of its own accord. Learning to look past what you're working *with* and seeing what you're working *for* is key to learning CG art. So don't view this as learning a software package but as learning a way of working. As you begin learning 3D with Maya, you acquire a new language, a new communication. Keep in mind that the techniques you acquire should remain only a means to the end of expression. In short, relax and enjoy yourself.

Computer tools begin with logic and explicit numbers; your exploration of Maya, however, need not be limited to such a logical path. Your exploration is about learning what *you* can do and not what the *software* can do. Don't make this a lesson in how to make a software program work; make it about how you work with the software.

CG studios hiring professional 3D artists look primarily for a strong artistic sense, whether in a traditional portfolio or a CG reel. It is paramount, then, to fortify the artist in yourself and practice traditional art such as life drawings, photography, painting, sculpture, and so on as you learn CG, beginning with the core principles introduced in this first chapter. Keep in mind that the computer you'll be using for 3D work is nothing more than a tool. You run it; it does not run you.

In the past decade, interest in 3D has surged, partly as a result of the availability of powerful machines with lower costs. Since 3D can be resource intensive on the entire computer system, few machines have been powerful enough all around and accessible enough until relatively recently. Beginning with the late 1990s, production-level equipment has become available to the home market at reasonable prices, helping to spur interest in 3D.

With that emergence of powerful, cheap computing, a lot of artists are adding the language of CG to their skill set. And before embarking on learning a staple tool of CG, it's important to already grasp fundamental issues inherent to CG.

Computer Graphics

CG is simply the abbreviation for computer graphics imagery, also known as CGI. CG refers to any picture or series of pictures that is generated with the aid of a computer. By convention, CG and CGI generally refer to 3D graphics and not to images created using 2D image or paint programs such as Photoshop or Painter. Most 2D graphics software is bitmap based, and all 3D software is vector based. Bitmap software creates an image as a mosaic of pixels, filled in one at a time. Vector software creates an image as a series of mathematical instructions from one calculated or graphed point to another. This much more powerful method for creating graphics is behind all the impressive CG images you've seen—and the ones you'll soon create with Maya. You'll learn more about vectors and bitmaps in the section "Computer Graphics Concepts" later in this chapter.

If you're familiar with 2D graphics software such as Adobe Illustrator or Macromedia Flash, you already know something about vectors. What Maya and other 3D graphics tools add are calculations of depth. Instead of being drawn on a flat plane, objects are defined in three-dimensional space. This makes the artist's job fairly cerebral and very different than it is with 2D art; there is more of a cross chat between the left and right sides of the brain. When working in 3D, you get a better sense of working with and manipulating objects as opposed to working with lines, shapes, and colors used plainly to create images.

A Preview of the 3D Process

The process of creating in 3D requires that you model or shape objects in a scene, give them color and light, and render them through a virtual camera to make an image. In essence, you create a scene that tells the computer what objects are where, what colors and textures they have, what lighting there is, and what camera to use; it's a lot like directing an actual production, but without all the actor tantrums over bottled water.

Instead of a canvas on which to paint or copy and paste images, you have a 3D space—an open area in which you define your objects, set their colors and textures, and position lights as if you were setting up for a real photo shoot. CG is actually remarkably analogous to the art and practice of photography and filmmaking.

Photographers lay out their scene by placing the subjects to form the frame. They light the area for a specific mood and account for the film stock and lens they use and for the colors of the scene. They choose the camera, film, and lenses according to their desired result. They snap a picture, develop the negative, and print it to paper. Through this process, a photo is born.

Once you build your scene in 3D using models, lights, and a camera, the computer *renders* the scene, converting it to a 2D image. Through setup and rendering, CGI is born. And with a little luck, a CG artist is also born.

Rendering is the process of calculating lights and shadows, the placement of textures and colors on models, the movement of animated objects, and so on to give you a sequence of 2D pictures that effectively "shoot" your virtual scene. Instead of an envelope of 4×6 glossy prints, you get a sequence of 2D computer images (or a movie file like a QuickTime or AVI [Audio Video Interleave] file) that sit on your hard drive waiting to be seen, and invariably commented on by your know-it-all friends.

And that, in a nutshell, is the CG process. It requires planning and patience, as CG follows conventions that are so different than those for painting programs and image editors. Its work flow is entirely based in building, arrangement, and relationships. But it is an easy work flow to pick up and eventually master. And it can be done by anyone with the desire and the patience to give it a try.

Fairly soon, you will begin to see CG as a bigger part of the everyday computing environment, as we are seeing with image editors and digital-video editing software now. The more familiar you are with it, whether with Autodesk Maya or another package, the greater your part in the computing future. The day will soon be on us when we can custom-make our own environments for our 3D Windows desktops.

Animation

Although Maya can be used to produce remarkably lifelike 3D still images, most Maya artists also work with a fourth dimension, time. That is, most Maya art is animated. Simply put, *animation is change over time.* A solid foundation in animation involves understanding the simulation of something changing over a period of time. Underlying all animation, from paper flipbooks to film and on to Maya, is the following principle: when we see a series of rapidly changing images, we perceive the changing of the image as continuous motion.

In creating CG animation yourself, you have to create scene files with objects that exhibit some sort of change, whether through movement, color shift, growth, or other behavior. But just as with flipbooks and film animation, the change you are animating occurs between static images, called *frames,* an analogy with film. You define the object's animation using a "timeline" measured in these single frames.

You'll learn more in the section "Basic Animation Concepts" later in this chapter.

The Stages of Production

The CG animation industry has inherited from the film industry a work flow, or pipeline, a way of doing things that consists of three broad stages: preproduction, production, and postproduction. In film, *preproduction* is the process in which the script and storyboards are written, costumes and sets are designed and built, actors are cast and rehearsed, a crew is hired, and the equipment is rented and set up. In the *production* phase, scenes are taped or filmed in the most efficient order. *Postproduction* (simply called "post") describes everything that happens afterward: the scenes are edited into a story; a musical score, sound effects, and additional dialogue are added; special visual effects may also be added. (In a film that has special effects or animation, the actual CG creation is usually completed in post but may have started in the preproduction phases of the film or project itself.)

Although the work performed at each stage is radically different, this is a useful framework for understanding the process of creating CG as well.

Preproduction

Preproduction for a CG animation means gathering all reference materials, motion tests, layout drawings, model sketches, and such together to make the actual CG production as straightforward as possible.

Since the CG artist must define 3D scenes in the program, it is essential to have a suc-
cinct plan of attack for a well-organized production. The more time spent planning and
organizing for CG, the better. Entering into production without a good plan of attack is
not only going to cause you trouble, it will stunt the growth of your project.

In the real world, preproduction is part of every CG animation project. For the tutorial
projects in this book, you'll work with sketches and other files supplied on the accompanying CD as your preproduction. Even for these tutorials, however, you're encouraged to
gather as much information as you can about the objects you'll create, even more than what
is presented to you. As with disappointing movies with terribly flawed preproduction stages,
a poorly thought-out CG production will invariably end in headaches and wasted time.

The Script

To tell a story, CG or not, you need to put it in words. A story need not contain dialogue
for it to benefit from a script. Even abstract animations can benefit from a highly detailed
explanation of timings and colors laid out in a script. The script serves as the initial blueprint for the animation, to lay forth the all-important *intent*. It is then fleshed out.

The Storyboard

A storyboard is a further definition of the script. You break the script into scenes, and
then you break those scenes into shots. You then sketch out each shot on a panel of a storyboard. The panels are laid out in order according to the script to give a visual and linear
explanation of the story. Storyboards are useful for planning camera angles (framing a
shot), position of characters, lighting, mood, and so on. Even rudimentary boards with
stick figures on notebook paper are useful to a production.

The Conceptual Art

Conceptuals are the design elements that are needed for the CG production. Typically, characters are drawn into character sheets in three different neutral poses from the front, from
the side, and from an angle called a 3⁄4 view. Some are even sculpted into clay for better
reference. Color art can also be created of the various sets, props, and characters to better
visualize the colors, textures, and, later on, the lighting that will be needed. Props and sets
are identified from the script and boards and sketched out into model sheets. The better the
conceptual art is visualized, the easier it will be to model, texture, and light everything in CG.

Production

Production begins when you start creating the models from the boards, model sheets, and
concept art. You model the characters, the sets, and the props, and you assign textures
(colors, patterns). The animators take the models and animate everything according to the
boards and script. The sequences are rendered in low quality for dailies and checked for
accuracy and content.

CG production itself has an involved number of steps that are usually defined by the needs of the production. We'll peer into 3D work flow in the next section, but to make a long story short, 3D scenes are created, lit, and animated in the production phase. Most of the CG techniques you'll learn in this book are part of the production phase.

Postproduction

Once all the scenes have been set up with props and characters and everything is animated, postproduction can begin. Postproduction for a CG project is similar to postproduction for a film. This is where all of a CG film's elements are brought together and assembled into final form.

Rendering

All CG scenes need to be rendered to their final image or movie files. Again, this is the process by which the computer calculates how everything in the scene should look and displays it. It is a process that makes great processing demands on your computer, usually requiring the full attention of your PC, and it can take a good amount of time. As you'll learn throughout this book, decisions you make in creating the objects in a scene can make a big difference in how the rest of the process goes.

You can render one scene while another scene is in production, but working on a system that is rendering is not advisable unless you're using a dual-processor machine with plenty of memory. When everything is rendered properly, the final images are sorted and the assembly of the CG project begins. Rendering is the subject of Chapter 11. Three more postproduction activities are advanced topics, beyond the scope of *Introducing Maya*: compositing, editing, and adding sound; you will find a multitude of books on these topics available for further study.

Compositing

Quite often, CG is rendered in different layers and segments and needs to be put back together. In a particular scene, for example, multiple characters interact. Each character is rendered separately from the others and from the backgrounds. They are then all put together in *compositing*, the process of bringing together scene elements that were created separately, to form the final scene. Maya makes this process easier with Render Layers, which you will experience in Chapter 11, "Maya Rendering."

Compositing programs such as Shake and After Effects not only allow you to compose CG elements together, they also give you some additional control over color, timing, and a host of other additions and alterations you can make to the scene. Compositing can greatly affect the look of a CG project; professionals consider it an integral part of CG creation.

One of the biggest problems students new to the CG process have is their need to generate their scene in one fell swoop. It is important to realize the component nature of CG and how you can use that to your advantage in rendering items separately and compositing them together in the finishing stage.

Editing

The rendered and composited CG footage is collected and edited together to conform to the script and boards. Some scenes are cut or moved around to heighten the story. This process is essentially the same as in film editing, with one big difference: the amount of footage.

Live-action filmmakers shoot much more footage than is needed for the film, to make sure they have adequate coverage for all their scenes and to leave extra room for creativity in the editing. The editor and the director sift through all the scenes and arrange them to assemble the film in a way that works best with what they have shot. A typical film uses a small fraction of all film or video that is shot.

Because CG creation and rendering is much more time-consuming and expensive to generate than shooting most live action, scenes and shots are often tightly arranged in preproduction boards so not much is wasted, if any. The entire production is edited with great care beforehand, and the scenes are built and animated to match the story, almost down to the frame. Consequently, the physical editing process consists mostly of assembling the scenes into the sequence of the story.

Sound

Sound design is important to CG. Viewers like to associate visuals with audio. A basic soundtrack can add a significant punch to a simple animation by helping provide realism, mood, narrative, and so on, adding a greater impact of gestalt to the CG.

Sound effects such as footsteps are added to match the action on the screen; this type of sound is also known in film as *foley sound*. Music is scored and added to match the film. Again, this is much the same procedure as in film, with one exception. In the event that a CG project requires dialogue, the dialogue must be recorded and edited *before* CG production can begin. Dialogue becomes a part of the preproduction phase as well as post. This is because animators need to hear the dialogue being spoken to match the lips of the characters speaking, known as *lip-synch*. Quite often, the dialogue or musical score inspires a character's actions or body language as well.

How It All Works Together

The process behind making a *South Park* episode makes for a perfect pipeline example. Although the show appears to be animated using paper cutouts, as was the original Christmas short, the actual production work is now done using Maya. In preproduction on a typical episode, the writers hammer out the script, and the voice talent records all the voices before the art department creates the visuals for the show. The script is storyboarded, and copies are distributed to all the animators and layout artists.

Beginning the production phase, each scene is set up with the proper backgrounds and characters in Maya and then handed off for lip-synch, the first step in the animation of the scene. The voices are digitized into computer files for lip-synch animators who animate the mouths of the characters. The lip-synched animation is then passed to character animators who use the storyboards and also the soundtrack to animate the characters in the Maya scene.

The animation is then rendered to start the post, edited together following the boards, and sent back to the sound department for any sound effects and such to round out the scene. The episode is assembled and then sent off on tape for a broadcast.

The CG Production Work Flow

Because of the nature of CG and how scenes must be built, a certain work flow works best. Modeling almost always begins the process, which then can lead into texturing and then animation (or animation and then texturing). Lighting should follow, with rendering pulling up the rear, as it must. (Of course, the process isn't completely linear; you'll often go back and forth adjusting models, lights, and textures throughout the process.) Chapters 4 through 12 follow this overall sequence, presenting the major Maya operations in the same order you'll use in real-world CG projects.

Modeling

Modeling, the topic of Chapters 4 through 6, is usually the first step in creating CG, and one that garners a lot of coverage in publications and tends to capture the interest of most budding CG artists. You most often start a CG scene by creating the objects you need to occupy your space. It can end up taking the majority of the time in your process.

There are many modeling techniques, and each could be the subject of its own series of books. The choice of which to use usually depends on the modeler's taste and preferred work flow. As you'll see, the choices are among NURBS modeling (Chapter 4), polygon modeling (Chapter 5), and a third method that combines elements of the first two, subdivision surface modeling (Chapter 6).

It helps a great deal in figuring out how to proceed with the modeling to have a good idea of your whole story via a storyboard. Knowing how an object is used in a scene gives you its criteria for modeling. You never want to spend more time on a model than needed. Beginning with a highly detailed model for a far-away shot will waste your time and expand rendering times. If a park bench is to be seen in a wide shot from far away, it does not need abundant detail or complicated surfacing. You can usually create any required details for it by just adding textures. However, a park bench that is featured prominently in a close-up needs as much detail as possible since viewers will see more of the bench. You'll learn more about this aspect of modeling in Chapter 4, but the more you use models in scenes, the better eye you will develop for knowing exactly how much detail to give them. As you begin your CG experience, however, it's a good idea to lavish as much attention on detail as you can. The detailing process will teach you perhaps 70 percent of what you can learn of modeling, which in turn will benefit your overall speed and technique. And with some more experience, you will be able to discern exactly how much detail to add to a scene and not go overboard.

Character Modeling

Character modeling usually involves organic forms such as animals, humans, aliens, and such. Practically anything that will be animated to be a character in a scene can be referred to as a character model. You need to create these with animation techniques in mind, as well as accuracy of form.

Some organic characters (as opposed to robots with mechanical parts and hard edges, for example) are built with patches of surfaces stitched together or as a single object that is stretched and pulled into shape. Character models need to look seamless since most character animation requires the model to deform in some way—to bend and warp at certain areas such as the joints.

A character modeler needs to keep the future of the character in mind to allow for particular character animation methods that will be used. Always try to build your characters with the proper amount of detail appropriate to the scene. Quite frequently, you will create several models for a character to account for different uses of that character and to keep the scene efficient and workable. You might create one character with fine facial detail for the close-up speaking scenes and another with hardly any details for walk cycles in distant shots. Listen to your mother: put only as much as you need on your plate.

Architectural and Environment Modeling

Architectural and environmental modeling includes architectural previsualization for the design of buildings as well as the generation of backgrounds for sets and environments. Typically, it involves modeling buildings or interiors as well as mountains or anything that is required for the scenery, such as benches, chairs, lampposts, and so on.

You should not create incredibly detailed environments if they are not featured in a shot, especially environments that use a lot of geometry. The greater the amount of geometry, the slower your computer will run and the longer rendering will take. You can create a good deal of the environment using clever textures on simple geometry. Detailed maps on bare surfaces are used frequently for game environments. The rule of thumb for all kinds of CG is "use whatever works."

> Since your computer stores everything in the scene as vector math, the term *geometry* refers to all the surfaces and models in a scene.

Props Modeling

Props modeling covers almost everything else needed in the scene. In theater and film terms, a *prop* is an object used by a character in the action; anything relegated to the scenery or background is a *scenic*. For example, a prop can be a purse a character is carrying, a leash on an animated dog, or a car a character is driving. If the car or purse were just sitting in the background, it would be considered a scenic.

Texturing

Once the models are complete, it's a good idea to begin *texturing* and *shading*, the process of applying colors and textures to an object to make it renderable. When you create an object in Maya, for example, a simple gray shader is automatically assigned to it that will let you see the object when you light and render the scene.

Because the textures may look different after animating and lighting the scene, it's wise to leave the final adjustments for later. Just as a painter will pencil in a sketch before adding details, you don't need to make all the shading adjustments right away since you can return to any part of your scene in Maya and adjust it to fine-tune the picture.

You'll learn more about texturing in Chapter 7.

Animation

Although modeling can take the biggest part of a CG artist's time, you can really make or break your scene with its animation.

We all have an innate sense of how things move. Culled from years of perception and observation, we understand how physics applies to things and how people and animals move around. Because of this, viewers tend to be much more critical of CG's motion than of anything else. Put bluntly, you know when something doesn't look right, and so will people watching your animation.

To animate something properly, though, you might need quite a lot of setup beyond just modeling. Depending on the kind of animating you'll be doing, you might need to set up the models for however you'll be animating them. For example, for character animation you will need to create and attach an armature, or skeleton, to manipulate to make the character move, like a puppet, and do your bidding.

Taking the models you've spent hours detailing and reworking and giving them life is thrilling and can make any detailed modeling and setup routine well worth the effort.

Chapters 8 and 9 cover animation techniques in Maya.

Lighting

Lighting can be the most important part of CG. During this step, you set up virtual lights in your scene to illuminate your objects and action. Lighting can drastically alter the look of your scene; it greatly affects the believability of your models and textures and creates and heightens mood.

Although you can set up some initial lights during the texturing of the scene, the serious lighting should be the last thing you do, aside from changes and tweaks.

The type and number of lights you use in a scene greatly affect not just the look of your scene, but also the amount of time the scene takes to render. Lighting becomes a careful dance between pragmatics and results. It is perhaps the subtlest part of CG to master.

Once you gain more experience with lighting, you'll notice it will affect every part of your CG creation. You'll find that you'll start modeling differently—modeling with the final lighting of the scene in mind. Texturing will change when you keep lighting techniques in mind. Even your animation and staging will change a bit to take better advantage of efficient, powerful lighting.

This is because *CG is fundamentally all about light.* Manipulating how light is created and reflected is what you're doing with CG. Without light we would not see anything, so it makes sense that simulating light is the most influential step in CG.

As you'll learn in Chapter 10, virtual lights in Maya are similar to lights used in the real world, from a single point of light such as a bulb to directed beams such as spotlights.

Rendering

At this stage, your computer takes your scene and does all the computations to create raster images for your movie. Rendering time depends on how much geometry is used in the scene, as well as on the number of lights, the size of your textures, and the quality and size of your output. The more efficient your scene, the better the render times.

A lot of people ask how long they should expect their renders to take or how long is too long for a frame to render. It's a subjective question with no answer. Your frames will take as long as they have to take for them to look the way you want. Of course, if you have tight time or budgetary constraints, you want simple scenes to keep the render resources and times to a minimum. But the general rule in production is, you're always out of time, so the most efficient pipeline will be your savior, and eventually your producer or boss will tire of hearing, "But I'm still rendering."

As you learn, use as many lights and as much geometry as you can handle for your scenes. The more experience you pick up, the better your eye will become for efficiency. It's important to understand *how* a scene is put together before you learn to *efficiently* put a scene together.

Core Concepts

3D animation draws from many disciplines. In learning Maya, you'll work with concepts derived not only from computer graphics but also from design, film and cinematography, and traditional animation. Here's a summary of the most important of those concepts as they apply to Maya.

Computer Graphics Concepts

Knowing a bit about the general terminology and methodology of computer graphics will help you understand how Maya works. Let's begin with the crucial distinction between raster (bitmapped) and vector graphics and how this distinction affects you as a Maya user.

Raster Images

Raster images (synonymous with bitmapped images) make up the world of computer images today. These images are displayed through the arrangements of colored pixels on screen or dots on a print to display an image. Everything you create in Maya will eventually be seen as a raster image, even though you create it using vectors.

Raster image programs such as Painter or Photoshop let you adjust existing settings such as color, size, and position for all or part of an image. They let you paint onto a scanned picture or a virtual canvas to adjust or create the pixels yourself. These programs essentially affect pixels directly, giving you the tools to change pixels to form images. For instance, you can use a scanned photo in Photoshop to paint the side of your house red to see what it might look like before you run down to the local paint store.

Recall from the beginning of this chapter that a raster or bitmap image is a mosaic of pixels, each pixel corresponding to a mosaic tile. The *resolution*—fineness of detail—of an image is defined by the number of pixels per inch (or other unit of measure) in the horizontal and vertical directions. Because they are based on a grid of a fixed size, raster images do not scale up well. The closer you get to a raster image, or the larger a raster image is scaled, the bigger the pixels become, making the image look blocky, or *pixelated*. To make large raster images, you need to use a higher resolution to begin with. The higher the resolution, the larger the file size. Figure 1.1 shows what happens when you blow up a raster image.

In light of this limitation, you might wonder why raster images are used. The answer lies in *how* these images are generated. Most common raster displays are television or computer screens. In fact, the term *raster* originally referred to the display area of a television or computer monitor. To form an image, the electronics in these devices essentially paint it as a grid of red, green, and blue pixels on a glowing screen. Every image generated by a computer, therefore, must either begin as a raster image or be rasterized as part of rendering for display.

Vector Images

Vector images are created in a wholly different way. Vector images are created using mathematical algorithms and geometric functions. Instead of defining the color of each and every pixel in a grid of a raster image, a vector image uses coordinates and geometric formulas to plot points that define *areas, volumes,* and *shapes.*

Popular vector-based image applications include Illustrator and Flash, as well as practically all computer-aided design (CAD) programs such as AutoCAD or SolidWorks. These programs let you define shapes and volumes and add color and texture to them through their toolsets.

They store the results in files containing coordinates and equations of points in space and the color values that have been assigned. This vector information is then converted into raster images (called *rasterization*) through rendering so you can view the final image or animation.

Figure 1.1

A raster image at its original size (left) and blown up two to three times (right)

When scaled, vector graphics do not suffer from the same limitations as raster images. As you can see in Figure 1.2, vectors can be scaled with no loss of quality; they will never pixelate.

Motion in vector programs is stored not by a long sequence of image files, but through changes in positions of the geometry and in the math that defines the shapes and volumes. When a Flash cartoon is played on a website, for example, the information downloaded and fed into your computer is in vector form. It contains the position, size, and shapes of all the characters and backgrounds of the animation. Your computer then renders this information on-the-fly, in real time, into a raster display that you can enjoy on your screen.

Figure 1.2

A vector image at its original size (left) and blown up to 200 percent (right)

In Maya, however, you work with vectors that are displayed as wireframes. When you finish your scene, Maya renders the image, converting the vector information into a sequence of raster images.

When a vector file is edited, its geometric information is altered through the tools of the vector program. This allows for easy manipulation and handling of changes and is perfect for design industries in which collaboration and efficiency in changes are a necessity. Only when the editing is finished will the vector file be rendered into a new sequence of raster images by the computer.

Image Output

When you're done with your animation, you'll want as many people as possible to see it; to make that happen, you have to render it out into a file sequence or a movie file. The file can be saved in any number of ways, depending on how you intend it to be viewed.

COLOR DEPTH

An image file stores the color of each pixel as three values, representing red, green, and blue. Image type depends on how much storage is allotted to each pixel (the *color depth*). These are the color depths common to image files in CG production:

Grayscale The image is black and white with varying degrees of gray in between, typically 256. Grayscale images are good for rendering out black-and-white subjects; no extraneous color information is stored in the image file.

16-Bit Color Display or High Color – 5-Bit Image File Each color channel (red, green, blue) gets 5 bits of space to store its value, resulting in an image that can display a maximum of 32,768 colors. Each color channel has a limited range of shades but still gives a nice color image. You might notice the gradation in the different shades of each color that can result in *color banding* in the image.

8-Bit Image File Commonly referred to as 24-bit color display or True Color, each color channel is given 8 bits for a range of 256 shades of each red, green, and blue channel for a total of 16 million colors in the image. This color depth gives the best color quality for an image and is widely used in most animation applications. It is said that the human eye cannot see quite as many shades of color as there are in a True Color image. Most of your renders from Maya will probably be as 24-bit color files.

16-Bit Image File Used primarily in film work using such file types as Cineon format or TIFF16, the image file holds 16 bits of information for each color channel, resulting in an astounding number of color levels and range. Each file can exceed several megabytes even at low resolutions. These files are primarily used in the professional workplace and are standard for film work since outputting CG to film can require high levels of color and brightness range in the image.

COLOR CHANNELS

As mentioned, each image file holds the color information in channels. All color images have a red, green, and blue color channel. Each channel is a measurement of how much red, green, or blue there is in areas of the image. A fourth channel, called the *alpha* channel, is used as a transparency channel. This channel, also know as the matte channel, defines which portions of the image are transparent or opaque. Not all image files have alpha channels. You can read more about alpha channels in Chapter 7.

FILE FORMATS

In addition to image type, several image file formats are available today. The most common perhaps is JPEG (Joint Photographic Experts Group), which is widely used on the Internet.

The main difference between file formats is how the image is stored. Some formats compress the file to reduce file size. However, the greater the compression, the poorer the image's color.

The popular formats to render into from Maya are TIFF (Tagged Image File Format), SGI (Silicon Graphics Inc.), Maya IFF (Maya Image File Format), and Targa. These file formats maintain a good 24-bit color depth using an 8-bit image file, are either uncompressed or hardly compressed (lossless compression), and are frequently used for broadcast or film work. These formats also have an alpha channel, giving you better control when you later composite images together. To see an animation rendered in a file sequence of TIFFs, for example, you must play them back using a frame player such as Fcheck or compile them into a movie file.

Ultimately, your final image format depends on the next step in your project. For example, if you plan to composite your CG, you'll need to output a format that can be imported by your compositing or editing program. TIFF files are perhaps the best format to use as they are widely compatible, store uncompressed color, and have an alpha channel.

MOVIE FILES

Animations can also be output to movie files such as AVI or QuickTime. These usually large files are self-contained and hold all the images necessary for the animation that they play back as frames. Like image files, movie files can be compressed to keep their sizes to a minimum, but they suffer from quality loss as well.

Maya can render directly to an uncompressed AVI movie format, saving you the seeming hassle of having to render out a large sequence of files as TIFFs or such. Although this might seem like a good idea, you shouldn't render directly to a movie file. It is best to render a sequence of files, which can easily be compiled into a movie file later using a program such as After Effects, Premiere, or even QuickTime Pro.

The reason is simple: nothing is perfect, and neither is rendering on your computer. At times, your render will crash or your machine will freeze. In such an event, you need to start your AVI render from the beginning, whereas with TIFFs you can pick up right after the last rendered frame. With a sequence, you also have the option of reordering the frames or easily adjusting a few individual frames' properties such as hue or saturation without affecting the entire movie file.

Color

Color is what we perceive as the differences in the frequency of light. The wide range of colors that we see (the visible spectrum) results when any of three *primary colors* of light—red, green, and blue—are "mixed" together. Color can be mixed in two ways, subtractive and additive. These color definitions are most often displayed in *color wheels*, which place primary colors equally spaced around a ring and place the resultant colors when primaries are mixed in between the appropriate primaries.

Knowing more about color will help you understand how your CG's color scheme will work and help you to design your shots with greater authority. (See the reading list at the end of this chapter for some books that expound on color theory and color's impact on composition.)

SUBTRACTIVE AND ADDITIVE COLOR

Subtractive color mixing is used when the image will be seen with an external light source. It's based on the way reflected light creates color. Light rays bounce off colored surfaces and are tinted by the different pigments on the surface. These pigments absorb and reflect only certain frequencies of the light hitting them, in essence *subtracting* certain colors from the light before it gets to your eyes. Pile up enough different colors of paint and you get black; all the color is absorbed by the pigment and only black is reflected.

With subtractive color mixing for painting, the traditional color wheel's primary colors are *red*, *blue*, and *green*. These three pigments can be mixed together to form any other color pigment. This is the basis for the color wheel most people are exposed to in art education. However, in the world of print production, a CMYK (Cyan, Magenta, Yellow, and blacK) color wheel is used, which places cyan, yellow, and magenta ink colors as the primary colors used to mix all the other ink colors for print work.

Projected light, however, is mixed as *additive color*. Each light's frequency adds upon another's to form color. The additive primary colors are *red*, *green*, and *blue*. These three colors, when mixed in certain ratios, form the entire range of color. When all are equally mixed together, they form a white light.

A computer monitor uses only additive color, mixing each color with amounts of red, green, and blue (RGB). Output for print is converted to a CMYK color model.

Warm colors are those in the magenta to red to yellow range, and *cool colors* are those in the green to cyan to blue range of the additive color wheel. Warm colors seem to advance from the frame, and cool colors seem to recede into the frame.

HOW A COMPUTER DEFINES COLOR

Computers represent all information, including color, as sets of numeric values made up of binary 0s and 1s (bits). In a 24-bit depth RGB color image, each pixel is represented by three 8-bit values corresponding to the red, green, and blue "channels" of the image. An 8-bit binary number can range from 0 to 255, so for each primary color you have 256 possible levels. With three channels you have $256 \times 256 \times 256$ (16.7 million) possible combinations of each primary color mixed to form the final color.

But color value can also be set on the hue, saturation, and value (HSV) channels of a color. Again, each channel holds a value from 0 to 255 (in a 24-bit image) that defines the final color. The hue value defines the actual tint (from red to green to violet) of the color. The saturation defines *how much* of that tint is present in the color. The higher the saturation value, the deeper the color. Finally, value defines the brightness of the color, from black to white. The higher the value, the brighter the color.

HSV and RGB give you different methods to control color, allowing you to use the method you prefer. All the colors available in Maya, from textures to lights, are defined as either RGB or HSV values for the best flexibility. You can switch from HSV to RGB definition in Maya at any time.

CMYK COLOR SPACE

A CMYK color wheel is used for print work, and this is referred to as the four-color process. Color inkjet printers produce color printouts by mixing the appropriate levels of these inks onto the paper.

All output from a computer, which is RGB based, to a printer goes through a CMYK conversion as it's printed. For professional print work, specially calibrated monitors are used to better preview the CMYK color of an RGB image before it is printed. Fortunately, only the print professionals need to worry about this conversion process because most of it is handled by our graphics software to a fairly accurate degree.

VIEWING COLOR

The broadcast standard for North America is called NTSC, as listed in the next section. One joke in the industry is that the acronym means Never The Same Color, referring to the fact that the color you see from one TV screen to another will be different. The same will hold true for computer monitors, especially flat panel displays. It's important to keep this in mind; all displays are calibrated differently, and what you see on one screen may not be exactly what you see on another screen. If it's important that the color matches on different screens, say between home and school, you can use traditional color bars downloaded from the Internet or your own custom-made color chart to adjust the settings of the monitors you work with so they match more closely.

Resolution, Aspect Ratio, Frame Rate

Resolution denotes the size of an image in the number of horizontal and vertical pixels, usually given as # × #, such as 640 × 480. The higher the resolution, the finer the image detail.

You will adjust your final render size to suit the final medium for which you are creating the animation. The following are some standard resolutions:

VGA (Video Graphics Array)	640 × 480	Formerly the standard computing resolution and still a popular television resolution for tape output.
NTSC D1 (National Television System Committee)	720 × 486	The standard resolution for broadcast television in North America.
NTSC DV	720 × 480	Close to the NTSC D1 resolution, this is the typical resolution of digital video cameras.
PAL (Phase Alternation Line)	720 × 586	The standard broadcast resolution for most European countries.
HDTV (High Definition TV)	1920 x 1080	The emerging television standard, sometimes also referred to as 1080i.
1K Academy (1K refers to 1000 pixels across)	1024 × 768	Typically the lowest allowable resolution for film production at Academy ratio. Since film is an optical format (whereas TV is a raster format), there is no real set defined resolution for film. Suffice it to say, the higher the better.
2K Academy (2K refers to 2000 pixels across)	2048 × 1556	Most studios output CG for film at this resolution, which gives the best size-to-performance ratio.
4K Academy (4K is 4000 pixels across)	4094 × 3072	A high resolution for film, used for highly detailed shots.

Any discussion of resolution must include the matter of *aspect ratio*. Aspect ratio is the ratio of the screen's *width* to its *height*, and of course, there are standards:

Academy Standard	1.33:1 or 4:3	The most common aspect ratio. The width is 1.33 times the length of the height. This is the NTSC (National Television Standards Committee) television aspect ratio as well as the aspect ratio of 16 mm films and some 35 mm films, especially classics such as *Gone with the Wind*.
Widescreen (a.k.a. Academy Flat)	1.85:1 or 16:9	The most often used 35 mm film aspect today. When it's displayed on a television, horizontal black bars appear above and below the picture so that the edges are not cropped off (letterbox).
Anamorphic Ratio	2.35:1	Using a lens (called an anamorphic lens), the image captured to 35 mm film is squeezed. When played back with a projector with an anamorphic lens, the image is projected with a width at 2.35 times its height. On a standard TV, the letterboxing would be more severe to avoid cropping the sides.

How many frames are played back per second determines the *frame rate* of the animation. This is denoted as *fps*, or frames per second. The following shows the three standard frame rates for media:

- NTSC: 30fps
- PAL: 25fps
- Film: 24fps

Knowing your output medium is important when beginning an animation project. Though not crucial, it can affect how you design your framing, create your movements, determine how to render, and so on. You can change the frame rate and render resolution at any time in Maya, but it's always better to know as best you can what the final resolution and fps will be before you begin.

Playing back a 24fps animation at 30fps will yield a slower-moving animation and will either necessitate the repetition of some frames to fill in the gaps or end the animation early. Conversely, playing a 30fps animation at 24fps will create a faster-moving animation that will either skip some frames or end later than it should.

3D Coordinate Space and Axes

It is essential with a 3D program to know where you are at all times. You can do so if you understand the toolset you're working with and the 3D space in which you're working. 3D space is merely the virtual area in which you create your models and execute your animation. It is based on the Cartesian coordinate system, a geometric map of sorts developed by René Descartes.

Space is defined in three axes—X, Y, and Z—representing width, height, and depth. The three axes form a numeric grid in which a particular point is defined by its *coordinates* set forth as (#,#,#) corresponding to (X,Y,Z).

At the zero point of these axes is the *origin*. This is at (0,0,0) and is the intersection of all three axes. The 3D space defined by these three axes is called the *World Axis,* in which the XYZ axes are a *fixed reference.* The axis in *World Space* is always fixed and is represented in Maya by the XYZ axis icon in the lower-left corner of the perspective windows.

But since objects can be oriented in all sorts of directions within the World Axis, it's necessary for each object to have its own width, height, and depth axis independent of the World Axis. This is called the *Local Axis.* The Local Axis is the XYZ coordinate space that is attached to every object in Maya. When that object rotates or moves, its Local Axis rotates and moves with it. This is necessary to make animating an object easier as it moves and orients about in the World Axis.

You'll get a hands-on introduction to Maya's Cartesian coordinate space in the tutorial in Chapter 3, where you'll re-create the solar system with the sun placed at the origin, the planets orbiting the World Axis and rotating on their own Local Axes, and moons orbiting the planets and also rotating (see Figure 1.3).

Basic Design Concepts

How you lay out your scene and design your colors is what composition is about. Creating a dynamic frame that not only catches the eye but informs and intrigues is itself an art form.

Some background in basic design is definitely helpful, and you'll want to look at some design books as you further your education in 3D. Understanding the fundamentals of layout and design makes for better-looking scenes and easier setup. The concepts presented here will get you started.

Figure 1.3

The sun at the origin, Earth and other planets orbiting the World Axis and also rotating on their own axes, and the moon orbiting Earth

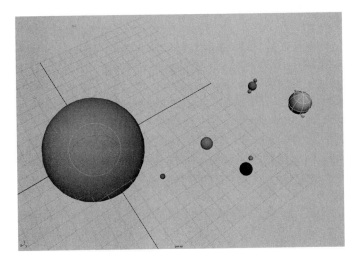

Form, Space, and Composition

Space is defined as your canvas or frame. Since ultimately your canvas will be a rendered image, your design space becomes your image frame. Whether that frame falls into a tiny web window or a huge IMAX screen, the basics of design always apply: how you arrange your forms and divide your space says a lot.

A *form* in design is anything that can be seen; it has some sort of shape, color, or texture that distinguishes it from its frame. Basically any object you model or animate becomes a form in your frame when you render the scene. How these objects lie in the frame defines your composition. The space behind and between what is rendered out is the ground, or background plane. Objects become *positive space*, and the background becomes *negative space*.

To viewers, positive space tends to proceed forward from the frame, while negative space recedes. Playing with the position of positive and negative space greatly affects the dynamics of your frame. Add to that the element of motion and you have a terrific chance to play with your canvas.

Design a static frame in which the objects are all centered and evenly spaced and your viewer will wonder why they're looking at your composition. Arrange the composition so that your subjects occupy more interesting areas of the frame, in which they play with negative space and the eye can travel the frame, and you create a dynamic composition, with or without animation.

In the tutorial in Chapter 10, you'll use light and shadow to make a still life of fruit a dynamic and interestingly composed frame.

Balance and Symmetry

Balance in a frame suggests an even amount of positive space from one side of the frame to the other. A frame that is heavier on one side can create a more dynamic composition.

Symmetrical objects in a frame are mirrored from one side to another and create a certain static balance to the frame. An asymmetrical composition, therefore, denotes movement in the composition.

A popular technique used by painters, photographers, and cinematographers is called *framing in thirds*, in which the frame is divided into a grid of thirds vertically and horizontally. Interesting parts of the frame or focal points of the subjects are placed at strategic locations in the grid. Placing your subject in the lower third would make it seem small or insignificant. Placing it in the upper third would make the viewer look up to it, magnifying its perceived scale or importance. Figure 1.4 illustrates the difference between a static, symmetric frame and a frame based on thirds.

Contrast

Contrast in design describes how much your foreground subject "pops" from the background. As you can see in Figure 1.5, when you create an area in your frame that contains little variation in color and light, the image will seem flat and uneventful. Using dark shadows and light highlights increases the perceived depth in the image and helps pop out the subject from the background. Animating contrast can help increase or decrease the depth of your frame.

As you'll see in Chapter 10, light plays an important role in creating dynamic contrasts within your frame.

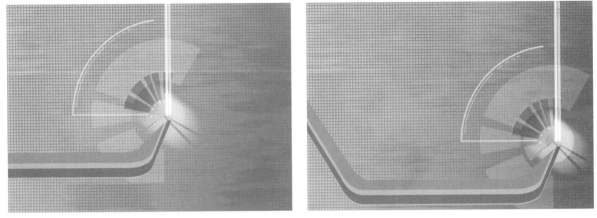

Figure 1.4
A purely symmetric frame looks static, but framing in thirds helps create a sense of motion.

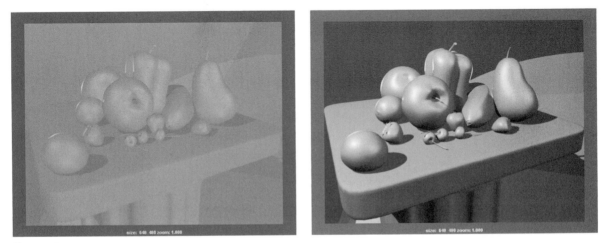

Figure 1.5
With low contrast, the subject seems to disappear into the background. Add shadows and highlights, and the subject will "pop out."

Color

Your use of color also plays a big part in creating impact in your frame. Warm colors tend to come out toward you, and cooler colors recede into the frame. Placing a warm color on a subject on a cool background creates a nice color contrast to help the dynamics of your frame.

Colors opposing each other on the color wheel are *complementary* colors and usually clash when put together. Using complementary colors can create a wide variation of contrast in your scene.

Design theory may not seem specifically pertinent to CG right now, but recognizing that there is indeed a way to quantify design elements of a pretty picture greatly helps the design student progress.

Basic Film Concepts

In addition to the design concepts used in framing a shot, you'll want to understand some other filmmaking concepts.

Planning a Production

Understanding the paradigm filmmakers use for their productions will make it easier to plan, create, and manage your own shorts. Most narrative films are broken into acts, which comprise sequences made up of scenes that are made up of shots.

> A *narrative film* is a film that tells a story of a hero called a *protagonist* and his or her struggle against an *antagonist*.

Narrative films are typically divided into three *acts*. The first act establishes the main characters and the conflict or struggle that will define the story. Act II covers most of the action of the story as the hero attempts to overcome this conflict. Act III concludes the film by resolving the action in the story and tying up all the loose ends.

Acts can be separated into *sequences,* which are groups of sequential scenes that unite around a particular dramatic or narrative point.

A *scene* is a part of a film that takes place in a specific place or time with specific characters to present that part of the story. Films are broken into scenes for organization purposes by their locations (that is, by where or when they take place). Don't confuse the scene in a film with the word *scene* in CG terms, which refers to the elements in the 3D file that make up the CG.

Scenes are then broken into *shots*, which correspond to a particular camera angle, or *framing*. Shots break up the monotony of a scene by giving different views of the scene and its characters. Shots are broken by *cuts* between the shots.

Shots are defined by angle of view, or the POV (point of view) of the camera. Shots change as soon as the camera's view is changed.

CG productions of even the simplest topics can follow this simple organization. By following a similar layout in the scripting and storyboarding of your own short, you will find the entire production process will become easier and the effect of your film stronger.

Lighting

Without lights, you can't capture anything on film. How you light your scene affects the contrast of the frame as well as the color balance and your overall design impact. For the most part, a typical lighting solution called the *three-point system* is the basis from which to at least begin when lighting a scene. This method places a *key* light in front of the scene as the primary illumination and to cast the shadows in the scene. The key light is typically placed behind the camera and off to one side to create a highlight on one side of the object for contrast's sake. The rest of the scene is given a *fill* light. The fill acts to illuminate the rest of the scene but is typically not as bright as the key light. The fill also helps soften harsh shadows from the key light. To pop the subject out from the background, a *back* light is used to illuminate the silhouette of the subject. This is also known as a *rim* light because it creates a slight halo or rim around the subject in the scene. It's a faint light compared with the key or fill lights.

Create lights in your scene that are too flat or even and you can greatly weaken your composition and abate your scene's impact. The more you understand how real lights affect your subjects in photography, the better equipped you will be in CG lighting. Although CG lighting techniques can vary wildly from real life, the desired results are often the same. You'll learn more about Maya lighting techniques in Chapter 10.

Basic Animation Concepts

As mentioned at the beginning of this chapter, animation is the representation of change over time. That's a simple view of an amazing art that has been practiced in one way or another for some time. Although this section cannot cover all of them, here are a few key terms you will come across numerous times on your journey into CG animation.

Frames, Keyframes, In-Betweens

Each drawing of an animation, or in the case of CG, a single rendered image, is called a *frame*. A frame also refers to a unit of time in animation whose exact chronological length depends on how fast the animation will eventually play back (frame rate). For example, at film rate (24fps), a single frame will last 1/24 of a second. At NTSC video rate (30fps), that same frame will last 1/30 of a second.

Keyframes are key frames at which the animator creates a pose for a character (or whatever is being animated). In CG terms, a keyframe is a frame in which a pose, a position, or some other such value has been saved in time. Animation is created when an object travels or changes from one keyframe to another. You will see how creating poses for animation works firsthand in Chapter 9, when you create the poses for a simple walking human figure.

In CG, a keyframe can be set on almost *any* aspect of an object—its color, position, size, and so on. Maya will interpolate the *in-between* frames between the keyframes set by the animator. In reality, you can set several keyframes on any one frame in CG animation. Figure 1.6 illustrates a keyframe sequence in Maya.

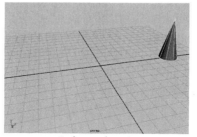

Keyframe at frame 1

Figure 1.6

Keyframing. In the first frame of this sequence, a keyframe is set on the position, rotation, and scale of the cone. On frame 30, the same properties are again keyframed. Maya calculates all the movement in between.

Frame 5

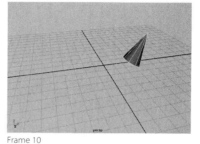

Frame 10

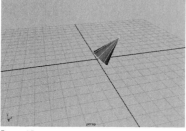

Frame 15

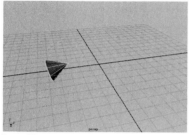

Frame 20

Frame 25

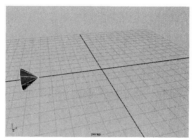

Keyframe at frame 30

Weight

Weight is an implied facet of design and animation. The weight of your subject in the frame rests on how it is colored and its contrast, shape, and location in the frame and the negative space around it. In animation, the idea of weight takes on a more important role. How you show an object's weight in motion greatly affects its believability. As you'll see in the axe tutorial in Chapter 8, creating proper motion to reflect the object's weight goes a long way toward creating believable animation.

Weight in animation is a perception of mass. An object's movement and how it reacts in motion and to other objects need to convey the feeling of weight. Otherwise the animation will look bogus, or as they say, "cartoonish."

Weight is created with any number of techniques developed by traditional animators over the years that in some ways distort the shape of the character to make it look as if it is moving. Although it may seem strange to distort an object's dimensions as with *squash and stretch*, it lends more realism of motion to the character. Chapter 8 will touch more on creating weight in animation; here's a quick preview.

SQUASH AND STRETCH

This technique makes a character responds to gravity, movement, and inertia by literally squashing down and stretching up when it moves. For example, a cartoon character will squeeze down when it is about to jump up, stretch out a bit while it is flying in the air, and squash back down when it lands to make the character look as if it is reacting to gravity.

EASE-IN AND EASE-OUT

Objects never really suddenly stop. Everything comes to some sort of rest in its own time, slowing before the complete stop in most cases. This is referred to as ease-out.

As objects don't suddenly stop, they also don't immediately start motion either. Most everything needs to speed up a bit before reaching its full speed. This is ease-in. The bouncing ball tutorial in Chapter 8 illustrates ease-in and ease-out.

FOLLOW-THROUGH AND ANTICIPATION

Sometimes exaggerating the weight of an object is necessary in animation. Objects ending an action typically have a follow-through in some way. For example, a cape on a jumping character will continue to move a bit even after the character lands and stops moving. This is similar to the movement of gymnasts. When they land, they need to bend a bit at the knees and waist to stabilize the landing.

Likewise, you can create a little bit of movement in your character or object *before* it moves. Anticipation is a technique in which a character or object winds up before it moves, like a spring that coils in a bit before it bounces. The axe tutorial in Chapter 8 will introduce you to these two concepts.

SUGGESTED READING

The more you know about all the arts that inform CG, the more confident you'll feel among your peers. To get started, check out the following excellent resources.

ART AND DESIGN

These books provide valuable insights into the mechanics and art of design. The more you understand design theory, the stronger your art.

Bowers, John. *Introduction to Two-Dimensional Design: Understanding Form and Function*. New York: John Wiley & Sons, 1999.

Itten, Johannes. *Design and Form: The Basic Course at the Bauhaus and Later*. New York: John Wiley & Sons, 1975.

Ocvirk, Otto G., and others. *Art Fundamentals: Theory and Practice*. New York: McGraw-Hill, 1997.

Wong, Wucius. *Principles of Form and Design*. New York: John Wiley & Sons, 1993.

CG

CG has an interesting history and is evolving at breakneck speeds. Acquiring a solid knowledge of this history and evolution is as important as keeping up with current trends.

Kerlow, Isaac Victor. *The Art of 3-D: Computer Animation and Imaging*. New York: John Wiley & Sons, 2000.

Kundert-Gibbs, John, Dariush Derakhshani, et al. *Mastering Maya 7*. San Francisco: Sybex, 2006.

Kuperberg, Marcia. *Guide to Computer Animation*. Burlington: Focal Press, 2002.

Masson, Terrence. *CG 101: A Computer Graphics Industry Reference*. Indianapolis: New Riders Publishing, 1999.

Periodicals

Computer Graphics World (free subscription for those who qualify)   `cgw.pennnet.com`

cinefex   `www.cinefex.com`

HDRI3D   `www.hdri3d.com`

3D World   `www.3dworldmag.com`

Websites

`www.animationartist.com`

`www.awn.com`

`www.highend3d.com`

`www.3dcafe.com`

`www.learning-maya.com`

Film

Block, Bruce. *The Visual Story: Seeing the Structure of Film, TV, and New Media*. Burlington: Focal Press, 2001.

Must Read

Myers, Dale K. *Computer Animation: Expert Advice on Breaking into the Business*. Milford: Oak Cliff Press, 1999.

Physics

You'll see in Chapter 12 that one of Maya's most powerful features is its ability to simulate the dynamics of moving objects. To use that capability effectively, you need a general awareness of the properties of physics—how objects behave in the physical world.

NEWTON'S LAWS OF MOTION

There are three basic laws of motion. Sir Isaac Newton set forth these three laws, summarized here:

- An object in motion will remain in motion, and an object at rest will remain at rest unless an external force acts upon the object. This is called inertia, and understanding it is critical to good animation. You'll find more on this in Chapters 8 and 9.

- The more massive an object is, the more force is needed to accelerate or decelerate its motion. This law deals with an object's momentum.

- Every action has an equal and opposite reaction. When you press on a brick wall, for example, the wall exerts an equal amount of force back to your hand. That way your hand doesn't smash through the wall.

Everyone in animation should and will definitely come to understand the first two laws to a good degree since they play a large part in how your animations should look.

MOMENTUM

In particular, it's important to understand what momentum is all about. When an object is in motion, it has momentum. The amount of momentum is calculated by multiplying the mass of the object by its velocity. The heavier something is, or the faster it is moving, the more momentum it has and the bigger the bruise it will leave if it hits you.

That's why a tiny bullet can cause such a great impact on a piece of wood, for example. Its sheer speed greatly increases its momentum. Likewise, a slow-moving garbage truck can bash your car, relying on its sheer mass for its tremendous momentum.

Basically, when one moving object meets another object that is moving or not, momentum is transferred between them. That means when something hits an object, that target is somehow moved if there is sufficient momentum transferred to it. For more on this notion, see the axe-throwing exercise in Chapter 8.

Summary

In this chapter, you learned the basic process of working in CG, called a *work flow* or *pipeline*, which is similar to the process of working on a typical production. In addition, this chapter covered the core concepts of CG creation and the fundamentals of digital images. Some important ideas in design foundation as well as traditional animation concepts were also covered.

Now that you have a foundation in CG and 3D terminology and core concepts, you are ready to tackle the software itself. Maya is a capable, intricate program. The more you understand how *you* work artistically, the better use you will make of this exceptional tool.

It seems as if there is a lot to think about before putting objects into a scene and rendering them out. With practice and some design tinkering, though, all this becomes intuitive to the artist. As you move forward in your animation education, stay diligent, be patient, and never pass up a chance to learn something new. And above all else, have fun with it.

CHAPTER 2

The Maya Interface

This chapter takes you on a guided tour of all the elements visible on the Maya screen. You will visit the menus, the icons, and the shelves, just to get an idea of what everything is. You'll learn how to work with these tools later in this book, but it's a good idea to go into this at least knowing what everything is called and its purpose. Don't get nervous, though; you won't need to retain all this information at once. Think of this more as a nickel tour.

This chapter can also serve as a good reference for later, when you're wondering what a particular icon does. If you are already familiar with the Maya interface, you might want to skip this chapter.

Topics include:

- **Navigating in Maya**
- **A Screen Roadmap**
- **Panels and Frequently Used Windows**
- **Maya Object Structure**

Navigating in Maya

The key to being a good animator, with Maya software or with any other tool, is not necessarily knowing where to find all the tools and buttons. It's about knowing *how* to find the features you need. Don't let the interface intimidate you; it's much friendlier than you might initially think, and there is more than one way to get something done through the UI.

Maya is intricate and multifaceted, with layers upon layers of function sets and interface options, separated into categories. The purpose of this chapter is to help you get to know Maya and how it operates rather than how to use it. You may even wish to jump ahead to the solar system exercise in the next chapter if you're looking to get your feet wet right away; you can then check back in for explanations of UI elements and windows in this chapter.

The best way to start is to explore the interface. Using your mouse, check out the menus, the menu sets, and the tools. Just be careful not to change any settings; the rest of this book and its projects assume your Maya settings are all at the default. Just in case you do change some settings, it's easy to revert to the default. Choose **Window → Settings/Preferences → Preferences**. In the Preferences window, choose **Edit → Restore Default Settings**. Now, all the settings and interface elements are restored to the default state.

A Screen Roadmap

Let's get to the basics of how Maya is laid out (see Figure 2.1). Running across the top of the screen, right under the application's title bar, are the *main menu bar*, the *Status line*, and the *shelf*.

To the left of the screen, running vertically, is the *Tool Box*, offering quick-view selections, and across from it is the *Channel Box/Layer Editor* and sometimes the *Attribute Editor* (not displayed in Figure 2.1). Running horizontally at the bottom of the screen (from the top down) are the *Time Slider*, the *Range Slider*, the *Character Set menu*, the *Auto Keyframe button*, and the *Animation Preferences button*.

In the middle of all these elements is the *workspace*, which is host to your *panels* (or scene windows) and their menu options, also known as views or viewports in some other 3D packages. This is where most of your focus will be; this is where you create and manipulate your 3D objects.

MOUSE CONTROLS

Maya requires the use of a three-button mouse, even on a Macintosh system. The scroll wheels on most mice can be used as the third button. The scroll wheel also has the ability to zoom into or out of a view panel as well as being the third (middle) button.

In Maya, holding the Alt key on a PC or the Option key on a Mac along with the appropriate button allows you to move in the View Panel. The left mouse button (LMB) acts as the primary selection button (as it does in many other programs) and allows you to orbit around objects when used with the Alt key, the right mouse button (RMB) activates numerous shortcut menus and lets you zoom with the Alt key, the middle mouse button (MMB) with the Alt key lets you move within the Maya interface, and the mouse's wheel can be used to zoom in and out as well.

The Main Menu Bar

Starting with the menu bar, shown here, you'll find a few of the familiar menu choices you've come to expect in many applications, such as File, Edit, and Help.

One difference in Maya, however, is that menu choices depend on what you are doing. By switching *menu sets,* you change your menu choices and hence your available toolset. The menu sets in Maya Complete are Animation, Polygons, Surfaces, Rendering, and Dynamics; Maya Unlimited adds the Cloth and Maya Live menu sets to those five. You'll find more in-depth information about these later in this chapter.

No matter which menu set you are working in, the first six items are constant: File, Edit, Modify, Create, Display, and Window. The last menu, Help, is also constantly displayed, no matter which menu set you choose.

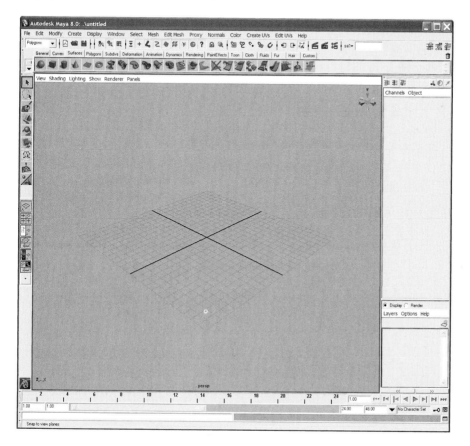

Figure 2.1

The initial Maya screen

When searching for a particular tool, keep in mind that each menu set controls particular functions. The following menus are always visible:

File Deals with file operations, from saving and opening to optimizing scene size and export/import.

Edit Contains the commands you use to edit characteristics of the scene, for example, deleting and duplicating objects or undoing and redoing actions.

Modify Lets you edit the characteristics of objects in the scene, such as moving or scaling them or changing their pivot points.

Create Lets you make new objects, such as primitive geometries, curves, cameras, and so on.

Display Contains commands for adjusting elements of the GUI (graphical user interface) in Maya as well as objects in the scene, allowing you to toggle, or switch on or off, the display of certain elements as well as components of objects, such as vertices, hulls, pivots, and so on.

Window Gives you access to the many windows you will come to rely on, such as the Attribute Editor, Outliner, Graph Editor, and Hypergraph broken down into submenus according to function, such as Rendering Editors and Animation Editors.

Help Gives you access to the help files.

You'll notice two different demarcations to the right of some menu items: arrows and boxes (called *option boxes*). Clicking an arrow opens a submenu that contains more specific commands. Clicking an option box (❏) opens a dialog box in which you can set the options for that particular tool.

ADVANCED TIP: FLOATING MENUS

In Maya you can "tear off" menus to create separate floating boxes, which you can place anywhere in the workspace, as shown here.

This makes accessing menu commands easier, especially when you need to use the same command repeatedly. Let's say, for example, that you need to create multiple polygonal spheres. You can tear off the **Create ➞Polygon Primitives** menu and place it at the edge of your screen. You can then click the **Sphere** command as many times as you need without opening the dual-layered menu every time. To tear off a menu, click the double line at the top of the menu, and drag the menu where you want it.

Click here and drag to tear off a menu.

The Status Line

The Status line (see Figure 2.2) contains a number of important and often used icons.

The Status line begins with a drop-down menu that gives you access to the menu sets in Maya. Selecting a menu set changes the menu set in the main menu bar. You will notice immediately after the Menu Set drop-down menu, and intermittently throughout the Status line, black vertical line breaks with either a box or an arrow in the middle. Clicking a break opens or closes sections of the Status line.

Figure 2.2

The Status line

Scene File Icons

The tools in the first section of the Status line deal with file operations:

ICON	NAME	DESCRIPTION
	New Scene	Creates a new, blank scene file
	Open Scene	Displays a window in which you can find and open any scene file you've saved
	Save Scene	Displays a window in which you can specify a filename and location to save a new scene or, if the current scene has already been saved and named, saves it to that location

Selection Modes

The second section between the black horizontal lines is the *Selection Mode field*. This drop-down menu lets you use presets for *selection masks*. Selection masks give you the chance to pick one kind of an object, but not another, so you can, for example, select all the particles in the scene and none of the polygon models.

> Using a selection mask, you can select some object types in a scene and not others. For example, in a heavily layered scene, you might want to select only the faces of a polygon and not any other object or object component. You can use a selection mask to isolate polygonal faces as the only selectable object on the screen and click away!

This Selection Mode field gives you some presets that optimize the selection modes for your convenience. But you might prefer to use the individual selection mask icons farther down the Status line; they give you more control—you can turn on and off selectability for individual object types, such as particles, NURBS, polygons, and so on.

The next group of icons lets you click into three distinct selection modes. Selection modes allow you to select different levels of an object's hierarchy. For example, using a selection mode you can select an entire group of objects, only one of the objects in that group, or even points on the surface of that object, depending on the selection mode you're in.

ICON	NAME	DESCRIPTION
	Hierarchy Mode	Lets you select groups of objects or parts of a group
	Object Mode	Lets you select objects such as geometry, cameras, lights, and so on
	Component Mode	Lets you select an object's components, such as vertices, faces, or the Control Vertices (CVs) of NURBS surfaces

To switch between object and component modes, press the F8 key, the default hot key.

Click Hierarchy Mode, for example, to select the topmost node of a hierarchy or group of objects. If you have grouped several objects together, being in this mode and clicking any of the member objects selects the entire group. For more on hierarchies, see the section "Maya Object Structure" later in this chapter.

Individual Selection Masks

The next set of icons between the section breaks deals with individual selection masks, which give you control over which objects or components you want to select. Exactly which icons are displayed here depends on the selection mode you're currently in. If you have many objects in your scene and you are having difficulty selecting a certain type of object with your cursor, you can use these filters to single the object(s) out:

ICON	NAME	DESCRIPTION
	Set Object Selection Mask	Turns on or off all selection icons
	Select by Handles	Allows selection of object handles
	Select by Joints	Allows selection of joints
	Select by Curve	Allows selection of curves
	Select by Surfaces	Allows selection of surfaces
	Select by Deformations	Allows selection of lattices and other deformers
	Select by Dynamics	Allows selection of particles and dynamic objects
	Select by Rendering	Allows selection of rendering nodes and objects such as lights and cameras
	Select by Miscellaneous	Allows selection of miscellaneous objects such as locators and dimensions
	Lock Selection	Keeps selected objects locked in as selected
	Highlight Selection Mode	Turns off the automatic display of components when selecting in selection mode

You'll work with these filters throughout the book. For a quick preview, roll your mouse over each of the icons to see a tooltip that gives the icon name and describes its function. As you gain experience, you'll find these masks helpful in your work flow.

Snapping Functions or Snaps

The icons with the magnets are called snaps, which allow you to snap your cursor or object to specific points in the scene. You can snap to other objects, to CVs or vertices, and to grid intersections and more by toggling these icons. Thus, you can precisely place your objects or points. You'll be using snaps in the next chapter to make a solar system.

ICON	NAME	DESCRIPTION
	Snap to Grids	Lets you snap objects to intersections of the view's grid.
	Snap to Curves	Lets you snap objects along a curve.
	Snap to Points	Lets you snap objects to object points such as CVs or vertices.
	Snap to View Planes	Lets you snap objects to view planes.
	Make the Selected Object Live	This has nothing to do with snapping. It lets you create objects such as curves directly on a surface.

Input and Output Connections

The first two icons following the filters list the input and output connections of an object; the third icon toggles on/off construction history. Briefly, objects in Maya can connect with each other for animation purposes. When an object is being influenced by an attribute of another object or node in Maya, it has an input connection. When the node's own attribute(s) is influencing another object, it has an output connection. Construction history is a feature that keeps track of the nodes and attributes that help make up an object, making it easier to edit those objects that have history. These subjects are covered in more detail later in this book.

ICON	NAME	DESCRIPTION
	Input Connections	Lets you select and edit all the input connections for the selected object. That is, you can select and edit any object that directly influences the selected object.
	Output Connections	Lets you select and edit the output connections or any objects the selection affects.
	Construction History	Toggles on/off the construction history.

Render Controls

The next three icons give you access to render controls:

ICON	NAME	DESCRIPTION
	Render Current View	Renders the active viewport at the current frame.
	IPR Render Current View	Renders the active view at the current frame into Interactive Photorealistic Rendering (IPR). You can change certain shading and texturing settings and view real-time updates in the IPR window.
	Render Settings	Opens a window that gives you access to all the rendering switches such as resolution, file type, frame range, and so on.

The Name Selection Field

You use this input window on the Status line to enter object names to make selections. You can enter exact names as well as wildcards such as "sphere*" just in case you forget part of the name of the object. This is useful for selecting objects you can't see in the panels or if you want to select a large number of objects all with similar names.

The Channel Box/Layer Editor

The last part of the Status line deals with the area defined earlier in the chapter as the Channel Box/Layer Editor. These buttons toggle through three views in that area on the right side of the screen. Clicking the first button displays the Attribute Editor, with which you can edit Maya's object attributes. Clicking the second turns on a window called Tool Options in that column, giving you access to options for the currently active tool. Clicking the last icon restores the Channel Box/Layer Editor, showing you the commonly keyed attributes of an active object as well as the display layers in your scene. These windows are discussed in detail later in this chapter. Feel free to skip ahead if you want and then come back for the next area of the interface, the shelf.

ICON	NAME	DESCRIPTION
	Show/Hide Attribute Editor	Displays the Attribute Editor in this area
	Show/Hide Tool Settings	Displays the current tool's settings
	Show/Hide Channel Box/Layer Editor	Displays the Channel Box and Layer Editor

The Shelf

The *shelf*, shown in Figure 2.3, is an area where you keep icons for tools. It is divided into tabs that define functions for the tool icons in the shelf. Typically Maya will start with the Surfaces tab displayed, showing you icons to create often-used NURBS primitives such as a sphere or a cube or often-used tools such as loft and extrude tools. For more on these

Figure 2.3
The shelf

NURBS surface tools, see Chapter 4. You can change the shelf display by clicking the tabs to switch to the functions you'll be using. The final tab on the right is empty so that you can create your own custom shelf, populating it with the tools you find most useful.

Pointing to the icons in the shelf displays a tooltip that gives you the name and a description of that tool.

Don't worry too much about the shelf right now; it may be better to use the commands from the menus first before turning to icons and shelves. This will get you in the habit of knowing where tools are and also gives you the chance to explore further every time you open a menu. You'll find that after using Maya for a while, you will create a group of your favorite tools in your own shelves and find the shelf area an invaluable asset to your work flow.

The Tool Box

The Tool Box, shown in Figure 2.4, displays the most commonly used tools: Select, Lasso Select, Translate (or Move), Rotate, Scale, Universal Manipulator, Soft Modification, and Show Manipulator. In addition to the common commands, it displays several choices for screen layouts that let you change the interface with a single click. This is quite convenient because different animations call for different view modes. Experiment with the layouts by clicking any of the six presets in the Tool Box.

ICON	NAME	DESCRIPTION
	Select	Lets you select objects
	Lasso Select	Allows for a free-form selection using a lasso marquee
	Paint Selection Tool	Enables the Paint Selection Tool
	Translate (Move)	Moves selection
	Rotate	Rotates selection
	Scale	Scales selection
	Universal Manipulator	Allows for translation, rotation, and scale within one tool
	Soft Modification	Allows you to modify an area with a gradual drop-off of its effect
	Show Manipulator	Displays an object's specific manipulators
	Current Tool Display	Shows the currently selected tool (shown as blank)

Figure 2.4
The Tool Box

ADVANCED TIP: CUSTOMIZING THE SHELF

Once you have established a set of favorite Maya tools for routine tasks, you might want to customize the shelf to make those tools immediately accessible. Clicking the Menu icon (▼) opens a menu that you can use to edit the shelf to your liking. To add a menu item to the shelf, press Ctrl+Alt+Shift and select the command from the menu (for Mac users, press Ctrl+Option+Shift). It will appear on the current shelf. To get rid of an item, MMB drag it to the Trash icon. You can create multiple shelves, stack them on top of each other, and access them by clicking the Shelf Tab icon (▭) above the Menu icon to the left of the shelf.

The Channel Box/Layer Editor

The area running vertically to the right of the screen is most usually used for the *Channel Box*. This key element of the interface lists an object's channels—that is, the attributes of an object that are most commonly animated and used for keyframing—as well as an object's input and output connections. When an object is selected in one of the main views, its name appears at the top of the Channel Box and its channels are listed vertically below with their names to the left and their values to the right in text boxes. In the Channel Box, you can edit all the channel values and rename the object itself. Below these values are the names of the nodes or objects to which the selection has input and output connections.

Immediately under the Channel Box is the Layer Editor. This arrangement is convenient for scenes that require multiple objects and require layered animations. You can place some objects on display layers that might be turned on or off to help organize a scene. Get familiar with this feature early on, as it will be a valuable asset when you find yourself animating complicated scenes.

To create a new layer, click the Create New Layer icon (▨). To add items to a layer, right-click on the layer and choose **Add Selected Objects**. You can also use the layers to select groups of objects by choosing **Layers → Select Objects In Selected Layers**. To change the name and color of a layer, simply double-click the layer to open the Edit Layer dialog box.

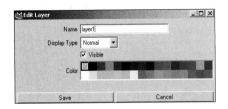

You can easily resize this area by clicking either of the double arrow buttons at the bottom of the panel. You can also switch between the Channel Box and the Layer Editor by toggling one of the icons in the upper-left corner. (See Figure 2.5.)

ICON	NAME
	Show the Channel Box
	Show the Layer Editor
	Show the Channel Box and the Layer Editor

The reason this area of the screen is "most usually" used for the Channel Box and the Layer Editor is that you can replace this panel with one of two other windows—the Attribute Editor or the Tool Settings—by clicking one of the three icons in the upper-right corner as seen in Figure 2.5. This gives you quick access to the three windows you find most useful to have onscreen all the time. You might want to display the Channel Box all the time.

Time Slider/Range Slider

Running horizontally across the bottom of the screen are the Time Slider and the Range Slider, shown in Figure 2.6. The Time Slider displays the range of frames available in your animation and gives you a gray bar, known as the *current time indicator*, that you can click and then drag back and forth in a scrubbing motion to move through time in your sequence. (When instructed in this book to "scrub" to a certain point in your animation, use this indicator to do so.)

The text box to the right of the Time Slider gives you your current frame, but you can also use the text box to enter the frame you want to access. Immediately next to the current time readout is a set of VCR playback controls that you can use to playback your animation.

Below the Time Slider is the Range Slider, which you use to adjust the range of animation playback for your Time Slider. The text boxes on either side of this slider give you readouts for the start and end frames of the scene and of the range selected.

You can adjust any of these settings by either typing in these text boxes or lengthening or shortening the slider with the handles on either end of the bar. When you change the range, you change only the viewable frame range of the scene; you don't adjust any of the animation. This lets you zoom into sections of the timeline, which makes adjusting keyframes and timing much easier, especially in long animations. When you zoom into a particular section of your time frame, the Time Slider displays only the frames and keyframes for that portion, making it easier to read.

Figure 2.5

The Channel Box/Layer Editor

Figure 2.6

The Time Slider and the Range Slider

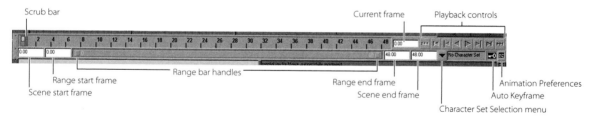

Command line   Command feedback   Script Editor button

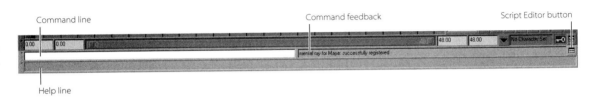

Help line

Figure 2.7

The Command line and the Help Line

To the right of the Range Slider are the Character Set Selection menu (which deals with the automation of character-animated objects), the Auto Keyframe button (which sets a keyframe automatically when an animated value is changed), and the Animation Preferences button. You'll find information on these features later in this book.

Command Line/Help Line

Maya Embedded Language (MEL) is the user-accessible programming language of Maya. Every action you take invokes a MEL command or script that runs that particular function. You can write your own commands or scripts, using either the Command line or the Script Editor. Use the Command line (see Figure 2.7) to enter single MEL commands directly from the keyboard in the white text box portion of the bar. The Command line also displays command feedback and messages from the program in the gray portion of the bar. Try entering the following into this box: **sphere**. A new sphere should pop up in your Maya panels. You've created a basic sphere using the MEL command. To delete it, click it to select it and then press Delete.

Clicking the icon at the end of the Command line opens the Script Editor, in which you can enter more complicated MEL commands and scripts.

OPENING THE ATTRIBUTE EDITOR IN ITS OWN WINDOW

By default, the Attribute Editor opens in the right-hand side of the UI area of the screen whenever you start Maya. The preferred configuration in this book is to open the Attribute Editor as a separate window instead. To follow along in this book, you'll also want this configuration.

To configure the Attribute Editor to open in its own window, choose **Window → Settings/Preferences → Preferences** to open the Preferences dialog box.

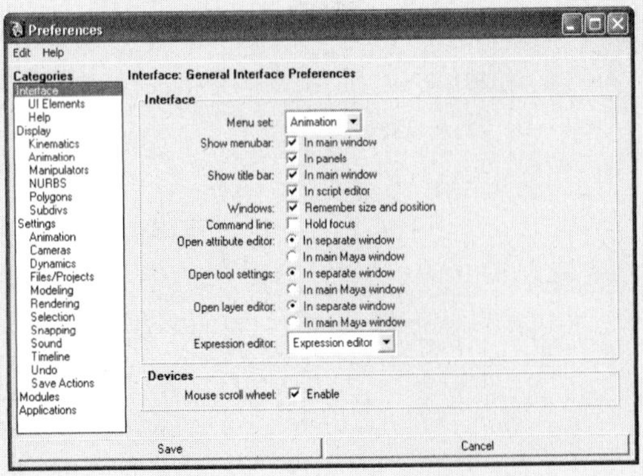

Under the Interface section, set Open Attribute Editor to In Separate Window, and set Open Tool Settings to In Separate Window. If any of your screen elements are missing, you can toggle them on and off through this dialog box.

Below the Command line is the Help line. This bar provides a quick reference for most everything on the screen. For the most part, it's a readout of functions when you point to icons. It also prompts you for the next step in a particular function or the next required input for a task's completion.

The Help line is most useful when you're not really sure about the next step in a command, such as which object to select next or which key to press to execute the command. You'll be surprised by how much you'll learn about tool functions by reading the prompts displayed here.

Panels and Frequently Used Windows

The main focus of Maya is, of course, its work windows—the perspective and orthographic views. You use these windows to create, manipulate, and view 3D objects, particles, and animations. By using the mouse, you can navigate in these views rather easily. Navigation in almost all work windows involves a combination of mouse control and keyboard input.

Perspective/Orthographic Windows

The default Maya layout begins with a full-screen perspective view, as shown in Figure 2.8. This view is essentially the view from a camera and expresses real-world depth through the simulation of perspective. In this window, you can see your creation in three dimensions and move around it in real time to get a sense of proportion and depth.

Figure 2.8

The full perspective view

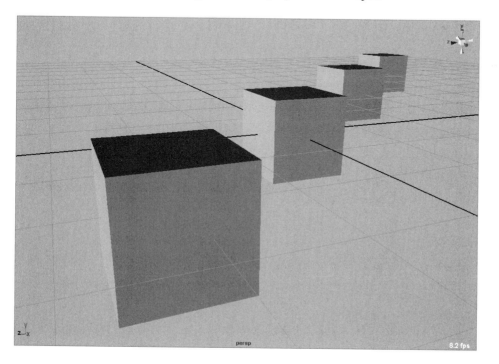

SHORTCUTS TO VIEWING

Here's a summary of the most important keyboard shortcuts. Keep in mind that the Option key is used on a Macintosh in place of the Alt key on a PC:

Alt+MMB

Tracks around a window. Tracking moves left, right, up, or down in two dimensions; just hold down the Alt key, press and hold the MMB, and drag the mouse.

Alt+LMB+MMB or Alt+RMB

Dollies into or out of a view. A dolly physically moves the camera in and out of the view, practically zooming in and out. However, this is different from an actual zoom in that a zoom function changes the *focal length* of the view's camera lens as opposed to moving the camera closer or farther away. Changing the focal distance can distort the image and change the viewing angle. To dolly, hold down the Alt key, press and hold both the LMB and the MMB, and drag the mouse.

Scroll Wheel

The scroll wheel, in addition to being a middle mouse button, can also dolly into or out of a view just as the Alt+LMB+MMB or Alt+RMB mouse/button combination described earlier. Scrolling up will dolly in, and scrolling down will dolly out.

Alt+LMB

Rotates or orbits the camera around in a perspective window. Orbiting lets you get around your object to observe it from different vantage points. To orbit, hold down the Alt key and the LMB. This move is called a tumble. You cannot tumble your view in an orthographic panel.

Alt+Ctrl+LMB Drag

Dollies your view into the screen area specified in your mouse drag. Hold down the Alt and Ctrl keys while using the LMB to outline a window in the panel to execute this "bounding box dolly." This action is commonly referred to as a window zoom in other applications.

The View Compass

This addition to the Maya 8 user interface lets you easily change your current panel view from, for example, perspective to side, top, and back to perspective with just a click. By clicking an area of the compass ( ), you can switch to other views inside that panel. Clicking one of the conical axis markers gives you an orthogonal view from that direction. Clicking the center square gives you the perspective view. You can toggle the View Compass in any panel. In that panel view's menu, choose **View → Camera Settings → View Compass**.

Macintosh Keys

The major difference in keys between a PC and a Mac, as far as Maya goes, is that the Alt key on a PC is the Option key on a Mac. Although a few Ctrl key combinations may work on a Mac by using the Command key, Mac users will use the Ctrl key for their key combinations just as PC users do.

By pressing the spacebar, you can switch your view from the full-screen perspective to the four-panel layout shown in Figure 2.9. Pressing the spacebar again returns your active view panel to full-screen mode.

Orthographic views (top, front, and side) are most commonly used for modeling, because they are best at conveying exact dimensions and size relationships. Even though the cubes in the perspective window are all the same size, the perspective view, by definition, displays the cubes farther away as being smaller than those closer to you. Orthographic views, however, display exact proportions so that you can see the four cubes as being identical in size and shape.

The four-panel layout gives you accurate feedback on the sizing and proportionality of your models. In general, you'll probably prefer to start your modeling in orthographic view and use the perspective view(s) for fine-tuning and finishing work and for setting up camera angles for rendering.

You can easily adjust the panel layouts of your screen by using any of the six presets in the Tool Box on the left side of the screen or by choosing **Window → Saved Layouts**. Furthermore, you can replace each view panel by choosing another panel name from the list in the Panels menu in the bar at the top of each view. From this menu, you can choose any modeling view, orthographic or perspective, or another window to best suit your work flow. You can also change the size of these windows by clicking and dragging the separating borders between the panels.

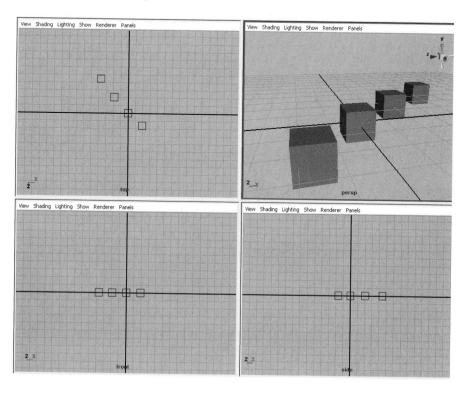

Figure 2.9

The four-panel screen layout

By default, each panel displays a grid that you can adjust by choosing **Display → Grid** ☐. The grid is made of actual units of measure that you can adjust. Choose **Window → Settings/ Preferences → Preferences** to open the Preferences dialog box, and in the Settings section make your adjustments.

Try This In the four-panel layout (click the second layout icon in the Tool Box), create a NURBS sphere by choosing **Create → NURBS Primitives → Sphere**. A sphere should appear and be selected, as shown in Figure 2.10. You will notice its primary attributes in the Channel Box.

Now, press 2, and you will see the wireframe mesh get denser. Press 3, and the mesh gets even denser. You can view all NURBS objects in three levels of display, such as this sphere. Pressing 1, 2, or 3 toggles between detail levels for any selected NURBS object.

NURBS is a type of surface in Maya that can adjust its detail level at any time to become more or less defined as needed. The display detail keys (1, 2, 3) adjust the level of NURBS detail seen in the panels only.

When you're working in the windows, you can view your 3D objects as either wireframe models (as in Figure 2.10) or as solid, hardware-rendered models, called *shaded mode* (see Figure 2.11). Wireframe mode is the fastest since the computer doesn't have as much computational overhead. But, depending on your graphics card and your system processor, you'll be surprised at how fast shaded mode can actually be.

Within the shaded mode, you can select from varying degrees of shading detail. You can cycle through the levels of detail by pressing 4, 5, 6, and 7. Wireframe mode is 4, shaded mode is 5, texture shaded mode is 6, and lighted mode is 7.

Pressing 4 or 5 toggles between wireframe and shaded mode in any of the modeling windows. Texture shaded mode (6) displays the actual image textures that have been applied to the object as long as Hardware Texturing is already enabled (in the view panel choose **Shading → Hardware Texturing** and make sure it is checked on). Lighted mode (7) is a hardware preview of the object or objects as they are lit in the scene. The detail level hot keys for NURBS objects (1, 2, 3) apply in shaded mode as well. Here's a summary:

KEY	FUNCTION
4	Toggles into wireframe mode
5	Toggles into shaded mode
6	Toggles into textured mode
7	Toggles into lighted mode

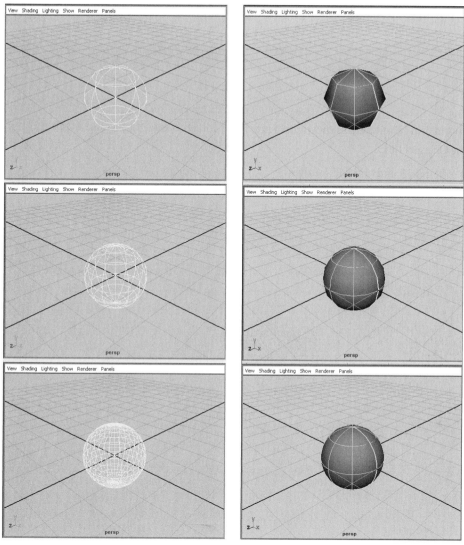

Figure 2.10

NURBS display smoothness

Figure 2.11

Shaded NURBS display detail

It's always good to toggle between the wireframe and shaded modes to get a feel for the weight and proportion of your model as you are building it. The texture mode is good for the rudimentary lining up of textures, but typically it's better to rely on fully rendered frames for that. The IPR renderer in Maya is also great for previewing work because it updates areas of the frame in good quality renders at interactive speeds. Chapter 11 covers IPR.

The lighted mode, however, is useful for spotting proper lighting direction and object highlights when you first begin lighting a scene. It helps to see the direction of lights within your scene without having to render frames all the time. How many lights you see in the modeling window depends on your computer's graphics and overall capabilities. Chapter 10 covers lighting and makes frequent use of this mode.

Other display commands you will find useful while working in the modeling windows are found under the view panel's View menu. **Look At Selection** centers on the selected object or objects, **Frame All** (press A as a keyboard shortcut) moves the view in or out to display all the objects in the scene, and **Frame Selection** (press F as a keyboard shortcut) centers on and moves the view in or out to fully frame the selected object or objects in the panel.

> When using the keyboard shortcuts in the preceding paragraph, *don't* press Shift to generate the capital letter like A or F. Keyboard shortcuts in Maya are described as "case sensitive" because in many cases pressing a single letter key has a different effect than pressing Shift plus that letter (the "uppercase" letter). This book shows all single letters as capitals (the same way they appear on your keyboard), and the Shift key is included when it's part of the shortcut. If you find yourself wondering why pressing a hot key isn't working, it may be that the Caps Lock is enabled, capitalizing your entries.

The Manipulators

The next thing you should know about the interface deals directly with objects. *Manipulators* are onscreen handles that you use to *manipulate* the selected object, hence the name. Figure 2.12 shows the three distinct and most common manipulators for all objects in Maya: Move, Rotate, and Scale. You use these manipulators to adjust attributes of the objects visually and in real time. Additionally, you can use some manipulators, called special manipulators, or special *manips*, to adjust specific functions while using certain tools or with some objects, such as a spotlight.

You can access the manipulators using either the icons from the Tool Box or the following hot keys:

KEY	FUNCTION
W	Activates the Move tool
E	Activates the Rotate tool
R	Activates the Scale tool
Q	Deselects any translation tool to hide its manipulator and reverts to the Select tool

It may seem strange for the default hot keys to be W, E, and R for Move, Rotate, and Scale, but since the keys are right next to each other on the keyboard, selecting them is easy. These are without a doubt the hot keys you will use the most, since they activate the tools you will be using the most.

Try This Select the Move tool (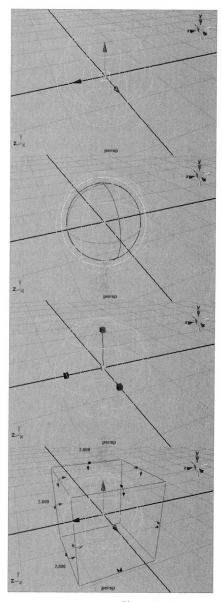)from the Tool Box, and the first manipulator shown in Figure 2.12 appears in the middle of the object. The three arrows represent the three axes of movement possible for the object.

Red is for the X axis, green is for the Y axis, and blue is for the Z axis. Cyan is for free movement in both axes of the active panel view.

Clicking any one of the three arrows lets you move the object *only* on that particular axis. The square in the middle of the manipulator lets you move the object freely about the plane of the view panel, regardless of the axis. When you select a manipulator handle for movement, it turns yellow. The free movement box in the center then turns back to its regular color, cyan.

Next select the Rotate tool ( ) from the Tool Box, and you will see the second manipulator in Figure 2.12. The three colored circles represent the three axes of rotation for the object—red for X, green for Y, and blue for Z. Select a circle to rotate the object on that axis. The yellow circle surrounding the three axis circles lets you freely rotate the object on all three axes. The free rotation handle also turns cyan when an axis handle is active.

Now try selecting the Scale tool ( ) to see the third manipulator in Figure 2.12. By selecting one of the axis handles and dragging the mouse, you can nonuniformly scale the object in that axis, while the middle cyan box will scale the object uniformly on all three axes.

Try selecting the Universal Manipulator. This one tool acts in place of all three that you just tried. Grabbing the familiar arrows translates the sphere. Selecting any of the curved arrows in the middle of the box edges of the manipulator lets you rotate the sphere in that axis. Last, selecting and dragging the cyan boxes in the corners of the manipulator box lets you scale the sphere. If you hold down the Ctrl key as you drag, you can scale the sphere in just one axis.

Figure 2.12

Using manipulators

It is much easier to use the default hot keys defined for these transformation tools rather than selecting them from the Tool Box. If the keys ever seem not to work, make sure Caps Lock is off. Be sure you are using the lowercase keys.

The one major difference here is that the Universal Manipulator interactively shows you the movement, rotation, or scale as you manipulate the sphere. Notice the coordinates that come up and change as you move the sphere. When you rotate using this manipulator, you'll see the degree of change. And notice the scale values in dark gray on the three outside edges of the manipulator box as they change when you scale the sphere.

Finally, try using the Soft Modification tool. This allows you to select an area on your surface or model and make any adjustments. The adjustments you make will gradually taper off away from the initial place of selection, giving you an easy way to "soft modify" an area of a model. For instance, create a NURBS plane by choosing **Create → NURBS Primitives → Plane ❑**. This opens the options for creating a plane. Set both the **U Patches** and **V Patches** sliders to 10 and click Create.

This places a plane on the grid. Select the Scale tool and scale it up to about the size of the grid. Then, select the Soft Modification tool ( ) from the Tool Box and click the plane, somewhere just off the middle. This will create an "S" and a special manipulator to allow you to move, rotate, or scale this soft selection.

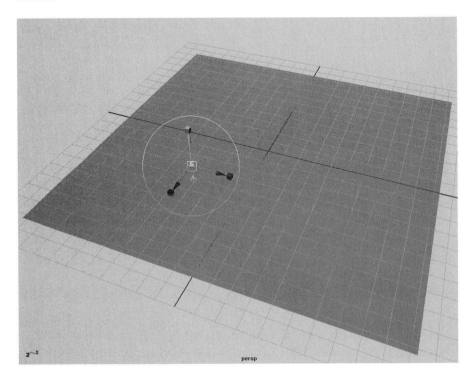

Grab the cone handle and drag it up to move the soft selection up. Notice the plane lifts up in that area only, gradually falling off, in effect as if you are picking up a tablecloth.

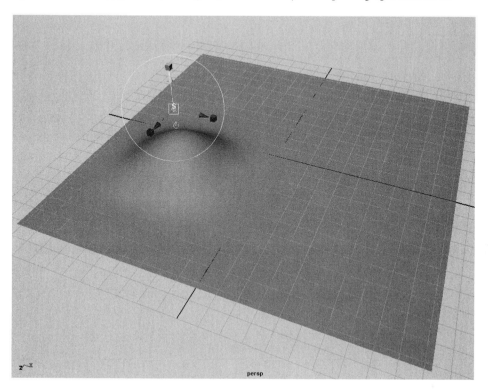

Grabbing the cube handle will scale the soft selection, and dragging on the circle will rotate it. Once you're done making your soft adjustments, you can go back to that soft selection by selecting the "S" on the surface for later editing. You can place as many soft selections as you need on a surface.

> You can scale the manipulator handles to make them more noticeable or less obtrusive. Press the plus key (+) to increase a manipulator's size, and press the minus key (–) to decrease it.

The Attribute Editor Window

Window → Attribute Editor (Ctrl+A)

The Attribute Editor is arguably the most important window in Maya. Every object is defined by a series of attributes, and you edit these attributes using the Attribute Editor. This window displays every attribute of an object, and you can use it to change them, set keyframes, connect to other attributes, attach expressions, or simply view the attributes.

The Attribute Editor has tabs that correspond to the object's node structure. You'll learn more about Maya's object structure later in this chapter, so don't worry about what the tabs mean just yet. As you can see, though, each tab displays different attributes of the object.

Try This Press Ctrl+A to open the Attribute Editor for the sphere (shown in Figure 2.13), and click the makeNurbSphere1 tab.

Now, you'll notice that the Channel Box has the primary attributes (**Translate X**, **Translate Y**, **Translate Z**, **Rotate X**, and so on) of the sphere already listed. Below that, you'll find listed the Shapes node named *nurbsSphereShape1* and the Inputs node *makeNurbSphere1*. If you click the *makeNurbSphere1* entry in the Channel Box, it will expand to show you select attributes from the tab of the same name in the Attribute Editor. These attributes, despite being shown in two places, are the same. If you edit one in the Channel Box, it will be reflected in the Attribute Editor, and vice versa. The Channel Box is essentially a quick reference, giving you access to the most likely animated attributes of an object, while the Attribute Editor goes into detail, giving you access to everything that makes up that object and the other nodes that influence it.

Figure 2.13

The Attribute Editor

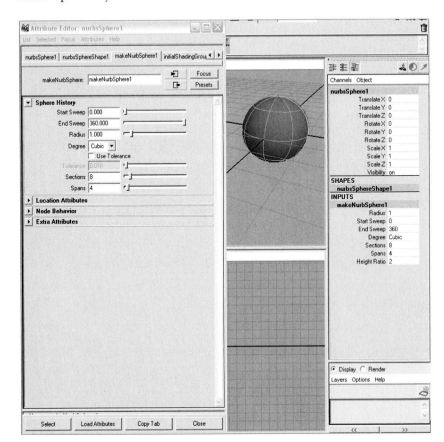

Try changing some of the settings in this window and see how that affects the sphere in the view panels. For example, changing the **Radius** attribute under the nurbsSphereShape1 tab changes the size of the sphere Click the nurbsSphere1 tab next, and you will see the primary attributes listed. Try entering some different values for the **Translate** or **Scale** attributes to see what happens to the sphere in the view panels.

On the flip side, press W to activate the Move tool, and move the sphere around one of the view planes. Notice that the respective **Translate** attributes update in almost real time in both the Attribute Editor and the Channel Box. Makes you kinda giddy, doesn't it?

At the bottom of the Attribute Editor, you'll see an area for writing down any notes. This is handy since you can remind yourself of important events such as how you set up an object or even a birthday or an anniversary. If you drag the horizontal bar, you can adjust the size of the notes view.

Because you'll use the Attribute Editor constantly, you might want to keep the window open all the time and just move it around, or you can press the Ctrl+A hot key to open the window easily.

Outliner/Hypergraph

These two very different windows serve similar functions. They are best used for organizing and grouping scene objects. Basically, these windows let you see every object node in your scene in either outline form or flowchart/graph form.

When you are steeped in an animation or a model, you will invariably have several elements to your scene. Without a roadmap, it becomes difficult to find the correct object to select or manipulate. Both windows provide this service.

Your needs will typically determine whether you use the Outliner or the Hypergraph. The Outliner is perfect for organizing, for grouping objects, for renaming nodes, and so forth. The Hypergraph displays all the connections between nodes and is perfect for editing the relationships between nodes and locating hard-to-find nested nodes in a big scene.

The Outliner

Window → Outliner

The Outliner (see Figure 2.14) displays all the objects in your scene as an outline. You can select any object in a scene by simply clicking its name.

The objects are listed by order of creation within the scene, but you can easily reorganize them by MMB dragging an object to a new location in the window, allowing you to group certain objects in the list. This is a fantastic way to keep your scene organized.

Figure 2.14
The Outliner

Additionally, you can easily rename objects by simply double-clicking their Outliner entry and typing their new name. It's crucial to an efficient animation process to keep things well named and properly organized. By doing so, you can quickly identify parts of your scene for later editing and troubleshooting.

A separator bar in the Outliner lets you split the display into two separate outline views. By clicking and dragging this bar up or down, you can see either end of a long list, with both ends having independent scrolling control.

The Hypergraph

Window →Hypergraph Scene Hierarchy

By contrast, the Hypergraph Scene Hierarchy (referred to as just the Hypergraph from here on) displays all the objects in your scene in a graphical layout similar to a flowchart (see Figure 2.15). You can see more directly the relationships between the objects in your scene. This window will perhaps be somewhat more difficult to decipher for the novice, but it affords the user great control over object interconnectivity, hierarchy, and input and output connections. The Hypergraph Input And Output Connections window is technically called the Hypergraph window, but it shows you the interconnections of attributes among nodes as opposed to the layout of nodes and node hierarchy within the scene. For the most part throughout this book, we will be dealing with the Hypergraph Scene Hierarchy and referring to it as the Hypergraph.

Navigating the Hypergraph is the same as navigating any modeling window using the familiar Alt key and mouse combinations for tracking and zooming. The following chapters focus much more on these two windows, so have a quick look here at the windows and their icons, and look back here as needed.

Figure 2.15
The Hypergraph

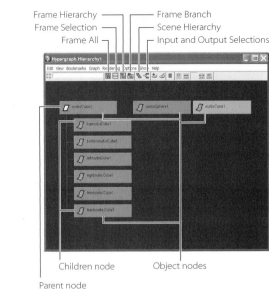

Multilister/Hypershade

As the Outliner and Hypergraph list the objects in the scene, the Multilister and Hypershade windows list the textures and shaders of your scene. Shaders are assigned to objects to give them their visual appearance—their look and feel, in other words. Through either of these windows, you can create and edit custom shaders and assign them to any object in the scene. Advantages are associated with each of these two windows, and which you use will depend on personal preference and the particular task.

> Maya uses render nodes to create shaders and shader networks for assignment to objects. Render nodes define the characteristics of shaders, which in turn are applied to objects to define how they will look when they're rendered. Shader networks are complex shaders that rely on a network of render nodes to achieve special rendering or texturing effects.

The Multilister

Window → Rendering Editors → Multilister

The Multilister (see Figure 2.16), true to its name, lays out not just the shaders of your scene, but also lights and cameras and the shaders' textures in a table format. All the shaders in the scene are displayed under their respective tabs in this window and are represented by named thumbnail icons.

Double-clicking any of the names under the thumbnails lets you change the name of the shader or render node. Remember, keeping objects—including shaders—properly named is critical to good animation work flow and will keep your coworkers happy when you're working in a group.

Clicking any of the thumbnails themselves selects the shader for use, and double-clicking a thumbnail opens its Attribute Editor. Commands for assigning and such are all located in the Multilister's menu bar, but you can access them by RMB clicking to activate the shortcut menus as well.

The Multilister is in two panels. Both panels let you select what type of shading/render node is displayed. By default, the top panel displays all the shaders in the scene on its General tab—with materials, lights, and camera nodes under their respective tabs. The bottom panel is typically reserved for the display of texture nodes that are available for use or are already connected to shaders.

You can customize both panels using the Display and Filter menus.

Figure 2.16

The Multilister

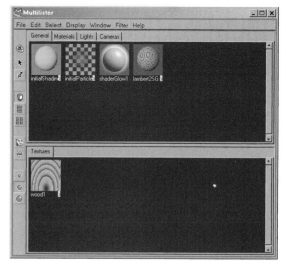

The Multilister is perfect for quick reference of shaders and lights, but it lacks the muscle to easily edit shaders as the Hypershade can. You might want to work more with the Hypershade window and use the Multilister as a quick reference now and then.

The Hypershade

Window → Rendering Editors → Hypershade

The Hypershade (see Figure 2.17) displays the shaders and textures in your scene in a graphical flowchart layout similar to the Hypergraph window. You can easily connect and disconnect render nodes to create anything from simple to complex shading networks. The Hypershade window is in three main areas: the *Create/Bins panel*, the *render node display*, and the *work area*. The three icons in the upper right let you easily switch views.

Figure 2.17

The Hypershade

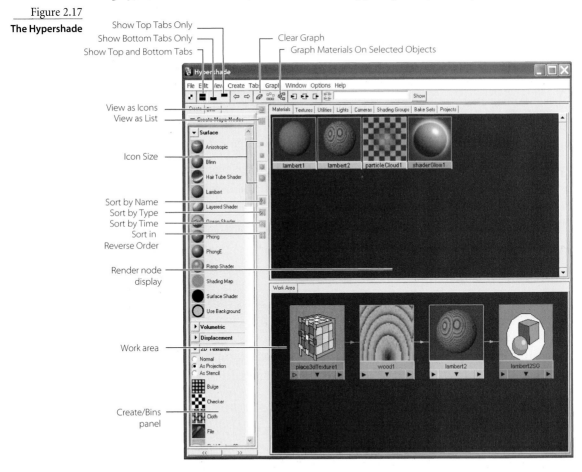

THE CREATE/BINS PANEL

The Create/Bins panel is divided into two tabs: Create and Bins. Selecting the Create tab gives you access to a variety of render nodes. The Bins tab adds a level of organization by letting you store sets of shaders in different bins, to sort them. By default, the Create tab is selected. Here you can create any render node and its supporting textures by simply clicking the icon for the desired shader or texture. The bar at the top switches between Create Maya Nodes and Create mental ray Nodes. You will deal exclusively with Maya shaders in this book, as the mental ray renderer is a more advanced topic. In the Create Maya Nodes panel, render nodes are divided into sections for their types, such as Surface (or material nodes), 2D Textures, Lights, and so on.

THE RENDER NODE DISPLAY AREA

After you create a render node, it appears in the display area as a thumbnail icon as well as in the work area and is available for editing. Clicking a render node's icon selects that node for use. Double-clicking the icon opens the Attribute Editor. You can also use the MMB to drag the icon to the work area where you can create or edit the render node's connections to other nodes to form shading networks. Navigating in this area of the Hypershade, as well as the work area, is similar to navigating the Hypergraph and work windows in that you use the Alt/Option key and mouse controls.

THE WORK AREA

The work area is a free-form workspace where you can connect render nodes to form shading networks that you can assign to your object(s) for rendering. This is by far the easiest place to create and edit complex shaders, because it gives you a clear flowchart of the network. You can add nodes to the workspace by MMB dragging them from either the display area of the Hypershade or even the Multilister window.

The Graph Editor

Window → Animation Editors → Graph Editor

Maya's Graph Editor (see Figure 2.18) is an unbelievably powerful tool for the animator, and you use it to edit keyframes in animation.

Since 3D data is stored digitally as vector information—in mathematical form—every movement that is set in Maya generates a graph of value vs. time. The Graph Editor gives you direct access to the curves generated by your animation, which means that you have unparalleled access to editing and fine-tuning your animation.

The Graph Editor is divided into two sections. The left portion, which is much like the Outliner, displays the selected objects and their hierarchy with a listing of their animated channels or attributes. By default, all of an object's keyframed channels are displayed as colored curves in the display to the right of the list. However, by selecting an object or an object's channel in the list, you can isolate only those curves you want to see.

Figure 2.18

The Graph Editor

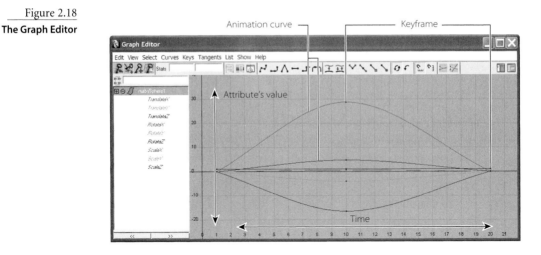

The Graph Editor displays these animation curves, also known as function curves, as value vs. time, with value running vertically and time horizontally. Keyframes are represented on the curves as points that can be freely moved about to adjust timing or value. You'll want to tune and refine animation through the Graph Editor, because it gives you the utmost in control over value, timing, and finesse.

The concept of the Graph Editor and the process of editing animation using graph curves may seem daunting at first, especially if you are not mathematically inclined, but this window is truly an animator's best friend. Intimate knowledge of this process will come to you as you use the Graph Editor, and you will find it much easier to deal with animation. Most, if not all, animation programs make extensive use of a graph or function curve editor. You will be making great use of the Graph Editor a little later on in the book.

Figure 2.19

The Script Editor

The Script Editor

Window → General Editors → Script Editor

You can access the Script Editor (see Figure 2.19) by clicking the icon in the bottom-right corner of the screen at the end of the Command line or by choosing it from the menu. Since almost everything in Maya is built on MEL, every command you initiate generates some sort of MEL script or MEL argument. A history of these comments is available in the Script Editor.

This window is handy when you need to reference a command that was issued or an argument or a comment that was displayed. It is also useful in *scripting*, or creating macros of MEL commands to execute compound actions. When you want to create a custom procedure, you can copy and paste MEL from this window to form macros.

> The Script Editor is essential in learning how to script. But scripting is a fairly advanced function that you might never need for your work. In any case, tackle scripting only after you establish a comfortable working repertoire in Maya.

The window is in two halves. The top half is the Script Editor's feedback history, and the bottom half is its Command line, where new MEL commands can be issued. By highlighting text in the upper window, you can copy and paste the command back into the Command line. You can easily add newly issued commands or macros of commands to the shelf by choosing **File → Save Script To Shelf**.

Using the Script Editor is also a good way to check on error messages that are too long to fully view in the Command line's feedback box. If you see an error message pop up and something goes wrong, open the Script Editor to see what sort of error(s) have scrolled by.

The Connection Editor

Window → General Editors → Connection Editor

You can use the Connection Editor (see Figure 2.20) to easily connect attributes between almost any two objects. Thus, you can set up almost any sort of relationship between any number of objects. For example, the height of a cube in the Y axis might control the X-axis translation of a sphere through a simple click of the mouse. You can set up more complicated connections to automatically rotate the tires of a car as the car moves forward, for example.

The Connection Editor window is separated into two vertical columns, each representing one of two objects. By selecting an object and clicking the Reload Left button, you can load into the Connection Editor's left column all the attributes of the selected objects. By selecting a second object and clicking Reload Right, you can

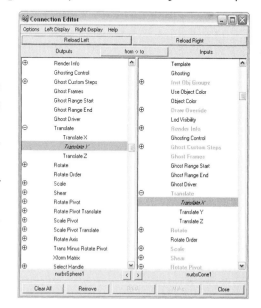

Figure 2.20

The Connection Editor

load the attributes of the second object. Clicking attributes in both columns creates a direct relationship between the two objects' attributes.

Connections are the cornerstone of animation and a significant reason for animation being so open-ended in Maya. You can create any kind of relationship between almost any attributes of almost any object to create highly complex, interconnected animations as well as automate animations to simplify a job. And who would argue with simplifying a job?

The Hotbox

The hotbox (see Figure 2.21) gives you convenient access to all menu commands in Maya.

To display the hotbox, press and hold down the spacebar in any modeling panel. All the menu commands that are available from the main menu bar are also available through the hotbox. To access a command, simply click it. You can display some or all of the menu headings to give you quick access to whatever commands and features you use most.

As you can see in Figure 2.22, the hotbox is separated into five distinct zones, delineated by the black diagonal lines: North, East, West, South, and Center. Activating the hotbox and clicking a zone displays a set of shortcut menu commands called *marking menus*, discussed in the next section.

If you don't see all the menu options when you invoke the hotbox, or if you want to restrict the menu display to specific menu sets, simply invoke the hotbox, click **Hotbox Controls**, and mark the selection of menus you would like from the marking menu from Hide All to Show All and everything in between.

Figure 2.21

The hotbox and marking menus

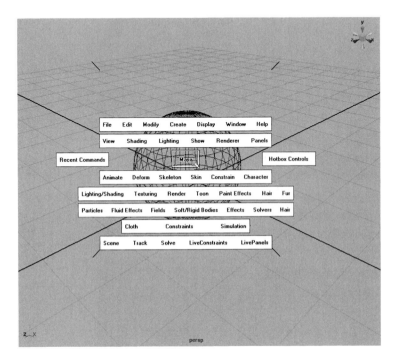

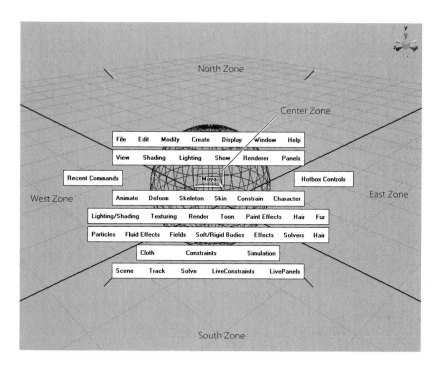

Figure 2.22

Hotbox zones

Marking Menus

In addition to menu selections, the hotbox has *marking menus* in each of the five zones. Using marking menus is yet another way to quickly access the commands you use the most. By default, the marking menu sets deal with changing your selection masks (which objects you can and cannot select), Control Panel visibility, and the type of panel that is being displayed. You can also access predefined (but customizable) key/mouse strokes through the hotbox.

A WORD TO THE WISE ABOUT THE HOTBOX

Only when you are comfortable with the interface and you've begun to establish a work flow for yourself should you use the hotbox/marking menus. Once you do, however, you'll find them pleasantly efficient. Many animators prefer to turn off the menu bar entirely to increase screen space for modeling and animating, using the hotbox exclusively. Others use both.

But again, use the main menu bar at the top of the screen instead of the hotbox when you're first starting out. It is better to find out where the commands are first. It also helps cut down the clutter of commands and the possibility of confusion about where and how to find them.

Menu Sets

Recall that menu sets are organized according to function. These menu sets are Animation, Polygons, Surfaces, Dynamics, and Rendering in Maya Complete, with Maya Unlimited adding the Cloth and Maya Live menu sets to those five. Each menu set gives you access to the commands associated with its broader function set. The Animation menu set, for example, displays in the main menu bar all the menu headers that correspond to animation functions, such as the Deform and Skeleton menus.

The menu set drop-down is the first thing on the Status line. Changing between menu sets is easier if you use the default hot keys.

KEY	FUNCTION
F2	Animation menu set
F3	Polygons menu set
F4	Surfaces menu set
F5	Dynamics menu set
F6	Rendering menu set

Switching back and forth between menu sets may feel a little strange at first, but it makes for a much more organized workspace than having all the menu headers staring at you across the top of the window as you animate. Besides, you can access all the functions through the hotbox anywhere on the screen.

When you find yourself wondering where a particular toolset is, all you need to do is ask yourself, What phase of CG would that function fall under? Since the menu sets are organized in phases of computer animation work flow—modeling (Polygons and Surfaces), animating, dynamics, and lighting/rendering—the task dictates which menu set includes its toolset.

Maya Object Structure

Now, on top of everything that you see in Maya—its interface—there is a layer that you don't see: the code. The layer of code keeps the objects in Maya organized through a network of nodes. How you relate these nodes defines how you've built your scene. In short, using Maya is essentially programming your computer directly to create 3D objects and animation.

So, having a solid understanding of how Maya defines objects and how they interact is essential to an efficient and successful animation process. This involves getting an intrinsic understanding of how nodes relate, whether it's a straightforward parent-child hierarchy in which one affects the other directly or a more complicated script-driven expression connecting 15 attributes of several objects to simplify a task.

When you're beginning to work with a robust program, the learning curve occasionally spikes. With Maya, these spikes typically involve nodes and their interconnections. Although the interface automates much of the node creation and relationship process, the sooner you are exposed to the implications of the node level of objects, the easier it will be for you to overcome the typical learning curve. Even though you may not actively see that you're making root level connections between nodes and attributes, you indeed are with every click of a command.

Understanding Nodes

At its core, Maya relies on packets of information called *nodes*, and each node carries with it a group of attributes that in combination define an object. These attributes can be spatial coordinates, geometric descriptors, color values, and so on. Taken together, an object's attributes define it and how it animates. You can define, animate, and inter-connect any or all of these attributes individually or in concert, which gives you amazing control over a scene.

Nodes that define the shape of a surface or a primitive are called *creation nodes* or *shape nodes*. These nodes carry the information that defines how that object is created. For example, a sphere's creation node has an attribute for its radius. Changing that attribute changes the radius of the sphere at its base level. Shape nodes are low on the hierarchy chain and are always child nodes of *transform nodes*. The sphere listens to its creation node attributes first and then moves down the chain to its other nodes' attrib-utes (such as position, rotation, or scale).

Not all primitives are created with shape nodes, so changes at the creation level may not be possible on certain objects; some objects are created without a creation node. When you create a new primitive or an object, make sure the History button ( ) is turned on. If it is crossed out, the primitive will be created without a shape node.

The most visible and used nodes are the transform nodes, also known as DAG nodes. These nodes contain all the transformation attributes for an object or a group of objects below it. Transformations are the values for translation (position), rotation, and scale. These nodes also hold hierarchy information on any other children or parent nodes to which they are attached. When you move or scale an object, you adjust attributes in this node.

Try This As an example of working with transform nodes, you can create a sphere and see what happens in the Attribute Editor as you adjust its position and size. Follow these steps:

1. Press Ctrl+A to open the Attribute Editor. (Ctrl is the same on PC as it is on Mac, so Mac users should also use their Ctrl key).

   The tabs along the top of the window let you switch between the nodes that are attached to this object. The current tab should be on the sphere's shape node called nurbsSphereShape1. This node contains specific information about the object, but it is not typically a node that you edit.

2. Press W to select the Translate tool. With the sphere still selected, click the nurbsSphere1 tab in the Attribute Editor to access the sphere's transforms node. Move the sphere a little bit in the X direction. Notice in the Attribute Editor that the **Translate** attribute for X has changed. You should also see the change in the Channel Box.

3. Press R to select the Scale tool. Scale the sphere uniformly, meaning equally, in all directions by clicking and dragging the center manipulator handle, the cyan box. Notice that the **Scale X**, **Scale Y**, and **Scale Z** attributes of the sphere change in the Attribute Editor. In the Attribute Editor, enter **1.0** for the X, Y, and Z scale values to reset the sphere to its original size.

4. In the creation node of makeNurbsSphere1, change the radius from 1.0 to 2.0. The sphere doubles in size since its radius is doubled. Switch back to the transform node (nurbsSphere1) and take note that the **Scale X**, **Scale Y**, and **Scale Z** attributes are unchanged. This is because you affected the size of the sphere through its **Radius** attribute in the creation node, at its root level and not through the **Scale** attributes in a higher node. Any changes you make to the **Scale** attributes take effect after changes in the lower node. This is a perfect example of how one node's output (here, the **Radius** attribute) changes another node.

Parents and Children

A parent node is simply a node that passes its transformations down the hierarchy chain to its children. A child node inherits the transforms of all the parents above it. For example, in the next chapter, you will create a simulation of the solar system. By using hierarchies, you will create a nested hierarchy of parents and children to animate the orbital rotation of the nine planets and some of their moons.

By creating parent-child relationships, you can easily animate the orbit of a moon around a planet while the planet orbits the sun. With the proper hierarchy, the animation of the planet orbiting the sun automatically translates into the moon. In effect, the planet takes the moon with it as it goes around the sun.

Child nodes have their own transformations that can be coupled with any inherited transforms from their parent, and these transformations affect them and any of their children down the line.

The rotation of one of the planets around the sun takes with it its moon, but that moon can have its own animation to spin itself around its planet. It may seem premature to explain this before you see it in practice, but understanding parent-child relationships and hierarchies in general is essential. The more you hear about these concepts in different contexts, the easier they will be.

Figure 2.23 features the Outliner and Hypergraph views with a simple hierarchy of objects for your reference. A top parent node called group1 holds its children nurbsCone1, nurbsSphere3, and the nested group node group2. The node group2 is the parent node of nurbsSphere2 and nurbsSphere1. Chapter 3 will have more information on hierarchies.

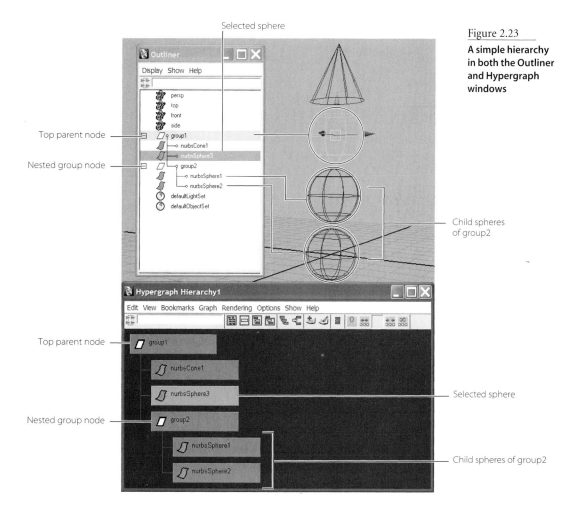

Figure 2.23

A simple hierarchy in both the Outliner and Hypergraph windows

Summary

In this chapter, you learned about the user interface and the primary windows you will work with in Maya. The user interface combines mouse and keyboard input as well as plenty of menu and tool icons you can select and use to accomplish your tasks.

Okay, you'll be quizzed in 10 minutes. You got it all memorized? Honestly, don't worry in the slightest if you haven't absorbed all of the information in this chapter. Now that you've had some exposure to the Maya user interface, you'll have some familiarity with the various windows once you really get to work.

Figure 2.24

The best menu...ever!

You can always come back to this chapter to refresh your memory. Remember, you should learn the Maya program using its default settings as in Figure 2.24. To start, concentrate on using the menus to access most commands. Once you are really comfortable working in Maya, you can start using hot keys and shortcuts. At this stage, though, focus on getting a clear understanding of the tools and what they do. You will be introduced to some hot keys and shortcuts as you work through the exercises in this book.

CHAPTER 3

Your First Maya Animation

In this chapter you're going to start using Maya software and get things moving. The last chapter showed you how the Maya interface works and how some of the windows operate, and that's really all you need to know to get started. The rest comes with practice and experience, so let's get started!

This chapter will take you through the creation of the solar system and the mechanics of animating orbits. With the solar system exercise, you'll dive into creating simple objects, setting keyframes, and stacking your animation to get planets and moons to orbit each other and the sun. This exposes you to object creation, simple modeling, object components, pivot point placement, grouping and hierarchies, basic keyframing, and timing. Topics include:

- **Project Overview: The Solar System**
- **The Preproduction Process: Planning**
- **Creating a Project**
- **The Production Process: Creating and Animating the Objects**
- **Using the Outliner**

Project Overview: The Solar System

This project focuses on familiarizing you with the fundamentals of object creation, hierarchy, and pivots, all very important points to understand before animating. You will create and animate a simple simulation of our working solar system. This time-tested tutorial is fantastic practice for getting used to object hierarchies and selections. It will show you how to set up hierarchies and give you experience in working with the proper nodes within a group to create hierarchically layered animation. The focus in this example is getting used to working with objects and hierarchies.

The Preproduction Process: Planning

As with any good animation, you need to begin with a good plan. The more research and information you gather, the better equipped you'll be. For this simple animation, you'll need to find out where each of the nine planets are in relation to the sun and each other, how they orbit, and how many moons they have.

Starting with the sun in the center, the planets in order are Mercury, Venus, Earth, Mars, Jupiter, Saturn, Uranus, Neptune, and Pluto. They all orbit the sun in ellipses, but you'll be fine with circular orbits for this exercise. Most planets have a number of moons that orbit them, and one has a large ring that circles around it.

Earth	1 moon
Mars	2 small moons
Jupiter	16+ moons
Saturn	3 large rings and 18+ moons
Uranus	18 moons
Neptune	8 moons
Pluto	1 moon

It may seem overwhelming to create and animate all those objects, but it's a great exercise in getting comfortable with Maya animation. Since the essence of the project is attainable without making every moon, you'll cut most of them out of your scene.

Creating a Project

Start by creating a new project for this assignment. Choose **File → Project → New** to open the New Project window. (Figure 3.1 shows the Windows version; the Mac OS X version has the same fields.) In the Maya software, files are organized in a particular way. The top level of this organization is the *project folder*. Within the project folder are numerous file folders that hold your files. The two that stand out are the Scenes and Images folders. The Scenes folder stores your scene files, which contain all the information for your scene, and the Images folder stores images you've rendered out from your scene. As with clothing and other items around your house, keeping your files and projects organized is a good practice.

> The scene files mentioned in this chapter are all included on the CD in a project layout explained here. You can copy the scene files into your own project folders once you create the project.

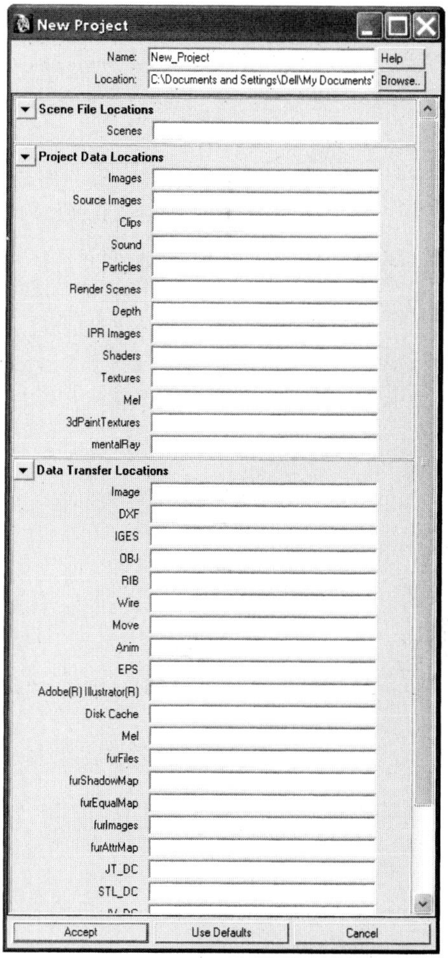

Figure 3.1

The New Project window on a Windows system. Maya automatically creates a new file system structure for your project.

To create a new project, follow these steps:

1. In the Name field in the New Project window, enter **Solar_ System** as the name for your project. In the Location box, type the location where you want to store your projects.

   The default location for Windows is My Documents\maya\projects; for Macs, the default location is Home (/Users/<*yourname*>) in the Documents/maya/projects/default folder. If you prefer, you can put projects in a folder on your second hard drive to keep them separate from your operating system; this allows for easier backup and is generally a safer environment.

2. On a Windows system, create a folder called Projects (on drive D, for example) through Windows Explorer. On a Mac, select a drive from the Choose a Folder dialog box (drag the bottom slider all the way to the left to display all your attached and networked hard drives) and create a folder in it called Projects. In the New Project window, click the Browse button and select D:\Projects (Windows) or <*Hard Drive Name*>/Projects (Mac) for the location. All the other fields will be filled in for you with defaults; just click the Use Defaults button. Click Accept to create the necessary folders in your specified location. Figure 3.2 shows the completed New Project window in Windows; except for the drive name, the values are the same on a Macintosh.

How much disk space you require depends on the project. Depending on the complexity and extent of your models and animation, your scene files will typically be small. Real disk space starts being consumed when you render out hundreds of frames at a time. You'll need about 10 to 15MB free for this project.

After you create projects, you can switch between them by choosing **File → Project → Set** and selecting the new project. Maya then uses that project's folders until you switch to or create another project. You may also select a recent project by choosing **File → Project → Recent Projects.** Maya by default lists four of your recent projects and scene files on the File menu for easy access.

The Production Process: Creating and Animating the Objects

As discussed in Chapter 1, production is typically divided into phases to make work flow easier to manage. In this project, you'll first create the sun, the planets, and their moons; then you'll animate their respective orbits and rotations.

Creating the Sun and the Planets

The first thing we're going to do is create the sun and the planets. Follow these steps:

Figure 3.2

The completed New Project window

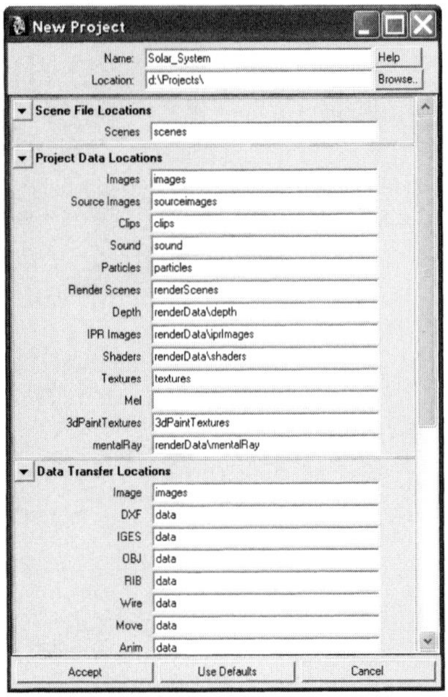

1. Choose **File → New Scene** (or press Ctrl+N). Maya will ask if you want to save your current scene. Save the file if you need to, or click Don't Save to discard the scene.

2. By default, you should begin in an expanded Perspective view. Press the spacebar to enable the four-panel view. Now, in the four-panel view, press the spacebar with the cursor inside the top view panel to select and maximize it.

3. To create the sun, choose **Create → NURBS Primitives → Sphere**. This will place a NURBS sphere at the origin—that is, at a position of 0,0,0 for X,Y,Z. The origin of the workspace will be the center of the solar system.

4. Select nurbsSphere1 in the Channel Box, and type **Sun**.

Keep in mind that Maya is case sensitive. An object named *sun* is different from an object named *Sun*.

Naming your objects right after creation is a necessary habit to establish. It makes for a cleaner scene file and a more organized workspace. This is particularly important if anyone needs to alter your scene file; proper naming will keep them from wanting to punch you in the nose when they work on your scene.

Maya typically uses an object naming structure called a humpback style, where the first letter of new words is capitalized. An example is the name indoorPatioScene. Maya uses this structure when naming nodes, such as the node name nurbsSphere1.

5. Press R to activate the scale manipulator and uniformly scale it up to about twice its current size. For more precision, you can instead highlight the entry fields (the white window next to the attribute) for the **Scale X**, **Scale Y**, and **Scale Z** channels in the Channel Box and enter the 4 in any of the three fields. A scale of 4 will be entered in all three fields, as shown in Figure 3.3, and your sun will expand in size by a factor of 4. Entering exact values in the Channel Box is a way to scale the sphere precisely. Using the manipulator does the same job but may not be as precise.

Creating the Planets

Next create the planets. Follow these steps:

1. Create a NURBS sphere for Mercury and name it as such.

2. Press W to activate the move manipulator, and move Mercury a few grid units away from the sun in the positive X direction. (Click the red arrow and drag it to the right.) Leave about two grid units between Mercury and the sun.

3. Since Mercury is the second smallest planet and is tiny compared with the sun, scale it down to 1/20 the size of the sun, or 0.2 in all three axes of scale.

4. Repeat steps 1 through 3 to create the rest of the planets and line them up, each progressively farther out in the X axis. Be sure to keep about 2 grid units of space between each of them. Scale each one to be proportional as follows:

Venus	0.5
Earth	0.5
Mars	0.4
Jupiter	1.0
Saturn	0.9
Uranus	0.7
Neptune	0.7
Pluto	0.15

Now of course this is not a precise proportion to the solar system, but it will do nicely here. Figure 3.4 shows how your solar system should look now.

Figure 3.3

The sun's Scale values in the Channel Box

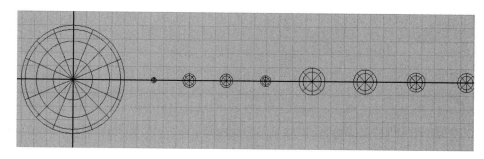

Figure 3.4

Top view—all the NURBS spheres lined up in place

Using Snaps

This would be the perfect time to start using *snaps,* the icons you looked at in the previous chapter.

Icon	Name	Description
	Snap to Grids	Snaps objects to intersections of the view's grid
	Snap to Curves	Snaps objects along a curve
	Snap to Points	Snaps objects to object points such as CVs or vertices
	Snap to View Planes	Snaps objects to view planes

You use *snaps* to snap objects into place with precision, by placing them by their pivot points directly onto grid points, onto other object pivots, onto curve points, and so on. Here you will slightly reposition all the planets to center them on the nearest grid line intersection. Follow these steps:

1. Select the first planet, Mercury, and toggle on the *grid snaps* by clicking the Snap to Grids icon ( ).

2. The center of the move manipulator turns from a square to a circle, signaling that some form of snapping is active. Grab the manipulator in the middle by this circle, and move it slightly to the left or right to snap it onto the closest grid intersection on the X axis.

3. Select the remaining planets, and snap them all to the closest grid intersection on the X axis, making sure to keep about two grid spaces between each of them. Since the sun was created at the origin and you haven't moved it, you don't need to snap it onto an intersection.

Making Saturn's Ring

You will now create the ring for your Saturn. Follow these steps:

1. Choose **Create → NURBS Primitives → Torus** to get a donut shape. Snap the ring to the same grid intersection as Saturn. This will ensure that both the planet and its ring are on the same pivot point; they share the same center.

2. Select the torus shape you've created, and name it Ring (if you haven't already done so).

3. While the torus shape is still selected, press the spacebar to display the four-panel layout, and maximize the perspective window.

4. Press F to *focus* the perspective display on the ring—and on Saturn as well.

5. Press 5 to get into shaded mode, and with the torus selected, press 3 to increase the resolution display for the ring.

6. Press R to display the scale manipulator, and scale it down to 0 or close to 0 in the Y axis to flatten it.

SAVING MULTIPLE VERSIONS OF YOUR WORK AND INCREMENTAL SAVE

As you're working on a project, you may want to save multiple versions of your files at various stages of completion. When working in the professional world, you'll find that clients and art directors often reconsider animations you've created, sometimes, it seems, just to make you crazy. So it's always good to keep as many versions of an animation as you can. Scene files are reasonably small, and hard disk space is inexpensive. Just keep your scene folder organized well—for example, by keeping older versions of scenes in separate subfolders—and you should have no problems.

Maya's *Incremental Save* feature makes a backup of your scene file every time you save your scene. To enable it, choose **File → Save Scene** □ and click the Incremental Save option box. Once you've done this, Maya creates a new folder within your Scenes folder with the name of your current scene file. It then creates a backup of your scene in that folder and appends a number to the filename; for example, planets_001.mb. Every time you save your file, Maya creates a new backup until you disable the feature by choosing **File → Save Scene** □.

The scene files for the projects in this book are provided on the accompanying CD to give you a reference point for the major stages of each project. These files use a slightly different naming system than the names generated by Incremental Save (for example, on the CD is planets_v1.mb instead of planets_001.mb), so there is no risk of files overwriting each other.

For important real-world projects, you might decide to supplement the incremental save backups by using Save Scene As to create manually named files, perhaps following a similar naming system with a version number appended, at the stages where you've made significant changes. Whether you do this or use Incremental Save, it's a good idea to keep written notes about the differences in each version of a scene file so whenever you make a significant change to a file, you have a record of your work. (If you do name files manually, be sure to use an underscore (_) between the filename and version number instead of a space. Using spaces in your filenames can create problems with the software and with the operating system, especially when you're rendering out a scene.)

You'll notice that the ring is too fat and is cutting into the planet. You need to edit the attributes of the ring to increase the inside radius of the donut shape and create a gap between the planet and the ring.

7. Press Ctrl+A / [⌘]+A to open the Attribute Editor, and then click the make-NurbTorus1 tab to select its creation node. (See Figure 3.5.)

8. Increase the **Radius** attribute to about 1.5, and decrease the **Height Ratio** attribute to about 0.25 to get the desired effect.

Now all your planets are complete and you can move on to the moons.

Changing the original attributes or parameters of an object as you've just done with Saturn's ring is often referred to as *parametric modeling*.

Saving Your Work

Now save your work, unless you like to live on the edge. Saving frequently is a critical habit to establish. Power failures and other unforeseen circumstances (like your pet jumping onto your keyboard) may not happen often, but they do happen, and usually just at the wrong time. (As mentioned in the sidebar "Saving Multiple Versions of Your Work and Incremental Save," Maya's Incremental Save feature makes it easy to maintain backups of your work.) Because you created this as a new project, the Save File window will direct you to the Scenes folder of that project. Save your scene as planets in the .mb (Maya Binary) format. (If you're working in Maya PLE, you can only save your files as .mp files.)

The file Planets_v1.mb in the Scenes folder of the Solar_System project on the CD shows what the scene should look like at this point.

Creating the Moons

Figure 3.5

Changing the creation attributes of the NURBS torus in the Attribute Editor

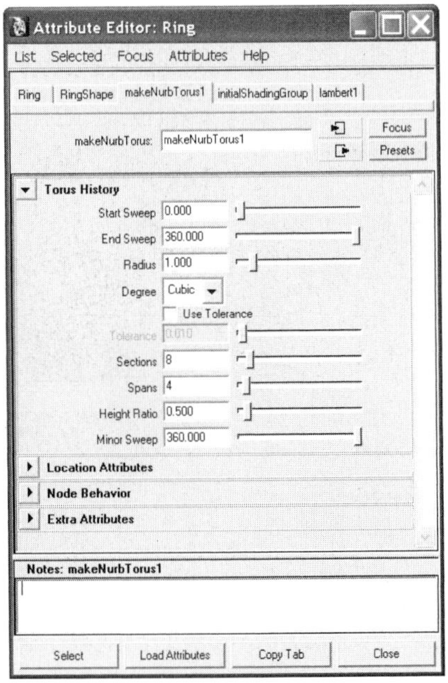

For the planets with moons, create a new NURBS sphere for each moon. For simplicity's sake, create a maximum of only two moons for any planet. However, feel free to make all the moons for all the planets once you get a handle on this exercise.

The first moon will be Earth's. Use the top view to follow these steps:

1. Create a NURBS sphere and scale it to about half the size of Earth using the scale manipulator. You can just visually estimate the size of the moon.

2. Move the sphere to within half a unit of Earth using the move manipulator by the X axis. There's no need to snap it to a grid point, so toggle off the Snap to Grids icon (⊞).

3. Repeat steps 1 and 2 for the remaining moons, placing them each within half a grid unit from their respective planets. When placing two moons, place one on either side of the planet.

4. Once you're done with all the moons and their placements and sizes, select all the elements in the scene and press 3 to increase the display resolution on all the spheres. When you're done, you should have a scene similar to Figure 3.6 in perspective view. If you don't, it's clear Maya is trying to kill you.

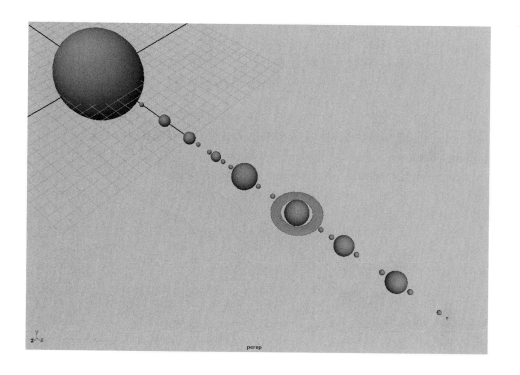

Figure 3.6

The planets and moons in position in perspective view

Applying a Simple Shader

To help distinguish one gray planet from another, attach simple shaders to each of the planets. You can easily take care of this task using the Hypershade window. Follow these steps:

1. Choose **Window → Rendering Editors → Hypershade** to open the Hypershade window. You will notice three default (or initial) shader icons already loaded. (See Figure 3.7.)

2. In the Create Maya Nodes Panel on the left of the Hypershade window and under the Surface heading, click the Lambert icon (a gray sphere) to create a new Lambert shader node. It will appear in the top and bottom of the Hypershade window. Click it another eight times to create a total of nine Lambert shading groups in the Hypershade window.

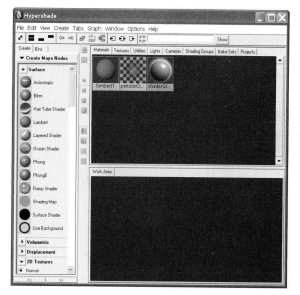

Figure 3.7

The Hypershade window

3. Click the first of the new Lambert nodes (lambert2) in the Hypershade window, and then double-click its icon to open the Attribute Editor. At the top, replace lambert2 with Mercury_Color to identify this material as the one you will use for Mercury.

4. Name each of the remaining eight planets in your animation (Venus, Earth, Mars, Jupiter, Saturn, Uranus, Neptune, and Pluto).

To rename a node in the Hypershade window, you can also right-click the node's icon and choose **Rename** from the shortcut menu that appears.

Again, keeping a well-named and organized scene is paramount in a smooth animation experience. It's so much more of a chore to root through dozens of unnamed nodes to find the one you want. When you're done with naming all the material nodes, save your work.

Once you've created the shaders, you can assign the appropriate colors to each of them according to the planet they represent.

1. Double-click Mercury to open its Attribute Editor if it's not currently open (see Figure 3.8).

2. To change the color of the shader, click the gray box next to the **Color** attribute. This opens the Color Chooser window, from which you can choose a new color from the color wheel or by adjusting values with the HSV sliders. Since Mercury has a brownish red appearance, go with an orange, such as in Figure 3.9.

SETTING KEYFRAMES

As with many other functions in Maya, you can set a keyframe in several ways. The best way when you're first starting to learn Maya is to choose **Animate → Set Key** ❐ to display the Set Key Options dialog box:

If you simply choose **Animate → Set Key** instead, Maya sets a keyframe for every single keyable attribute for the selected object. Although this may seem convenient, it makes for a sloppy scene, especially if the scene must be heavily animated.

Having keyframes for attributes that may not actually be animated creates unnecessary clutter. In the Set Key Options dialog box, set the Set Keys On option to All Keyable Attributes instead of the default All Manipulator Handles and Keyable Attributes. Set Channels to From Channel Box instead of the default All Keyable. (These attributes will remain grayed out until you change to All Keyable Attributes.) Now when you choose **Animate → Set Key**, you will set only a keyframe for the channels that you specify explicitly through the Channel Box, giving you greater control and efficiency. All you have to do is highlight the channel you want to keyframe in the Channel Box and then choose **Animate → Set Key**. Save your settings by choosing **Edit → Save Settings**, and then click Close to close the dialog box.

3. Change the remainder of shaders as follows:

Mercury	Orange Brown
Venus	Beige Yellow
Earth	Blue
Mars	Red Orange
Jupiter	Yellow Green
Saturn	Pale Yellow
Uranus	Cyan
Neptune	Aqua Blue
Pluto	Bright Gray

Figure 3.10 shows the shading groups. Next you will apply shaders to each of the planets.

4. Select a planet in the perspective window and RMB click its corresponding material in the Hypershade window to open a marking menu. Drag up to highlight **Assign Material to Selection** and release the button to select it. You can also MMB drag the material from the Hypershade window to its planet, although assigning materials in this way is not preferable. Leave the moons the default gray color. When you're finished, you should have a scene similar to Figure 3.11.

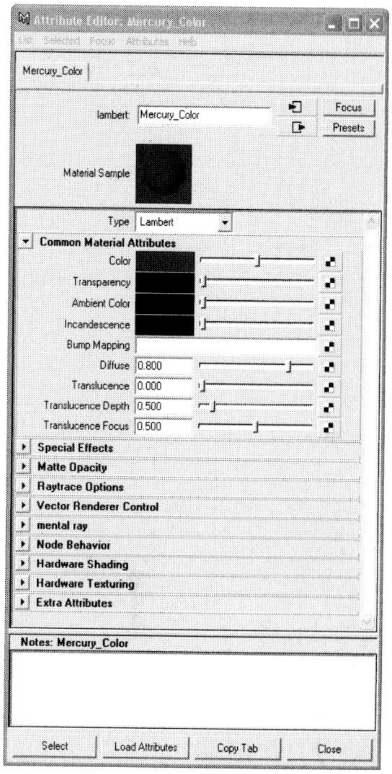

Now that you're done, you're ready to animate! Just save this file, and if you've enabled Incremental Save as recommended earlier, it won't be replaced with subsequent saves. If you get lost in your animation and need to start fresh, you won't have to create everything from scratch again. You can just return to a previous version of the file and start your animation again.

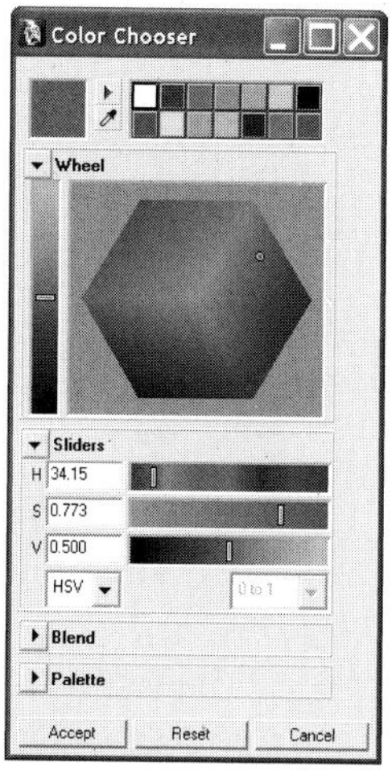

Figure 3.8

Mercury's shading group in the Attribute Editor

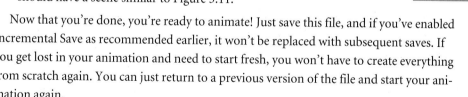

Figure 3.9

The Color Chooser window

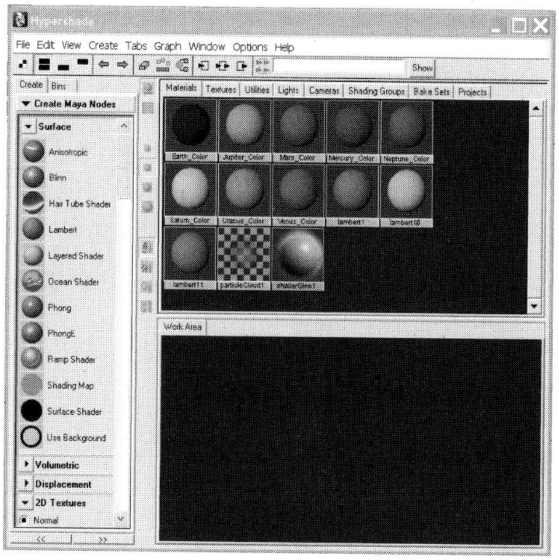

Figure 3.10

The Hypershade window with all the colored planet shading groups

Figure 3.11

The shaded planets in perspective view

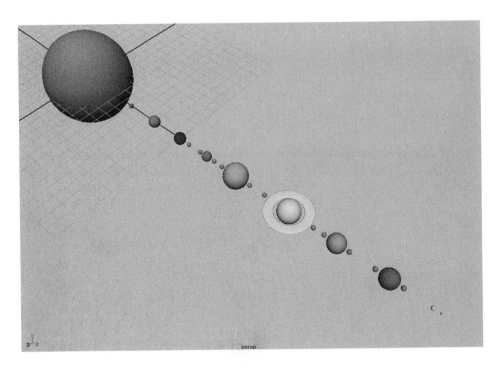

Creating the Animation

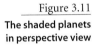

To begin this phase of the project, load the file `Planets_v2.mb` in the Scenes folder of the Solar_System project on the CD, or continue with your own scene file. The animation you'll be doing for the orbits is straightforward. Basically you will rotate the planets around their own axes, then you'll animate the moons around the planets, and finally you'll send the planets with their moons to orbit the sun.

The premise of this exercise deals with hierarchy and pivot points. A *pivot point* is an object's center of balance of sorts. Every object or node that is created in Maya has a pivot point set at the origin. Since most objects, such as the spheres you created for the planets, will appear at the origin upon creation, their pivot points are automatically centered.

Once you move an object, as you have done to position the planets and moons, the pivot point moves with it. Thus, all your planets' and moons' pivot points are already correctly positioned at the center of each planet and moon.

Now you'll set up your scene file's animation settings:

1. Press F2 to open the Animation menu set.

2. With the Range Slider, set your animation to go from 1 to 240.

3. Click the Animation Preferences icon (🖼), click Settings, and set Time to 30 frames per second, or *NTSC* video speed.

4. Verify that Up-Axis is set to Y and not Z. This ensures that you have designated the Y axis to be pointing "up" in the perspective window or pointing out at you from the monitor in the top view. "Y up," as it's called, is Maya's default, but it never hurts to make sure.

> Choose **Window → Settings/Preferences → Preferences** to open the Preferences window. Under Settings: Undo, check the circle for Undo to On (if it isn't already), and set Queue to Infinite. Setting Queue to Infinite takes a little more system memory, but it's worth it. With this configuration, you can undo (press Ctrl+Z / ⌘+Z or just Z) as many times as it takes to undo any blunders. To close the Preferences window, click Save.

Mercury's Rotation

Now you're ready to animate Mercury's rotation. Follow these steps:

1. Select Mercury first, and press E to activate the rotation manipulator. Press F to focus on it in the perspective view, or zoom in on it manually.

2. Make sure you are on frame 1 of your animation range. For Mercury, you'll be setting your initial keyframe for the Y-axis rotation. In the Channel Box, click the attribute **Rotate Y** to select it and choose **Animate → Set Key**. If you followed the advice in the sidebar "Setting Keyframes," only **Rotate Y**'s attribute box will turn orange to indicate a keyframe. If you have left the Set Key command at its defaults, choosing **Animate → Set Key** will set keys on all the attributes, turning them all orange.

3. With the Range Slider, go to frame 240. Grab the rotation manipulator handle by the Y axis and turn it clockwise a few times to rotate the sphere.

4. Choose **Animate → Set Key** with the **Rotate Y** attribute still selected in the Channel Box.

5. To playback your animation, you can *scrub* your Timeline. Scrubbing refers to using the mouse to move the time marker back and forth to watch the animation playback in a window. Click in the Timeline, hold down the left mouse button, and move your cursor side to side to scrub in real time. You'll see Mercury rotating around itself in your active view panel.

Clicking so many things just to set two keyframes may seem like a lot of work, but you're doing this the long way right now; you're not yet using any shortcuts or hot keys. You'll start using those for the next planet.

You have the self-rotation for Mercury worked out, and since there's no moon for Mercury, let's get it orbiting the sun.

Grouping Mercury for a New Pivot Point

You've learned that every object created in Maya is created with a pivot point around which it rotates, from which or to which it scales, and which acts as the placement point for its XYZ coordinates. If the pivot point for Mercury is already at the center of itself, how can you rotate it around the sun?

One idea is to move its current pivot point from the center of itself to the center of the sun. That would, however, negate its own rotation and it will no longer spin around its own center, so you can't do that. What you need to do is to create a new pivot point for this object by creating a new parent node above it in the hierarchy. For more on object nodes and hierarchy, refer to the end of Chapter 2. If you're new to CG animation, take your time with the following section.

To create a new pivot point by making a new parent node, follow these steps:

1. With Mercury still selected, choose **Edit → Group**. The Channel Box displays the attributes for the node called group1. In addition, the rotation manipulator handle jumps from where it was originally, centered on Mercury, to the origin—where the zero points of the X, Y, and Z axes collide. Figure 3.12 shows the new Mercury group and its new pivot location.

You essentially created a new Maya object by grouping Mercury to itself and hence also created a new pivot point, placed by Maya at the origin by default. Since an object's manipulator always centers on its pivot point, yours jumped to the origin. That's fortunate for you because that just happens to be the center of the sun, exactly where you need it to be for Mercury to orbit it properly.

Figure 3.12

Grouping Mercury to itself creates a new pivot point at the origin.

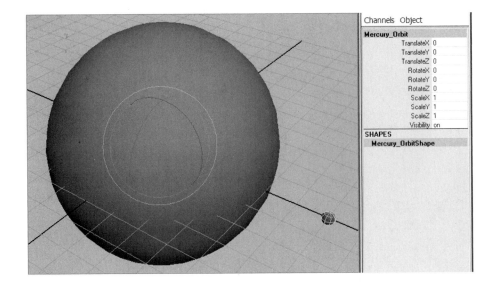

2. Without unselecting Mercury, click the word *group1* in the Channel Box and change the name of this new group to Mercury_Orbit.

3. Now click anywhere in an empty space in your view window to unselect Mercury_Orbit. Try selecting it again. Notice that when you click Mercury, you select only the planet and not the new parent node Mercury_Orbit, the group that has its pivot point at the center of the sun. This happens because you are in object selection mode (a.k.a. object mode).

> To select the group Mercury_Orbit, you need to switch into hierarchy mode by toggling its icon (🔲) on the Status line. Just remember to switch back to object mode (🔲).

4. Go back to frame 1 of your animation and set a keyframe for Mercury_Orbit's **Rotate Y** attribute by choosing **Animate → Set Key**.

5. Go to frame 240, grab Mercury_Orbit's rotate manipulator handle by the Y axis, and spin it around the sun twice. You could also type **720** in the **Rotate Y** attribute field in the Channel Box.

6. Choose **Animate → Set Key** to set a keyframe at frame 240 for Mercury_Orbit. Scrub your animation to play it back.

   One down, eight to go.

Creating Venus

For your next planet, Venus, follow the same procedure as for Mercury and animate it so that it orbits itself. Then create a new pivot point (placed by default at the origin) by grouping it to itself, and call the new node Venus_Orbit. Lastly, animate Venus_Orbit to rotate around the sun.

Earth and the Moon

You will animate the third planet (That's the Earth. Hey, I can see my house from here!) in much the same way, except that this time there is the added complication of a moon. In addition, instead of choosing **Animate → Set Key** to set your keyframes, you'll use the keyboard hot key S.

> Whenever you press S when an attribute is highlighted in the Channel Box, you are essentially choosing **Animate → Set Key**. In the Set Key Options dialog box, be sure that you have changed Set Keys On to All Keyable Attributes instead of the default All Manipulator Handles and Keyable Attributes and that you've set Channels to From Channel Box instead of the default All Keyable as mentioned in the earlier sidebar.

To animate Earth and the moon, follow these steps:

1. Select Earth and give it its self-rotation animation as with Mercury, but this time select the rotation channels in the Channel Box and press S instead of choosing **Animate → Set Key** to set rotation keyframes. Again, if you have left the **Animate → Set Key** ❑ at its defaults, pressing S will set keys for all attributes, but if you followed the advice given previously, only the selected channels will be keyframed.

2. Select the moon and give it its self-rotation animation by spinning it around itself and keyframing it as you've just done with Earth.

3. To spin the moon around Earth, do what you did earlier in this chapter to spin a planet around the sun: group the moon to itself by choosing **Edit → Group** and name it Moon_Orbit.

This time, however, you need the pivot point to be at the center of Earth and not at the center of the sun, where it is currently. Follow these steps:

1. Turn on the grid snap, and then press the Insert key to activate the pivot point. For a Macintosh, press the Home key. The moon's manipulator changes from a rotation handle to the *pivot point manipulator*. This manipulator acts just like the move manipulator, but instead of moving the object, it moves the object's pivot point.

2. Grab the yellow circle in the middle of the manipulator and move the pivot point to snap it to the grid point located at the center of Earth (see Figure 3.13).

3. Press the Insert key again (or the Home key on a Macintosh) to return to the rotation manipulator for Moon_Orbit. At frame 1, set a keyframe for the moon's Y-axis rotation. Then, at frame 240, rotate the moon about the Y axis and set a keyframe. Return to frame 1.

Figure 3.13

Moving the moon's pivot point to the center of Earth

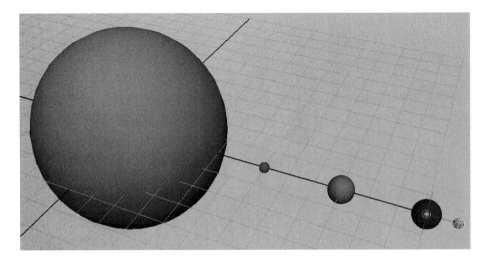

GROUPING THE MOON WITH EARTH

To animate Earth's orbit of the sun, you need to make sure the moon will also follow Earth around the sun. So, instead of just selecting Earth and grouping it to itself as you've done for the other two planets, you need to include Moon_Orbit. Follow these steps:

1. Select Earth and then Shift+click the group Moon_Orbit while in hierarchy mode to make sure you get the topmost node of the moon, and then choose **Edit → Group**. Name this Earth_Orbit. Remember, when you simply select either Earth or the moon in object mode, the Earth_Orbit node is not selected. If you select Earth and then Shift+click the moon, you do select both objects, but you will still not select Earth_Orbit, the group that contains both these objects and has its pivot point at the center of the sun. So make sure you select the right group.

> Make sure you use hierarchy mode (🔣) when you click the moon object to select Moon_Orbit and not just the moon sphere. Otherwise, you will lose the animation of the moon orbiting Earth.

2. Set a keyframe for Earth_Orbit's **Rotate Y** attribute at frame 1 by highlighting **Rotate Y** in the Channel Box and pressing S for the Set Key command. This assumes you have changed the defaults in **Animate → Set Key ❑** as discussed earlier.

3. Go to frame 240, spin Earth and the moon around the sun a few times, and set a keyframe there as well.

Now the first three planets are going around themselves and around the sun, with a moon in there too. If you haven't been saving your work, save it now. Just don't save over the un-animated version from before.

CREATING THE OTHER PLANETS' MOONS

Repeat this animation procedure for the remaining planets and moons, but leave out Pluto for now. (Poor Pluto, always last.)

> If you find that one of your moons is left behind by its planet or that it's no longer rotating around the planet, you most likely made an error when grouping the moon and planet. Undo until you're at the point right before you grouped them, and try again. If that still doesn't work, start over from the earlier version of the file you saved just before you started animating it. You'll learn how to fix it in the section "Using the Outliner" later in this chapter.

AUTO KEYFRAME

You can also use the Auto Keyframe feature when animating the planets and moons. Auto Keyframe automatically sets a keyframe for any attribute that changes from a previously set keyframe. For example, an initial keyframe for an attribute such as **Y-Axis Rotation** needs to be set at some point in the animation. The next time the **Y-Axis Rotation** is changed, Maya will set a keyframe at the current frame automatically.

To turn on Auto Keyframe, click the Auto Keyframe icon (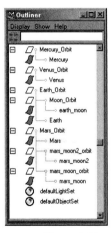), which is to the right of the Range Slider. When the icon is red, Auto Keyframe is active.

To use Auto Keyframe to animate Mars's moon orbiting Mars, follow these steps:

1. Turn on Auto Keyframe.

2. Start at frame 1. Select Mars's moon and set a keyframe for its Y rotation by highlighting **Rotate Y** in the Channel Box and pressing S.

3. Got to frame 240. Rotate the moon around Mars several times. Maya will automatically set a frame for Y rotation at frame 240. Save your file.

Using the Outliner

Now let's look at how to use the Outliner to illustrate the hierarchies for the planets and moons. When all is good and proper, the Outliner should look like Figure 3.14. Choose **Window → Outliner** and take a peek at what you have. If you haven't yet properly named everything, such as the moons, take this opportunity to do so.

Let's take a look at the planet Mars and its layout in the Outliner to better understand the hierarchy for all the planets. All the other planets should be laid out exactly like Mars (except for the planets that have just one or no moons).

At the bottom of the hierarchy are Mars's two moons, mars_moon and mars_moon2. Each of those moons is spinning on its own pivot point. You grouped each moon to itself, creating the mars_moon_orbit and mars_moon2_orbit nodes, and you placed their pivot points at the center of Mars to animate their orbits of Mars.

Mars is spinning on its own pivot point, but it needed another pivot point to be able to orbit the sun. Since you needed to make the moons go with it around the sun, you selected Mars, mars_moon_orbit, and mars_moon2_orbit (the top nodes of the moons that circle the planet Mars) and grouped them all together, placing that pivot point at the center of the sun. This node you called Mars_Orbit. This is the *parent node* since it is the topmost node for this group. Where this parent node goes, so follow the children nodes that are grouped under it.

Hierarchy such as this is a cornerstone of Maya animation. It is imperative to be comfortable with how it works and how to work with it. If you find yourself scratching your head even just a little bit, try the exercise again. A proper foundation is critical. And remember, this learning 3d thing is not easy, but patience and repetition help a lot.

Correcting Hierarchy Problems Using the Outliner

One of the most common problems you will run into with this project is a planet rotating around the sun without its moon. The following steps will force you to make this error

Figure 3.14
The Outliner view of the planet hierarchies

with the planet Pluto, to illustrate how to fix it using the Outliner—as opposed to undoing and redoing it as suggested earlier. Sometimes, you just learn more from mistakes.

Go to Pluto, start the same animation procedure as outlined earlier, and then follow these steps:

1. Create Pluto's own rotation by spinning it around itself.

2. Do the same for its moon's rotation.

3. Group the moon to itself and grid-snap the pivot point at the center of Pluto to create the moon's orbit of Pluto.

Once Pluto's moon (pluto_moon) is orbiting Pluto, you're ready to group the moon's orbit and Pluto together to create an orbit of the sun for them both.

4. Here is where you make your mistake. In object mode, select the sphere for Pluto's moon and select the sphere for Pluto. Your error is that you are remaining in object mode instead of switching to hierarchy mode.

5. Choose **Edit → Group** to group them together, and call that new node Pluto_Orbit like the others.

6. Animate Pluto_Orbit rotating around the sun.

7. Playback the animation.

Notice that the moon is no longer orbiting the planet. This is because you didn't include pluto_moon_orbit in your group Pluto_Orbit. The animation of the moon going around Pluto is stored in that node, and since it is no longer attached to your Pluto_Orbit, there's no moon orbit of Pluto.

Figure 3.15 shows the hierarchy of Pluto and how it's different from the other planets (with Earth showing as an example). The moon's orbit node has been left out of the group.

Using the Outliner, you can easily fix this problem. You will place the pluto_moon_orbit node under the Pluto_Orbit node. Go to frame 1 of the animation, grab the pluto_moon_orbit node in the Outliner, and MMB drag it to the Pluto_Orbit node so that it has a black horizontal line above and below it to show a connection, as in Figure 3.16.

You have just grouped pluto_moon_orbit under Pluto_Orbit, a practice known as parenting. Now you need to parent pluto_moon under pluto_moon_orbit as well. MMB drag pluto_moon onto pluto_moon_orbit. When you playback the animation, you will see that the moon is rotating around the planet as Pluto and the moon both orbit the sun. Now the layout in the Outliner for Pluto is similar to the other properly working planets.

The file `Planets_v3.mb` in the Scenes folder of the Solar_System project on the CD will give you an idea of how this project should now look. The first five planet systems are grouped and animated as reference, leaving the final four for you to finish.

Figure 3.15

Pluto's incorrect hierarchy

Figure 3.16

Regrouping objects in the Outliner

GROUPING TERMINOLOGY

Grouping terminology can be confusing. Grouping Node A under Node B makes Node A a *child* of Node B. Node B is now the *parent* of Node A. Furthermore, any transformation, or movement, applied to the parent Node B will be *inherited* by the child Node A.

When you *group* Node A and Node B, both nodes become *siblings* under a newly created parent node, Node C. This new node is created just to be the parent of Nodes A and B and is otherwise known as a *null node*. To group objects, select them and choose **Edit → Group**.

Parenting nodes together places the first selected node under the second selected node. For example, if you select Node A, Shift+select Node B, and then choose **Edit → Parent**, Node A will group under Node B and become its child. This is the same procedure as MM dragging Node B to Node A in the Outliner as you did with Pluto's moon and Pluto itself.

You can add objects to a group by MMB dragging their listing onto the desired parent node in the Outliner. You can also remove objects from a group by MMB dragging them out of the parent node to a different place in the Outliner.

Summary

In this chapter, you have learned how to start working in Maya by creating a new project, creating basic objects, such as primitives, and placing objects in the scene. You then learned how to place pivot points for objects and how to use snaps to place points precisely. You had some experience with the Channel Box and Attribute Editor to set an object's attributes. You then went on to create simple shaders for your objects and set keyframes to animate a solar system. Finally, you went over object hierarchy and grouping conventions to better organize and set up your scene.

The planet animation you created is based on a system of layering simple actions on top of each other to achieve a more elaborate result. If you work slowly and in segments, animation is more straightforward to produce and generally is of a higher quality. Much of your time in actual animation—as opposed to setup or modeling—will be spent adjusting the small things. These small things give the scene life and character. You will find that finishing 85 percent of a scene will take about 15 percent of the time. The remaining 85 percent of the time goes into perfecting the final 15 percent of the scene.

CHAPTER 4

Modeling with Polygons

Modeling is the process of creating 3D objects, whether for animation or otherwise. Simple objects call for simple models, and complicated objects call for a complex of simple models. One of the toughest decisions is how to represent an object in 3D. Just like a sculptor, you must analyze the object and deconstruct its design to learn how it exists.

Maya software uses three types of modeling: polygons, NURBS, and subdivision surfaces. All three types require a process that begins with deciding how best to achieve your design, though it is common to mix modeling methods in a scene.

To help you decide where to begin, this chapter starts with an overview of modeling, briefly describing the three methods and how they differ. You'll also learn about Maya's primitives, which are available with all three modeling methods. The second part of the chapter takes a detailed look at modeling with polygons. (The next two chapters cover the process of modeling with polygons and subdivision surfaces and bringing them all together in one model.)

Topics include:

- **Planning Your Model**
- **Polygon Basics**
- **Poly Editing Tools**
- **Putting the Tools to Use: Making a Simple Hand**
- **Creating Areas of Detail on a Poly Mesh**
- **The Insert Edge Loop Tool**
- **Combine Meshes and Merge Vertices**
- **The Sculpt Polygons Tool**
- **Modeling Complex Objects: The Steam Locomotive**
- **Suggestions for Modeling Polygons**

Planning Your Model

The first step in making any object is understanding how it's constructed. The best training for a CG modeler is to visualize the elements that make up an object. By dissecting the components of an object into primitive shapes, perhaps, you can translate its re-creation into 3D terms. You create the elements in Maya and then join them to form the desired object.

Gather as much information as you can about the object you want to model. Take pictures from many angles, get sizes and dimensions, and even write a detailed description of the object; try to re-create it in a sketch or a simple clay or balsa wood model, for example. Maya has a rich toolset for creating models, so it's important to choose the methodology that best matches the modeling task at hand. Be prepared with sketches, pictures, and whatever information you can gather before you sit down to realize your CG model.

How detailed should your model be? This is a crucial question, because a model that's too complex or a scene that has too much detail wastes precious computing time and power, greatly increasing render times.

Begin by deciding the purpose for your model. Then find out to what level of detail it will be *seen* in your CG scene. For example, consider the two scenes in Figure 4.1. If you need to create a park bench that is shown in a far shot (left), it will be a waste of time and effort to model all the details like the grooves in the armrest. If, however, your park bench is shown in a close-up (right), you'll need those details after all. It is important to plan your model to the level of detail it requires.

If you aren't certain how much detail you will eventually need, it is best to create a higher level of detail that you can easily pare down if it becomes unnecessary in the scene.

Figure 4.1

The level of detail you need to include in a model depends on how it will be seen in the animation.

Keep in mind that you can add detail to your model in the texturing phase of production. You would be amazed at the richness of detail a model can achieve with simple geometry and well-painted texture maps. (Chapter 7 covers texturing.) It's also important to keep in mind that in the rendering phase, you can run into memory shortcomings if you have too many scene models or they're overly detailed. Finding the right balance is tough, but it comes with time and experience.

As the geometry detail increases in a model, the performance demands on your PC can skyrocket. If a slower machine or a weaker graphics card limits you, your models will have to be better thought-out in terms of their level of detail. Equipped with this decision and hopefully a number of photos, Web pictures, and sketches, you will find your modeling experience more productive.

An Overview of Polygons, NURBS, and Subdivision Surfaces

A fundamental decision you'll make in planning is choosing a modeling method. Maya can define a model in three ways: polygons (the subject of this chapter), NURBS (the subject of Chapter 5), and subdivision surfaces (an advanced technique introduced in Chapter 6). Although NURBS modeling is traditionally what Maya modeling is renowned for, polygons are the simplest to describe.

Polygon Modeling

Polygons are made up of *faces*. A single polygon *face* is a flat surface made when three or more points called *vertices* are connected. The position of each *vertex* defines the shape and size of the face, usually a triangle. The line that connects one vertex to another is called an *edge*. Some polygonal faces have four vertices instead of three, creating a square face instead of a triangular one.

Polygonal faces are attached along their polygonal edges to make up a more complex surface that constitutes your model (as shown with the polygonal sphere in Figure 4.2). A camping tent is a perfect example. The intersections of the poles are the faces' vertices. The poles are the edges of the faces, and the cloth draped over the tent's frame is the resultant surface.

Polygon models are the simplest for a computer to render, so they are used for gaming applications, which need to render the models as the game is running. The gaming artists create models with a small number of polygons—called *low-count poly models*—that a PC or game console can render in real time. Higher-resolution polygon models are frequently used in television and film work. In fact, a number of science fiction TV shows use polygonal

Figure 4.2

A polygonal sphere and its components

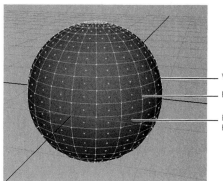

Vertex

Edge

Face (with selection handle visible)

models almost exclusively for their special effects. And because even complex polygon models can be made of a single surface, they are useful for character animation work as well. Since models in character animation bend and warp a good deal, having a single surface that will not separate at the seams can be advantageous. You'll get hands-on practice with polygon modeling later in this chapter.

NURBS Modeling

NURBS modeling is based on mathematics that is more complicated than the mathematics for polygons. Because NURBS modeling requires more processing, this method is typically used for applications in which the rendering is done in advance, such as animation for film or television. *NURBS modeling* excels at creating curved shapes and lines, so it is most often used for organic forms such as animals and people, as well as highly detailed cars and the like. These organic shapes are typically created with a quilt of NURBS surfaces, called *patches*. Patch modeling can be powerful in creating complex shapes such as characters.

NURBS is an acronym for *Non-Uniform Rational B-Spline*. NURBS geometry is based on Bezier curves, a math concept originally developed by the French engineer Pierre Bézier. Bezier curves are drawn between *control vertices (CVs)* based on equations using cubic polynomials.

In essence, Bezier curves are created with a starting and an ending CV and at least two CVs in between that provide the curvature. As each CV is laid down, the curve or spline tries to go from the previous CV to the next one in the smoothest possible manner.

As shown in Figure 4.3, CVs control the curvature. The *hulls* connect the CVs and are useful for selecting multiple rows of CVs at a time. The starting CV appears in Maya as a closed box, and the second CV, which defines the curve's direction, is an open box, so you can easily see the direction in which a curve has been created. The curve ends, of course, on the end-point CV. The start and end CVs are the only CVs that are always actually on

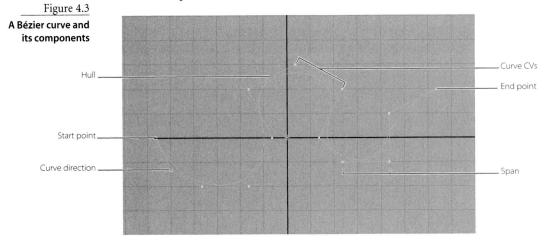

Figure 4.3

A Bézier curve and its components

Hull

Start point

Curve direction

Curve CVs

End point

Span

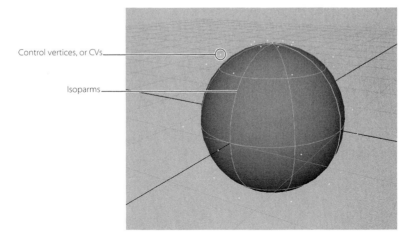

Figure 4.4

NURBS surfaces are created between isoparms. You can sculpt them by moving their CVs.

Control vertices, or CVs

Isoparms

the curve. Whereas CVs control the curvature of a Bezier spline, NURBS surfaces are defined by curves called *isoparms* that are created with CVs. The surface is created between these isoparms to form *spans* that follow the surface curvature defined by the isoparms, as in Figure 4.4. The more spans, the greater the detail and control over the surface; but this added detail makes greater demands on the computer, especially during rendering.

A NURBS surface deformation is based on the interpolation of curves, unlike a polygonal model, which must interpret a deformation of polygons as a collection of faces created from straight edges. For that reason it is easier to get a smooth deformation on a NURBS surface with few CVs. To get the same smooth look on a polygon would take much more surface detail.

As you can see in Figure 4.5, NURBS yield a smoother deformation, whereas polygons can become jagged at the edges.

If your model requires smooth curves and organic shapes, use NURBS. When in doubt, however, it is better to begin modeling with NURBS. You can convert NURBS to polygons at any time, but converting back to NURBS can be tricky.

You'll get plenty of hands-on practice with NURBS modeling as well as NURBS patching in the next chapter.

Try This Open a new scene (choose **File → New Scene**). In the new scene you'll create a few curves on the ground plane grid in the perspective panel (*persp*). Maximize the perspective view by moving your cursor to it and pressing the spacebar. Choose **Create → CV Curve Tool**. Your cursor will turn into a cross. On the grid, lay down a series of points to define a curved line. Notice how the actual Bezier curve is created between the points (CVs) as they are laid down.

Figure 4.5

A NURBS cylinder
(left) and a polygo-
nal cylinder (right)
bent into a C shape.
The NURBS cylinder
remains smooth,
while the polygon
cylinder shows its
edges. A NURBS
object retains its
smoothness more
easily, though it is
possible to create a
smooth polygon
bend with increased
surface faces.

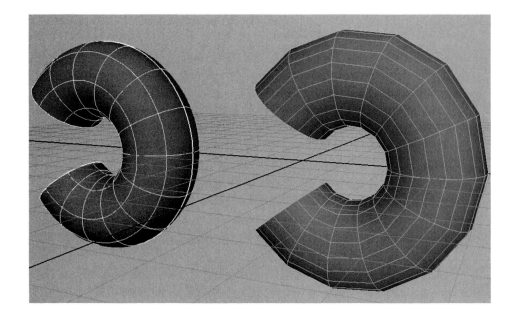

Subdivision Surfaces

Subdivision surfaces incorporate the best of polygons and NURBS modeling to give you the ease of polygon creation with the smoothness and organic forms of NURBS geometry.

Subdivision surfaces usually start as polygonal surfaces. You then use NURBS math to smooth the rough polygon surfaces by subdividing them according to how the model needs to look. For example, you can easily turn a poly cube into a sphere by using subdivisions to subdivide the faces into smaller and smaller faces that are rearranged to form the sphere along smooth curves used to define this new surface.

With this technique, you can create simple poly models quickly and then overlay them with levels of detail to define the new smooth surface. At any time you can go back to the original poly model to make large-scale changes quickly and efficiently.

Furthermore, with subdivision surfaces you have the added advantage that your surface will not tend to crease or tear at the seams as NURBS models made of patches of surfaces are prone to do. This leads to better models with which to animate organics.

The disadvantage of subdivision surfaces is that they require even more computation than NURBS and keeping models in subdivisions will cost you a lot of memory. Subdivisions (subDs) are almost always better converted back to polygons or even NURBS patches. You'll get hands-on practice with subdivision surface modeling in Chapter 6.

Choosing a Method

Maya provides highly effective tools for all three types of modeling, so you can make a model with any type and it can be as detailed as necessary. The choice depends on how you prefer to model.

Polygons are a welder's tool. Polygon modeling involves tearing and extruding from larger pieces and welding several surfaces together to form a desired whole. Orthogonal models, models with straight lines and sharp corners, are more easily created with polys.

A clay sculptor might prefer NURBS. Pushing and pulling CVs to create subtle curves on the surface is like working soft clay with your fingertips; you are nurturing something into shape with the fine art of pressure.

Subdivision surfaces combine the best of both worlds. An artist can begin with a rough shape, chiseled out coarsely, and then switch to finely detailed sculpting by adding levels of detail to the sculpture only when and where needed. Subdivision surface modeling excels at creating organic shapes out of single surfaces.

And in the end, it's almost always preferred to convert it all back to polygons. Why? The available renderers all turn everything to polygons when they render the scene (called tessellation), so you can save yourself some memory and time and be master of your own models by trying to go back to polys as often as is reasonable.

Using Primitives

Primitives are the simplest objects that you can generate in Maya (or indeed in any 3D application). *Primitives* are simple geometric shapes—which can be polygons, subdivisions, or NURBS—and are typically used to sculpt out models, as you saw in Chapter 3 with our solar system project.

Primitives offer great sculpting versatility (through vertex or CV manipulation) because you can define the level of detail of the primitive's surface. You can create polygonal primitives with practically any level of subdivisions to define the number of vertices and faces. NURBS primitives can be created with almost any number of *sections* and *spans* to define the number of isoparms and CVs.

> *Spans* are isoparms that run horizontally in a NURBS surface; *sections* are isoparms that run vertically in the object.

Starting with primitives, a modeler can create highly complex and detailed models. You may find it easier to analyze your modeling subjects into forms and shapes that fit in with Maya primitives to get a better sense of how to begin a modeling assignment. Figure 4.6 shows all of Maya's primitives, NURBS, polygons, subdivisions, and volume primitives. Quite different from geometry primitives, volume primitives are used for lighting and atmosphere effects such as fog or haze and do not play a part in modeling.

Figure 4.6

The Maya primitives

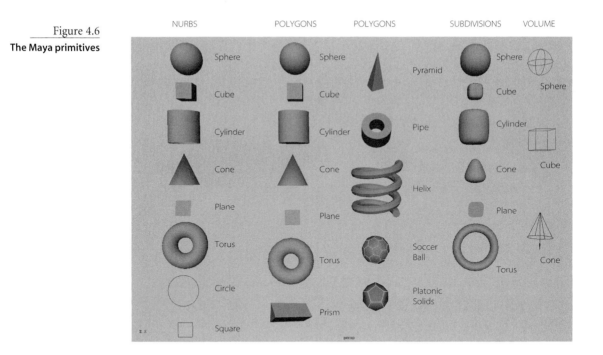

Figure 4.6

The Maya primitives

Polygon Basics

As well as being more memory friendly in rendering, polygon modeling is popular because its resulting models are usually one piece of geometry with many facets. You can therefore deform polygon models without fear of patches coming apart, as can happen with NURBS. Polygons, however, have a finite detail limitation and can look jagged up close or when scaled up. One solution to this problem in the Maya software is the Smooth tool. Many 3D applications support only this form of modeling, so it is a popular exchange method among platforms as well.

Polygons are inherently better for orthogonal models, mechanical objects, and the like. Character modeling with polygons, however, is quite powerful once you understand the tools to edit polygons. A popular method of polygonal modeling, sometimes called box modeling, involves creating a base object, such as a simple cube, and pulling and pushing faces to draw out angles to create more faces. Whereas NURBS typically need the creation of curves to start, complex polygons are usually created from basic-shaped polygons such as primitives.

Another method for creating poly surfaces uses the same curves that NURBS surfaces use or even convert a completed NURBS surface model to polygons. We'll take a look at these procedures in the next chapter. A third method is to create poly surfaces directly with the Polygon tool, which allows you to outline the shape of each face.

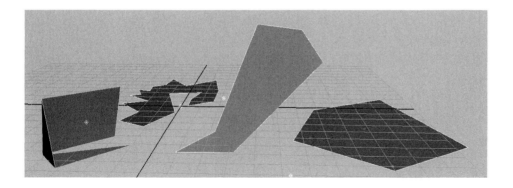

Figure 4.7

Polygon faces created with the Polygon tool

Creating Polygonal Primitives

Choosing **Create → Polygon Primitives** gives you access to the poly version of most of the NURBS primitives. Opening the option box for any of them gives you access to their creation options. To see an example, choose **Create → Polygon Primitives → Sphere** and open the option box.

The most notable difference between the options for a NURBS primitive and a poly primitive are the options for surface detail. With a NURBS surface, sections and spans define detail. With a poly surface, detail is defined by *subdivisions*, which are the number of rows and columns of poly faces that run up, down, and across. The more subdivisions, the smoother the surface.

First make sure that history is turned on or there will be no creation node; then click Create to make the poly sphere. Open the Attribute Editor and switch to its creation node, called polySphere1. In the creation node polySphere1, just as in the option box, you'll find the Subdivisions Axis and Subdivisions Height sliders to retroactively change the surface detail.

The Polygon Tool

You use the Polygon tool (choose **Mesh → Create Polygon Tool**) to create a single polygon face by laying down its vertices. When you select this tool, you can draw a polygon face in any shape by just clicking down the position of each point or vertex. Aside from creating a polygon primitive by choosing **Create → Polygon Primitives**, this is the simplest way to create a polygon shape. Figure 4.7 shows some simple and complex single faces you can create with the Polygon tool.

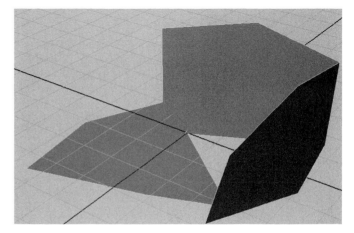

Once you've laid down all your vertices, press Enter to create the poly face and exit the tool. On complex shapes, you might want to create more than just the single face so that you can manipulate the shape. For example, you might want to fold it.

Try This The poly shown here was created with the Polygon tool and has only one face. Thus, adjusting or deforming the surface is impossible. For example, to fold this object,

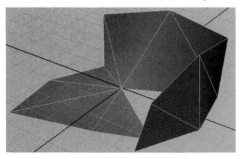

you need more faces and the edges between them. Make your own intricate poly shape with the Polygon tool by clicking vertices down in the different views to get vertices in all three axes.

With the surface selected, choose **Mesh → Triangulate**. The surface will now have more faces and edges and can be edited easier, but it was still simple to create first as a single face. If you need a uniquely shaped poly, start with this tool, and then triangulate it into several faces.

Poly Editing Tools

Here's a brief preview of what to expect in the world of poly editing. You should experiment with using each tool on a primitive sphere as each tool is introduced; then you'll take the new skills into two different poly models. As you've learned, you can easily create complex models by adjusting existing, simpler poly objects with some of the poly editing tools Maya provides.

For most of the work in this chapter, you will be in the Polygons menu set. Open the **Edit Mesh** menu and tear it off to get a good look at the tools and functions. You can access all the following tools from that menu.

The Poly Extrusion Tools

The most often used poly editing tool has to do with extrusion. You can use *Extrude* to pull out a face or an edge of a polygon surface to create additions to that surface. The tool itself is accessed at **Edit Mesh → Extrude**. Maya will make the distinction between edge or face Extrude based on what you have selected, faces or edges. Follow these steps:

1. Select a face or multiple faces of a polygon, and choose **Edit Mesh → Extrude**. The regular manipulator will change to a special manipulator as shown (below left).

2. Grab the Z axis move handle (the blue arrow), and drag it away from the sphere (below center).

3. Using the scale handles (the boxes) will scale the faces of the extrusion. The cyan circle will rotate the face (below right).

The face(s) you selected pull out from the sphere, and new faces are created on the sides of the extrusion(s). This is an exceptionally powerful tool in that it allows you to easily create additions to any poly surface in any direction. It is particularly useful in modeling characters and creatures. Later in this chapter you'll use it to make a simple human hand.

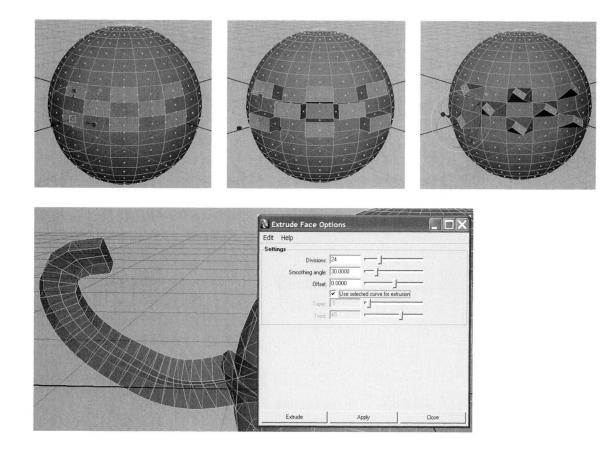

4. Choosing the **Extrude** command again without deselecting the faces will let you extrude even farther, keeping the original extrusion shape and building on top of that.

5. Selecting the edges of the poly surface instead of the faces and choosing **Edit Mesh →
Extrude** will extrude flat surfaces from the edges selected. The special manipulator works the same way as **Extrude** does for poly faces.

You can also use the direction and shape of a curve to extrude faces. Create a curve in the shape you want your extrusion to take, select the curve along with the face(s), and choose **Extrude ❐**. Taper decreases or increases the size of the face as it extrudes. Twist rotates the face as it extrudes, and Divisions increases the smoothness of the resulting extrusion. Once you have your settings for those attributes, click Use Selected Curve for Extrusion. Notice however, that the **Taper** and **Twist** options become grayed out when you select Use Selected Curve For Extrusion. This seems to be strange behavior, but the **Twist** and **Taper** values are taken into account in the extrusion. You can just edit these values when you uncheck Use Selected Curve For Extrusion, but you can check it back on after you enter values for **Twist** and **Taper**. If your faces aren't extruding to the shape of the curve, increase the number of **Divisions**.

The Wedge Face Tool

Similar to extruding faces, **Wedge Face** pulls out a poly face, but in an arc instead of a straight line. For this tool, you need to select a face and an edge of the selected face for the pivot point of the corner. Follow this step:

Select a face, Shift+select one of its edges, and choose **Edit Mesh → Wedge Face □**. (To select face and Shift+select an edge, right-click the sphere to display the marking menu.

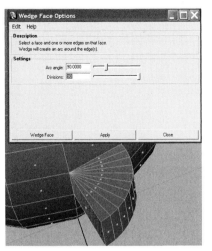

Choose **Face** and select a face. Right-click again and choose **Edge** on the marking menu. Then Shift+select one of its edges.)

In the option box you will notice some help for the tool under the Description heading. Under the Settings heading, you can select the degree of turn in the arc angle (90 degrees is the default) as well as the number of faces used to create the wedge (by moving the **Divisions** slider).

To more easily access selection filters, you can right-click an object to display a marking menu. Drag the cursor in the direction of the selection type you want and release the mouse button. Then click or Shift+click your selection.

The Wedge Face tool is useful for items such as elbows, knees, building archways, tunnel curves, and so on.

The Poke Face Tool

Use the Poke Face tool to easily add detail to a face. Select a face, and then choose **Edit Mesh → Poke Face**.

A vertex is added to the middle of the face, and a move manipulator appears on the screen. This lets you move the point to where you need it on the face. You can add bumps and depressions to your surface as well as create regions of extra detail. By selectively adding detail, you can subdivide specific areas of a polygon for extra detailed work, leaving lower poly counts in less-detailed areas for an efficient model.

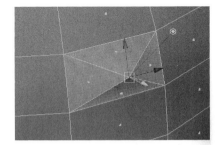

Poke Face is great for creating detailed sections of a mesh (poly surface) and bumps or indentations.

The Bevel Tool

The Bevel tool used for editing polygons is similar to the NURBS version, but only if it is used to round sharp corners. The Bevel tool requires that you select an edge or multiple edges and then use them to create multiple new faces to round that edge or corner. The Bevel tool has new controls added in Maya 6.

Select an edge or edges and choose **Edit Mesh → Bevel ❑** to adjust your bevel. The **Width** slider sets the distance from the edge to the center of where the new face will be. This basically determines the size of the beveled corner. The Segments number defines how many segments are created for the bevel. The more segments, the smoother the beveled edge. Leaving Segments at 1 creates a sharp corner.

The setting of the Roundness slider specifies the roundness of the corner. Setting the number too high will make the beveled edge stick out, as shown in Figure 4.8, though that can be a valid design choice. You can allow Maya to automatically set the roundness based on the size of the geometry being beveled. Check the Automatically Fit Bevel To Object check box to disable the Roundness slider. Move the Segments slider to set the number of new faces that are created on the bevel: the more segments, the smoother the bevel.

Use the Bevel tool to round polygonal edges and, in some cases, add extra surface detail, since Bevel creates more faces on the surface.

Putting the Tools to Use: Making a Simple Hand

Starting with a simple polygonal cube, you will create a basic human hand.

Now, either create a new project called Poly_Hand, or copy the entire project from the CD and use that. Follow these steps:

1. Begin by creating a polygonal cube. Open the Attribute Editor, and in the Polycube1 tab, set **Subdivisions Width** to 4, **Subdivisions Height** to 1, and **Subdivisions Depth** to 3. If you don't have that tab in the Attribute Editor, click Undo, turn history on, and re-create the cube.

Figure 4.8

A poly bevel's roundness set too high

2. Scale the cube to 1 in X, 0.25 in Y, and 1.3 in Z so that it looks as shown in Figure 4.9.

3. Enter component mode (press F8) and turn on the Faces filter ( ) in the Status line. You can also right-click the object and choose **Face** from the marking menu, although it might be easier to use the icons for a little while to become more accustomed to the interface.

4. Select the front face that is in the corner closest to you by clicking its little blue handle box. You will extrude the face to make the first part of the index finger. Before you extrude, though, rotate the face a little bit out in the Y axis away from the rest of the hand to angle the extrusion out toward where the thumb would be.

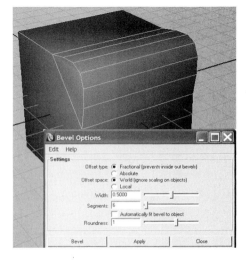

Figure 4.9

The poly cube in position to make the hand

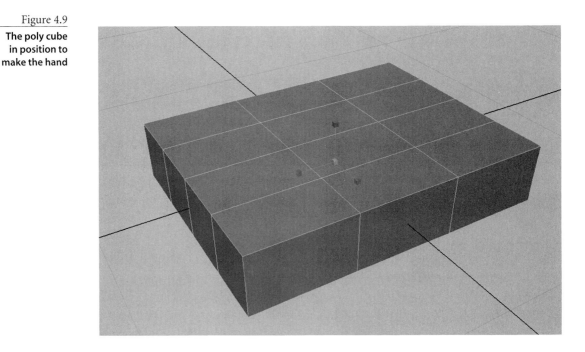

Figure 4.9

The poly cube in position to make the hand

5. Choose **Edit Mesh → Extrude**, and use the Z axis translate handle to pull out the face to a distance of 0.4 in the **Local Translate Z** attribute in the Channel Box. This is the first segment of the index finger. Select the Extrude command for a new extrusion. Extrude the second segment of the finger out to 0.4 in **Local Translate Z**. Use Extrude again for the tip of the index finger, pulling that out to 0.3. Figure 4.10 shows the full index finger with the slight rotation away from the hand.

 Save your work and compare it to the scene file `poly_hand_v1.mb` in the Poly_Hand project on the CD.

6. Repeat steps 4 and 5 for the remaining three fingers. Remember, if you rotate the initial face of each finger a little bit away from the previous finger, the extrusions will have small gaps in between them, as shown in Figure 4.11. Otherwise, the fingers will extrude right next to each other, like a mitt.

Use the following guide for the extrusion lengths:

Finger	1st	2nd	Tip
Middle	0.45	0.45	0.3
Ring	0.45	0.4	0.3
Pinkie	0.35	0.3	0.3

 The scene file `poly_hand_v2.mb` shows the hand with the four fingers created.

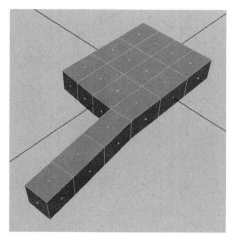

Figure 4.10

The index finger

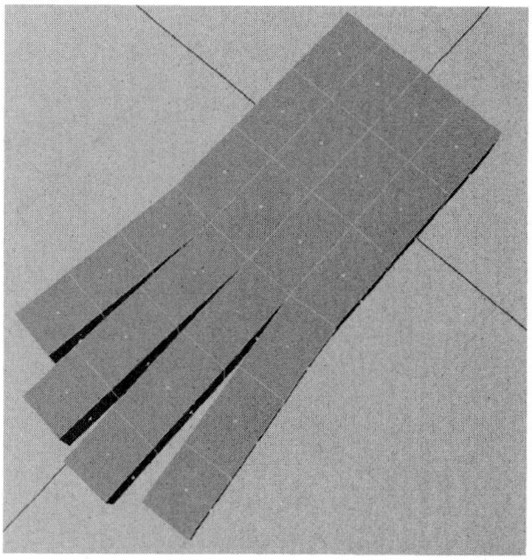

Figure 4.11

Four fingers

7. Now for the thumb. First you'll need to move a couple of edges to make room for where the thumb attaches to the hand. Select the three edges on the index finger side of the hand and move them up toward the tip of the hand, as shown in Figure 4.12. This will create an elongated face to start the thumb.

8. You will use the Wedge Face tool to start the thumb. Select the elongated face. Right-click the object to display the marking menu, and choose **Edge**. Shift+select the edge on the left side of that face. (See Figure 4.13.)

Figure 4.12

Creating an elongated face for the thumb

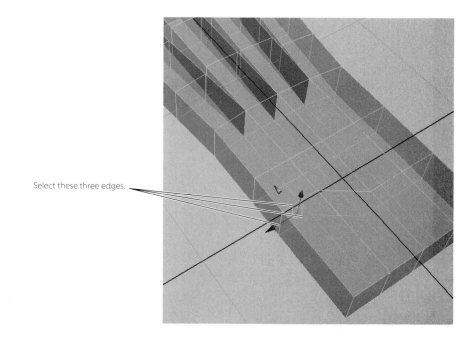

Select these three edges.

9. Choose **Edit Mesh → Wedge Face** ▢. In the option box, set **Arc Angle** to 65 and set **Divisions** to 5. Click Wedge Face. With that wedged face still selected, scale it down in the X axis to just under half its width to make it less broad, and rotate it toward the hand a bit (below left).

10. To make the thumb itself, extrude that face first to 0.5 and then to 0.4 in **Local Translate Z**. The hand looks a bit awkward right now, especially the thumb area (below right).

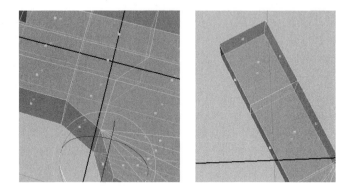

11. Select the faces along the meaty part of the thumb, and move and rotate them to round out the hand. While you're at it, squeeze in the tips of the fingers a bit to point them all by selecting and scaling the very top face of each finger.

12. Select the pinkie finger edges (not faces), and scale them in to narrow the pinkie.

13. Select the edges that make up the knuckle of each finger (one by one), and scale them out in the X axis to fatten the knuckles a bit. Your results should be similar to Figure 4.14.

14. Now to add a bit more detail to the hand, you'll raise the knuckles. You'll have to create new vertices for the knuckles where each finger meets the hand. For this, the Split Polygon tool is perfect. Go back into object mode (press F8) and select the hand. Choose **Edit Mesh → Split Polygon Tool.** Your cursor will change to a sharp triangle. Use it to select a point on the hand where the index finger starts. Click the opposite edge on that face along the back of the hand. A line will be drawn between the two points (top left).

Figure 4.13

Select the face and edge for the Wedge Face function.

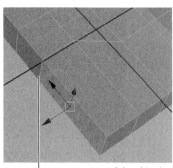

Select this edge.

15. If you press Enter, that line becomes a single new edge on that face. While you have the Split Polygon tool active, select three more points along the back of the hand as shown (top right).

16. Press Enter to add four new edges and, hence, four new faces along the back of the hand for the knuckles. Select each of those new faces, and choose **Edit Mesh → Poke Face** to subdivide them into four triangles, with a vertex in the center. A special manipulator will appear. Use the Z translate handle to pull those middle vertices up to make knuckles. (See Figure 4.15.)

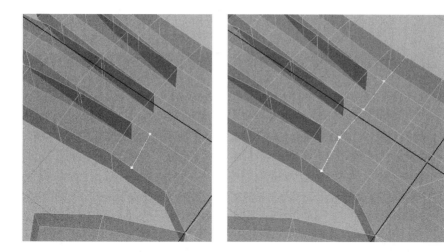

Figure 4.14

Better-proportioned fingers and knuckles

Scale these edge pairs out for bigger knuckles.

Figure 4.15

Use the Poke Face
tool to raise the
knuckles.

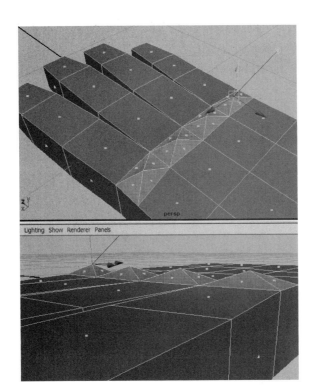

17. Now that you have a simple hand, you'll want to smooth out the mesh to make it less
    boxy. In object mode, select the hand and choose **Mesh → Smooth** ❑. In the option box,
    set **Division Levels** to 2 and leave the other options at their defaults, as shown here.

18. Click Smooth and your hand should take on a smoother, rounder look, more like a
    real hand. Notice in Figure 4.16 all the nodes listed under INPUTS in the Channel
    Box. This is because history has been on for the entire duration of this exercise. At

    any time, you could select one of those nodes
    and edit the extrusion of the pinkie, for
    example. You won't need any of that, so with
    the hand selected, choose **Edit → Delete By
    Type → History** to get rid of them all. Feel
    free to edit any of those nodes through the
    Attribute Editor if you'd like.

    Save your file again. To verify that you've been
    working correctly, you can load the finished hand
    file (with its history intact) poly_hand_v3.mb from
    the CD.

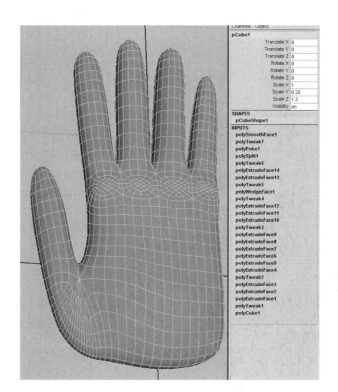

Figure 4.16

The smoothed hand with all its history nodes

Creating Areas of Detail on a Poly Mesh (Surface)

As you saw with the hand, it became necessary to add more faces to parts of the surface to create various details. The hand takes on better form when time is devoted to detailing it. The hand shown here was begun using the previous steps, but it was detailed by creating

faces using the tools discussed in this section and moving vertices, in addition to adding fingernails. The most intricate of objects begin from the simplest models. You merely need time and effort to create them. Don't expect yourself to model like that right from the start, unless you already have modeling experience from another package. Recognizing how to detail models take a good amount of time and experience; just stay with it.

Maya provides several ways to add surface detail or increase a poly's subdivisions.

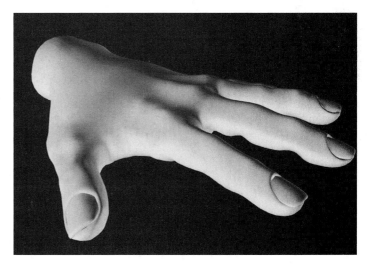

The Add Divisions Tool

You can use the *Add Divisions* tool to increase the number of faces of a poly surface by evenly dividing either all faces or just those selected. Select the poly surface, face, or faces, and choose **Edit Mesh → Add Divisions**. In the option box, you can adjust the number of times the faces are divided by moving the **Division Levels** slider. The **Mode** drop-down menu gives you the choice to subdivide your faces into quads (four-sided faces, as on the left) and triangles (three-sided faces, as on the right).

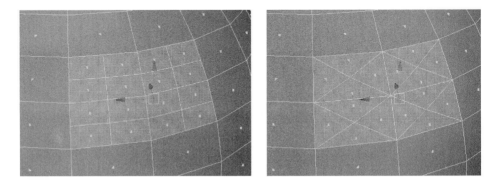

You can also select a poly edge to divide. Running this tool on edges divides the edges into separate edges along the same face. It will not divide the face; rather, you use it to change the shape of the face by moving the divided edges as shown here.

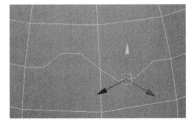

You use the **Add Divisions** tool to create regions of detail on a poly surface. It is a broader approach than using the Poke Face tool, which adds detail for more pinpoint areas.

The Split Polygon Tool

Another way to create detail is to use the *Split Polygon Tool*, which does exactly what its name suggests. As you've seen, when you choose **Edit Mesh → Split Polygon Tool**, your cursor changes to a triangle. Use this cursor to select two points along two edges of a face. That creates a straight line from the first to the second point, which serves as a new edge to divide the face into two halves. Notice in the lower left in the Help Line that there is a percentage readout that gives your relative position of the tool along the current edge. You can use this readout to help position the new split.

Press Enter, RMB to create the new edge and faces, or continue to select new points for more edges. Using the RMB makes for a much faster work flow when adding multiple new edges. Simply pick the first two points, and then RMB. The tool will still be active for the next split.

Using the Split Polygon Tool is a flexible, accurate, and fast way to create surface subdivisions for your model.

The Insert Edge Loop Tool

This handy tool quickly adds edges to a poly selection, much the same as the Split Polygon Tool does, but it works much faster by working along the entire poly surface, along common vertices. The Insert Edge Loop Tool automatically runs a new edge along the poly surface perpendicular to the subdivision line that you click, without requiring you to click multiple times as with the Split Polygon Tool. We will use this tool in the Locomotive exercise shortly. You'll find it indispensable in creating polygonal models as it creates subdivisions quickly.

For instance, subdividing a polygonal cube is quicker than using the Split Polygon Tool. With a poly cube selected, choose **Edit Mesh → Insert Edge Loop Tool**. Click an edge, and the tool places an edge running perpendicular from that point to the next edge across the surface and across to the next edge. If you click and drag along an edge, you can interactively position the new split edges.

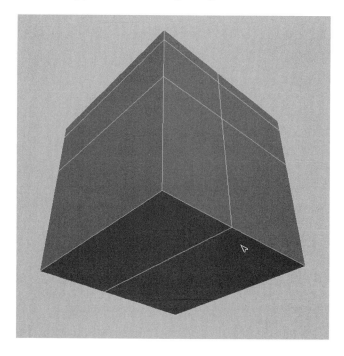

The Offset Edge Loop Tool

Much like the Insert Edge Loop Tool, the Offset Edge Loop Tool inserts not one, but two edge loop rings of edges across the surface of a poly. Edges are placed on either side of a selected edge, equally spaced on both sides. For example, create a polygon sphere and select one of the vertical edges as shown here. Maya displays two dashed lines on either side of the selected edge. You simply drag the mouse to place the offset edge loops and release the mouse button to create the two new edge loops.

Offset Edge Loop Tool is perfect for adding additional detail symmetrically on a surface quickly.

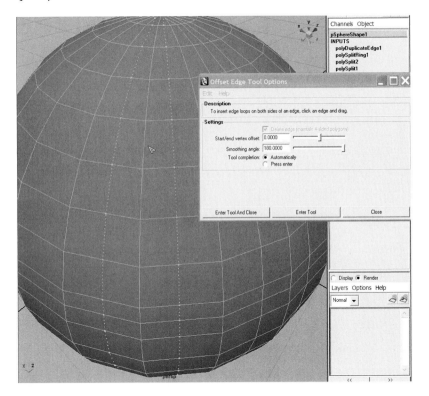

The Combine and Merge Functions

The Combine function is important in cleaning up your models, and creating a unified single mesh out of the many parts that make it up. When modeling, you'll find yourself sometimes using several different polygon meshes and surfaces to generate your final shape. Using Combine, you can create a single polygonal object out of the pieces.

Similarly, the Merge tool is important when you are creating a polygon model because it fuses multiple vertices that are at the same point into one vertex on the model. Frequently when you are modeling a mesh, you will need to fold over pieces and weld parts together. Doing so often leaves you with several vertices occupying the same space. Merging them simplifies the model and makes the mesh much nicer to work with from rigging to rendering.

In the following simple example, we will create two boxes that connect to each other along a common edge, and then combine and merge them into one seamless polygonal mesh. To begin, follow these steps:

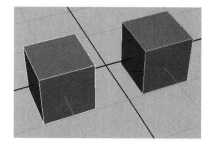

1. In a new scene, create two poly cubes and place them apart from each other as shown here, more or less.

2. Select the bottom edge of the cube on the right that faces the other cube and choose Edit Mesh > Extrude. Pull the edge out a little bit to create a new face as shown here. This will be a flange connecting the two cubes. It is not that important where you pull the edge out to; you will be connecting the two cubes together by moving the vertices manually.

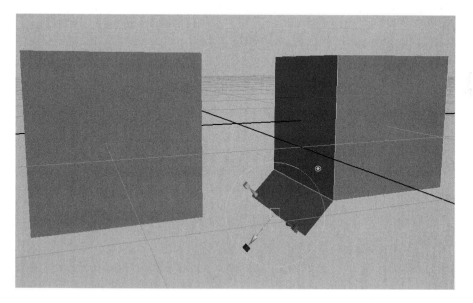

3. Select the first corner vertex on the newly extruded face, and snap it into place on the corner vertex of the other cube as seen here. Remember, you can press the **Snap to points** icon ( ) to snap the vertex onto the cube's corner.

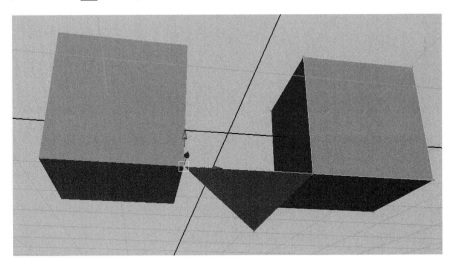

4. Snap the other vertex to the opposite corner so that the cubes are connected with a flange, along a common edge as seen here.

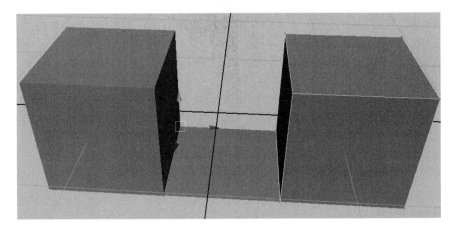

Even though the cubes seem to be connected at a common edge, they are still two separate polygonal meshes. You can easily select just one of the vertices and disconnect the connective face of the two cubes. What we need to do now is to merge the common vertices of the cubes. But, the **Merge** function will not work on vertices from two separate meshes. So first, we must **Combine** the cubes into a single poly mesh. The following steps continue our task:

5. Select the two cubes (one has the extra flange on the bottom, of course) and choose **Mesh > Combine**. This will make a single poly mesh out of the two cubes. You will now be able to use the Merge function.

6. Even though the cubes are now one mesh, you still have two vertices at each of the connecting corners of the cube on the left. As you can see here, the flange is disconnected by selecting a vertex at the corner and moving it. If you do move a corner vertex, just hit the Z key to undo and return the flange to its connected position.

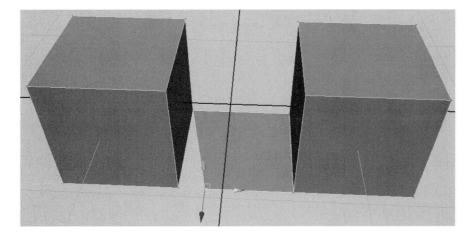

7. To merge the vertices at the corners, select both the vertices at the near corner first (you can use a marquee selection), and then choose Edit Mesh > Merge. These two vertices are now one. Repeat the procedure for the far corner. Your connected cubes are now a single mesh with no redundant vertices. As you can see here, if you select a vertex at a corner and move it, the cube and the flange both move, and there is no disconnect.

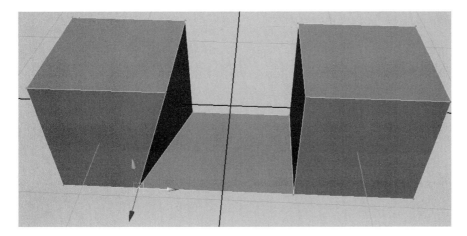

If you need to separate a poly mesh back into its component meshes after you combine them, you can simply select the mesh and choose **Mesh > Separate**. You will not be able to use Separate if the mesh you have combined has merged vertices, however.

Keeping your meshes simple and organized is important to a clean and efficient workflow. You will notice fewer errors and issues with clean models when you animate, light, and render them. Combining meshes together makes it easier to deal with a mesh, and Merge cuts down on unwanted vertices and makes the mesh cleaner and the surface easier to work with. You will find the more you model with polys, the more useful Merge becomes to creating great models.

If the Merge function is not working on vertices in your work, make sure the model you are working on is a single mesh; merging vertices with this tool does not work on separate meshes.

The Cut Faces Tool

Known as a poly knife in other 3D applications, the *Cut Faces Tool* lets you cut across a poly surface to create a series of edges for subdivisions, to pull off a section of the poly, or to simply delete a section. (See Figure 4.17.) Select the poly object, and choose **Edit Mesh →** **Cut Faces Tool**. Click the option box if you want to extract or delete the section .

You can use the Cut Faces Tool to create extra surface detail, to slice portions off the surface, or to create a straight edge on the model by trimming off the excess.

Figure 4.17

You can use the Cut Faces Tool to create the edges, to pull apart the poly object, or to cut off a whole section.

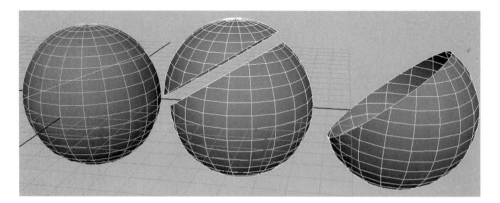

The Duplicate Face Tool

Select one or more faces, and choose **Edit Mesh → Duplicate Face** to create a copy of the selected face(s). You can use the manipulator that appears to move, scale, or rotate your copied face(s).

The Extract Tool

The *Extract* tool is similar to the Extrude tool, but it does not create the extra faces. Select the face(s), and choose **Mesh → Extract** to pull the faces off the surface. With the **Separate Extracted Faces** option on, the extracted face will be a separate poly object; otherwise, it will remain as a part of the original.

You can use the Extract tool to create a hole in an object and still keep the original face(s). When you use this tool with the Split Polygon Tool to make custom edges, you can create cutouts of almost any shape.

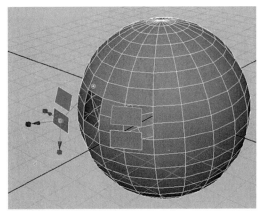

The Smooth Tool

The *Smooth* tool (choose **Mesh → Smooth**) evenly subdivides the poly surface or selected faces, creating several more faces to smooth and round out the original poly object.

The Sculpt Geometry Tool

You can use a Maya feature called Artisan to sculpt polygonal surfaces. Artisan is a painting system that allows you to paint attributes or influences directly onto an object. With the Sculpt Geometry Tool usage of Artisan, you paint on a polygon surface to move the vertices in and out to essentially mold the surface.

To access the tool in polygon modeling, select your poly object, and choose **Mesh → Sculpt Geometry Tool ❑**. For more on sculpting, see the section "Using Artisan to Sculpt NURBS" toward the end of Chapter 5. Though the work flow is much the same with sculpting NURBS, the only difference with sculpting polygons is that the surface will behave slightly differently when sculpted. Unlike the NURBS sphere, where the brush strokes give smooth curves in and out, a polygon surface is more jagged. Of course, if you create the poly with a large number of subdivisions, you'll have a smoother result when using the Sculpt Geometry Tool. (See Figure 4.18.)

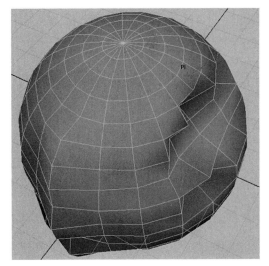

Figure 4.18
The Sculpt Geometry tool deforms the surface.

Modeling Complex Objects: The Steam Locomotive

This exercise will demonstrate the following polygonal modeling techniques:

- Extrusion
- Insert Edge Loop and Wedge Face tools
- Object duplication
- Pivot placement
- CV curves and revolved surfaces
- Complex model hierarchy

You're going to create a rather complex-looking object, an old-fashioned steam locomotive, using mostly polygons. You will create one of the detailed parts using NURBS patches in the following chapter. You'll use a schematic printout of the final model as a reference for your model. Since this is a fairly complicated object, it's much better to start with good plans. This, of course, involves some research, web surfing, image gathering, or sketching to get a feel for what it truly is you're trying to make.

To begin, create a new project for all the files called Locomotive, or copy the Locomotive project from the CD to your hard drive. If you do not create a new project, set your current project to the copied Locomotive project on your drive. Choose **File → Project → Set** and select the Locomotive. If you forget, your rendered images and scene files will be saved into your last project. When you create a new project, Maya automatically sets it as the current project. Remember that you can enable incremental save to make backups at any point in the exercise.

Now on to modeling a design already sketched and modeled. To begin with, study the schematic printout of the final model included in the source images folder of the project. This will help orient you to what we're building. Typically, you would be using sketches or downloaded images and such.

Beginning in Chapter 8 and following into Chapter 9, you'll set up and animate the locomotive. When building any model, it's important to keep animation in mind, especially for grouping related objects in the scene hierarchy so that they will move as you intend. Creating a good scene hierarchy will be crucial to a smooth animation work flow; so throughout this exercise you'll use the Outliner to keep the locomotive's component pieces organized as you create them.

The Production Process

The trick with a complex object model is to approach it part by part. Deconstruct the major elements of the original into distinct shapes that you can approach one by one. The locomotive can be broken down to five distinct objects, each with its own subobjects:

- Engine
- Cabin
- Wheels
- Cowcatcher

You will model each part separately based on the detailed schematic in Figure 4.19.

The Boiler Engine

The most prominent part of a steam locomotive is the steam engine, or boiler. Take a look at the boiler and you will quickly see that we can start with a simple cylinder and work from there. To start building the boiler engine, follow these steps:

1. Create a polygonal cylinder by choosing **Create → Polygon Primitives → Cylinder**. Leave all the creation option settings at their defaults.

2. Rotate the cylinder 90 degrees in the X axis to place it on its side. Scale the cylinder to about 1.8 in all axes. Then lengthen the cylinder until Scale Y is at about 8.9.

Figure 4.19

A schematic diagram of the finished model

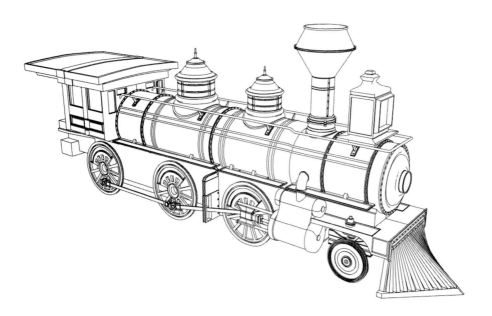

3. Now we will use the Insert Edge Loop Tool mentioned earlier in this chapter to insert edges into the cylinder to make one end smaller. Select the cylinder, and choose **Edit Mesh → Insert Edge Loop Tool □**. In the option box, make sure **Maintain Position** is set to Relative Distance From Edge and **Auto Complete** is turned on. Your cursor will turn into a triangle pointer. In two separate actions, click one of the horizontal subdivisions to create two new vertical edges about one-third of the way in from the right end of the cylinder, as shown in Figure 4.20.

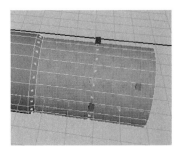

4. RMB the cylinder and choose Face from the marking menu. Select the end faces and scale them down a bit as shown. This gives us the main part of the boiler engine.

5. Make a new poly cylinder as before. Scale the cylinder to make it a flat plate and place it on the boiler. The cylinders will need to be scaled to fit snugly over the boiler as you see fit. This will give us a simple weld plate to provide the boiler with some simple detail. Choose **Edit → Duplicate Special □** to copy the plate four times in one action. In the option box, set **Number of copies** to 4. Now move these duplicates one by one back along the boiler cylinder and place them through the skinny section of the boiler. Space the total of five plates along the boiler as shown.

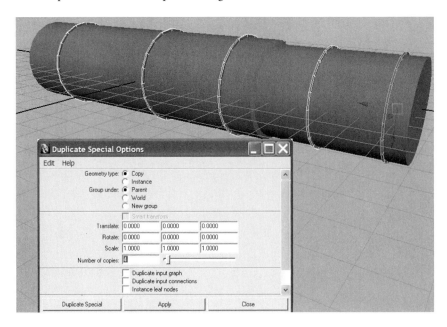

Boiler Front Cap

Now we will create the boiler's front cap. Here we will use a NURBS curve to create a NURBS surface using a technique called Revolve, which is covered further in the next chapter. First switch to the Surfaces menu set and then follow these steps:

1. Choose **Create → CV Curve Tool**, and in the side view panel, lay down CVs as shown in Figure 4.21 from the top of the curve down. Make sure you begin the curve about 1.5 units from the Z-axis so you can end the curve on the Z axis line, as shown in Figure 4.21. When you have placed your last CV, press Enter to complete the curve. Don't worry if it is not exactly like the curve shown.

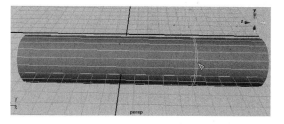

Figure 4.20

The Edge Split tool creates subdivisions quickly.

> When you finish the curve in step 1, you should notice that Maya no longer displays its CVs in the panel. To display the CVs on a NURBS object, such as this curve, select the object and choose **Display → NURBS → CVs**. You can toggle the CVs off by choosing the same menu items again.

2. This curve is called the profile curve and will essentially spin around to sweep a surface for the boiler cap. We need to revolve the curve around its bottom end to sweep a proper surface. Since you created the curve to end on the Z axis, and the pivot point for the curve is by default at the origin, simply select the curve and choose **Surfaces → Revolve ❑**. Set **Axis Preset** to Z. Click Revolve to create the boiler cap.

Now that you have created the boiler cap, select the curve and move it in the scene. You will notice that the surface changes. This is the history on the resulting surface. As touched on in Chapter 3, history keeps a record of how the object was made, as long as the Construction History icon in the Status line is on, of course.

3. We don't want history on the object, so select the boiler cap and choose **Edit → Delete by Type → History**. This will erase the history so the curve no longer affects the surface. Move the boiler cap into place at the front of the boiler. Scale it as needed to fit the cylinder's skinny end. (See Figure 4.22.)

Adding Details

Now we'll include a bit of detail by adding bolts to the front boiler cap and the weld plates. This will introduce you to the process of copying multiple objects into position automatically, otherwise know as copying into an array. To create the bolts, follow these steps:

1. Create a poly sphere by choosing **Create → Polygon Primitives → Sphere ❑**. In the option box, set both **Subdivisions Around Axis** and **Subdivisions Along Height** to 6. Click Create. This makes a crude sphere at the origin, perfect for a bolt. Scale the sphere down to 0.07 in all axes to make it the right size.

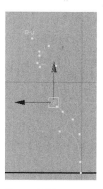

Figure 4.21

Draw a curve to create an outline for the boiler front cover.

2. Now we need to duplicate this bolt many times to place it around the boiler cap and the weld plates. Instead of moving them into position one by one, we will create an array of bolts already placed in a circle that we can group together and slap on the boiler. Move the bolt to the boiler cap, and place it on the left side of the boiler cap, halfway into the surface as shown here.

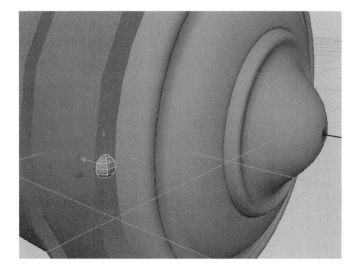

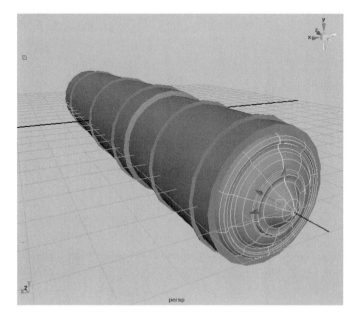

Figure 4.22

Fit the boiler cap onto the boiler engine.

3. Enter pivot placement mode by pressing Insert/Home to move the pivot of the bolt to the center of the boiler cap, and then exit pivot mode by pressing Insert/Home again. We will copy 19 more bolts to go around the boiler cap at 18-degree intervals, pivoting around the center of the boiler cap. Select the bolt and choose **Edit → Duplicate Special □**. In the option box, set **Number Of copies** to 19, and set a value of 18 for **Rotate Z**, as shown in Figure 4.23. Click Apply to copy the bolts all the way around the boiler cap. If you did not move the pivot point of the original bolt to the center of the boiler cap and made the copies, all 19 copies would end up in a different configuration than that nice circle. The copies arrayed themselves around their common pivot point (i.e., the center of the boiler plate) at 18-degree intervals.

4. Notice that the option box does not close when you click Apply. Make sure to reset Duplicate Options back to normal or the next time you try to duplicate an object, you will get 19 more of them! In the option box, choose **Edit → Reset Settings**.

5. In the Outliner, select the 20 bolts and choose **Edit → Group** (or press the hot key Ctrl+G) to group them. Call the new group boiler_bolts or something similar to keep organized. Center the pivot on the new group by choosing **Modify → Center Pivot**.

6. Select the boiler_bolts group, and duplicate it once for another set of bolts you can place on the welding plates. You will have to scale the duplicated boiler_bolts group up a bit to make all the bolts fit around the weld plates. Repeat for the other plates as shown here. Make sure you reset the duplicate options to keep from making 19 copies like before.

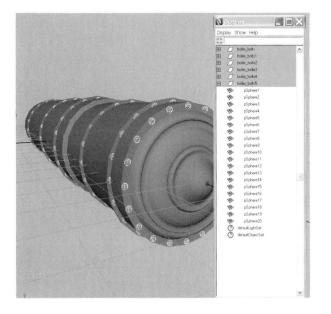

You can load the scene file `locomotive_v1.mb` from the Locomotive project on the CD to check your work or to jump to this point.

Figure 4.23

Multiple copies of the bolt are placed automatically.

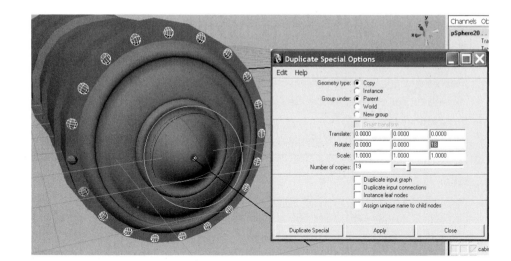

Figure 4.24

The schematic view of the boiler and undercarriage

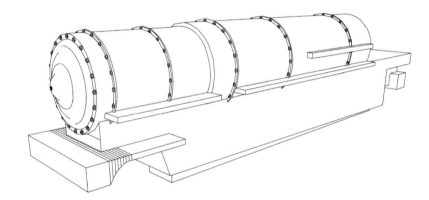

The Undercarriage

Now we can tackle the base on which the boiler sits. Take a look at Figure 4.24 , which shows a schematic view of the boiler sitting on the undercarriage of the train. Luckily we have the luxury of referring to the final model here to better visualize what we're modeling. Follow these steps to continue with the engine:

1. Create a poly cube and scale it to 2.7 in X, 2.95 in Y, and 17.55 in Z. This will form the main length of the undercarriage you see in Figure 4.19. Now we will use extrusions to create the ends. To make your view while you create the undercarriage easier, you could select all the boiler elements and place them on a display layer to hide them as you work on this section, or simply move the cube away from the boiler for the time being and move it back when you're finished.

2. Switch back to the Polygons menu set, and RMB the cube you just created, choose Face from the marking menu, and select the left end of the face. Choose **Edit Mesh → Extrude**. Using the transform manipulator on the special extrude manipulator, pull out the face slightly. Use the Scale Y manipulator (the green box) to scale the new face smaller in the Y axis and move it up as shown.

3. With the new face still selected, choose the Extrude tool again, and pull a new face out about 2.5 units to create a lip as shown here.

4. At the other end, we need to make a thinner lip. Select the poly object and choose **Edit Mesh → Insert Edge Loop Tool**. Place a horizontal edge about one-fifth of the way down from the top edge. Choose the Extrude tool (from the **Edit Mesh** menu or in the Polygons tab of the Shelf by using the 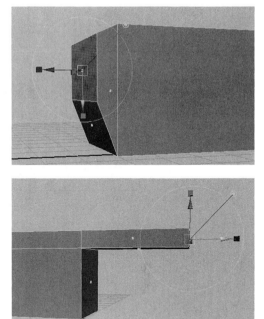 icon) and pull the newly divided face out 3.5 units as shown. This completes the main undercarriage piece.

5. Create three polygon cubes, and scale and position them at the right end of the undercarriage as shown. You can simply fit them in, without worrying about overlapping or interpenetrating geometry.

> If you would like to view your models as shown in the preceding image, with the wireframe lines showing in shaded mode, in the panel view toggle **Shading → Wireframe On Shaded** to on. This helps delineate the model for you.

6. For a finishing touch back there, we will round out the lip we created in step 4. Select the face on the end of the lip, and then RMB it again. This time choose Edge from the marking menu, and Shift+select the bottom edge as shown. Choose **Edit Mesh → Wedge Face □**. Set **Arc Angle** to 90 and **Divisions** to 6. Click Wedge Face, and you

will see a result similar to that shown in Figure 4.25. These little impromptu details help make your model nicer.

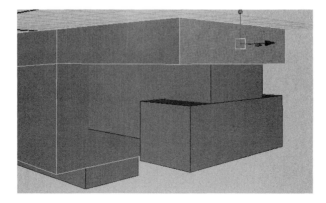

7. The next piece of the undercarriage fits on the left hand or front end and eventually attaches to the cowcatcher of the locomotive. Create a polygon cube, and scale it to 4.45 in X, 0.16 in Y, and 4.0 in Z. Using the Insert Edge Loop Tool, place nine equidistant subdivisions on the polygon slab as shown in Figure 4.26. Notice that if you click and hold with the Insert Edge Loop Tool, you can drag the location of the new edge line. This way you can more easily position the lines.

8. By selecting the bottom faces and moving them down individually, create an arc as shown in Figure 4.27. There's no need to extrude faces; simply moving them one by one is fine. Place the new piece at the front of the undercarriage as shown.

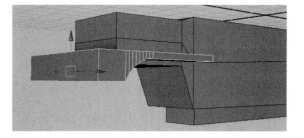

Figure 4.25

The rounded back lip of the undercarriage

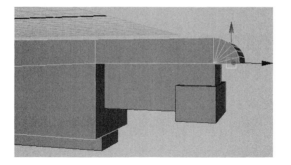

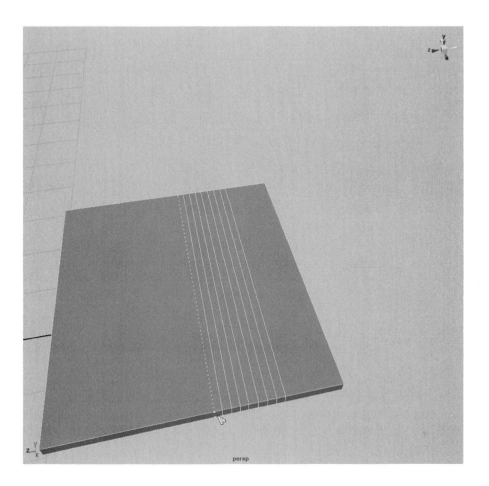

Figure 4.26
Place nine subdivisions on the poly slab.

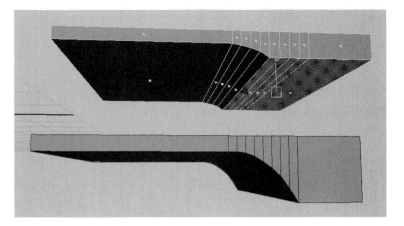

Figure 4.27
Create an arc by moving the bottom faces down individually.

9. Let's tackle the cowcatcher. Create a polygon cube with 8 subdivisions along the width. Scale the cube to 4.4 in X, 2.15 in Y, and 1 in Z. We will use this subdivided cube to pull vertices to make a cowcatcher shape. Enter component selection mode, pick the front top vertices, and move them down to make a wedge as shown.

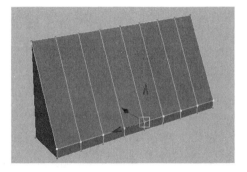

Figure 4.28

The cowcatcher in place

10. Select all the front vertices and the middle five back vertices along the bottom. Scale them in together in the Z axis and then in the X axis. Move them all forward to create the cowcatcher as shown. Place the cowcatcher at the front of the undercarriage, as in Figure 4.28.

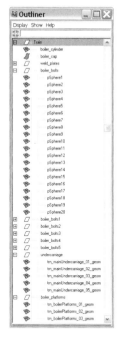

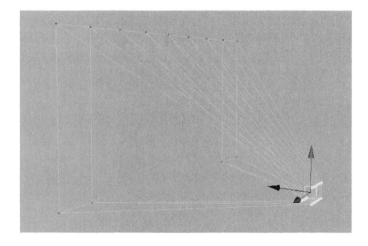

11. Place three poly cube slabs approximately as shown in Figure 4.29 for the boiler plat-forms. Group all these undercarriage pieces together and name them appropriately to stay organized. Also make sure to group the parts of the boiler in a logical manner. The Outliner is shown here with the organization of the model so far.

You can load the scene file `locomotive_v2.mb` from the Locomotive project on the CD to check your work.

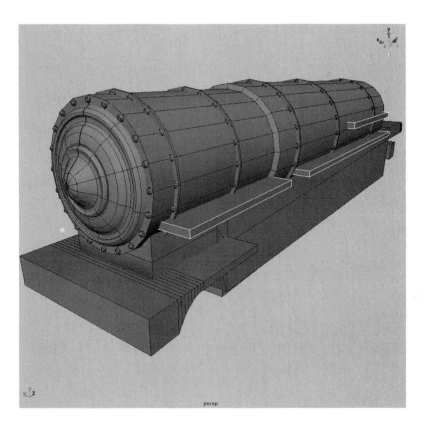

Finishing the Boiler

The fun parts of a steam locomotive are all the chimneys on top of the boiler. To create the main steam chimney with a revolve surface, follow these steps:

1. You will need to draw a profile curve for the smoke stack/chimney. Choose **Create →
   CV Curve Tool** ❒. In the option box, set **Curve Degree** to 1 Linear. This will allow
   you to create straight curves. In the top view panel, start from the bottom and lay
   down CVs similar to those shown in Figure 4.30. Press Enter when you finish. Make
   sure to reset the options to the defaults when you're done.

2. This profile curve should now be about five units tall in the z-axis in the top view
   panel and have its pivot point at the origin. Enter the Surfaces menu set, select the
   curve and choose **Surfaces → Revolve** ❒. Change **Axis Preset** to Z. Also, at the bottom
   of the window, change **Output Geometry** to Polygons. We will not create a NURBS
   surface as we did before with the boiler cap, but this time go for a poly revolve. Change
   Type from Triangles to Quads. This will create polygon faces that are rectangular as

opposed to triangular. Under **Tessellation Method**, select Standard Fit. Click Revolve and you will have a chimney similar to the one shown in Figure 4.31. You may need to orient the chimney to fit the boiler properly if it is lying flat.

3. Delete the history by selecting the chimney and choosing **Edit → Delete By Type → History**. Place the chimney as shown in Figure 4.31. You can move the vertices at the bottom of the chimney to fit it to the round engine boiler as shown. You can also set to the Polygons menu set.

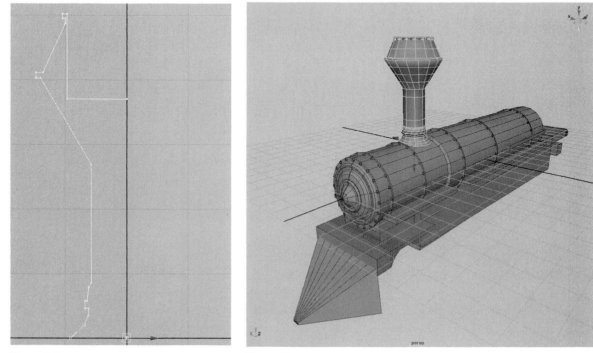

Figure 4.30

The profile curve for the chimney

Figure 4.31

The engine's chimney

Go Get 'em, Cowboy!

Here is where I kick you out into the cruel hard world and task you with creating the remaining pieces for the engine boiler before we move on to the steam pumps, main cabin, and the wheels and drive axles. We will set up the wheels in the animation chapters to follow.

Study the following figures and graphics to get an idea of how to create these pieces using the Revolve Surface tool and the other polygon toolsets used in this exercise and in this chapter. Figure 4.32 shows the extra pieces for you to build. You will find suggestions on how to create the individual pieces in this section.

You can build the light box shown here from a polygon cube by adding subdivision edges with the Insert Edge Loop tool and extruding or moving faces in and out. The light itself is a simple cylinder set into this shape.

You can draw the two topside boiler caps shown below by drawing a profile curve and then revolving the boiler caps as we did for the chimney.

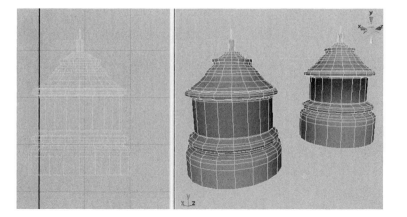

Figure 4.32
You're on your own!

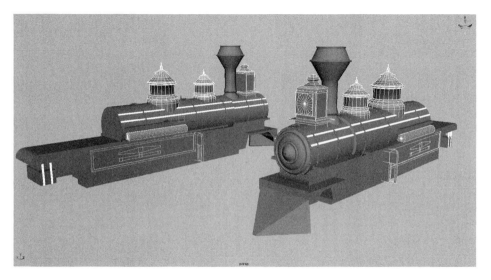

The piping and small tanks along the length of the engine boiler are simple cylinders placed in position as shown here.

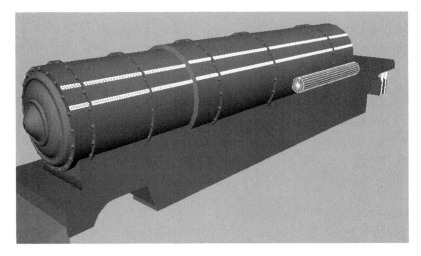

The side panel details are simple poly cubes that have some faces extruded, with a few faces cut out, as shown.

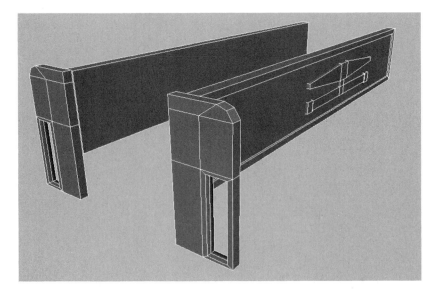

You can load the scene file locomotive_v3.mb from the Locomotive project on the CD to go over the models firsthand and get a much closer look. You can use the scene file to help build the pieces shown in this section to complete the engine boiler and its details. The following sections will cover the cabin and wheels.

The Cabin

All that remains now, as shown in Figure 4.33, are the main cabin, the wheels, and their drive system. We'll finish those parts in the following sections, and later we will move on to setup, or rig, the wheels for animation in Chapter 9. We'll start with the main cabin first.

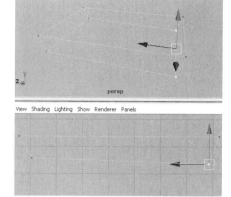

The cabin has two main sections, the cabin itself and the roof. Let's start with the roof and work our way down. Follow these steps:

1. Make a poly cube and scale it to about 5.6 in X, 1 in Y, and 7.7 in Z. Then select the front vertices (shown to be the right side of the cube in the image here), and move them back a bit in Z to angle the edge a bit. Do the same to the rear bottom vertices, giving the cube a tapered look in the Z axis as shown here.

2. We need to subdivide the cube. This time we will use the Add Divisions tool. Select the cube and choose **Edit Mesh → Add Divisions** ❑. Make sure **Division Levels** is set to 1 and **Mode** to quads. Click Add Divisions, and Maya will place edges that cut through the middle of the faces.

Figure 4.33

The remaining bits to make of the locomotive

3. RMB the cube to enter component selection mode, and choose Edge from the marking menu. Select the edges as shown here, and move them toward the back (to the left of the image here) of the roof.

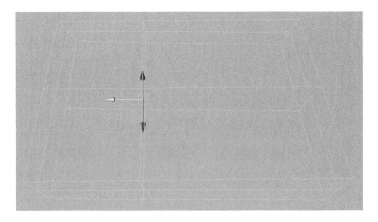

4. Using vertices, shape the roof to match the one shown here.

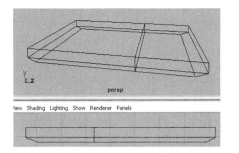

5. Select the bottom two faces and extrude them down once. Select the back face again, and extrude that down one more time to match the shape shown here.

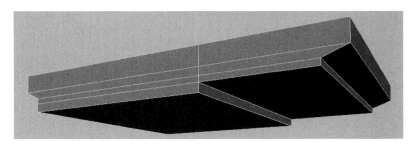

6. Use the Insert Edge Loop Tool to create more subdivisions running along the long sides of the roof, and then move the corner vertices down to angle the side edges of the roof down a little bit to complete the roof, as shown in Figure 4.34.

7. The cabin is a simple cube that is subdivided with the Insert Edge Loop Tool, as shown in Figure 4.35. To make the windows and the open back, simply select the faces in component mode that make up the openings, and delete them.

8. Place the roof on top of the cabin, and you're done! Figure 4.35 shows the completed main cabin.

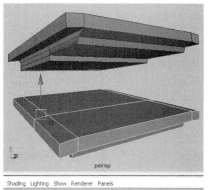

Figure 4.34

The roof is finished.

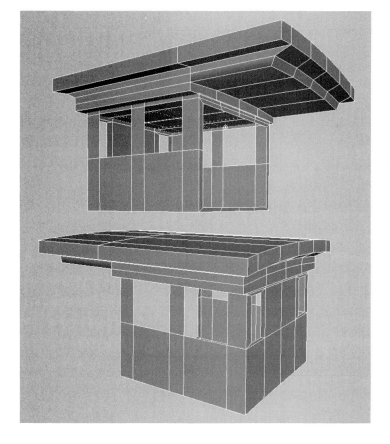

Figure 4.35

The cabin is a simple cube with some deleted faces.

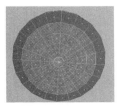

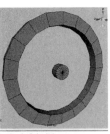

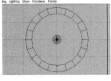

The Wheels

What's a locomotive without wheels? We will have two types of wheels, large ones that are driven by the steam pumps and a pair of small wheels in front of the boiler as shown previously in Figure 4.33.

To make the large wheels, follow these steps:

1. First, we'll create the outer rim of the wheels. Create a poly cylinder with **Subdivisions On Caps** set to 5 in the option box and **Subdivisions Around Axis** set to 20. Scale the cylinder to 1.87 in X and Z, and squash it down to 0.145 in Y. Turn it up on its side by rotating it 90 degrees in Z.

2. To hollow it out, select the inner faces on the caps as shown here and delete them.

3. Now you should see a wheel rim similar to that in Figure 4.36. It is hollow on the inside, so we'll need to close the inside rim. Select the front edges of the inside rim, as shown in Figure 4.36, and choose **Edit Mesh → Extrude**. Extrude the edges toward the back side of the rim to close the inside rim.

4. The wheel spokes are next. We'll create the hub of the spokes with a poly cylinder scaled to 0.25 in X and Z and 0.12 in Y to be slightly thinner than the thickness of the rim. Rotate the hub 90 degrees in Z, and place it in the middle of the rim. It helps to snap both the hub and the rim to the same grid point to make sure they are centered and line up, as shown here.

Figure 4.36

Close the inside rim using Extrude.

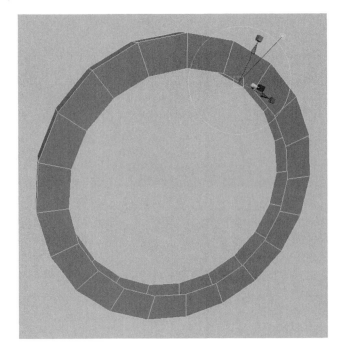

5. Choose **the Edit Mesh** menu, and make sure that the **Keep Faces Together** option at the top of the menu is unchecked. Select the outer ring of faces on the hub, and extrude them out to meet the rim, as shown in Figure 4.37.

6. Next, create a poly cube, and shape it as shown here to place it against the rim of the wheel on one side. This is where the steam drive's arm will connect to the wheel.

7. Group the pieces together and name the node large_wheel. Center the pivot right in the middle of the hub by choosing **Modify → Center Pivot**. If your geometry is not perfectly symmetrical, the pivot may not center properly and you will have to enter pivot mode (press Insert/Home) and move it manually to the center of the hub. If the top wheel node's pivot is not centered properly, animation will look weird. Duplicate and place the wheels as shown in Figure 4.38. Make sure they all face out properly and align as in Figure 4.38.

8. The wheel arms are next. These connect the wheels to the steam drive that runs the loco-motive. You can use simple poly cubes to make the arms in Figure 4.39. Place them as shown, and then rotate the appropriate wheels (using the top large_wheel node) so that they align with the connecting plates. Notice the arms go through the side panel detail you created earlier with the undercarriage. Group the arms together so that you have one group on either side of the train.

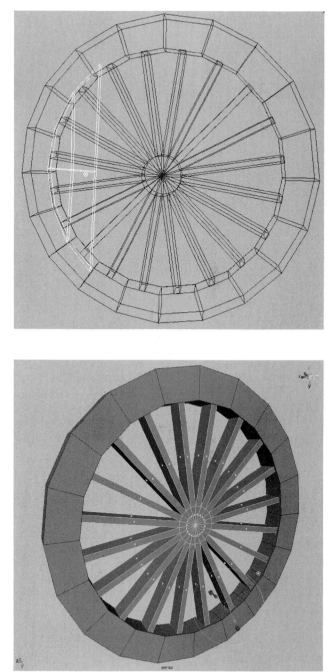

Figure 4.37

Extrude the outer faces of the hub to create the spokes.

Figure 4.38
Duplicate and place the wheels.

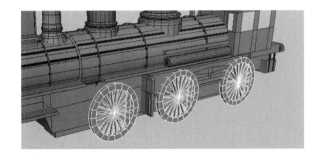

Figure 4.39
Add the wheel arms to the wheels to drive the locomotive.

The Small Wheels, the Axle, and the Steam Pumps

Sounds like a '50s rockabilly band, but it's actually the last part of the locomotive to build. The small wheels up front are exactly the same as the larger wheels, except they do not have the connector plate and they have a solid background. You simply copy one of the large_wheel groups and scale that top node down from 1.0 to 0.575. Delete the connector plate on the side, and place a cylinder behind the wheel to close the back. Remember to group this new closing cylinder into the top node. Call the group small_wheel. Figure 4.40 shows a small wheel in position.

The axle that holds the front wheels is simple to make using basic shapes. Using Figures 4.41 and 4.42 as a guideline, build the axle assembly using simple poly shapes made with primitives and a few subdivision tools and extrusions.

Figure 4.40

A small wheel in position

Figure 4.41

The front axle

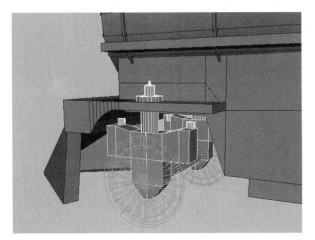

Figure 4.42

The front axle connected to the undercarriage

The steam pumps provide drive power to the wheel arms that in turn rotate the wheels to move the locomotive. These pumps are located on the sides of the engine between the small wheels and the first of the large wheels. They connect down from the boiler and through a drive mechanism to the first large wheel on both sides. This drive mechanism rotates the first wheel, which drives the wheel arm to turn the other wheels on the engine. We will look at how to set up this relationship in the animation chapters later in the book. For now, let's make the steam pumps using simple poly objects, as shown in Figures 4.43 and 4.44.

Figure 4.43

The steam pump is made of two cylinders and an extruded cube.

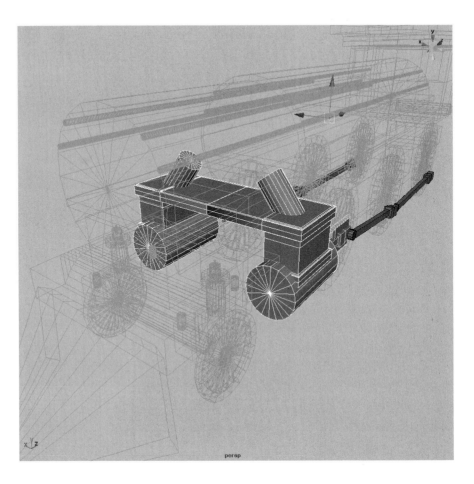

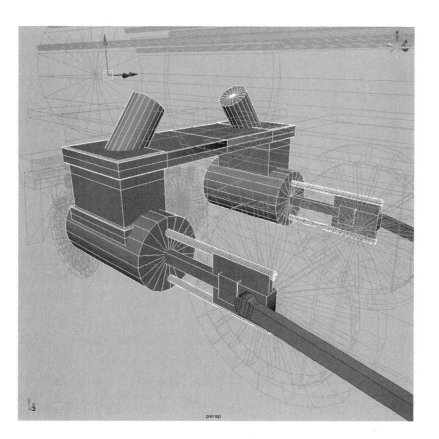

Figure 4.44
The drive mechanism is made of a couple of extruded cubes flanked by poly cylinder rods.

Connect the drive mechanism to the end of the wheel arm. This unit will animate in and out of the large pump cylinder, pulling the drive arm back and forth with it. Considering how your model will animate is an important aspect to modeling. The completed model is shown in Figure 4.45.

Carefully go through your scene and name, if not everything, the top nodes and important pieces of the model. Group items neatly so that everything makes sense. You will later learn in Chapter 8 how best to organize the hierarchy of the model to suit animation needs. Figure 4.46 shows the Outliner view of the organization of the final scene on the CD.

Figure 4.45
We built the whole thing!

Open the scene file `locomotive_model_v4.mb` from the Locomotive project on the CD to compare with your work and also to help complete your work. Comparing and contrasting are valuable learning aids. Sometimes figuring out how something was done by starting at the end and working backward to reverse engineer it will give you a great deal of information.

Suggestions for Modeling Polygons

Poly modeling lends itself nicely to a wide range of objects—practically anything you can think of, and some things you can't. Try modeling the following objects to fine-tune your skills and explore the toolset.

Dining room table and chairs This is an easy place to start. A good amount of leeway in the design gives you as much a challenge as you feel you can handle.

Computer monitor With all the angles and overall surface details, modeling a monitor makes for a great extrusion and face-editing exercise.

Desk lamp, floor lamp This can be a quick exercise, so try to keep it highly detailed.

Car This exercise can be a real challenge, so keep it simple at first and increase the amount of detail the next time you try a poly car. Try to keep your model to the overall shape of the car, and don't worry about doors and windows that actually operate. Try to model the faces such that parts of the car have different faces. Use NURBS surface tools to create poly patches to form the body of the car.

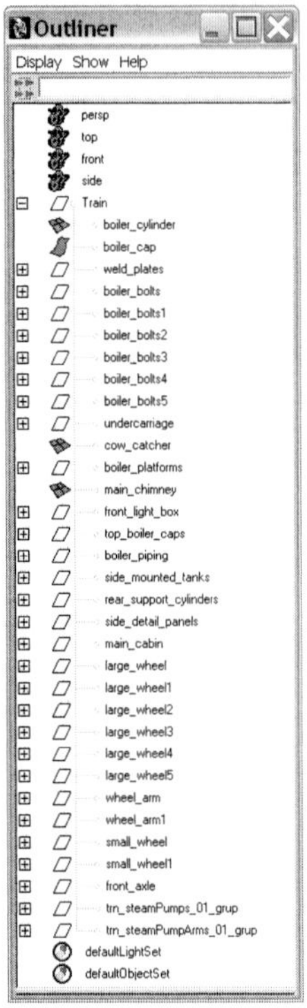

Summary

In this chapter you learned about the basic modeling work flows and how best to approach a model. This chapter dealt primarily with polygon modeling and covered several polygon creation tools as well as several polygon subdivision tools. You put those tools to good use building a hand and smoothing it out, as well as making a complex model system of an old-fashioned steam locomotive. This latter exercise stressed the importance of putting a model together step by step and understanding how elements join together to form a whole model.

Complex models become much easier to create once you recognize how to deconstruct them into their base components. You can divide even simple objects into more easily managed segments from which you can create a model.

The art of modeling with polygons is like anything else in Maya. The technique and work flow enhance with age and time. It is less important to know all the tricks of the trade than it is to know how to approach a model and interpret it into a wireframe mesh.

Figure 4.46

The Outliner view of the organized scene

CHAPTER 5

Modeling with NURBS

As you saw in the previous chapter, NURBS are based on more organic mathematics that allow you to create smooth curves and surfaces. NURBS models can be made of a single surface molded to fit or can be a collection of *patches* connected like a quilt. In any event, NURBS provide ample power for creating smooth surfaces for your models.

NURBS modeling depends on surfaces that are created using curves. Just as CVs are connected to form curved lines, NURBS surfaces are created by connecting (or *spanning*) curves. Therefore, typical NURBS modeling pipelines first involve the creation of curves that will define the edges, outline, paths, and/or boundaries of surfaces.

Once a surface is created, its shape is defined and governed by its isoparms. These surface curves—curves that reside solely on a surface—show the outline of a surface's shape much as the chicken wire in a wire mesh sculpture does. CVs on the isoparms define and govern the shape of these isoparms just as they would regular curves. So, in short, adjusting a NURBS surface involves manipulating the CVs of the object somewhat like sculpting.

Topics include:

- Ways to Make NURBS
- Creating an Axe
- Editing NURBS Surfaces
- Using NURBS Surfacing to Create Polygons
- Converting NURBS to Polygons
- Patch Modeling
- Using Artisan to Sculpt NURBS

Ways to Make NURBS

You can create a NURBS surface in several ways. The easiest way is to create a NURBS primitive. You can sculpt the primitive surface moving its CVs, but you can also cut it apart to create different surface swatches or patches to use as needed. A primitive need not retain its original shape. Using the surfacing tools available under the Surfaces menu set, you can detach, cut, and attach pieces into and out of a primitive to get the shapes you need.

You can also make surfaces in several ways without using a primitive. All these methods involve first creating or using existing NURBS curves (or curves on another surface) to define a part or parts of the surface and then using one of the methods described in the following sections to create the surfaces.

The Lofting Method

The most common surfacing method is *lofting*, which takes at least two curves and creates a surface span between each selected curve, *in the order in which they are selected*. Figure 5.1 shows the result of lofting two curves together.

Figure 5.1

A simple loft created between two curves

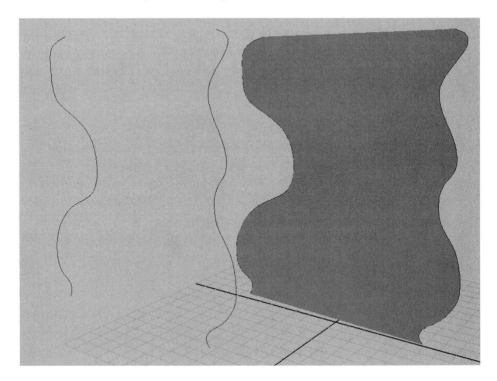

To create a loft, follow these steps:

1. Switch to the Surfaces menu set (press F4).

2. Draw the two curves.

3. Select the curves in the order in which you want the surface generated.

4. Choose **Surfaces → Loft** or click the Loft icon in the Surfaces shelf (🌀).

When you define more curves for the loft, Maya can create more complex shapes. The more CVs for each curve, the more isoparms you have and the more detail in the surface. Figure 5.2 shows how four curves can be lofted together to form a more complex surface. Indeed, you can use almost any number of curves for a lofted surface.

Lofting works best when curves are drawn as cross-sectional slices of the object to be modeled. It is used to make a variety of surfaces, which may be as simple as tabletops or as complex as human faces.

Revolved Surface

A *revolved surface* requires only one curve that is turned about a point in space to create a surface, like a woodworker shaping a table leg on a lathe. First you draw a *profile curve* to create a profile of the desired object, and then you revolve this curve (anywhere from 0 degrees to 360 degrees) around a single point in the scene to create the surface. The profile will revolve around the object's pivot point, which is typically placed at the origin but can be moved (as seen in the solar system exercise in Chapter 3), and sweeps a new surface along its way. On the left in Figure 5.3 is the profile curve for a wine glass. On the right is the complete revolved surface once the profile is revolved around the Y axis.

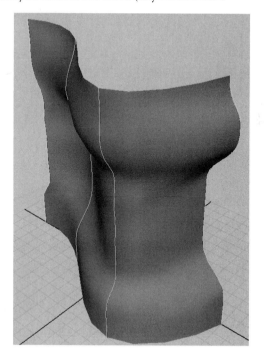

Figure 5.2

A loft created with four curves that are selected in order from left to right

To create a revolved surface, follow these steps:

1. Draw and select your profile curve.

2. Choose **Surfaces → Revolve**.

A revolved surface is useful for creating objects such as bottles, furniture legs, and baseball bats—anything that is symmetrical about an axis.

Figure 5.3

A profile curve is drawn in the outline of a wine glass in the Y axis. The curve is then revolved around the Y axis a full 360 degrees to create a wine glass.

Extruded Surface

An *extruded surface* uses two curves—a profile curve and a path curve. The profile curve is drawn to create the profile shape of the desired surface. It is then swept from one end of the path curve to its other end, creating spans of a surface along its travel. The higher the CV count on each curve, the greater the surface's detail. An extruded surface can also take the profile curve and simply stretch it to a specified distance straight along one direction or axis, doing away with the profile curve. Figure 5.4 shows the profile and path curves, and Figure 5.5 shows the resulting surface once the profile is extruded along the path.

Figure 5.4

The profile curve is drawn in the shape of an I, and the path curve comes up and bends toward the camera.

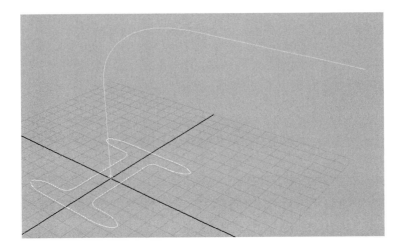

To create an extruded surface, follow these steps:

1. Draw both curves.

2. Select the profile curve.

3. Shift+select the path curve.

4. Choose **Surfaces → Extrude**.

An extruded surface is used to make items such as winding tunnels, a coiled garden hose, springs, or curtains.

Planar Surface

A *planar surface* uses one perfectly flat curve to make a two-dimensional cap in the shape of that curve. It does this by laying down a NURBS plane (a flat square NURBS primitive) and carving out the shape of the curve like a cookie cutter. The resulting surface is a perfectly flat, cutout shape, also known as a *trimmed surface* since the "excess" outside the shape curve is trimmed away.

To create a planar surface, follow these steps:

1. Draw and select the curve.

2. Choose **Surfaces → Planar**.

You can also use multiple curves within each other to create a planar surface with holes in it. On the left in Figure 5.6 is a simple planar surface. When a second curve is added inside the original curve and both are selected, the planar surface is created with a hole. On the right is the result when the outer curve is selected first and then the inner curve before **Surfaces → Planar** is chosen.

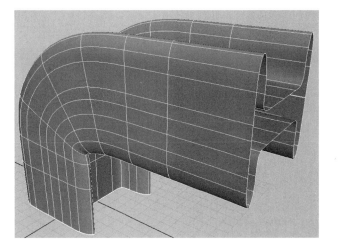

Figure 5.5

Once extruded, the surface becomes a bent I-beam.

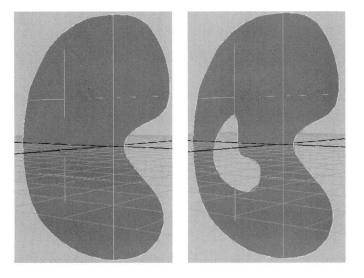

Figure 5.6

A planar surface based on a single curve (left). A planar surface based on a curve within a curve to create the cutout (right).

A planar surface is great for flat lettering, for pieces of a marionette doll or paper cutout, or for capping the ends of a hollow extrusion. Planar surfaces are best left as flat pieces, however, as deforming them may not give the best results. In addition, it sometimes is best to create the planar surface as a polygon. You will see how to convert surfaces to polygons later in this chapter. However, the following quick exercise will give you an idea of what to look out for when creating polygons from surfacing techniques:

1. In the Surfaces menu set, select **Create → NURBS Primitives → Circle** twice to create two circles.

2. Scale the second circle to about three times its original size, as shown.

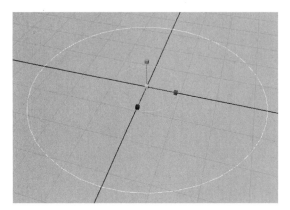

3. Select the larger circle first, then the smaller circle and select Surfaces → Planar ❒. In the option box, check Polygons for **Output Geometry,** Quads for **Type**, and General for **Tessellation Method** as shown here.

4. Depending on how you create the geometry as polygons, you will get different results, particularly around curves. Since Maya has to figure out where to put more faces to create a smother outline, you will have to set the **Number U** and **Number V** settings to best fit the curves of your resulting surface. At current settings, your planar surface will look as shown here. Notice the small gaps between the original outer NURBS circle and the surface outline.

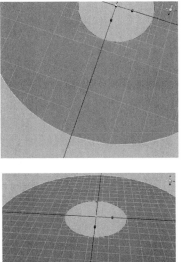

5. Try increasing the **Number U** and **Number V** values and you will get tighter results at curves, though with more faces on your model.

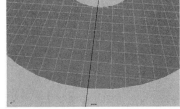

Keep this exercise in mind as you go through your modeling from here on. Whenever you need to create polygons from NURBS surfaces, which should be quite often for some, try the different creation methods for the best output. No one way works the best all the time.

> If you try creating a planar surface using a curve and notice that Maya does not allow it, verify that the curve(s) is perfectly flat. If any of the CVs are off the same plane as the others, the planar surface will not work.

Beveled Surface

The *bevel surface* function takes an open or a closed curve and extrudes its outline to create a side surface. It creates a bevel on one or both corners of the resulting surface to create an edge that can be made smooth or sharp (see Figure 5.7). The many options in the Bevel tool allow you to control the size of the bevel and depth of extrusion, giving you great flexibility. Once a bevel is created, you can easily cap the bevel with planar surfaces.

To create a bevel, follow these steps:

1. Draw and select your curve.

2. Choose **Surfaces → Bevel**.

Maya also offers a Bevel Plus surface, which has more creation options for advanced bevels. A beveled surface is great for creating 3D lettering, for creating items such as bottle caps or buttons, or for rounding out an object's edges.

Figure 5.7

**A curve before and
after it is beveled.
The beveled surface
is given a planar cap.**

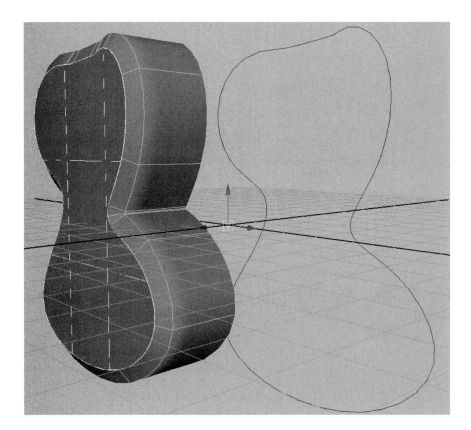

Boundary Surface

A *boundary surface* is so named because it is created within the boundaries of three or four
surrounding curves. For example, two vertical curves are drawn opposite each other to
define the two side edges of the surface. Two horizontal curves are then drawn to define
the upper and lower edges. These curves can have depth to them; they need not be flat
for the boundary surface to work, unlike the planar surface. Although you can select the
curves in any order, it is best to select them in opposing pairs. In Figure 5.8, four curves
are created and arranged to form the edges of a surface to be created. First, select the vertical pair of curves, as they are opposing pairs, and then select the second two horizontal
curves before choosing **Surfaces → Boundary**.

A boundary surface is useful for creating shapes such as car hoods, fenders, and other
formed panels.

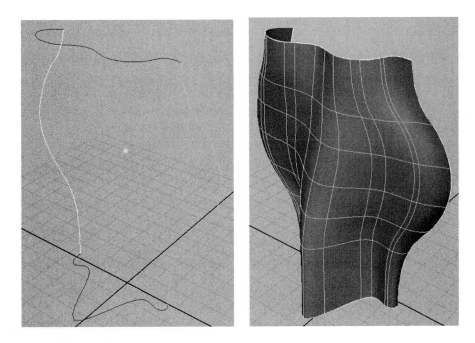

Figure 5.8

Four curves are arranged to create the edges for a surface (left). The resulting boundary surface from the four curves (right).

Combining Techniques

You can use certain surfacing techniques in conjunction to create intricate models. For example, whenever a curve is required for a surface, you can use an isoparm instead to create a surface between two existing surfaces.

Try This Take a couple of lofted surfaces and connect them with a third surface. Figure 5.9 shows two surfaces with two intermediate curves in between them. (Notice that the view panel's option **Shading → X-ray** is turned on so you can see through the shaded surfaces.) You will select an isoparm from the first surface (on the left), then the curve on the left, the curve on the right, and finally an isoparm on the second surface.

1. Either create two lofted surfaces and curves as shown in Figure 5.9, or load the Lofting_Exercise_1.ma file from the Lofting_Exercise project on the CD.

2. To select the first isoparm, press F8 for component selection mode and click the Lines Selection Filter button ( ) in the Status line to allow you to select isoparms. You can also RM click the surface and choose **Isoparm** from the marking menu to enter component mode for isoparms.

3. Select an isoparm close to the left edge. Press F8 to return to object selection mode (or you can RM click the first curve and choose **Object Mode** from the marking menu), and Shift+select the first curve and then the second curve. Press F8 again or use the marking menu again for component mode, and Shift+select an isoparm toward the left edge on the second surface, as in Figure 5.10.

4. Choose **Surfaces → Loft** to create the intermediate surface between the existing lofts. Figure 5.11 shows how the new surface snakes from the first loft to the second loft by way of the two curves.

Surface History

In Chapter 2 you learned that clicking the History icon ( ) toggles history on and off. *History* has to do with how objects react to change. Leaving history on when creating primitives, as you did in Chapter 2, gives access to the object's original parameters.

Leaving history on when creating NURBS surfaces allows the surface to update as any of its creation pieces changes. For example, the loft you just created will update whenever the two original surfaces or curves you used to create the loft move or change shape. If you were to move the original loft on the left and rotate it back a bit, the new loft would adjust to keep its one side attached to the same isoparm. If one or more of the input curves were to change, the loft would bend to fit.

You must toggle history on before you create the object(s) if you want history to be on the object(s).

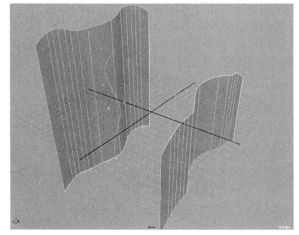

Figure 5.9

Two lofted surfaces with two curves in between

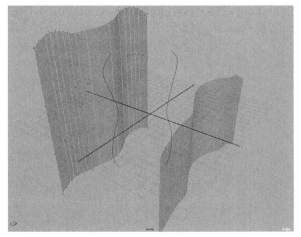

Figure 5.10

Selecting the isoparm

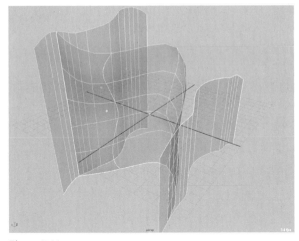

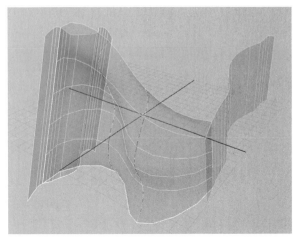

Figure 5.11

The spanning loft between the existing surfaces snakes from the first isoparm to the curves to the second isoparm.

Figure 5.12

History will update the newly created loft to keep it attached to the isoparms and curves used to create it, even when they've been moved or altered.

By lofting using isoparms and with history toggled on, you can keep the new surface permanently attached to the original loft, no matter how the isoparms move, as in Figure 5.12. This technique works with all surface techniques, not just with lofting, as long as history is turned on. History is useful for making adjustments and fine-tuning a surface and can be handy in animation if several surfaces need to deform but stay attached.

Why wouldn't you want history turned on for everything? After a long day modeling, having history on every single object can slow down your scene file, adding unnecessary bloat to your work flow. But it is not typically a problem on most surface types unless the scene is huge, so you should leave it on while you're still modeling.

If you decide that you no longer want a surface or an object to retain its history, you can selectively delete it from the surface. Select the surface and choose **Edit → Delete by Type → History**. You can also rid the entire scene of history by choosing **Edit → Delete All by Type → History**. Just don't get them mixed up!

Creating an Axe Using NURBS

The exercise in this section will take you through the following NURBS modeling techniques:

· Image planes

· Lofting

· Revolves

· Boundary surfaces

- Trims
- Curve and surface attachment/detachment
- Object and curve duplication

In this exercise, you will model an axe using NURBS geometry. Instead of replicating in 3D a fully finished design, you will design the axe on-the-fly. But even when you're using Maya as a design tool, you'll need a good starting point. That involves research and some sketching to give you a good idea of where to start and which direction to head.

Getting Started

Create a new project called axe_model. In a real project, you would now gather any reference information, stills, and images on which to base your axe design. Typically, those reference images are placed in the *sourceimages* folder of your project. For this exercise, you will find all the source files in the axe_model project on the CD.

For this example, you will use a sketch of a simple axe design as a template for the model. Copy the file Axe_outline_1.tif in the sourceimages folder of the axe_model project from the CD into your project's sourceimages folder.

> It is unwise to work on files directly from the CD. As a matter of fact, you shouldn't work from or on files stored on any removable medium. Always copy files to the project folders set up on a local or network hard drive.

1. Choose **File → New Scene**. Open the Surfaces menu set either by selecting it in the menu or by pressing the default hot key F4.

2. Import the sketch of the axe into Maya. You will need to import it as an *image plane*. In your front window, choose **View → Image Plane → Import Image**.

An *image plane* is a bitmap picture, such as a TIFF or JPEG, that is displayed in one or all of your work panels as a reference guide. Image planes are extremely useful for modeling alone, but a sequence of files can be brought in to animate to or track motion as well (a.k.a. matchmoving, more on that later).

3. Point to Axe_outline_1.tif in your sourceimages folder and load it. The sketch will now display full screen in your front window and as a plane in the perspective window (see Figure 5.13).

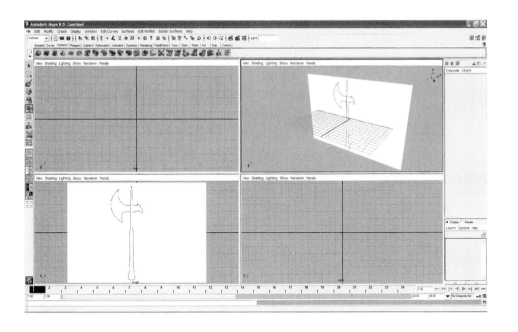

Figure 5.13

An image plane loaded into the front panel

Placing the Plane behind the Grid

In the next steps, you'll adjust the image plane settings to place the plane behind the grid. As it is now, the image plane should have loaded at the origin and on top of the grid in the front window. Move it back a few units to view the grid.

1. Choose **View** → **Image Plane** → **Image Plane Attributes** → **imagePlane1** to open the Attribute Editor for the image plane.

2. Under Placement Extras, change the **Center** Z value to –2.0. This will push the image plane back in the Z axis and reveal the grid once again. This will also allow you to create curves on the origin plane without losing sight of them behind the image plane. Figure 5.14 shows the proper settings.

3. If the clutter of seeing the image plane in the other windows bothers you, under Display at the top of the Attribute Editor, change the radio button selection from In All Views to Looking Through Camera. This setting will remove the image plane from the other windows.

> If you can't see the image plane, click Show in the view panel and make sure Cameras is set to Show.

Tracing the Outline

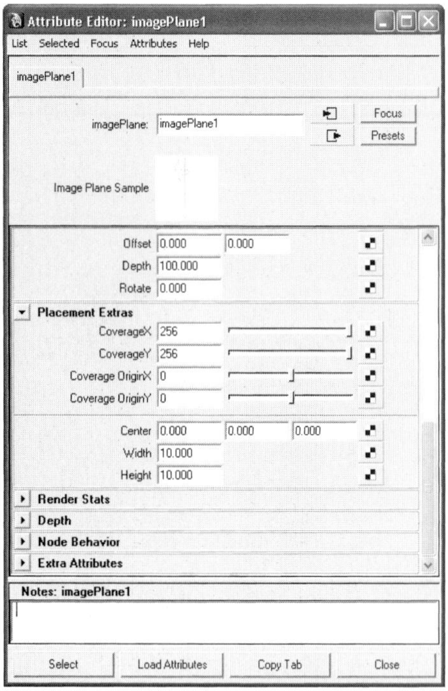

Figure 5.14

The Attribute Editor
for the image
plane settings for
placement

This is where coloring in the lines in kindergarten comes into play. In the front window, trace the outline of the axe using NURBS curves. Start with the axe head to the left of the handle. Also, make sure history is enabled. Follow these steps:

1. Select the CV Curve tool by choosing **Create → CV Curve Tool**.

2. Starting from the top of the axe head, a little bit behind where it meets the handle as shown in Figure 5.15, lay down a series of CVs to create a curve that follows the contours of the axe head counterclockwise. When you reach the top tip, you'll need to lay down three CVs directly on top of each other to make a sharp corner:

   • Lay down the first CV at the corner tip.

   • Turn on point snaps with the Snap to Points icon (✎).

   • Put down two more CVs, snapping them both on top of the first corner CV.

   • Turn off snaps.

3. Follow along the axe counterclockwise until you reach the bottom tip of the head. Place three CVs there, using snaps to make a sharp corner.

4. Follow the axe head's curvature into the handle and a little bit beyond where it meets the handle. Place three CVs at that point, and continue the curve up to meet the start of the curve.

It doesn't matter if you don't place the final CV directly on top of the first CV. As a matter of fact, place it just a little below it. You will close the curve using the Open/Close Curve command later. Using this command will ensure that the curve is geometrically closed. Otherwise, there would be two points at the closure point that could become separated, thereby opening the curve's loop.

5. Press Enter to create the curve.

6. With the curve selected, choose **Edit Curves → Open/Close Curves**. This command will complete the curve for you.

7. In component mode (press F8), adjust the CVs to make the curve better fit the sketch of the axe.

8. Save your work.

9. Load `Axe_model_v1.mb` in the axe_model project on the CD and compare your work up to this point.

By saving your own scene file before opening the other version, you've made sure you won't lose your work. When you open a new file or new scene, Maya asks you to save your current scene if you have not done so already. It's a good idea to save before opening a new file regardless. As discussed in Chapter 3, Maya's Incremental Save feature makes it easy to back up your work at any time.

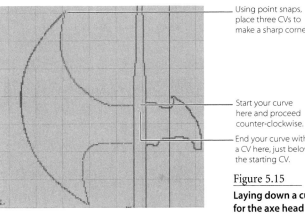

Using point snaps, place three CVs to make a sharp corner.

Turning Off the Image Plane

Now you can turn off the image plane. Go to the front panel and choose **View → Image Plane → Image Plane Attributes → imagePlane1** to open the Attribute Editor for the image plane. In the Display Mode menu, choose None to turn off the image plane in all views. To turn it back on, change the display mode back to RGB.

Start your curve here and proceed counter-clockwise.

End your curve with a CV here, just below the starting CV.

Figure 5.15

Laying down a curve for the axe head

Duplicating the Curve

We'll now make a copy of the outline curve to give the axe head depth. Follow these steps:

1. To duplicate the curve you've drawn, select it and choose **Edit → Duplicate** (or press Ctrl+D). The duplicate curve is now selected.

2. Move the curve back in the Z axis a little bit to give the axe head some depth. Figure 5.16 shows a good depth for the axe head's curves. Notice that the pivot point for both the original and duplicate curves are at the origin.

3. To quickly center their pivots (and to also center their manipulators), select them both and choose **Modify → Center Pivot**. You'll find this function useful.

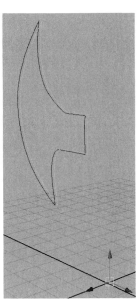

Figure 5.16

Positioning the duplicate axe head curve

If you get strange results from a menu command, open its option box and reset its settings by choosing **Edit → Reset Settings**.

Creating the Axe's Edge

To create the axe's edge, follow these steps:

1. Select the original axe curve and duplicate it. Move the new curve in between the two curves.

2. Select the original curve again, toggle into component mode (F8), and move the CVs on the front edge in about halfway toward the middle curve. Do the same with the third curve to get its CVs closer in to the middle.

3. Select the CVs on the front edge of the middle curve *except* for the corners, and move them out in the X axis away from the edge just a little bit, as in Figure 5.17. This will give a nice crisp edge for the axe when you loft the three curves together to form the sides of the axe head.

4. You're going to create a groove in the top and bottom sides of the axe head for a nice detail. Select the top and bottom CVs of the middle curve *without* the corners and bring them down and in by scaling them down in the Y axis and moving them to the left in X, as shown in Figure 5.18.

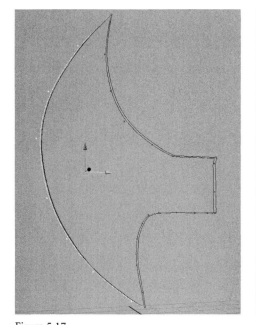

Figure 5.17

Positioning the middle curve CVs for the edge

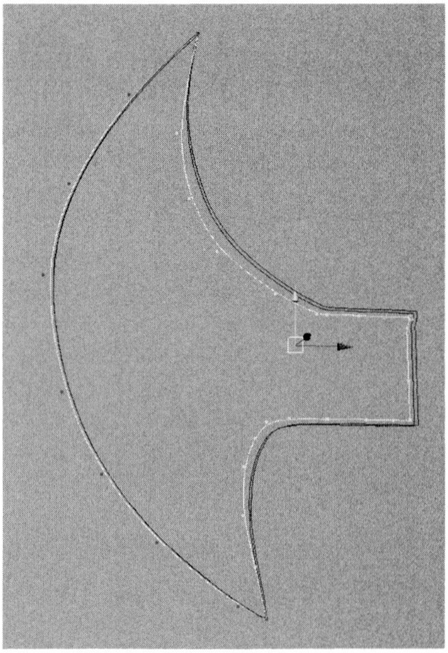

Figure 5.18

Creating a groove on the sides

Breakpoint

This is a perfect time to save a version of your work and take a walk to stretch your eyes a bit and grab a delicious peach smoothie. You have finished the preparation work and are now ready to move on to creating the NURBS surfaces themselves. It might also be a good time to go back to the beginning to redo the procedures in a new file to practice the prep work in the exercise up to this point. You'll find that, with practice, these procedures become almost second nature and afford you the opportunity to pick up something that may not have been clear the first time. Repetition is critical in learning a powerful package such as Maya (and in teaching an "old dog" new tricks).

Creating the Surfaces

You'll create a boundary surface for the faces of the axe head and lofts for its sides. You cannot use the planar surface for the axe's two faces because the curves you created are no longer flat. They push in slightly at the cutting edge to make the axe sharp. Planar surfaces must be perfectly flat.

First, to make the axe faces, you have to create four curves to make the boundary surface work properly. Instead of re-creating them all, you can detach the current curve into four separate curves. Follow these steps:

1. Select the top curve and toggle into component mode. You will need to pick curve points instead of CVs to cut apart the curve. Turn off the Points Filter (■) and turn on the Parm Points Filter (●) on the Status line. The curve will turn cyan, and little Xs called edit points will appear on the curve. You can select any point on the surface; it does not need to fall on an X.

> *Curve points* are points that actually make up the curve, as opposed to CVs, which control the shape of the curve. Choosing a curve point is choosing a precise location on the curve itself. *Edit points* are much like CVs in that they change the shape of the curve, but unlike CVs, they lie on the curve itself.

2. Click somewhere on the curve, and drag the little orange box that appears to the bottom corner of the cutting edge. Shift+click again, and drag that new point to the top cutting-edge corner. You now have two curve points selected at the top and bottom of the cutting edge. Shift+select/drag points for the remaining two corners of the axe, as shown in Figure 5.19. These points locate the exact position where you want to detach the curve into four new sections.

3. Choose **Edit Curves → Detach Curves** to cut the curves apart at the selected points. This will generate four separate curves so that you can make the boundary surfaces. The detached curves will be displayed as new curves in the Outliner and Hypergraph.

4. Let's hide these curves to make the work area more manageable:

    - In the Layer box right under the Channel Box, choose **Layers → Create Empty Layer.** Do this three times to create three layers.

    - Select the four new curves from the first axe profile curve and assign them to layer1 by right-clicking the layer and choosing **Add Selected Objects.**

    - To toggle visibility of this layer, click the V to the left of the layer1 name. This will take those curves off your screen to make it easier to work.

    - Select the middle curve and assign it to layer2, and then assign the third curve to layer3.

5. Turn off visibility for the first and second curves to work on the third profile curve. Repeat the curve detach procedure to cut apart the remaining outside axe profile curve. Repeat for the middle curve as well.

Once you detach the curves, Maya will place three of the detached curves into the default layer. You will have to select them and place them back in layer3.

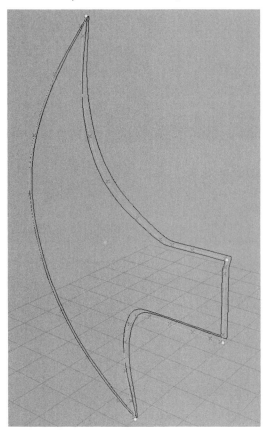

Figure 5.19

Selecting the corner curve points

6. Turn off layer3, and turn layer1 back on. Select the four curves and make a boundary surface by choosing **Surfaces → Boundary**.

The surface at this point does not fit in the boundaries because the spans on each curve don't line up. Some curves have more CVs than other curves. Since surfacing relies on the CVs on the input curves, you'll need to rearrange the axe profile curves to match up with each other.

7. Select all four curves and choose **Edit Curves → Rebuild Curve ❑**. In the window, leave **Rebuild Type** to Uniform and change **Number of Spans** to 10. This will rebuild the curves so that each has the same number of CVs and the surface will build properly. You might notice that some of the new CVs on the rebuilt curve are out of place, though, and the curve is now slightly misshapen.

8. In component mode, position those CVs to regain the original curve shape.

9. Select these rebuilt curves in opposite pairs, and create the boundary surface as shown in Figure 5.20. If necessary, refer to the section "Boundary Surface" earlier in this chapter. Once created, this surface will be your axe's front face. Assign it to layer1.

10. Turn off layer1 and turn on layer3. Rebuild these curves with the same settings as before.

11. Create a boundary surface to make the back face for the axe head.

Connecting the Axe Faces

Now that you have the faces for the axe, you'll need to connect them to create the side edges of the axe. Follow these steps:

1. Turn on layer2. You'll use these curves as the middle input curves for a loft between the two faces you've just made. This will give the sharp edge and the grooves on the sides.

> You can clean up your work window so that selecting is easier. In the *persp* panel, choose
> **Show → NURBS Surfaces** to toggle off NURBS surface display in this window. That will leave
> you with just the curves.

2. Rebuild these middle curves as you did the face curves.

3. Turn back on the NURBS Surfaces display in the panel by choosing **Show → NURBS Surfaces** (if you've turned them off previously).

4. Select the top curves from front to back and choose **Surfaces → Loft** to make the top side edge. Do the same for the bottom side curves. You should end up with something like Figure 5.21.

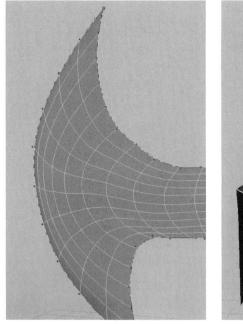

Figure 5.20

The front axe face surface

Figure 5.21

The axe's top and bottom grooved edges

5. To create a nice sharp edge, you'll make a slightly different version of a loft. Select the cutting edge curves from front to back and choose **Surfaces → Loft ❏**. In the window, change the Surface Degree option from Cubic to Linear. Click the Loft button to create the surface.

> NURBS can calculate at different level degrees. Cubic NURBS curves and surfaces are standard and create the smooth curves you've already seen. Linear degree will create direct, straight spans between CVs, creating sharp corners.

6. To adjust the cutting edge, select the middle curve in this new loft, and move it away from the axe a bit more. Surface history will stretch the cutting edge surface and make it sharper. Be sure you turn on history before you make these surfaces, though.

Fine-Tuning the Axe

Now it's time to make a few adjustments to the new surfaces. You'll notice that the top and bottom tips of the cutting edge flare out. Taper them by moving the CVs on the original curves in together. Follow these steps:

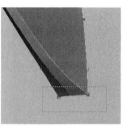

1. Select the bottom tip CVs for all four curves as shown here.

2. With CVs selected, go to Scale and scale them in toward each other in the Z axis to taper the bottom tip.

3. Select pairs of CVs up the edge and sides of the axe and scale them in Z (the blue locator handle) a bit to taper them in as well.

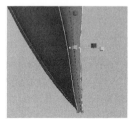

Break Point

This is another good time to take a break and save your work; grab a juice and flex your wrists.

Once you've saved, use the CD file `axe_model_v2.mb` to check your work up to this point. Make sure you understand the techniques used thus far. You have been exposed to a number of procedures, and it's a good idea to make sure they make sense before continuing. Although the process of creating this axe, and most CG, may seem daunting, taken one step at a time, creating CG is not as complex as you might think.

> You can either choose to manually save the file of your axe scene and rename it with a new version number to better keep track of your progress or rest assured that Maya will make a backup for you through Incremental Save. (Make sure the option is turned on through **File → Save Scene ❏**.)

Building the Back of the Axe Head

What remains now is the right side of the full axe head. Follow these steps:

1. Turn the image plane back on in the front view panel.

> An easy way to toggle the image plane view on and off in a work panel is to toggle camera display. As long as the image plane's display is set to RGB, choose **Show → Cameras** to toggle the image plane on and off.

2. In the same way you created the edge of the cutting side of the axe, create a curve to trace around the image plane, starting where the back of the axe head meets the handle up top and proceeding clockwise around the shape.

3. Close the curve by choosing **Edit Curves → Open/Close Curves**.

4. Duplicate the curve and move it to create a thickness to match the front of the axe head.

5. Pick the corner curve points and cut apart the curve into four parts by choosing **Edit Curves → Detach Curves**. (See Figure 5.22.)

6. Rebuild the curves by choosing **Edit Curves → Rebuild Curve**, and use 20 spans. You'll lose some definition, so you'll have to go in and adjust the CVs manually.

7. Create a boundary surface to make the faces, and use lofts to create the sides.

8. Now you'll try something different. Delete the original curves to leave behind the two faces of the axe head.

   To create the sides without curves to loft with, you'll need to use isoparms.

9. Switch to component mode and enable isoparm selection. Select an isoparm at the top edge of both faces and choose **Surfaces → Loft**.

10. Repeat with the remaining three sides. Figure 5.23 shows the completed surface.

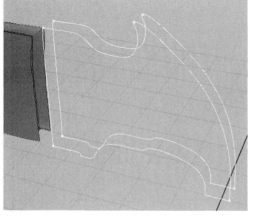

Figure 5.22

Select corner curve points to detach the curves.

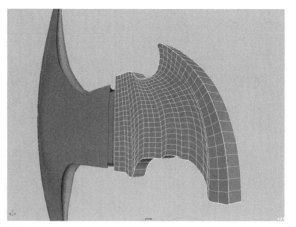

Figure 5.23

The back end of the axe head

Modeling with Deformers

Deformers are tools in Maya that allow you to easily change the shape of an object. As opposed to using CVs to manually distort or bend an object, you can use a deformer to affect the entire object. Popular deformers such as Bend and Flare can be powerful tools for adjusting your models quickly and evenly. For more on modeling with deformers, see Chapter 6.

To alter the shape of the axe head using a Flare deformer, follow these steps:

1. Select the two faces. Since the lofted edges have history, they will be affected when the faces are deformed.

2. Switch to the Animation menu set (press F2).

3. Create a Flare deformer by choosing **Deform → Create Nonlinear → Flare**. The Flare deformer appears as a cylindrical object.

4. Rotate the deformer 90 degrees in the Z axis.

5. Open the Attribute Editor (press Ctrl+A), click the flare1 tab to access the Flare controls, and enter the following values:

Attribute	Value
Start Flare Z	0.020
High Bound	0.50

Deformers use history to distort the geometry to which they're attached. You can animate any of the attributes that control the deformer shapes, but in this case you're using this deformer as a means to adjust a model. Once you get the desired shape as seen in Figure 5.24, you can discard the deformer. But simply selecting and deleting the deformer will reset the geometry to its original shape. You'll need to pick the geometry (not the deformer) and delete its history by choosing **Edit → Delete by Type → History**.

Figure 5.24

The back of the axe head with a Flare deformer attached

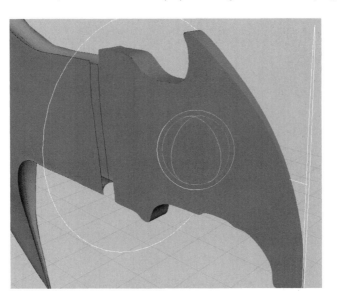

Now that we're done with the axe head, let's move on to the handle. Follow these steps:

1. Turn the image plane back on in the front view panel.

2. Create a curve to outline just the left *half* of the handle in the image plane. You'll revolve this surface to create the handle itself. Start at the top and work down to the middle of the bottom.

3. Once you make the curve, move its pivot point (toggle pivot mode with the Insert key) to the end CV at the bottom using Snap to Points ( ).

4. Select the curve and in the Surfaces menu set (press F4), choose **Surfaces → Revolve** ❏. In the options, make sure that Axis Preset is set to Y and that Pivot is set to Object (the default settings). Make sure that Start Sweep Angle is set to 0, that End Sweep Angle is set to 360, that Segments is set to 8, and that you're outputting a NURBS surface. Click Revolve to create your handle surface as in Figure 5.25.

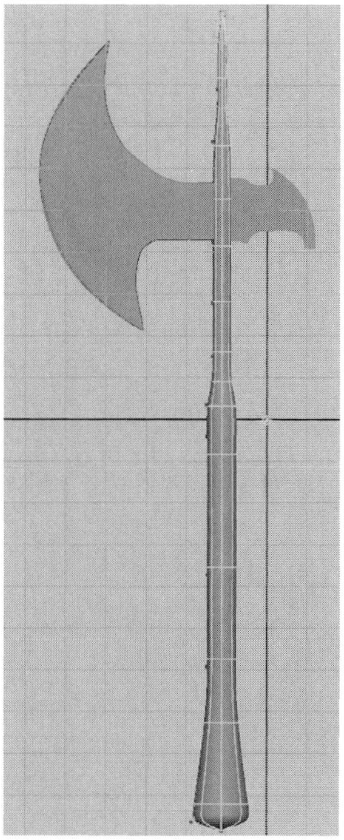

Save again and use the file axe_model_v3.mb on the CD to check your work.

See Chapter 6 for more on modeling with deformers, particularly the Lattice deformer.

Figure 5.25

The revolved surface handle completes the axe model.

Cleaning Up

Open the Outliner, and you'll see the long, unorganized list of curves and surfaces shown in Figure 5.26. Cleanup is probably the most overlooked part of the modeling process, but vital. Go though the nodes and group objects, and name everything in a consistent and straightforward manner, if you haven't been keeping track of items as you went along. With time, this will be routine.

Once you're done with the axe, all the original input curves will no longer be needed. You can delete them and the history on the surfaces you used them to make. Search through and select these curves from the Outliner to delete them, as shown in Figure 5.27. While in wireframe mode in the view panels, you will notice some of the surfaces turning magenta. That means the selected object has an output connection to that magenta object, most usually history. If that surface or object is final, you can safely delete the input. If you made a mistake, use the undo function (press Z or Ctrl+Z). You will usually notice a problem if you forget to delete history on some objects when you move or animate them. For more on this, see the sidebar "Testing the Geometry" in this chapter.

Figure 5.26

The Outliner full of nodes

Figure 5.27

The cleaner Outliner

Axe Conclusion

Surfacing techniques can yield powerful results. Using curves and isoparms, you can create intricately connected surfaces to model very detailed organic shapes with NURBS. History plays a huge part in modeling as it allows you to make easy adjustments to keep surfaces in certain harmony.

In the end you should have an axe similar to Figure 5.28. Feel free to adjust the design of the axe to try out a few more axes to brush up on NURBS techniques.

Using similar techniques you can create a hammer, a knife, or an arrowhead to further hone your skills.

Editing NURBS Surfaces

Maya provides numerous NURBS tools you'll find useful in editing your surfaces. Besides tools for moving CVs, some important functions and tools allow you to add realism to your model. This section gives you a quick preview of these tools; you'll need to try them for yourself.

Open and tear off the Edit NURBS menu and follow along here. The following functions are all accessed through it.

Project Curve on Surface

The ability to project a curve onto a surface allows you to cut out holes in the surface using the Trim tool (choose **Edit NURBS → Trim Tool).** It also allows you to create, using history, another surface that is attached, following the outline of your projected curve, as you saw in the section "Combining Techniques" earlier in this chapter.

Projected curves are also useful for tracing animation paths for objects to follow along a surface. For example, you can project a curve around a hilly landscape surface and assign a car to animate (drive) along that projected curve. The car will stick to the surface of the road with ease.

To use Project Curve on Surface, select the surface and the curve to project, and choose **Edit NURBS → Project Curve on Surface**.

Trim and Untrim Surfaces

Trimming a surface (choose **Edit NURBS → Trim Tool**) creates holes in your surface using curves that are either drawn or projected onto the surface.

If you have a surface that's already been trimmed, and it's too late to undo the function with Undo, you can use Untrim Surfaces to remove either the last trim performed or all trims the surface has by choosing **Edit NURBS → Untrim Surfaces**.

Attach Surfaces

Attach Surfaces will do exactly that—attach two contiguous NURBS surfaces along two selected isoparms. Select an isoparm on the edge of the first surface, Shift+select an edge isoparm on a second surface, and choose **Edit NURBS → Attach Surfaces** to create a new surface of the two. As shown in Figure 5.29, the attach point will be along the selected isoparms.

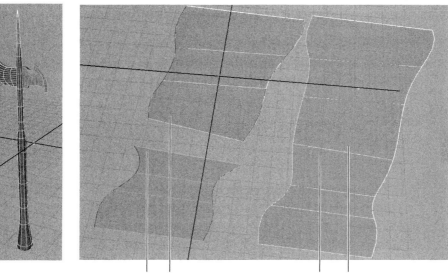

Selected edge isoparms   The attach point

Figure 5.28

The finished axe

Figure 5.29

Attach Surfaces connects surfaces along their selected isoparms.

TESTING THE GEOMETRY

Before you begin in earnest to texture the axe in a later chapter, select its top node in the Outliner and try moving or rotating the axe in the scene. You will notice in the file loaded from the book's CD, and quite possibly in your own file, that parts of the axe are moving or rotating separately from the whole axe. This is due to history on the object. Some of the surfaces you created earlier in this chapter were created with history. Now, because you are moving the entire axe and including surfaces with history in that group, you are creating "double transforms." This means the surfaces with history are moving because their parent node is moving, but they are also moving because their history is telling them to move. Simply select the Back_Axe node under the Axe_2 node in the Outliner and delete the history by choosing **Edit → Delete by Type → History**. Then select the Front_Axe_Head node and delete its history. Now if you select the Axe_2 top node and move or rotate it, those pieces will not fly off.

Detach Surfaces

Detach Surfaces is a highly useful tool for generating specific areas of a NURBS surface, or patches. Select an isoparm to define the line of detachment, and choose **Edit NURBS → Detach Surfaces**. The surface will be cut along that isoparm to create two distinct surfaces (see Figure 5.30). You will see plenty of Detach and Attach tools later in this chapter.

> To select an isoparm that is not displayed on the surface, click a viewable isoparm, and drag the mouse to place the isoparm selection elsewhere on the surface. Release the button to make the selection; a dashed isoparm line is now selected. This is a valid surface isoparm, but is not one used to define the number of spans in the surface.

Insert Isoparms

You'll inevitably come upon a modeling assignment for which you'll need extra surface definition (that is, more spans) on a NURBS object. Select an isoparm such as you did for Detach Surfaces earlier, and choose **Edit NURBS → Insert Isoparms**. This will create an isoparm and redefine the surface to add more spans. This function is used to make extra detailed parts of a NURBS surface to allow for smoother deformations, for example, adding an isoparm or two to the elbow joint of a model to make the arm bend with a cleaner crease (see Figure 5.31). You can either create a new isoparm between two already existing ones or add isoparms to your own defined area.

Figure 5.30

Detach Surfaces cuts a surface at the selected isoparms to create a new surface.

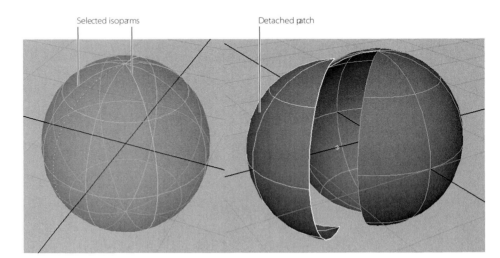

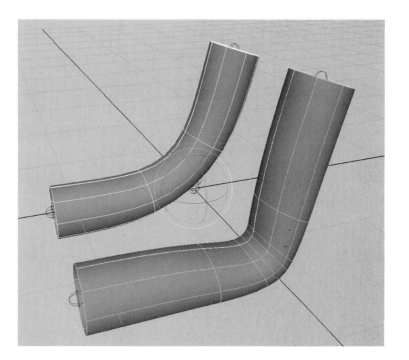

Figure 5.31

Inserting isoparms for a smoother deformation

Using NURBS Surfacing to Create Polygons

You can create swatches of polygon surfaces by using NURBS surfacing tools as well, as you saw with the earlier exercise on creating a planar surface in this chapter.

To create a polygonal surface with any of the surfacing techniques in this chapter, just open the option box for that particular NURBS tool. For example, create two simple curves. With both curves selected, choose **Surfaces → Loft □**. In the options for Output Geometry, click the Polygons button to display the options for creating the polygon surface and its detail level.

History for the surface will adjust the new polygonal surface. The detail of the surface will try to adjust as changes to the input curves are made. If you anticipate significant changes to the input curves, make sure to create the poly surface with a high poly count to accommodate major changes. This is probably the best way to create a single poly surface, especially if you prefer a NURBS work flow.

Try This Draw two CV curves as you did at the beginning of this chapter, both with the same number of CVs. Open the Loft option box and click the Polygons option for the **Output Geometry.** The creation options that appear at the bottom of the window affect the tessellation of the resulting surface; that is, you use them to specify the level of detail and the number of faces with which the surface is created. Generally speaking, the more faces, the more detail. That doesn't mean a detailed surface can't be efficient, with areas of high tessellation only where needed.

The default **Tessellation method** Standard fit will yield the fewest faces to create the surface without losing overall integrity. The sliders adjust the resulting number of faces in order to fit the finer curvature of the input curves.

The lower the **Fractional tolerance**, the smoother the surface and the greater the number of faces. The **Chord height ratio** determines the amount of curve in a particular region and calculates how many more faces to use to give an adequate representation of that curved area with polygons. This option would be best used with surfaces that have multiple or very intense curves.

It is not uncommon to create a surface, undo it, change slider settings, and re-create it again and again to get just the right tessellation. That's why you should click the Apply button, to keep the window open, as opposed to the Loft button (which closes the window after applying the settings).

The General **Tessellation method** creates a specific number of lines, evenly dividing the horizontal (U) and vertical (V) into rows of polygon faces. The Control points method tessellates the surface according to the number of points on the input curves. The more CVs and spans on the curves, the more divisions of polygons. The Count method simply relies on how many faces you tell it to make. The higher the count, the higher the tessellation on the surface. Experiment with the options to get the best poly surface results.

TESSELLATION

In the rendering phase, all 3D objects are broken into polygonal triangles that form the surfaces that shape your objects. This process—called *tessellation*—happens on all rendered surfaces, whether polygonal, subdivided, or NURBS.

The computer calculates the position of each significant point on your surface and connects the points to form a skin representing your surface.

Converting NURBS to Polygons

Some people prefer to model on NURBS curves and either create poly surfaces or convert to polygons after the entire model is done with NURBS surfaces. Ultimately you will find your own work-flow preference, but it helps greatly that you can use all surfacing methods. Most modelers choose one way or another but are familiar with both methodologies.

Try This Convert the NURBS axe into a poly model, as it might be needed in a game.

 Open your latest scene file from the axe_model project (or load `axe_model_v3.mb` from the CD). The toughest part of this simple process is getting the poly model to follow all the curves in the axe with fidelity, so you'll have to convert parts of the axe differently. Follow these steps:

1. Grab the handle and choose **Modify → Convert → NURBS to Polygons** ❐. Use the default presets (if need be, reestablish your settings by choosing **Edit → Reset Settings**), and the handle will convert well to polygons. Click Apply, and a poly version of the axe handle will appear on top of the NURBS version. Move it eight units to the right to get it out of the way. You'll move the other parts eight units as well to properly assemble the poly axe.

2. Select the back part of the axe head. Hopefully, you should have all the surfaces grouped together to make selection easy (as in the file on the CD); otherwise, select all the surfaces that make it up. The default settings will work for this part as well, so click Apply, and move it eight units to the left.

3. The front of the axe head holds a lot of different arcs, so you'll have to create it with finer controls. Change **Fractional tolerance** from 0.01 to 0.0005. This will yield more polygons, but finer curved surfaces. Figure 5.32 shows the result.

If you were following this process for a conventional game engine, you would normally be restricted to a low number of polygons, and your axe design would be different to better handle a low poly count.

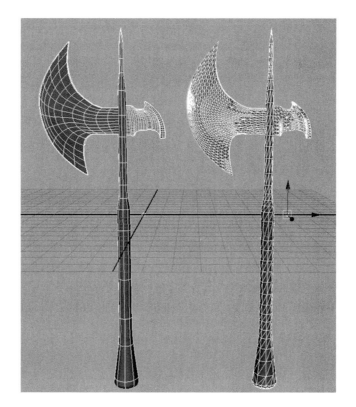

Figure 5.32

A faithful high-poly conversion (on the right) of the original NURBS axe

Patch Modeling

With NURBS modeling, you frequently need to attach surfaces so that a model does not split at the seams. This process of aligning and attaching NURBS patches is called *stitching*, and this kind of modeling is called *patch modeling*.

In this exercise, we jump back in time to create an element for the locomotive modeling exercise in the previous chapter. We will create a pump for the polygonal locomotive we made in Chapter 4 using patches that we will stitch together. This exercise gives you a good idea of how patches work to pull together an organic shape using NURBS shapes. The finished model is shown in Figure 5.33 to give you an idea of what we are aiming for.

Keep in mind, patch modeling is a fairly involved process. If you do not feel comfortable with modeling quite yet, skip this tutorial and move on to the next section in this chapter, "Using Artisan to Sculpt NURBS." You can always return to this section to bone up on your patch modeling later.

Starting the NURBS Pump

First, create a new project called Locomotive, or copy the Locomotive project from the CD to your hard drive and make it your current project.

To start the locomotive pump, follow these steps:

1. Create a NURBS cylinder with no caps by choosing **Create → NURBS Primitives → Cylinder ❑**. Under Caps in the option box, select None to create an open-ended cylinder. Set Axis to Z to create the cylinder on its side, and then click Create.

2. Size the cylinder down to 0.72 in X and Y and to 0.9 in Z. Now we will "reset" the cylinder so that its attributes are set back to normal. With the cylinder selected, choose **Modify → Freeze Transformations ❑**. In the option box, choose **Edit → Reset Settings** to set to reestablish the defaults, and then click Freeze Transform. *Freeze Transformations* just sets the numbers of the object's settings back to default (that is, it sets Translate and Rotate back to 0 and Scale back to 1). It does not reset the size or positions to the original, just the number values in the attributes. This is useful for getting an object back to default conditions without losing all the work done to it. This action is frequently referred to as freezing transforms as well as freezing transformations. You will find that freezing transforms will keep things clean as you work and is usually a good idea when working with patches. The cylinder, resized and after the application of Freeze Transformations, is shown in Figure 5.34.

Figure 5.33

The finished pump elements for the previous chapter's locomotive model are created in NURBS patches.

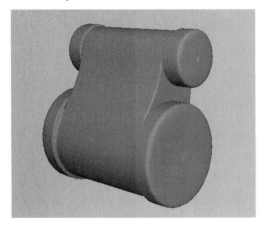

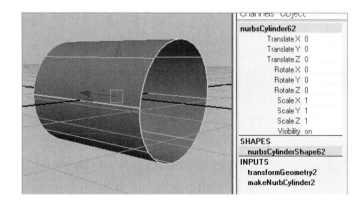

Figure 5.34

The first NURBS Cylinder, after Freeze Transforms

3. Now we'll create slightly larger end pieces for the cylinder. Duplicate the cylinder once, move the copy, and scale it as shown in the following illustration. Repeat to create the other end piece. The end pieces are roughly 1.075 in Scale X and Y and 0.18 in Scale Z and are moved just slightly past the ends of the cylinder, leaving a slight gap as shown. You should freeze transforms on the ends to reset their scale and positions back to the default.

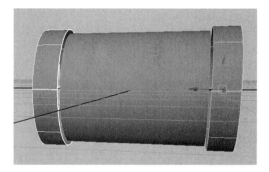

4. Now we will create a second copy of this assembly that is smaller in radius but is the same length. Duplicate the three cylinders, and change their respective scales to 0.55 in X and Y, but leave Scale Z set to 1. Remember, you froze their transforms, so their starting scales should have all been at 1. Now position the three cylinders as shown in the following illustration, slightly to the side and above the original larger cylinders. Freeze their transforms.

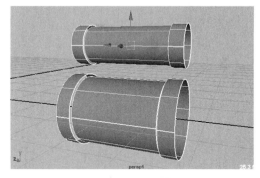

5. Next we will cut a couple of holes in the main cylinders. We will cut at the top two isoparms on the sides of the larger cylinder first. To select the first isoparm, RMB the cylinder, choose **Isoparm** from the marking menu, and click the isoparm to select it. Next Shift+select the isoparm on the other side so that both are selected.

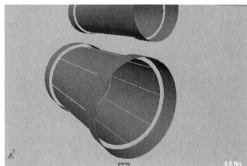

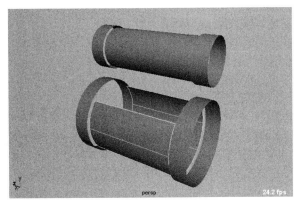

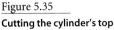

Figure 5.35

Cutting the cylinder's top

Figure 5.36

The cylinders cut

6. In the Surfaces menu set, choose **Edit NURBS → Detach Surfaces**. The surface between the isoparms you just selected is now its own surface and can be deleted. This will give you your first cut, as shown in Figure 5.35.

7. We will use the same procedure to cut the smaller cylinder, but at the sides so we can remove the bottom half entirely. Select the isoparms on the sides of the smaller cylinder, and detach the surface by choosing **Edit NURBS → Detach Surfaces** again. Delete the bottom surface, and your model should look as in Figure 5.36.

If detaching the surface does not work the first time, select the same isoparms again and detach surfaces again. This sometimes happens when you try to cut a NURBS surface at a side isoparm where the surface is beginning and ending.

End Caps

At this point, we will cap the ends of the cylinders to close them off. You can continue with your own file or load the file NURBS_pump_v01.mb from the Locomotive project on the CD and check your work so far. The trick here will be to add four isoparms using the Insert Isoparms function you read about earlier in this chapter to create the caps.

To cap the ends, follow these steps:

1. Select the end cylinder, RM click the geometry, and select **Isoparm** from the marking menu. Select four isoparms (make sure you hold down Shift while selecting the isoparms so as not to deselect them) as shown in the following illustration, and choose **Edit NURBS → Insert Isoparms ❑**. Make sure your settings match those in Figure 5.37. This will insert four isoparms into the end cylinder that you can use to close the end to make the cap.

2. We will select the end CVs to scale them down to close the cap. The easiest way to do this is to select the hull that controls all the edge CVs. RM click the end cylinder, and select Hull. Select the very edge hull, and scale it down as shown in the following illustration. This will close the end cap. Don't worry about leaving a small hole in the cap; we'll complete this pump as we complete the locomotive model.

3. Repeat the previous procedures to close off the other three end cylinders to create caps for both ends of both objects, as shown in Figure 5.38.

4. Next we need to connect and patch the end caps to their cylinders. To this end, we will need to line up a few new isoparms on the cylinders to allow us to stitch everything together properly. Using the previous work flow, add new isoparms to the bottom cylinder, as shown in Figure 5.39. (You may have to hide the end caps to create the isoparms on the cylinder. Select the end caps and use **Display → Hide → Hide Selection**. After you create the isoparms, select **Display → Show → Show All**.)

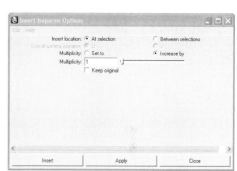

5. You will now need to prep the end cap to connect to the cylinder, by cutting a pie piece out of the cap itself, to line it up with the cut cylinder. On the end cap, select two isoparms to form a V that lines up with the cut edges of the main cylinder, as shown in Figure 5.40. Then choose **Edit NURBS → Detach Surfaces**. This will cut the V section out of the end cap. This aligns the end cap and the cylinder geometry at the edges so we can create a smooth connection between them in the next few steps.

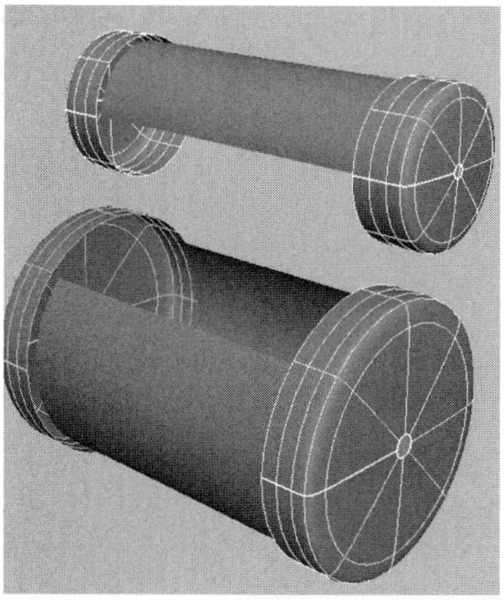

Figure 5.37

The default Insert Isoparm settings

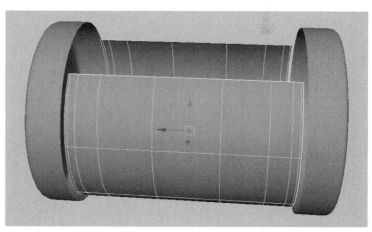

Figure 5.38

End caps for the pump pieces

Figure 5.39

Add isoparms as shown.

Figure 5.40

Select isoparms and detach surfaces.

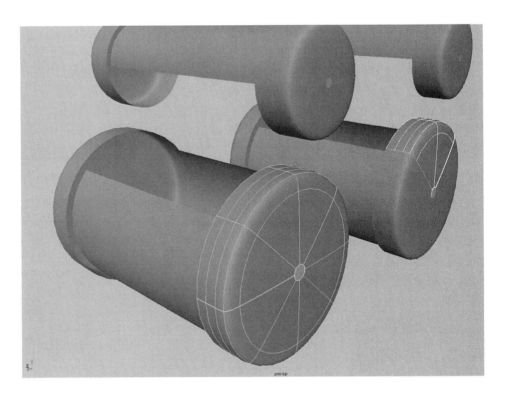

You can load the file NURBS_pump_v02.mb from the Locomotive project to compare your work or to skip the previous steps and proceed from here to attach the end cap.

6. We need to pull the end of the cylinder to line up with the edge of the end cap. Select the end four vertical hulls as shown and move them so that the edges of the cylinder and end cap align. Repeat this to line up the other end of the cylinder with the other cap.

7. Now we can create the pieces to connect the caps to the cylinder using lofts. RM click the cylinder, and choose Isoparm from the marking menu. Select the edge isoparm on the cylinder. Now RM click the end cap, and choose **Isoparm** from the marking menu. Shift+select the edge isoparm of the end cap as shown in the following illustration. Choose **Surfaces → Loft □**. Make sure you are using the default settings for the loft: in the option box, choose **Edit → Reset Settings**.

8. This creates a surface to bridge the cylinder and the end cap. You will notice it is rather jagged, almost a diamond shape as opposed to a smooth ring. With the loft selected, just press 3 on the keyboard to see it with smooth display in the panel. Figure 5.41 shows the loft.

Stitching and Tangency

In the next series of steps, we'll get into the real meat of patch modeling, which is all about creating smooth seams. The trick in making a good patch model is to make sure that all the patches line up; this is called *tangency*. In animation setup, it is important for characters that have been made with NURBS patches and for textures, to name but two instances, that tangency be correct; otherwise, you may notice tearing at seams during deformations or texture maps that don't line up quite right. It is a bit of a tedious process, but here is a taste of it. To continue with the patch model of the locomotive pump, follow these steps:

1. We will start by creating a smooth piece that connects the cylinder and the end caps using the lofts created in steps 7 and 8 in the previous section and shown in Figure 5.46. Select the cylinder and the connector loft, as shown in Figure 5.42, and attach them by choosing **Edit NURBS → Attach Surfaces** ☐. Make sure the tool is set to default (choose **Edit → Reset Settings**). Turn off Keep Originals and click Attach. This will blend the two surfaces into one, creating a smooth transition between them, and delete the original surfaces.

2. Now here's the funny part: we will be disconnecting them. Select the isoparm at the location where the patches originally met, and choose **Edit NURBS → Detach Surfaces**. Again, make sure the tool is reset to default so as not to keep the original patches. This gives you tangency across the two patches as well as a smooth transition in the model.

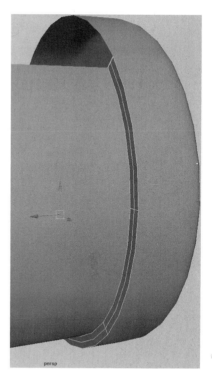

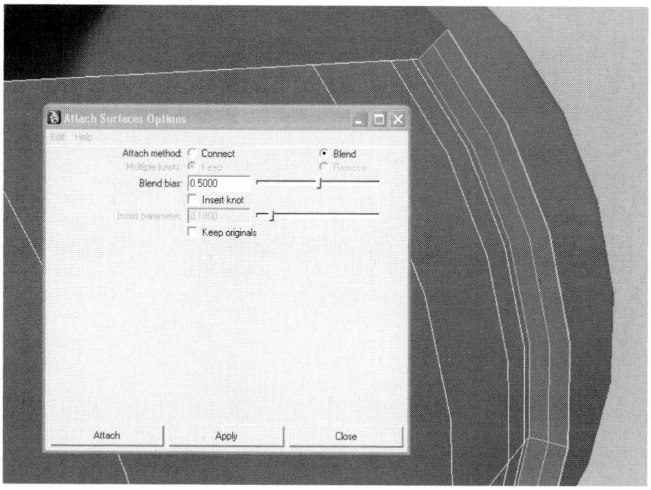

Figure 5.41

Lofting the end cap to the cylinder

Figure 5.42

Attach the patches.

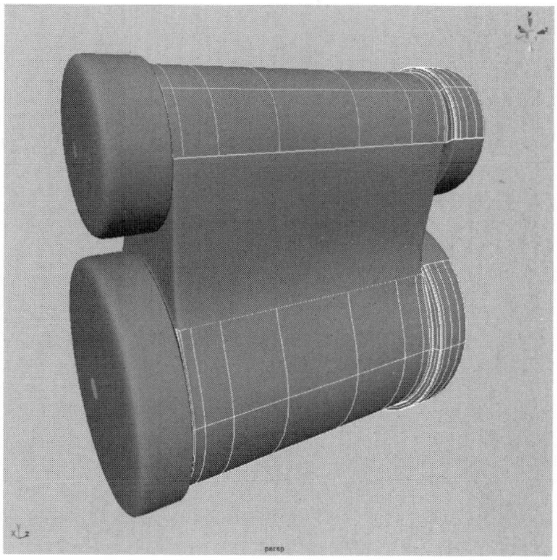

Figure 5.43

The end caps attach to the cylinders smooth as butter.

Figure 5.44
Lofting the two cylinders together

Figure 5.45
Closing the sides

3. Repeat steps 1 and 2 for the other end of the cylinder and its end cap and also for the upper cylinder and its two end caps. You should now have end caps with smooth attachments to the cylinders as in Figure 5.43.

4. Connecting the upper and lower cylinders is next. Select the edge isoparms of both cylinders and choose **Surfaces → Loft** ☐. This time the lofted surface will need more spans, so in the option box, set **Section Spans** to 3 and click Apply. Repeat to create a loft on the back side of the cylinders as well. Figure 5.44 shows the resulting surfaces.

5. Individually select the middle and then the lower middle hulls of the lofts and move them back to create a bit of curvature to surfaces as shown. Remember, you can select hulls by right-clicking the surface and using the marking menu.

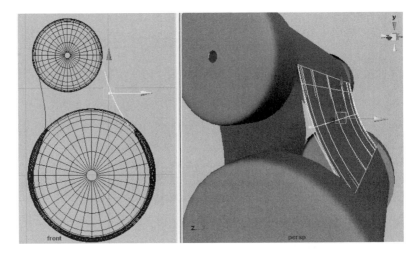

6. Select the edge isoparms of the lofts you just created, and loft between them with two spans. Make sure to reset the settings by choosing **Edit → Reset Settings** in the option box and then set **Section Spans** to 2 spans before you create the loft. Repeat for the other side. Figure 5.45 shows the closed ends.

7. Now go into CV mode, and move the CVs to line up the edges of the newly formed closed ends with the bottom and top cylinders. Repeat for the other side as shown here.

8. As we did in steps 1 and 2, attach and then detach the loft you just edited with CVs (we'll call it the side panel) and the front panel as shown here to set up a smooth transition and a tangency. Repeat for the back panel and the other end of the cylinders to make the other side panel.

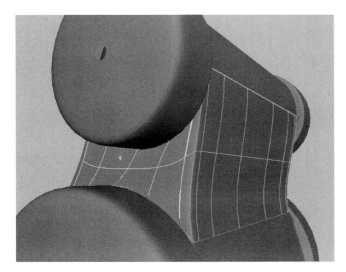

9. Now we'll shift the attention to one of the end caps on the lower cylinder. In step 5 in the previous section ("End Caps"), and shown in Figure 5.45, we detached a pizza slice shape out of the end caps. Select the detached slice, and insert two isoparms in between the existing ones. Your model should resemble the one in Figure 5.46 with the added isoparms. This is set up for another attachment coming up. Repeat for the other end cap on the lower cylinder.

10. Now select isoparms on the edges of the end cap and the side panel, and loft between them with two spans. Repeat for the other side. This will plug the hole between the end cap and the side panels. You can, if you wish, run another attach and detach to smooth out the groove between the end caps and the side panels. Figure 5.47 shows the end result of the groove.

11. You'll be kicked out into the cold now to run the same set of procedures on the upper cylinder and its end caps. These should be simpler as there are fewer sections to deal with, but go ahead and finish the model from here to form the connections shown in Figure 5.48 and to form the final model shown in Figure 5.49.

As you can see, there is quite a bit of lofting, attaching, and detaching between surface patches in patch modeling. The key to getting good here is to be able to line up isoparms easily and cleverly and to be able to attach them again smoothly. This type of modeling is not for the faint of heart and takes a lot of practice to get used to. You will make a lot of mistakes along the way, but that is how you will learn the most! It's easy to see how this kind of modeling will be useful for making organic shapes such as faces.

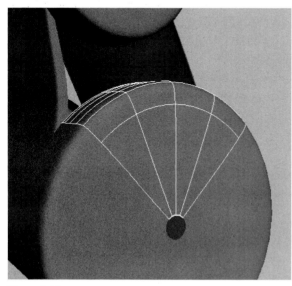

Figure 5.46
Insert isoparms into the end cap slice.

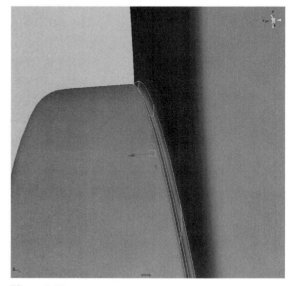

Figure 5.47
The groove connecting the end cap with the side panel

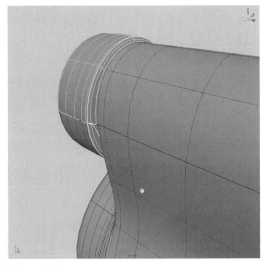

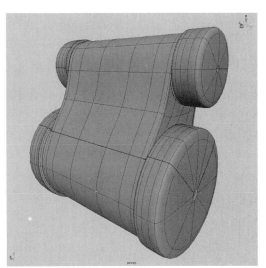

Figure 5.48

Finishing the top part of the NURBS pump

Figure 5.49

The finished pump

Using Artisan to Sculpt NURBS

Imagine that you can create a NURBS surface and just sculpt it using your cursor to mold the surface like hands on wet clay. Well, you can with a Maya module called Artisan, without the mess.

Try This Artisan is basically a 3D painting system that allows you to paint directly onto a surface. By painting on the surface with the Sculpt Surfaces tool, you are moving the CV points in and out to effectively mold the surface.

1. In shaded mode (press 5), maximize the perspective window (press the spacebar) for a nice big view. Create a NURBS sphere and open the Attribute Editor. In the sphere's creation node (makeNurbSphere1), set **Sections** to 24, and set **Spans** to 12. The greater the surface definition you have here, the more detailed the sculpting can be.

2. Select the sphere and choose **Edit NURBS → Sculpt Geometry Tool** ❐. Clicking the option box will open the tool settings. You'll need those almost every time you paint with Artisan, to change brush sizes and so forth.

Your cursor will now change to the Artisan brush as shown in Figure 5.50. The red circle around the brush cursor and the lettering display the type of brush you are currently using. When the red lines point outside the circle, and the lettering reads *Ps*, you're using the *push* brush, which will push in the surface as you paint it. The black arrow pointing toward the sphere's center is a measurement of the Max Displacement slider in the tool settings. This sets how far each stroke will push in the surface. The lower the number, the less the brush will affect the surface.

Figure 5.50

The Sculpt Surfaces Tool allows you to mold your surface by painting on it. Here the brush is set to push in the surface of the sphere as you paint.

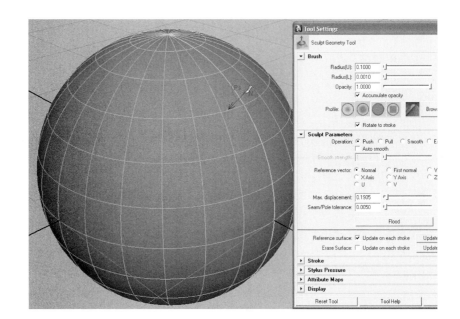

3. Click and drag the cursor across the surface of the sphere to get a feel for how the surface deforms under your tool. Use the Max Displacement slider to control the force of the brush, and use Radius (U) and Radius (L) to set the size of the brush.

4. Switch your brush type to *pull*. Your cursor will change to read *Pl*, and the red lines appear on the inside of the circle. You'll now be able to pull out the surface.

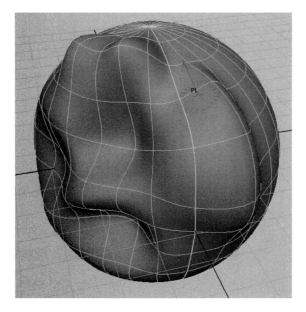

The Opacity slider also controls the force of the brush, but it is subtler than Max Displacement to give you greater control. Since this is, after all, a 3D painting tool, opacity controls how much *value* you paint onto the surface. The value in this case is not a color, but how far the surface is deformed. You'll see how Artisan comes back into play in other aspects of Maya later in the book.

5. *Smooth* will blend the pushed in and pulled out areas of the surface together to get a smoother result. *Erase* will simply erase the deformations on the surface, setting it back to the way it was before.

If you plan to sculpt a finely detailed surface, be sure to create the surface with plenty of surface spans and sections. If you only want to paint a specific area of a NURBS surface, choose **Edit NURBS → Insert Isoparms** to add extra detail to that area before you begin painting, though you can add isoparms after you paint. Once you begin to sculpt this way, going back into the surface's creation node to increase its sections and spans will ruin your results.

Summary

In this chapter we tackled NURBS modeling by going through the usual surfacing tools from lofting and revolving to bevels and boundary surfaces. Then we explored the implications of surface history and how surfaces will adjust to changes when history is enabled, and then we got to work building an axe using most of the surfacing techniques in the beginning of the chapter. During the axe exercise we also learned how to import an image plane to use as reference to build the axe, and how to model using deformers. Once the axe was finished, we learned about different editing methods for NURBS surfaces such as inserting isoparms and attaching surfaces together. The chapter next dealt with creating polygons from these NURBS tools and converting existing NURBS surfaces to polygons. Next, we put all the editing tools to use as we path modeled the steam pump for the locomotive exercise from Chapter 4, and learned how to stitch and line up tangencies on our patches. Finally, this chapter introduced you to the Artisan tool and how to use it for sculpting a NURBS surface.

Modeling is usually the first step of CG production. It is important to keep in mind the goal of modeling: to represent an object with CG. To that end, simplifying and deconstructing the object to be modeled into its simplest components puts the task of modeling into clearer perspective. For example, a car is not best modeled as a car per se, but as a collection of parts: tires, doors, seats, a hood, side panels, a trunk, and so forth. Learning to see how objects come together is invaluable in creating them in CG.

For further practice, use this chapter as a reference to create some of the following NURBS models.

Bathroom Sink Snap a few digital stills of your bathroom sink, or find some on the Internet. A sink will give you a great chance to explore NURBS surfacing, making pristine curves and smooth surfaces. It may be a bit involved, but it's not overwhelming.

Couch or Loveseat Cushy furniture is great for NURBS. Use lofting to make plush cushions, or just use a primitive. It's up to you, but try it. You'll only get better with practice.

Disposable Lighter Sounds simple, but try to get detailed with it.

Cartoon Head Use Maya Artisan and the Sculpt Surfaces tool to turn an ordinary sphere into a cartoonish head. You'll find it fun to use Sculpt Surfaces to model. Try to make the head using only Artisan.

CHAPTER 6

Further Modeling Topics: Deformers and Subdivision Surfaces

Once you've learned the basics of creating and editing poly and NURBS models, more advanced modeling techniques will easily become part of your toolbox. This chapter explains how to use deformations to adjust a model, as opposed to editing the geometry directly as you did with the previous methods, and introduces you to subdivision surface modeling, which fully incorporates this concept.

Topics include:

- **Modeling with Deformers: The Lattice**
- **Subdivision Surfaces**
- **Creating a Starfish**
- **Building a Teakettle**

Modeling with Deformers: The Lattice

As you have seen in the chapters that deal with NURBS and polygonal modeling, deformers are handy for creating and editing modeled shapes. Nonlinear deformers such as Bend and Flare create a simple shape adjustment for the attached geometry, such as bending it. When a model requires more intricate editing with a deformer, you will need to use a *lattice*.

A *lattice* is a scaffold that fits around your geometry. The lattice object controls the shape of the geometry. When you adjust the Lattice deformer, the geometry deforms to match. When a lattice point is moved, the lattice smoothly deforms the underlying geometry. The more lattice points, the greater control you have.

Lattices are especially useful when you need to edit a relatively complex poly mesh or NURBS surface that is too dense to efficiently edit directly with control vertices. You assign a lattice and use it to create changes without having to move the individual surface points.

Lattices can work on any surface type, and a single lattice can affect multiple surfaces at the same time. You can also move an object through a lattice (or vice versa) to animate a deformation effect, such as a golf ball sliding through a garden hose.

Creating a Lattice

Make sure you are in the Animation menu set. To adjust an existing model or surface, select the model(s) or applicable groups to deform and choose **Deform → Create Lattice**. Figure 6.1 shows the detailed polygonal hand model from Chapter 4 with a default lattice applied. The top node of the hand was selected, and the lattice applied.

Figure 6.1

A lattice is applied to the polygonal hand model.

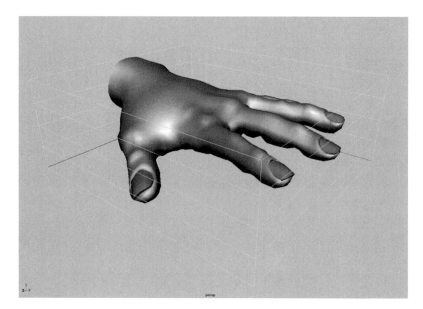

To experience how this works, you will remodel the detailed poly hand using a few different lattices. Your objective is to create an alien hand by thinning and elongating the hand and each of the fingers. Since it would take more time and effort to move the vertices of the poly mesh to achieve this, lattices are ideal.

To elongate and thin the entire hand, load the scene file `detailed_poly_hand.ma` from the Poly_Hand project on the CD and follow these steps:

1. Select the top node of the hand (poly_hand), and choose **Deform → Create Lattice**. This will create a default lattice that will affect the entire hand, fingernails and all, as seen in Figure 6.1. Although you can change the lattice settings in the options window upon creation, you will edit the lattice after it is applied to the hand.

2. The lattice will be selected once it's created. Open the Attribute Editor, and click the ffd1LatticeShape tab. The three attributes of interest here are **S Divisions**, **T Divisions**, and **U Divisions**. These sliders control how many divisions the lattice uses to deform its geometry. Set **S Divisions** to 3, set **T Divisions** to 2, and set **U Divisions** to 3 for the result shown in Figure 6.2. A 3 × 2 × 3 lattice refers to the number of division lines in the lattice as opposed to the number of sections; otherwise, this would be a 2 × 1 × 2 lattice!

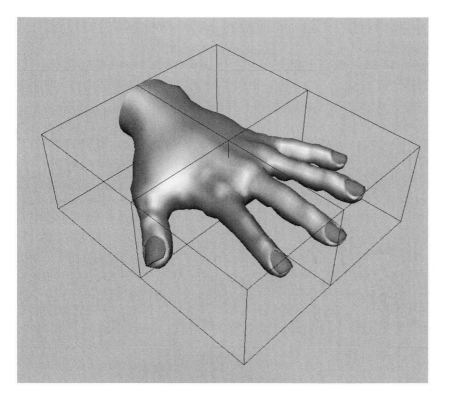

Figure 6.2

Changing the number of divisions for the lattice

3. With the lattice selected, switch to component mode (press F8) to display the lattice's points. These points act just like the vertices on a polygonal shape. You will use them to change the overall shape of the hand, without resorting to moving the vertices of the hand themselves. Select the vertices on the thumb side of the hand, and move them to squeeze in that half of the hand. Notice how only that zone of the model is affected by that part of the lattice.

4. Switch back to object mode (press F8), and scale the entire lattice to be thinner in the Z axis and longer in the X axis. Now the entire hand is deformed as the lattice is scaled.

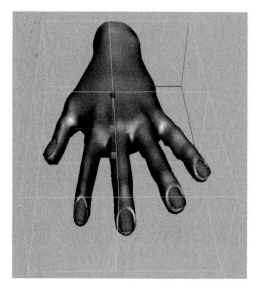

Now that you have altered the hand, you have no need for this lattice. If you delete the lattice, the hand will snap back to its original shape. Instead, to get rid of the lattice, you need to delete the construction history on the hand itself, as you did with the NURBS axe exercise in Chapter 5.

5. Select the top node of the hand, and choose **Edit → Delete by Type → History**.

The next step is to elongate the individual fingers and widen the knuckles. To begin with the index finger, follow these steps:

1. Select the top node of the hand, and create a new lattice as before. It will form around the entire hand.

Although you can divide the lattice so that its divisions line up with the fingers, it is easier and more interactive to scale and position the entire lattice to fit around just the index finger.

2. Since transforming the currently selected lattice will deform the geometry, you need to select the lattice and its base node as well to change the lattice without affecting the hand. In the Outliner, select both the ffd1Lattice and ffd1Base nodes.

3. With both nodes selected, scale, rotate, and transform the lattice to fit around the index finger, as shown in Figure 6.3.

4. Deselect the base and set the lattice **S Divisions to 7**, set **T Divisions** to 2, and set **U Divisions** to 3.

5. Adjust the lattice to lengthen the finger by pulling the lattice points. Pick the lattice points around each of the knuckles individually, and scale them up to widen them.

6. To delete the lattice and keep the changes to the finger, select the top node of the hand and delete its history. Repeat this entire procedure to adjust the other fingers to finish your alien hand.

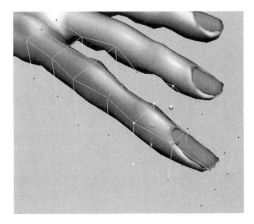

Adjusting the polygonal hand from this exercise, using only lattices, created the alien hand in Figure 6.4.

As you can see, lattices afford you powerful editing capabilities without the complication of dealing with surface points directly. They can help reshape an entire complex model quickly or adjust minor details on parts of a larger whole.

Lattices not only work on polygons, they can be used on any geometry in Maya at any stage in your work flow to create or adjust models as well as create animated effects such as the next exercise in this chapter. You will animate an object using another type of deformer in Chapter 8 as well as learn how to deform an object through a path. In many ways, deformers are the Swiss Army knives of Maya animation, except you can't open a bottle with them.

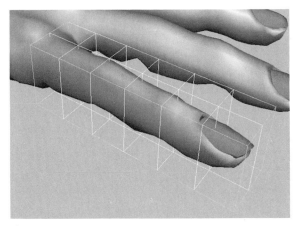

Figure 6.3
Position the lattice and its base to fit around the index finger.

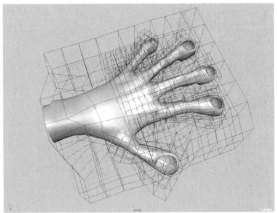

Figure 6.4
The human hand model is adjusted to be an alien hand using lattices to deform the geometry.

Animating through a Lattice

We will animate an object through a simple lattice. Before you deleted the last of your lattices in the previous example, and if you had a chance to move the hand geometry through the lattice while it was still applied to one of the fingers, you should have seen an interesting effect. The parts of the geometry of the hand would deform as the hand travels through the lattice. Think of ways you can use this warping effect in an animation. For example, you can create the effect of a balloon squeezing through a pipe by animating the balloon geometry through a lattice.

Try This We will create a NURBS sphere with 8 sections and 16 spans and an open-ended NURBS cylinder that has no end caps.

1. Choose **Create → NURBS Primitives → Cylinder** ❐ and check None for the **Caps** option. Scale and arrange the sphere balloon and cylinder pipe as shown in Figure 6.5.

2. Select the balloon and create a lattice for it. (In the Animation menu set, choose **Deform → Create Lattice**.) Set the S, T, and U divisions to 4, 19, and 4 respectively, as shown. This number of lattice divisions is set to create a smoother deformation when the sphere goes through the pipe.

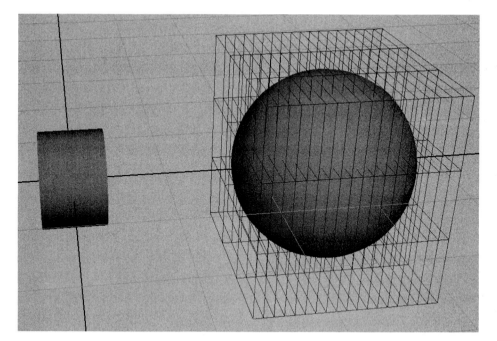

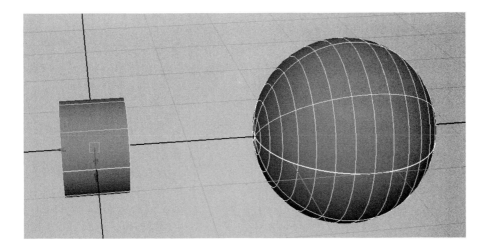

3. Select the lattice and its base in the Outliner (*ffd1Lattice* and *ffd1Base* nodes) to move the middle of the lattice to fit it over the length of the pipe as shown.

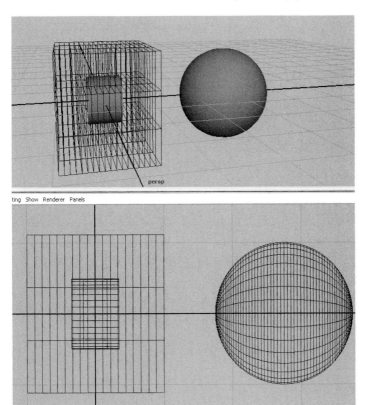

4. Deselect the lattice base, and enter component mode for the lattice itself. Select the appropriate points, and shape the lattice as shown to fit the middle of the lattice into the cylinder.

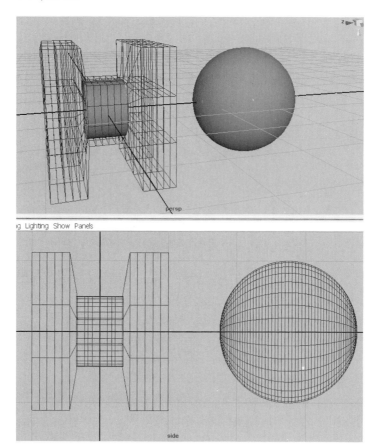

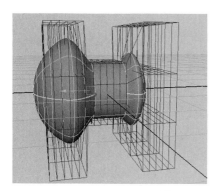

Figure 6.6

Squeezing the balloon through the pipe using a lattice deformer

5. Select the sphere and move it back and forth through the pipe and lattice. Notice how it squeezes to fit through. If you look closely, you will also notice that the sphere starts to squeeze a little before the pipe. Also, you'll see parts of the sphere sticking out of the very ends of the pipe. This is called *interpenetration*, in which geometry passes through itself or another surface. You can avoid this by using a more highly segmented sphere and lattice. If you try this exercise with a lower segmented sphere and/or lattice, you will notice the interpenetrations even more. Figure 6.6 shows the balloon squeezing through the pipe.

In a similar fashion, you can create a lattice along a curve path and have an object travel through it. We'll try this out in Chapter 8.

Subdivision Surfaces

Subdivision surfaces combine the best features of NURBS and polygonal modeling for intricate surfaces such as faces. Using subdivision surfaces, you can model complex characters and create models from single primitives as in polygonal modeling, but with perfectly smooth surfaces as in NURBS modeling.

Like lattices, *subdivision surfaces* rely on varying levels of editing detail that allow you to adjust a surface from a global level, where large parts of the model are modified, to a micro-level, where you have control over the most dense of surface points.

Typical subdivision work flow begins when you create a simple polygonal mesh of your model. The polygon is converted to a subdivision surface that you can edit using any number of subdivision detail levels. More often than not, the resulting subdivision surface is then converted back to a polygonal object for use in the production. Subdivision surfaces can also be converted to NURBS patches.

The Subdivision Surfaces (or SubD as they are called) toolset is found in the Surfaces menu set (press F4), so you will find yourself switching back and forth with the Polygons menu set (press F3). Just remember their hotkeys and you'll be switching like a pro in no time.

Creating a Starfish

You will create a starfish model starting with polygons, like the models you created in Chapter 4. You will then convert the polygon mesh to a subdivision surface to mold it into a proper starfish. Follow these steps:

1. Create a new scene and switch into the Polygons menu set. Create a polygon cube and scale it to be 8 wide, 8 deep, and 1.2 high.

2. Use the Split Polygon tool (choose **Edit Mesh → Split Polygon Tool**) to split one side of the box into half as shown. You can RMB click every time you finish one of the splits without exiting the tool. When you do, use the readout display in the feedback bar (lower-left side of the screen) to place the split at 50 percent along each edge to center the new edge.

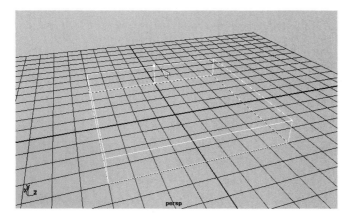

Figure 6.7

Figure 6.7

Once the pentagon
is created, split each
face into two.

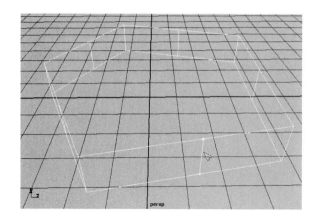

Notice that when you invoke the Split Polygon tool, Maya prompts you right in the view
panel to select along the first edge.

3. Reshape the box into an irregular pentagon as shown in Figure 6.7 by selecting the
   polygonal edges of the box in component mode (press F8) and moving them one by
   one. You needn't make sure each of the five sides is perfectly the same size. Starfish
   are irregular themselves, but be careful not to move any of the edges up or down in
   the Y axis. You'll want the pentagon to be flat.

4. Use the ever popular Split Polygon tool again to cut all five sides in half, as shown in
   Figure 6.7. You will be using these edges to create a polygonal star, from which you
   will convert to the subdivision surface.

5. Use the newly created edges to shape the pentagon into a star by moving the edges in
   toward the center as shown. This will be the basis for your starfish subdivision surface.

6. Save your work and compare it to the scene file Starfish_v01.ma in the Starfish project on the CD.

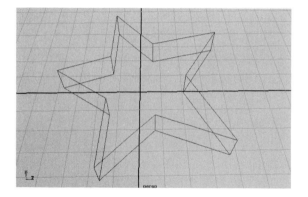

Converting to a Subdivision Surface

Now that you have the basic polygonal shape for the starfish, convert it to a subdivision surface. Follow these steps:

1. Select the star, and then choose **Modify → Convert → Polygons to Subdiv**. The star will turn into a smooth subdivision surface, as shown in Figure 6.8.

2. Although you have all but lost the points of the star in converting it to smooth subdivisions, you now have far greater control. Press the 3 key to increase the display resolution of the surface. As they do with NURBS objects, the keys 1, 2, and 3 set the display resolution of a subdivision surface.

3. With the starfish still selected, switch to the Surfaces menu set and choose **Subdiv Surfaces → Polygon Proxy Mode**. This will switch you to a low-level editing mode and restore the shape of the star as shown here. The star here is not the surface of the starfish, but a proxy that will shape the subdivision surface much as a lattice does. Switch to component mode (press F8), and you'll see vertices on the polygon proxy that you can move to shape the starfish.

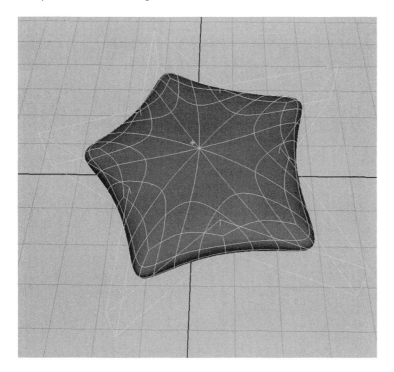

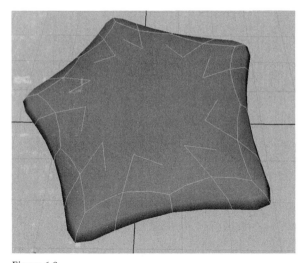

Figure 6.8

Converting the star shape to a subdivision

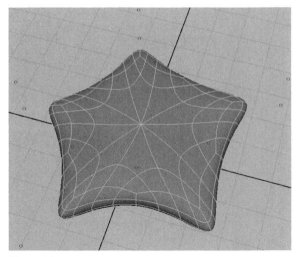

Figure 6.9

The zeros represent the zero level of detail on this subdivision starfish and correspond to the vertices on its polygon proxy.

4. Using the *polygon proxy* to shape the starfish is good for creating "broad strokes" when creating your final model. It will not yield good results by itself, however, so press F8 to go back to the object selection mode to select the starfish and not its vertices, and then switch back to standard mode (choose **Subdiv Surfaces → Standard Mode**). With the starfish still selected, enter component mode to select vertices. The vertices of the starfish will appear in the same location as the points on the polygon proxy and are represented with zeros, as in Figure 6.9.

5. Right-click the starfish to open a marking menu, and choose **Display Level → 1**. It is at this level of detail that you will define the arms of the fish. Select the vertices (now represented with 1s) between each point, and pull them in toward the center of the fish, as shown. This level of detail is automatically generated when you convert the poly starfish to a subdivision surface. As a matter of fact, you also have another level of detail (**Display Level → 2**), which you'll use later.

If by chance you do not see **Display Level → 2** as an option and **Display Level → 1** is the highest detail level you have, you can create this higher level of display by selecting all the level 1 vertices on the starfish in component mode and choosing **Subdiv Surfaces → Refine Selected Components** to create level 2 vertices. You will then be able to choose **Display Level → 2** when needed.

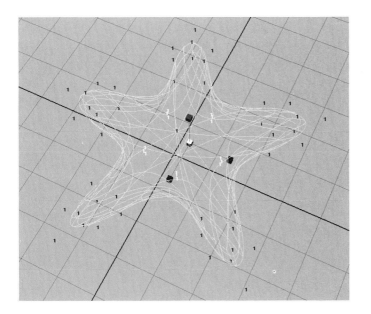

6. Save your file now and compare your work to the scene file `Starfish_v02.ma` in the Starfish project on the CD.

7. Right-click the starfish, and choose **Display Level → 2**. The vertices on the next higher detail level appear and are represented by 2s. With this level of detail, you can move these vertices to give your starfish more character. Try making the areas between the points on the star smoother, as shown in Figure 6.10. Also try to flatten the bottom of the starfish using either level 1 or 2 vertices.

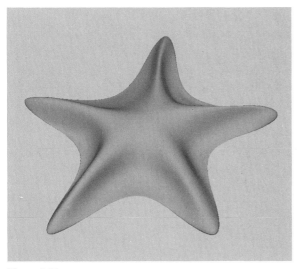

Figure 6.10

A molded starfish

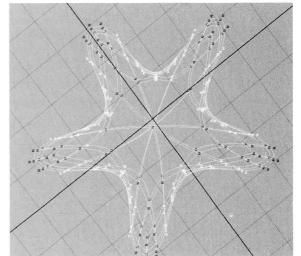

Figure 6.11

Select the area to be refined.

8. You may need to further detail your starfish in some areas to achieve the look seen in Figure 6.10, though. As it stands now, the starfish can be edited up to level 2. To create another level of detail, select the areas you want to refine by selecting the level 2 vertices along the outside of each star point, as shown in Figure 6.11.

9. With those vertices selected, right-click the selection and choose **Refine Selected** from the marking menu. Maya will add another level of detail to that area of the starfish with vertices marked as 3s. This allows you to make more detailed adjustments to the surface to mold it to your liking. Work the vertices at all levels to sculpt your starfish close to the one in Figure 6.10.

> RMB clicking the starfish and choosing **Refine Selected** is the same as selecting the vertices and choosing **Subdiv Surfaces → Refine Selected Components**. Choosing vertices in an area of your model and refining them beyond a display level of 2 will create more vertices for that area only. You can continue to refine your selection as needed. At any time, you can go back to polygon proxy mode to access the lowest level of detail to adjust the broad strokes of the model.

10. Save again, and load the scene file Starfish_v03.ma in the Starfish project on the CD to compare your work.

> You can use these same techniques to re-create the polygon hand from Chapter 4 with subdivision surfaces.

Building a Teakettle

Now that you have experienced the mechanics of subdivision surface modeling and editing, you're ready for another model. The next subdivision exercise is to create a teakettle. You'll fashion the kettle from simple polygon shapes and then refine it using subdivisions.

Creating the Base Polygon Model

To create the base poly mesh for the kettle, follow these steps:

1. The main body of the kettle will begin as a poly cylinder. Choose **Create → Polygon Primitives → Cylinder ❑** to open the options box. Set Subdivisions Around Axis to 8, and set Subdivisions Along Height to 4.

2. To create the lid, create another poly cylinder with 8 subdivisions around the axis and only 2 for the height. Scale it to fit as a lid for the first cylinder.

3. Select the upper row of poly edges on the lid, and scale them all in to create a bevel, as shown in Figure 6.12. Then select every other edge on the top surface and delete them, as shown in Figure 6.13.

4. Select the poly edges of the main cylinder, and scale them out increasingly larger as you work your way down. Delete every other edge of the top surface as you did with the lid. Your kettle should look as shown here.

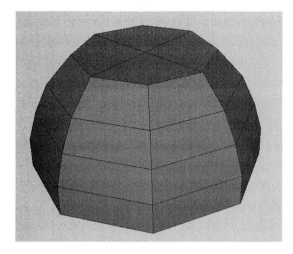

5. You are going to create a simple handle for the lid. Select the lid's top four faces. You will create the handle by extruding these faces and scaling them in. If you were to choose **Edit Mesh → Extrude** and use the special scale handles as shown in Figure 6.14, your faces may all separate.

Figure 6.12
Scale the outer edges inward.

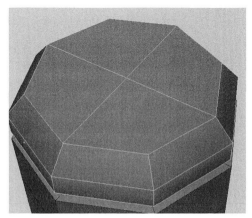

Figure 6.13
Delete every other edge of the top surface.

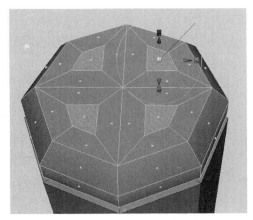

Figure 6.14

By default, faces will extrude separately.

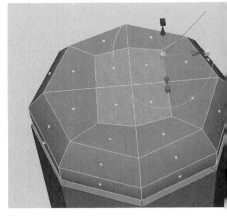

Figure 6.15

The Keep Faces Together command allows you to extrude the faces together.

Instead, you need to first make sure the option **Edit Mesh → Keep Faces Together** is enabled. This option lets you extrude these faces properly. Now select the four faces again and choose **Edit Mesh → Extrude ◻**. Choose **Edit → Reset Settings** to make sure the settings are correct, and click **Extrude**. Use the scale handles to scale the extruded faces in, as shown in Figure 6.15. The tool option you set keeps the poly faces together during the extrude operation.

6. With those four faces still selected, extrude faces again, but this time pull them up and scale them in a bit as shown (on the left).

7. Select the side faces of the lid's new handle, and extrude the faces inward using the scale handle to create detail on the handle as shown (on the right).

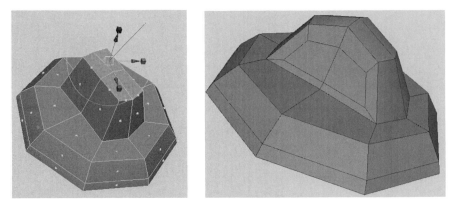

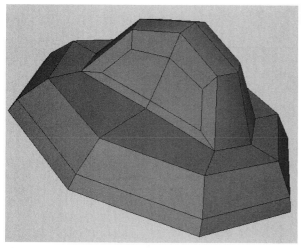

Figure 6.16

Round out the handle by moving the edges.

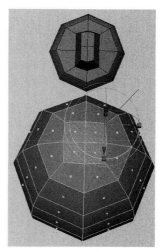

Figure 6.17

Rounding off the top of the kettle

8. Select the edges that make up the lid handle, and move them to round out the handle, as shown in Figure 6.16.

9. Select the four faces on the top of the kettle and extrude the faces. Scale the faces in, and pull them up to round the top of the kettle as shown in Figure 6.17.

10. Select the kettle and apply a lattice to it by choosing **Deform → Create Lattice** (in the Animation menu set). Set **S Divisions** to 2, set **T Divisions** to 3, and set **U Divisions** to 2. Adjust the lattice to bend the kettle back to create the front. Figure 6.18 shows the lattice's final position. Once you have the proper shape, select the kettle and delete its history to delete the lattice.

Figure 6.18

Use the lattice to bend the kettle.

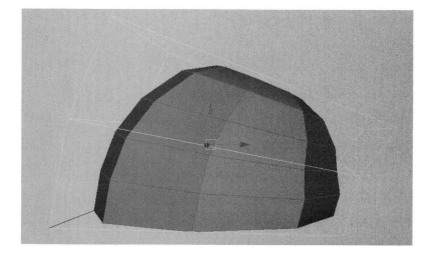

Figure 6.19

Use the Insert Edge Loop Tool to create a straight division line across the bottom.

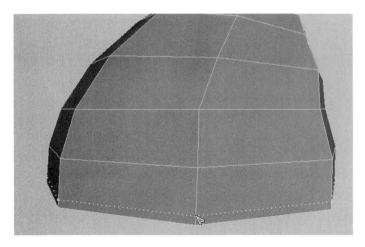

11. Just before you convert the kettle to a subdivision surface, you need to create more detail at the bottom of the kettle so that the subdivision surface won't round out and you will still have a flat bottom. In the side or front view panel, select the kettle. In the Polygons menu set, choose **Edit Mesh → Insert Edge Loop Tool**, and use the Insert Edge Loop tool to create a new division along the bottom of the kettle, as shown in Figure 6.19.

12. Select all the new faces along the bottom, and extrude them out to create a lip that runs around the kettle's bottom as shown here. Be sure that **Edit Mesh → Keep Faces Together** is still checked on; otherwise, the faces will separate. Luckily you see the **Keep Faces Together** option at the top of the **Edit Mesh** menu whenever you access the tools in that menu, so you can verify that it's checked on without too much bother.

13. Save your scene file and load the Kettle_Model_v01.ma file from the Tea_Kettle project on the CD to compare your work up to this point.

Converting to Subdivisions

Once you complete the base polygon model for the kettle, you can convert it to a subdivision surface to round it out and make it smooth. To convert the kettle, follow these steps:

1. Select the kettle, and choose **Modify → Convert → Polygons to Subdiv**. Then select the lid and convert it as well.

2. Select the converted kettle and the lid, and press 3 to view them in high-resolution mode. Position the lid to go on top of the kettle, and your model should be similar to that in Figure 6.20.

3. The only items that remain are the spout and a handle. For the handle, create a subdivision torus (choose **Create → Subdiv Primitives → Torus**). Scale, rotate, and place the torus above and around the lid, on top of the kettle.

4. With the handle selected, choose **Subdiv Surfaces → Polygon Proxy Mode** in the Surfaces menu set. Using the vertices on the polygon proxy, make the handle thinner and elongate it up, as shown in Figure 6.21.

5. Return to standard mode with the handle selected (choose **Subdiv Surfaces → Standard Mode**). To make the handle smoother, you will refine it and add more subdivisions. Switch to component mode, and the vertices of the handle will display as zeros. Right-click the handle and choose **Refine Selected** from the marking menu. New vertices will appear, and they will all read as 1s. The handle will be much smoother. Make any modeling adjustments to your liking, switching between level 0 and level 1 display as needed, using the right mouse button and the marking menu's **Display Level** command.

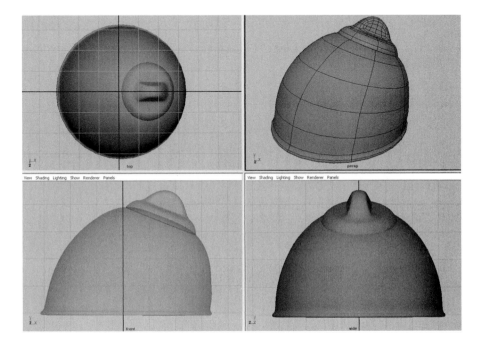

Figure 6.20

The subdivision kettle and lid

Figure 6.21

The kettle's handle

Figure 6.22

Hollow out the spout.

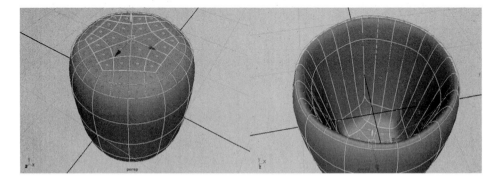

6. To create the spout, create a subdivision cylinder. Switch to component mode to select faces (not vertices). Right-click the cylinder, and choose display level 2. Select the inside circle of faces on the top of the cylinder, as shown in Figure 6.22. Move them down into the cylinder to hollow it out, but creating a thickness to the spout at the same time, also shown in Figure 6.22.

7. Position the spout on the kettle. Move vertices to flare out at the bottom of the spout where it meets the kettle. Figure 6.23 shows the completed kettle. Save your file.

Converting Back to Polygons

Most models created with subdivision surfaces should really be converted back to polygons once the modeling is finished and rendering setup is ready to begin. Since subdivisions are a more intricate surface type than polygons, it usually makes for much improved performance while animating to work with a polygonal model rather than a subdivision. Professionals frequently use subdivision tools and surfaces to create their models but convert back to polygons once they are finished to avoid any excessive memory usage while rendering.

Figure 6.23

The completed sub-division teakettle

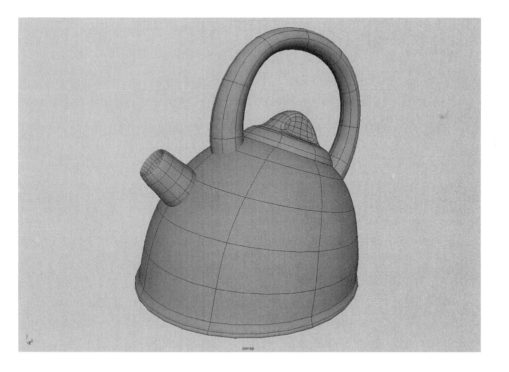

This is a simple procedure, similar to the Chapter 5 exercise in which you converted NURBS surfaces to polygons. Here you will convert the kettle back to polygons.

1. Select the subdivision kettle and its handle, spout, and lid, and choose **Modify → Convert → Subdiv to Polygons** ❐ to open the options box shown in Figure 6.24.

2. Next to Tessellation Method, select Adaptive. This usually will yield the best results.

3. The Divisions Per Face slider controls how smoothly the object is converted to polys. At a division factor of 1, your kettle will look jagged. Turn it up to 2, and you will notice a faithful conversion to polygons.

4. For best results, however, select each piece of the kettle separately, and convert the pieces one by one, adjusting the Divisions Per Face value appropriately. You will find that a division value of 2 will work for everything but the handle, which requires a division value of at least 3 to remain fairly smooth.

More often than not, you want to take a model as far as possible before you convert it to polygons, but the original subD version is still saved in case it needs to be modified. This way, you can revert to your subD file, make your changes, and reconvert to polygons to render out the changes.

Taking the Kettle Further

Try creating more detail for the kettle, or even experiment with your own designs. An easy addition is a whistle cap for the spout. Or try creating a matching set of tea cups and saucers with subdivision surfaces. With the skills you have acquired here, you should feel confident to tackle an entire kitchen full of models!

Also, try your hand at creating the models suggested at the end of Chapter 5 using subdivision techniques instead of NURBS. SubDs are a great way to make organic shapes, so try your hand at making the following objects using subDs:

Human Hand Use the polygon model example in Chapter 4, but this time convert the base poly model to subDs and then add detail to it.

Computer Mouse A PC or Mac mouse will make for a great subD model.

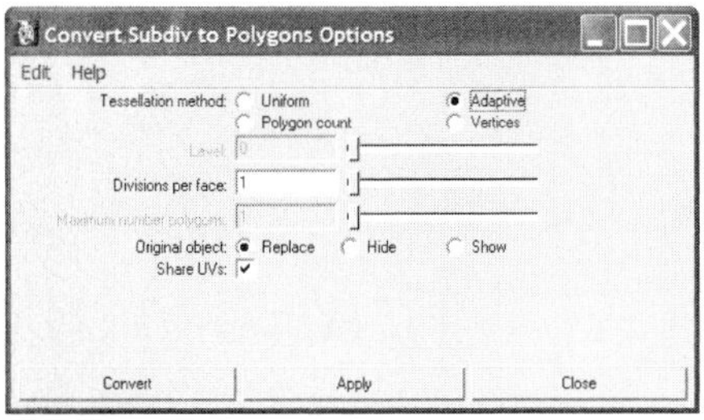

Figure 6.24

The Convert Subdiv to Polygons Options box

Office Chair This will require a few different pieces, of course, but find a good ergonomic chair to reference and go to task making the major if not all the components out of subDs, and then convert it to polys for good practice.

Character's Head This is quite a bit more complicated, and you might need to get some help from additional texts, but making the head of a person or a character is a way to hone your modeling skills. Making one out of subDs and converting it back to a low polygon count mesh will give you a great flavor for gaming modeling.

Summary

This chapter covered various modeling techniques that can help you out of the typical way of thinking. You learned how to use a lattice to adjust the polygon hand model into an alien hand as well as to animate a balloon pushing through a pipe. Moving on to a starfish model, you explored subdivision modeling techniques that are based on polygon modeling methods. Using polys and subDs hand in hand, you made a teakettle out of polygons at first and then refined the model using subdivision modeling. And finally, you learned how to convert subD models back to polygons.

Modeling is perhaps the most visible aspect of CG, since most CG projects need some form of modeling. It is almost always the first CG procedure students try to excel at before moving on to other aspects of CG, and it is usually the first aspect of CG to be taught in depth. Using other tools such as a lattice to shape your model is a fantastic way of not just making gross or overall changes to a model, but also adding fine detail in certain areas.

So as you have seen in this and the past two chapters, you can accomplish a modeling task in several ways. Different work flows give you great flexibility to choose your own modeling style. To make such a choice, however, you'll need to practice. Good modelers have a strong eye for detail and a high tolerance for work that is repetitious. But they also love assembling a complex object and seeing a grand result, and they are thrilled by the eventual outcome.

Keep at it; model everything you get your hands and eyes on. Try the same model a few different ways; switch between NURBS, polygons, and subdivisions to get comfortable with Maya's toolset. As you're doing that, keep on top of how you organize your nodes, and keep everything named and organized. Organization in your scenes is extremely important.

CHAPTER 7

Maya Shading and Texturing

Shading is the term in the Maya software for applying colors and textures, known as *shaders*. After you model your objects, Maya assigns a default shader to them with a neutral gray color. This is to allow them to render and display properly. Without any shader attached to a surface, an object cannot be seen.

Simply put, a shader defines an object's look: its color, tactile texture, transparency, luminescence, glow, and so forth.

Topics include:

- Shader Types
- Shader Attributes
- Texturing the Axe
- Textures and Surfaces
- UVs, Polygons, and Images: Color My Pear

Shading is the proper term for applying a renderable color, surface bumps, transparency, reflection, shine, or similar attributes to an object in Maya. It is closely related to, but distinct from, the term *texturing,* which is formally used when you apply a map or other node to an *attribute of a shader* to create some sort of surface detail. For example, adding a scanned photo of a brick wall to the color attribute of a shader that you assign to a model in Maya is considered applying texture. Adding another scanned photo of the bumps and contours of the same brick wall to the **Bump Mapping** attribute is also considered applying a texture. Nevertheless, since textures are often applied to shaders, the entire process of shading is sometimes informally referred to as texturing. Applying textures to shaders is also called *texture mapping* or simply *mapping.* You map a texture to the color node of a shader that is assigned or applied to a Maya object.

Shaders are based on nodes. Each node holds the attributes that define the shader. With shaders, akin to the hierarchies and groups of models, you create shader networks of interconnected nodes. These networks can be simple or they can be intricate and involved, as when several render nodes are used to create complex shading effects.

Each shader, also known as a shading group, comprises a set of material nodes. *Material nodes* are the Maya nodes that hold all the pertinent rendering information about the object to which they are assigned, such as the color, opacity, or shininess. The shading groups are the nodes that allow the connection between the surface and the material you've created. When you edit the shader through the Attribute Editor, as you will do later in this chapter, you edit its material node.

As you learn about shading in this chapter, you will deal primarily with the Hypershade as opposed to the Multilister. See Chapter 2 for the layout of these windows and then Chapter 3 for a hands-on introduction to the Hypershade. You can access either window by choosing **Window → Rendering Editors**. Through either of these windows you can create and edit your shaders.

Shading in Maya is almost always done hand in hand with lighting, which is the subject of Chapter 10. At the very least, textures are tweaked and edited in the lighting stage of production. Since the appearance of an object depends on light, in this chapter's exercise you'll create some lights as you create textures; then you'll learn more about lighting in Chapter 10.

Shader Types

Open the Hypershade by choosing **Window → Rendering Editors → Hypershade**. In the left column of the Hypershade window, you will see a listing of Maya shading nodes. The first section displays Surface nodes, a.k.a. material nodes or shader types.

Of these shader types, you'll find five that are common to other animation packages as well. You'll use two of these later in this chapter. To understand a bit more about shaders, take a look at what makes objects look as they do in the real world.

The short answer is light. The way light bounces off an object defines how you see that object. The surface of the object may have pigments that affect the frequency of light once it reflects off it, giving the surface color. Other features of that object's surface also dictate how light is reflected.

For the most part, shader types address the differences in how light bounces off surfaces. Most light, once it hits a surface, *diffuses* across an area of that surface. It may also reflect a hot spot called a *specular* highlight. The shaders in Maya differ in how they deal with specular and diffuse parameters. As you learn about the shader types, think of the things around you and what shader type would best fit them. Some Maya shaders are specific to creating some special effects, such as the Hair Tube shader or the Use Background shader. It is important to learn the fundamentals first, so we will cover the shading types you will be using right off the bat.

The Lambert Shader Type

The most common shader type is *Lambert*, an evenly diffused shading type found in dull or matte surfaces. A sheet of paper, for example, is a Lambert surface.

A Lambert surface diffuses and scatters light evenly across its surface, in all directions (bottom left).

The Phong Shader Type

Phong shading, named after its developer Bui Tuong-Phong in 1975, brings to a surface's rendering the notions of specular highlight and reflectivity. You'll find glossy objects such as plastics, glass, and most metals take well to Phong shading.

A Phong surface reflects light with a sharp hot spot, creating a specular highlight that drops off sharply (bottom right).

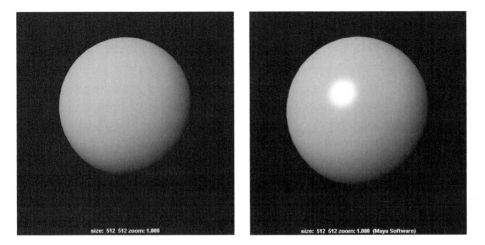

The Blinn Shader Type

Also named after its developer (James Blinn), the *Blinn* shading method brings to the surface a highly accurate specular lighting model with increased control over the specular's appearance. This creates a shader that is good for use on shiny surfaces and metallic surfaces.

A Blinn surface reflects light with a hot spot, creating a specular that diffuses somewhat more gradually than a Phong (top left).

The Phong E Shader Type

The Phong shading model is expanded to include more control over the specular highlight. This creates a Phong surface whose specular drops off more gradually and yet remains sharper than a Blinn. Phong E also has greater color control over the specular than does Phong and Blinn, giving you some more options for metallic reflections.

A Phong E surface reflects light much like a regular Phong but has more detailed control over the specular settings to adjust the glossiness of the surface (center left).

The Anisotropic Shader Type

The Anisotropic shader is good to use on surfaces that are deformed, such as a foil wrapper or warped plastic. *Anisotropic* is defined as having properties that differ according to direction. This creates a specular highlight that is uneven across the surface, changing according to the direction you specify on the surface. By contrast with Blinn and Phong types, the specular highlight is evenly distributed to make a circular highlight on the surface.

An Anisotropic surface reflects light unevenly and creates an irregular-shaped specular highlight that is good for representing surfaces with directional grooves like CDs (bottom left).

The Layered Shader Type

A *Layered* shader allows the stacking of shaders to create complex shading effects—useful for creating objects composed of multiple materials. By using the Layered shader to texture different materials to different parts of the object, you can avoid using excess geometry.

You control Layered shaders by using transparency maps to define which areas show which layers of the shader. You drag material nodes into the top area of the Attribute Editor and stack them from left to right, the left being the topmost layer assigned to the surface.

Layered shaders are valuable resources to control compound and complex shaders—perfect for putting labels on objects or adding dirt to aged surfaces. You will use a Layered shader for the exercise in this chapter (top right).

The Ramp Shader Type

A *ramp texture* is a gradient that can be attached to almost any attribute of a shader as a texture node. Ramps can create smooth transitions between colors and can even be used to control particles. (See Chapter 12 for how a ramp is used to control particles.) When used as a texture, a ramp can be connected to any attribute of a shader to create graduating color scales, transparency effects, increasing glow effects, and so on. You will use ramp textures later in this chapter.

The *Ramp shader* is a self-contained shader node that automatically has several ramp texture nodes attached to its attributes. These ramps are attached within the shader itself, so there is no need to connect external ramp texture nodes. This makes for a simplified editing environment for the shader because all the colors and handles are accessible through the Ramp shader's own Attribute Editor, as shown in Figure 7.1.

To create a new color in any one of the horizontal ramps, click in the swatch to create a new ramp position. Edit its color through its Selected Color swatch. You can move the position by grabbing the circle right above the ramp and dragging left or right. To delete a color, click the box beneath it.

Ramp textures are automatically attached to the **Color**, **Transparency**, **Incandescence**, **Specular Color**, **Reflectivity**, and **Environment** attributes of a Ramp shader. In addition, a special curve ramp is attached to the **Specular Roll Off** to allow for more precise control over how the specular highlight diminishes over the surface.

Figure 7.1

A ramp shader in its Attribute Editor

Shader Attributes

Shaders are composed of nodes just like other Maya objects. Within these nodes, attributes define what shaders do. Here is a brief rundown of the common shader attributes you'll be working with.

Color An RGB or HSV value that defines what color the shader is when it receives a neutral color light. For more on RGB and HSV, see Chapter 1.

Transparency The higher the **Transparency** value, the less opaque and more "see-through" the object becomes.

Although usually expressed in a black-to-white gradient, with black being opaque or solid and white being totally clear, transparency can have color. In a color transparency, the shader's color shifts because only certain of its RGB values are now transparent as opposed to the whole.

Ambient Color This color affects the **Color** attribute of the shader as more ambient light is created in the scene. Ambient color tends to flatten an object because **Ambient Color** evenly colors the object. This attribute is primarily used to create flat areas and should be used with care. The default is black, to keep the darker areas of a surface dark. The lighter the ambient color, the lighter those areas. A bright **Ambient Color** will flatten out an object.

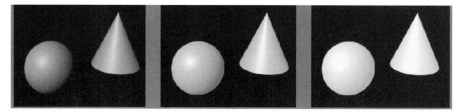

Ambient Color = Black   Ambient Color = Medium Gray   Ambient Color = White

Incandescence This is the ability to self-illuminate. Objects that seem to give off their own light, such as an office's fluorescent light fixture, can be given an incandescence value. It will not, however, light objects around it, nor will it create a glow. It will also serve to flatten the object into a pure color. **Incandescence**, as you will see in the next chapter, can also help light a scene in mental ray's Final Gather rendering: the value of incandescence (as well as the color) of an object is used to calculate the overall brightness in a Final Gather scene.

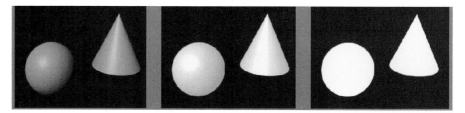

Incandescence = 0   Incandescence = 0.5   Incandescence = 1

Bump Mapping This attribute creates a textured feel to the surface by adding highlights and shadows to the render. It will not actually alter the surface of the geometry, though it will make the surface appear to have ridges, marks, scratches, and so forth. The **Bump Map** has to be a texture node such as a ramp, a fractal noise, or an image file. The more intense the variation in tones of that map, the greater the bump. **Bump Maps** are frequently used to make surfaces look more real, as nothing in reality has a perfectly smooth surface. Using bumps very close up may create problems, so bumps are generally good for adding inexpensive detail to a model that is not in an extreme close-up.

Close-up geometry, where you have to physically change the topology of the model using texture maps, will require displacement maps. We will cover displacement maps later in this chapter.

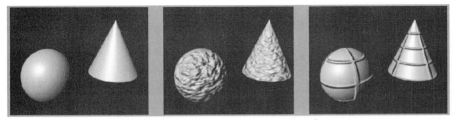

| No Bump Map | Fractal Texture Bump Map | Grid Texture Bump Map |

Diffuse This value governs how much light is reflected from the surface in all directions. When light strikes a surface, light disperses across the surface and helps to illuminate it. The higher this value, the brighter its object when lit, since more of the striking light is reflected from the surface. The lower the diffuse value, the more light will be "absorbed" into the surface, yielding a darker result, especially in areas not well lit. Metals have very low diffuse values since they rely on reflections and direct light.

| Diffuse = 0.8 (default) | Diffuse = 0.3 | Diffuse = 1 |

Translucence and Translucence Focus The **Translucence** and **Translucence Focus** attributes give the material the ability to transmit light through its surface, like a piece of canvas in front of a light. At a value of 1 for **Translucence**, all light shines through the object; at 0, none does. The **Translucence Focus** attribute specifies how much of that light is scattered.

A light material such as paper would have a high translucence focus, and thicker surfaces should have low focus rates.

Glow Intensity In the Special Effects section of the Attribute Editor, the **Glow Intensity** attribute adds a glow to the object, as if it were emitting light into a foggy area. We will add glow to an object in Chapter 10.

| Glow = 0 | Glow = 0.5 | Glow = 1 |

Matte Opacity Mode and slider Objects rendered through Maya generate a solid matte. Where there is an object, the *matte* is white; where there is nothing, the matte is black. This helps compositing programs separate rendered CG from their background to composite into a scene. Turning the slider down decreases the brightness of the object's matte, making it appear more transparent. This is usually used for compositing tricks or to make an object render in RGB but not appear in any composites. For more information about mattes, see both the sidebar "Image Mattes" in this chapter and Chapter 11.

Raytrace Options This subset of attributes allows you to set the raytracing abilities of the shader. With raytracing, you can achieve true reflections and refractions in your scene. See Chapter 11 for more on raytracing.

Some attributes are available only with certain shader types. Here are the attributes you'll see for the Phong, Phong E, and Blinn shaders.

Specular Color The color of the highlights on a shiny surface. Black produces no specular, and white creates a bright one.

Reflectivity The amount of reflection that is visible in the surface. The higher the value, the more reflective the object will render. Increasing this value increases the visibility of the **Reflected Color** attribute or of true reflections in the scene when raytraced.

Reflected Color Gives the surface a reflection. Texture maps are generally assigned to this attribute to give the object a reflection of whatever is in the image file or texture without having to generate time-consuming true reflections with a raytraced render. However, using raytracing to get true reflections is the only way to generate reflections of other objects in the scene.

Cosine Power Only available with a Phong shader. This attribute changes the size of the shiny highlights (a.k.a. specular) on the surface. The higher the number, the smaller the highlight will look.

IMAGE MATTES

As you learned in Chapter 1 (and will explore further in Chapter 11), image files are stored with a red, a green, and a blue channel that keep the amount of each color in each pixel of the image. Some image formats, including TIFF and TARGA, also have an alpha channel, also known as a *matte channel* or *image matte*. This is a grayscale channel that controls the opacity of an image. Completely white parts of the matte make those parts of the image opaque (solid), while black parts make those parts of the image fully transparent. Gray in the matte channel makes those parts of the image partly transparent. These mattes are used in compositing—bringing together elements created separately into a single composite scene. See Chapter 11 for an example of how an alpha channel works.

Roughness, Highlight Size, and Whiteness   Control the specular highlight on a Phong E surface only. They control specular focus, amount of specular, and highlight color, respectively.

mental ray attributes   Since mental ray was integrated with Maya, there is usually a set of mental ray options in the Attributes of an objects. Shaders are no different. If you open the mental ray heading in the Attribute Editor for a shader, you'll notice a few attributes from **Reflection Blur** to **Irradiance**, as well as a few ways to override Maya's shading attributes with mental ray's own.

A in-depth discussion of the mental ray attributes is beyond the scope of this introductory text, but it is a good idea to know this heading is here and available to you once you have more experience with rendering and wish to work with mental ray at its more implicit levels in Maya.

Texturing the Axe

In this section, you will add shaders to your NURBS axe to make it look real, and in the next chapter, you'll import the axe into an animation exercise. This is actually a fairly common practice, starting animation on a project and then replacing it with a finished and textured model.

Load axe_texture_A.mb from the axe_model project on the CD, or load the NURBS axe you modeled in Chapter 5.

You'll start by texturing the metal parts of the axe. Metal is one of the toughest materials to create and light since the look of real metals is greatly affected by their surroundings, that is, by the reflections of the environment.

Autodesk's website lists several premade shaders for your use. Maya also includes a shader library on its installation CD. Even though you can find a good metal to use for your axe head in one of these libraries, you will make it from scratch.

The Metal Axe Head

First, set up your render parameters so that you can render out your axe as you tweak the metal shader to get it right.

1. Choose **Window → Rendering Editors → Render Settings**, or click ⊞ in the menu bar to open the Render Settings window. Make sure Render Using is set to Maya Software.

2. In the Image Size section under the Common tab, set Presets to 640 × 480. In the Anti-aliasing Quality section under the Maya Software tab, use the Intermediate Quality Preset. This will give you a good look for the final render with a short render time.

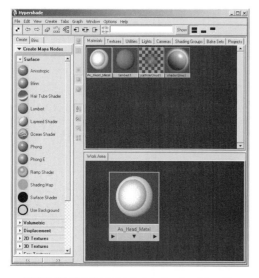

3. You can create the Metal shader in two ways:

   - Open the Hypershade window, and click Phong in the Create Maya Nodes section. A new Phong shader will show up in both the top and the bottom parts of the Hypershade window.

   - Open the Multilister, and choose **Edit → Create** to open the Create Render Node window. Click Phong to create a Phong shader type. A new Phong shader will appear in the Multilister.

4. Double-click the phong1 shader node in either the Hypershade or the Multilister window to open the Attribute Editor.

5. Click the gray swatch next to the **Color** attribute to open the Color Chooser. Select a light blue gray. In the Slider section, the HSV values should be something like H: 207, S: 0.085, and V: 0.80. Click Accept.

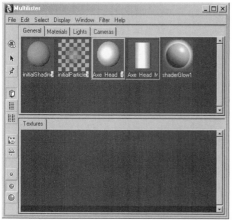

6. Back in the Attribute Editor for the shader, click the gray swatch for the **Specular Color**. By changing this color, you control the hue and brightness of the highlights on this surface. Use a bright faded blue with HSV values of H: 208, S: 0.20, and V: 0.90.

7. Increase the spread of the specular highlights by changing the **Cosine Power** from the default of 20 to 2.0. This creates a large area for the bright highlights, implying a polished reflective surface.

8. To assign the shader to the surfaces, select both sides of the axe head. In the Hyper-shade, RMB click the shader node (in either the upper or lower window), and choose **Assign Material To Selection** from the shortcut menu; or in the Multilister, choose **Edit → Assign**. Figure 7.2 shows the shader in both windows.

9. Make sure your perspective view is active, and click the Render The Current Frame button ( ) in the menu bar. Check out different angles of the axe, and render them to see how the metal axe head responds to the default lights Maya inserts into the scene for your render.

Figure 7.3

You can add a texture to a shader's attribute by clicking the checkered Map button.

This creates a simple Metal shader that will work well overall. To create a more polished look for the axe head, you can add a reflection to it using an environment texture node. This node creates a 3D texture node in the scene that will project its contents onto the material attribute to which it has been connected. As an object animates through the scene, different parts of the texture will be reflected on its surface.

10. In the Metal shader's Attribute Editor, click the Map button next to the **Reflected Color** attribute, as in Figure 7.3. This attaches a new node to create a reflection and opens the Create Render Node window. Click the Environment Textures section and select Env Chrome. An environment texture will provide an interesting reflection.

11. Move the **Reflectivity** slider from 0.50 to 0.85. The higher this number, the more prominent the **Reflected Color** will reflect in the surface. Figure 7.4 shows the axe before and after a reflection. The Env Chrome reflection texture makes the axe look polished by reflecting a grid representing the ground and a bright blue sky.

MULTILISTER VERSUS HYPERSHADE DISPLAYS

The Multilister and Hypershade accomplish the same shading tasks, although their method-ologies and layout are different. The Multilister lists shading nodes in tabbed pages, while the Hypershade gives you more options to lay out shaders and work with their connections and input/output nodes. Notice in the layout differences that the Multilister's round shader icons in the General tab are *shading group* nodes. The Hypershade's round shader icons show the *material node* of the shader.

The shading group is the node that assigns a shader to a surface, while the material node carries all the pertinent shader information such as Color, Transparency, Specular, and so on. The Hypershade by default shows only the material nodes since little editing is actually done to shading group nodes. (To display a shading group node, you need to select the material node and display its output connections.) To see the material node of a shader in the Multilis-ter, however, you must either click the Materials tab or, while in the General tab, click the small arrow in the lower right of the Shading Group icon to expand the material node.

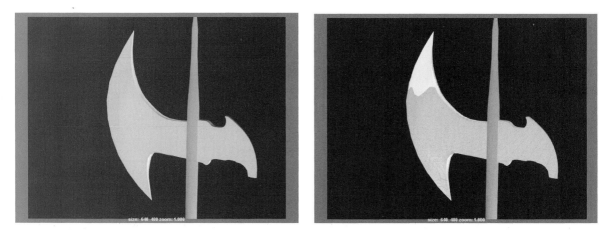

Figure 7.4

The axe head before and after a reflection is added

After you create the Env Chrome texture, you'll see a green object in the modeling windows at the origin, shown in Figure 7.5. This is the Env Chrome's placement node. You can manipulate this node just as you manipulate other Maya objects—in other words, move, rotate, and scale it.

Altering this will change how the environment chrome projects itself in the scene. For example, if you increase the size of this placement node, the grid showing in the reflection of the axe will get larger. For more on projections and placement nodes, see the section "Texture Nodes" later in this chapter.

The Wooden Handle

A glossy cherry wood would look good for the handle, so a Phong shader would be best.

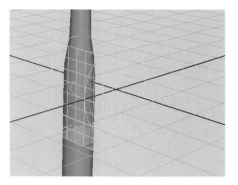

Figure 7.5

Use placement nodes in the scene to scale and position textures.

1. In the Hypershade, choose **Create → Materials → Phong**. Set **Diffuse** to 0.70, **Specular Color** to a light gray, and **Cosine Power** to 50.

2. Click the Map button for the color. In the Create Render Node window, in the 3D Textures section, select Wood. Figure 7.6 shows this texture in the Attribute Editor.

3. In the Wood's Attribute Editor, adjust **Filler Color** to a nice red brown with an HSV of 8.5, 0.85, 0.43. Change **Vein Color** to a darker version of the filler with an HSV of 8.5, 0.75, 0.08.

4. Change **Vein Spread** to 0.70, change **Layer Size** to 0.119, and darken **Grain Color** a bit by pulling the slider to the left, but not all the way. This will give you a nice dark cherry wood.

The Wood texture is a projected 3D texture; it's projected from a source onto the object using a 3D placement node, just like the Env Chrome on the axe head's reflection. To assign the Wood texture from the Hypershade, select the handle and RMB click the shader to select **Assign Material To Selection**, or you can MMB drag the icon onto the handle in the viewport. For more on projected textures, see the section "Texture Nodes" later in this chapter.

You can assign a shader to any object by MMB dragging its icon from the Multilister or Hypershade to the object in the viewport.

5. To see this dark texture on your object, create a new light in the scene. In the main menu, choose **Create → Lights → Ambient Light**. (For more on lights, see Chapter 10). Open the Attribute Editor for the light by pressing Ctrl+A or by double-clicking its icon on the Lights tab in the Multilister or Hypershade. Increase **Intensity** to 2.5.

6. Render a frame of the axe handle up close, as shown in Figure 7.7. Notice how the wood repeats on the handle and makes for an undesirable texture. Adjust the wood's texture placement.

7. To get to the Wood texture's placement node, open the Hypershade. Drag the Wood shader to the Hypershade work area (bottom half). RMB click the wood and choose **Graph Network** from the shortcut menu. You could also select it and click the Input Connections button ( ) at the top of the Hypershade. Figure 7.8 shows the shader nodes for the wood shader network in the Hypershade work area. The place3dTexture2 node connects to the wood2 node and gives it position information. The wood2 node then connects to the phong3 material node as a color texture map.

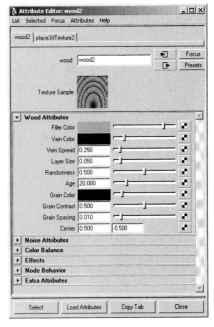

Figure 7.6

The Wood texture in its Attribute Editor

8. Double-click the place3dTexture node to open its Attribute Editor.

9. Click the Fit To Group Box button to automatically position the placement node for the wood around the handle. In your viewport, you'll see the green placement node around the handle, as in Figure 7.9.

10. Rendering a frame reveals that the wood still does not look quite right. Select the placement node in the viewport, and rotate it in Z to 90. Click the Fit To Group Box button again to rescale it to fit the handle. This will not rotate it back to the way it was; it will only scale it to fit the extent of the object to which it's assigned.

11. Render another frame, and you'll see the wood veins running the length of the handle. It looks more like wood now, but it still repeats too much.

Instead of moving and scaling the texture placement node and rendering multiple times to get the wood placement just right, you can use Maya's Interactive Photorealistic Rendering (IPR) to see your changes in real time. Click the IPR Render The Current Frame button (🎞) in the Status line, or choose **Render → IPR Render Current Frame**.

The Render View window shows a lower-quality render of the axe. It will prompt you to select a region to begin tuning. Drag a marquee selection in the Render View window around the handle. IPR refreshes that part of the window. Every change you make to the texture placement node prompts IPR to update that section of the render, giving a fast update on the positioning and scale of the wood texture.

12. Select the texture placement node and scale it up in the three axes until you get a good-looking grain. Figure 7.10 shows a well-spaced wood grain.

The scene file `axe_texture_B.mb` in the axe_model project on the CD will bring you up to this point.

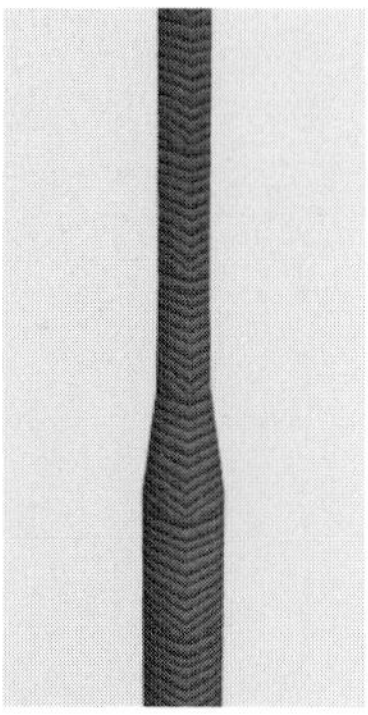

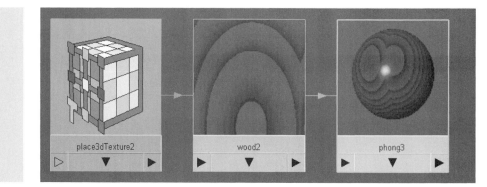

Figure 7.7

The Wood texture repeats too much by default.

Figure 7.8

The wood shader network

The Metal Spike

Currently, the entire length of the handle is shaded as wood, including the top spike. The spike on the axe head should be metal like the axe head.

You can approach this in two ways: with geometry and with shaders. If you manipulate geometry, you select a horizontal isoparm and detach the spike portion of the handle to make it a separate surface. You then assign a Metal shader to the new tip surface.

Using a shader instead of cutting up or creating more geometry can be desirable in many instances. For example, you may not be able to detach surfaces like this all the time.

The Layered shader is a normal surface shader that allows you to stack materials on top of each other to assign to a surface. You control which layer of material is exposed and by how much by assigning transparency values or textures to each layer. Use a Ramp texture to specify where on the handle the wood stops and the metal starts.

To create a Layered shader, follow these steps:

1. Select the axe handle, and choose **Lighting/Shading → Assign New Material → Layered Shader** to open the Attribute Editor, as in Figure 7.11. By default, the Layered shader contains a green layer in the top of the Attribute Editor window. From left to right, the layers are displayed in the order they appear from top to bottom as they are assigned to the surface. So the leftmost shader in the Layered shader is on top of all the others.

Choosing **Lighting/Shading → Assign New Material** is an easy way to create and assign a material without having to open the Hypershade or Multilister.

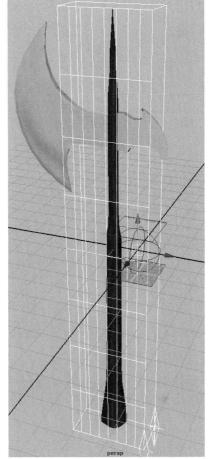

Figure 7.9

The wood's placement node

Figure 7.10

The wood handle after the texture has been scaled and placed

2. Using the Hypershade, MMB drag the metal material you've made into the top region of the Layered shader's Attribute Editor window. To delete the default green material, click the X'ed square beneath it. The Material Sample icon in the Attribute Editor turns into the metal.

3. MMB drag the wood material into the Layered shader's Attribute Editor. Make sure it is placed to the left of the metal material. If the materials are already in place, you can rearrange their order by MMB dragging them left or right of the other materials in the Attribute Editor. Notice in Figure 7.12 that the Material Sample icon changed to the wood material. The wood is now the top layer, so only it will show until you give it some transparency to reveal some metal at the tip.

> You can see the names of the materials in the Layered shader by pointing to the icons.

4. Click the wood shader icon in the Layered shader's Attribute Editor to highlight it. Notice that the Transparency Map button (as well as Color) is now a square with an arrow (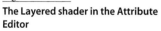) as opposed to the checkerboard you've seen before. Click this button to open the Attribute Editor for the wood material.

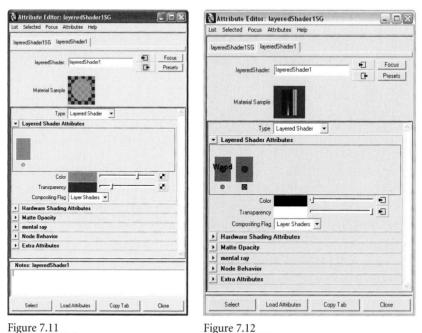

Figure 7.11

The Layered shader in the Attribute Editor

Figure 7.12

The Layered shader with the wood on top of the metal

When an attribute is already mapped, its Map button turns from a checkerboard to an input connection icon. Clicking it opens the Attribute Editor for whatever node is attached to that attribute. In this case, clicking the Map button opens its Attribute Editor since the wood material was assigned to this layer. Here you need to attach a transparency ramp to control where the metal tip starts and the wood handle ends.

5. Click the Map button for the wood's **Transparency** attribute. Create a ramp texture node. Make sure the Normal radio button is checked and not the As Projection or As Stencil radio button.

6. In the ramp's Attribute Editor, change **Interpolation** to None, and change **Type** to U Ramp.

7. Delete the middle (green) color by clicking the square to the right of green's position. Select the bottom (red) color by clicking its round handle on the left of the ramp. Change the **Selected Color** attribute to white. Drag it all the way to the bottom of the ramp.

8. Select the top color (blue) and change it to black. Drag the handle down the ramp to a **Selected Position** of 0.105. Figure 7.13 shows the ramp position and the axe. If you're in texture display mode in the perspective view (press the 6 key), you'll see that the tip of the model is a blue-gray color (the metal) and the bottom of the handle is a reddish brown (the wood). As you adjust the position of the white color on the ramp, notice how the spike and handle change.

9. In the Hypershade, choose **Edit → Delete Unused Nodes** to purge all unused shading nodes from your scene. Make sure your Layered shader and Metal shader are assigned, of course.

10. Render out a frame of the axe. Save this frame in the render buffer by clicking Keep Image (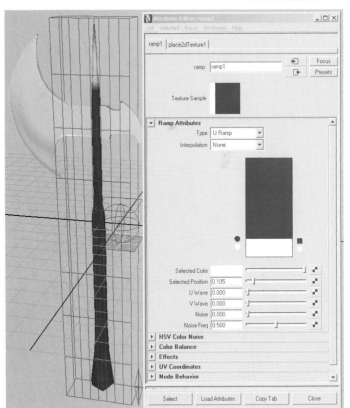) in the Render View window. This will keep the image so that you can scroll back to it for reference. A scroll bar will appear at the bottom of the Render View window.

Figure 7.13

The ramp texture set on the wood's Transparency attribute controls where the wood and metal meet.

11. Select the axe's top node and rotate it about 45 degrees in Z to angle it. Render a frame at this point. Notice how the grain of the wood has changed. Use the scroll bar to toggle back and forth and compare these two images, as in Figure 7.14.

When a projected texture, such as the wood, does not "stick" to an object and the object seems to move through the texture, the object is "swimming" through the projection. The wood is being projected by the 3D placement node that you positioned to get the grain just right, so you'll need to group the texture node under the axe's top node. When the axe moves, the texture will stick with it, maintaining its orientation with the axe.

12. Rotate the axe back to 0 in Z. Select the place3dTexture2 node from either the viewport (it's the green texture you scaled to fit the handle as you see here) or the Outliner. Be careful not to use the Env Cube's 3D placement node you used for the axe head reflection. In the Outliner, MMB drag it under the axe's topmost node.

The file axe_texture_C.mb in the axe_model project on the CD has the final textured axe for your reference.

Now you have a fully textured axe. By using a Layered shader, you did not need to build another piece of geometry to represent a metal tip. You can embellish a model a lot at the texturing level. Although you may first consider using geometry, you can accomplish a number of tasks by using simple texturing tricks, such as the axe handle and its metal spike. The more you explore and experience shaders and modeling, the better you'll be at juggling modeling with texturing to get the most effective solution.

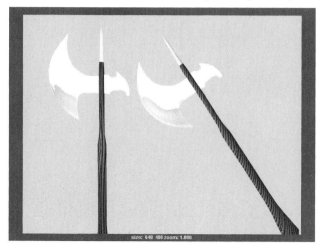

Try loading the locomotive model from Chapter 4 and texturing it from top to bottom. A great deal of independent geometry needs textures, some to be carefully placed with 3D placement nodes. Experiment with as many different ways of shading the locomotive as you can.

Figure 7.14

The wood grain changes as the axe moves.

Textures and Surfaces

Texture nodes generate maps to connect to an attribute of a shader. There are two types of textures: procedural and bitmapped (or simply, maps). *Procedural* textures use Maya's own nodes' attributes to generate an effect, such as ramp, checkerboard, or fractal noise textures. You can adjust each of these procedural textures by changing their attribute values.

BAKING A TEXTURE PROJECTION

In the axe handle texturing exercise, you grouped the 3dplacement node for the wood grain to the handle of the axe to make the texture stick to the handle. But you can also "bake" the texture onto the axe handle by converting the texture projection to a file node. By baking the texture node, you are converting the 3dplacement node into an image file that is then mapped to the color channel of the material, discarding the projection node altogether, so you needn't group it with the handle as you did earlier.

Follow these steps to bake that wood grain texture to the axe:

1. Open the Hypershade.

2. Click to select the axe handle's Layered shader node and MMB drag it to the work area of the Hypershade.

3. RMB click it and select **Graph Network** to see all the nodes of the Layered shader (bottom left).

4. Select the axe handle geometry and then Shift+select the wood2 node in the Hypershade.

5. Choose **Edit → Convert To File Texture (Maya Software)** ☐. In the option box, select an **X Resolution** and a **Y Resolution** of 512 each and click Convert and Close. If you get an error when you convert, you can choose **Edit → Delete Unused Nodes** and try again. The shader will rebuild itself to create a texture file, material, and a shading group node that is automatically assigned to the selected geometry. Delete all unused nodes again to clean up the Hypershade window, and your new shader network should look as pictured here (bottom right).

Notice that the 3dplacement node is removed from the scene as well as the Hypershade view. Your axe handle's texture will now stick to the handle as a mapped file texture.

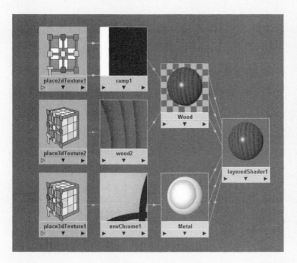

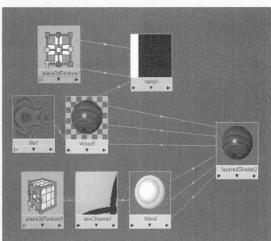

A *map*, on the other hand, is a saved image file that is imported into the scene through a file texture node. These files are pregenerated through whatever imaging programs you have and include digital pictures and scanned photos. You need to place all texture nodes onto their surfaces through the shader. You can map them directly onto the surfaces' UV values or project them.

UV Mapping

Just as 3D space is based on coordinates in XYZ, surfaces have coordinates denoted by U and V values along a 2D coordinate system, for width and height. The UV value helps a texture position itself on the surface. The U and V values range from 0 to 1, with (0,0) UV being the origin point of the surface.

Maya creates UVs for primitive surfaces automatically, but frequently you need to edit UVs for proper texture placement, particularly on polygonal meshes once you have edited them. In some instances, placing textures on a poly mesh will require projecting the textures onto the mesh, since the poly UVs may not line up as expected once the mesh has been edited. See the next section, "Using Projections."

If you find that the placement of your texture or image is not quite right, simply use the 2D placement node of the texture node to position it properly. See the section "Texture Nodes" later in this chapter for more information.

Simply put, UV mapping places the texture directly on the surface and uses the surface coordinates for its positioning. In this case, you must do a lot of work to line up the UVs on the surface to make sure the images created line up properly. For a sense of UV mapping, see the section "UVs, Polygons, and Images: Color My Pear" at the end of this chapter.

Using Projections

You need to place textures on the surface. You can often do so using UV placement, but some textures need to be projected onto the surface. It is common to project textures (when texturing polys, for example). A projection is what it sounds like. The file image, ramp, or other texture being used can be "beamed" onto the object in several ways.

You can create any texture node as either a normal UV map or a projected texture. In the Create Render Node window, select the method—Normal (for UV mapping) or As Projection—by clicking the appropriate radio button before you create the texture.

When you create a projected texture, a new node is attached to the texture node. This projection node controls the method of projection with an attached 3D placement node, which you saw in the axe exercise. Select the projection node to set the type of projection in the Attribute Editor (see Figure 7.15).

Setting the projection type will allow you to project an image or a texture without having it warp and distort, depending on the model you are mapping. For example, a planar projection on a sphere will warp the edges of the image as they stretch into infinity on the sides of the sphere.

Try This In a new scene, create a NURBS sphere and a NURBS cone and place them side by side. Create a Blinn shader and assign it to both objects. In the Blinn shader's Attribute Editor, set its **Color** attribute to a checkerboard pattern. Make sure Normal is checked to create a UV-mapped checker texture (see image on the bottom left).

Now try removing the color map from the Blinn shader. In the Blinn shader's Attribute Editor, right-click and hold the attribute's title word *Color*, and then choose **Break Connection** from the shortcut menu. This severs the connection to the checker and resets the color to gray. Now re-create a new checker map for the color, but this time create it as a projection. In the illustration on the right, you see the perspective view in texture mode (press the 6 key) with the two objects and the planar projection placement node. Try moving the planar placement object around in the scene to see how the texture maps itself to the objects. On the left are the rendered objects (see images on the bottom center and right).

Try the other projection types to see how they affect the texture being mapped.

Projection placement nodes control how the projection maps its image or texture onto the surface. Using a NURBS sphere with a spherical projected checker, with U and V wrap turned off on the checker texture, you can see how manipulating the place3dTexture node affects the texture.

In addition to the Move, Rotate, and Scale tools, you can use the Special Manipulator tool (press T to activate or click the Show Manipulator Tool icon in the toolbar) to adjust the placement. Figure 7.16 shows this tool for a spherical projection.

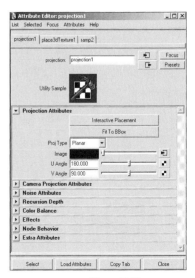

Figure 7.15

The projection node in the Attribute Editor

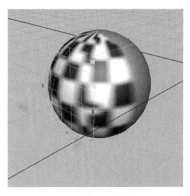

Figure 7.16

The spherical projection's Manipulator tool

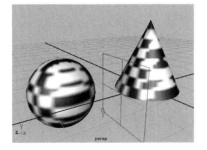

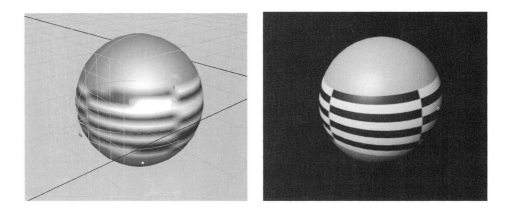

Drag the handles on the special manipulator to change the coverage of the projection, orientation, size, and so forth. All projection types have special manipulators. Figure 7.17 shows the special manipulator wrapping the checker in a thin band all the way around the sphere.

To summarize, projection textures depend on a projector node to position the texture onto the geometry.

Texture Nodes

You can create a number of texture nodes in Maya. This section covers the most important. All texture nodes, however, have common attributes that affect their final look.

Open the Attribute Editor for any texture node. The two top sections affect the color balance of the texture. The Color Balance and Effects sections are described here.

Color Balance This set of attributes adjusts the overall brightness and color balance of your texture. Use these attributes to tint or brighten a texture without having to change all the individual attributes of the shader itself.

Effects You can invert the texture's color space by clicking the Invert check box. This changes black to white and white to black in addition to inverting the RGB values of colors.

You can map textures to almost any shader attribute for detail. Even the tiniest amount of texture on a surface's bump, specular, or color increases its reality.

Place2dTexture Nodes

2D texture nodes come with a 2D placement node that controls their repetition, rotation, size, offset, and so on. Adjust the setting in this node of your 2D texture in the Attribute Editor, as shown in Figure 7.18, to position it within the shader network. You used a similar approach when dealing with the wood's 3D placement node in the axe exercise earlier this chapter.

The **Repeat UV** setting controls how many times the texture is repeated on whatever shader attribute it is connected to, such as color. The higher the wrap values, the smaller the texture will appear but the more times it will appear on the surface.

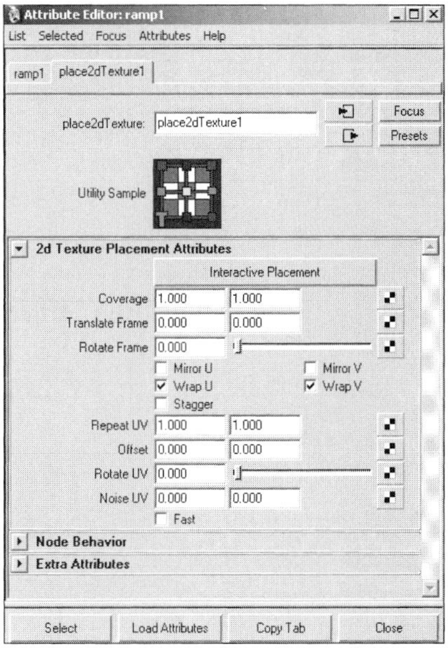

The **Wrap U** and **Wrap V** check boxes allow the texture to wrap around the edges of their limits to repeat. When these are turned off, the texture will only appear once and the rest of the surface will be the color of the **Default Color** attribute found in the texture node itself.

The **Mirror U** and **Mirror V** settings allow the texture to mirror itself when it repeats. The **Coverage**, **Translate Frame**, and **Rotate Frame** settings control where the image is mapped. These are useful for positioning a digital image or a scanned picture.

Figure 7.18

A 2D placement node in the Attribute Editor

Ramp Texture

A ramp is a gradient in which one color transitions into the next color. You've already seen how useful it can be in positioning materials in a Layered shader. It's also perfect for making color gradients, as shown in Figure 7.19.

Use the round handles to select the color and to move it up and down the ramp. The square handle to the right deletes the color. To create a new color, click inside the ramp itself.

> The ramp texture is different from the Ramp shader. The Ramp shader automatically has several ramp textures mapped to some of its attributes.

The **Type** setting allows you to create a gradient running along the U or V direction of the surface, as well as make circular, radial, diagonal, and other types of gradients. The **Interpolation** setting controls how the colors grade from one to the next.

The **U Wave** and **V Wave** attributes let you add a squiggle to the U or V coordinate of the ramp, and the **Noise** and **Noise Freq** (frequency) attributes specify randomness to the placement of the ramp colors throughout the surface.

Using the **HSV Color Noise** attributes, you can specify random noise patterns of Hue, Saturation, and Value to add some interest to your texture. The HSV Noise options are great for making your shader just a bit different, to enhance its look.

Figure 7.19

The Ramp shader

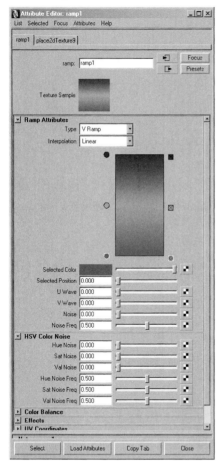

Fractal, Noise, and Mountain Texture

These textures are used to create a random noise pattern to add to an object's **Color**, **Transparency**, or any other shader attribute. For example, when creating a surface, you'll almost always want to add a little dirt or surface blemishes to the shader to make the object look less CG. These textures are commonly used for creating bump maps.

Bulge, Cloth, Checker, Grid, and Water Textures

These textures help create surface features when used on a shader's **Bump Mapping** attribute. Each creates an interesting pattern to add to a surface to create tactile detail, but you can also use them to create color or specular irregularities.

When used as a texture for a bump, grid is useful for creating the spacing between tiles, cloth is perfect for clothing, and checker is good for rubber grips. Placing a water texture on a slight reflection makes for a nice poolside reflection in patio furniture.

The File Node

You use the file node to import image files into Maya for texturing. For instance, if you want to texture a CG face with a digital picture of your own face, you can use the file node to import a Maya-supported image file.

Importing an Image File as a Texture

To attach an image to the color attribute of a Lambert shader (for example), follow these steps:

1. Create the Lambert shader. (Phong, Blinn, or any of the shaders will do.)

2. Click the Map button to map a texture on the **Color** attribute of the new Lambert shader. Select the file node as a normal texture. (You can also use a projected texture with an image file.) The Attribute Editor will show the attribute for the file node.

3. Next to the **Image Name** attribute, click the folder icon to open the file browser. Find the image file of choice on your computer. (It's best to put images to use as textures in the sourceimages folder of the project. As a matter of fact, the file browser will default directly to the sourceimages folder of your current project.) Double-click the file to load it.

4. After you import the image file, it connects to the **Color** attribute of that shader. You can position it as you please by using its Place2dTexture node or by manipulating the projection node, if you created the file texture node as a projection.

You can attach an image file to any attribute of a shader that is mappable, meaning it can accept a texture node. Frequently, image files are used for the color of a shader as well as for bump and transparency maps. You can replace the image file by double-clicking the file texture node in the Hypershade and choosing another image file with the file browser. Maya disconnects the current image file and connects the new file.

Using Photoshop Files: The PSD File Node

Maya can also use Adobe Photoshop PSD files as image files in creating shading networks. The advantage to using PSD files is that you can specify the layers within the Photoshop file to different attributes of the shader as opposed to importing several image files to map onto each shader attribute separately. This, of course, requires a modest knowledge of Photoshop and some experience with Maya shading. As you learn how to shade with Maya, you will come to appreciate the enhancements inherent in using Photoshop networks.

Try This You will create a single Photoshop file that will shade this sphere with color as well as transparency and a bump. Again, this is instead of creating three different image files (such as TIFFs) for each of those shading attributes.

1. Create a NURBS sphere in a new scene, and assign a new Lambert shader to it. You can do this through the Hypershade or the Multilister, or by choosing **Lighting/Shading → Assign New Material → Lambert** in the Rendering menu set. This creates a new shader and assigns it to the selection, in this case your sphere.

2. Select the sphere, and choose **Texturing → Create PSD Network**. In the option box that opens, select color, transparency, and bump from the list of attributes on the left side, and click the right arrow to move them to the Selected Attributes list on the right.

3. Select a location and filename for the image. By default, Maya will place the PSD file it generates under the sourceimages folder of your current project, named after the surface it applies to. Click Create.

4. In Photoshop, open the newly created PSD file and you'll see three layers grouped under three folders named after the shader attributes you selected when creating the PSD file. There will be a folder for lambert2.bump, lambert2.transparency, and lambert2.color, as well as a layer called UVSnapShot. The UVSnapShot layer gives you a wireframe layout of the UVs on the sphere as a guideline to paint your textures. Since the sphere is an easy model, you won't need this layer, so turn it off. You will use UVSnapShots later in this chapter. You can now paint whatever image you want into each of the layers to create maps for each of the shader attributes, all in one convenient file. Save the PSD file. You can save over it or create a new filename for the painted file.

5. In Maya, open the Hypershade and open the Attribute Editor for the Lambert shader assigned to the sphere (in this case, Lambert2). If you graph the connections to the Lambert shader in the Hypershade work window, you'll see that the PSD file you generated is already connected to the color, bump, and transparency attributes of the shader, with the proper layering all set for you.

6. Open the file nodes for the shader and replace the PSD file with your new painted PSD file. If you saved your PSD file with the same name, all you need to do is click the Reload File Texture button to update the psdFilenode.

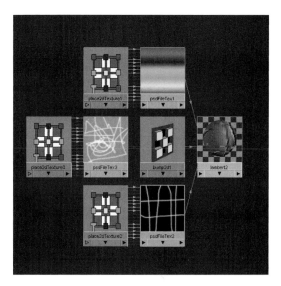

If you decide that you need another attribute added to the PSD file's layering, or if you need to remove an attribute, you can edit the PSD network. Select the shader in the Hypershade and choose **Edit → Edit PSD Network**. In the options window, you can select new attributes to assign to the PSD file, or you can remove existing attributes and their corresponding Photoshop layer groups. Once you click Apply or Edit, Maya saves over the PSD file with the new layout.

3D and Environment Textures

As you saw earlier with the axe, 3D textures are projected within a 3D space. These textures are great for objects that need to reflect an environment, for example.

Instead of simply applying the texture to the plane of the surface as 2D textures do, 3D textures create an area in which the shader is affected. As an object moves through a scene with a 3D placement node, its shader looks as if it swims, unless that placement node is parented or constrained to that object, as you saw with the wood handle of the axe. (For more on constraints, see Chapter 9.)

Disconnecting a Texture

You will find that sometimes the texture you've applied to an object is not what you want and you need to remove it from the shader. To do so, double-click the shader in the Hypershade to open its Attribute Editor.

You can then disconnect an image file or any other texture node from the shader's attribute by RMB clicking the attribute's name in the Attribute Editor and choosing **Break Connection** from the marking menu.

UVs, Polygons, and Images: Color My Pear

Texturing polygons can involve the task of defining UV coordinates for them so you can more easily paint their textures. When you create a NURBS surface, UV coordinates are inherent to the surface. At the origin (or the beginning) of the surface, the UV coordinate is (0,0).

When the surface extends all the way to the left and all the way up, the UV coordinate is (1,1). When you paint an 800×600 pixel image in Photoshop, for example, it's safe to assume that the first pixel of the image (at $X = 0$ and $Y = 0$ in Photoshop) will map directly to the UV coordinate (0,0) on the NURBS surface, while the topmost right corner pixel in the image will map to the UV (1,1) of the surface. To that end, mapping an image to a NURBS surface is fairly straightforward. The bottom of the image will map to the bottom of the surface, the top to the top, and so on. Figure 7.20 shows how an image is mapped onto a NURBS plane and a NURBS sphere. The locations in the image, marked by text, correspond to the positions on the NURBS plane. The sphere, since it is a surface bent around spherically, shows that the origin of the UV coordinates is at the sphere's pole on the left and that the image wraps itself around (bowing out in the middle) to meet at the seam along the front edge shown.

When creating polygons, however, this is not always the case. You will frequently have to create your own UV coordinates on a polygonal surface to get a clean layout on which to paint. While poly UV mapping becomes fairly involved and complicated, it is a concept that is important to grasp early on. When poly models are created, they do have UV coordinates; however, these coordinates may not be laid out in the best way for texture image manipulation.

Figure 7.20

An image file is mapped to a NURBS plane and a NURBS sphere. Notice the locations marked in the image and how they map to the locations on the surface, with the pixel coordinates directly corresponding to the surface's UV coordinates.

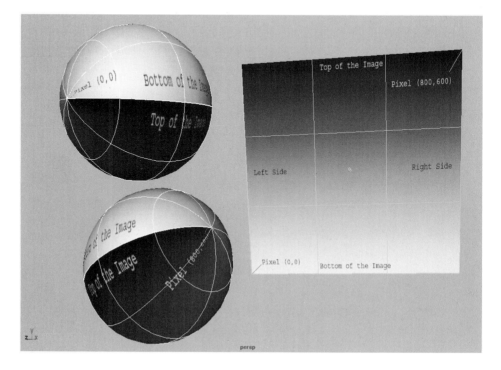

Open the scene file `pear_texture_v01.mb` from the Lighting project on the CD. This file contains a poly model of a pear, seen in examples throughout this book. Select the pear in the perspective window, and in one of your orthogonal views, choose **Panels → Panel → UV Texture Editor**. The viewport now turns into the UV Texture Editor and displays the UV layout for the selected pear (bottom left).

In practice, to color this poly pear you would need to paint an image file so that the colors and pixels of the image line up with the layout you see in the UV Texture Editor. This is not a very clean UV layout and will make for an impossible time painting in Photoshop. You can alter the UV set and give the pear a cleaner UV layout to make your image painting much easier.

With the pear still selected, enter the Polygons menu set and choose **Create UVs → Cylindrical Mapping**. This will create a cylindrical projection node to fit around the pear. By default it should be placed around the pear to create a new UV layout that will make it far easier to paint a texture image to map to the pear. It will, however, be a little too wide to fit into a typical UV axis, so in the UV Texture Editor, select **Polygons → Normalize** to fit the wireframe layout to within a range of 0 to 1 UVs (bottom right).

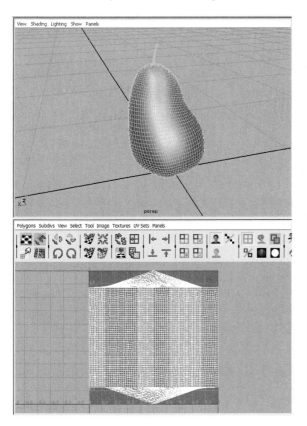

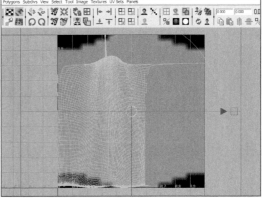

To be able to see this wireframe layout in an image editor such as Photoshop, make sure the pear is selected, and in the UV Texture Editor window, choose **Polygons → UV Snapshot**. In the option box, select the location of the output file, and change Size X and Size Y to 512 each. Change Image Format to TIFF for the widest compatibility with image programs, and click OK. This will write out the wireframe UV layout you see in the UV Texture Editor to a TIFF file so you can use it as a guideline to paint your pear's texture. The resulting image file is shown in Figure 7.21.

Once you open this TIFF file in Photoshop or another editor, use it as a blueprint to paint the pear as if you're painting a piece of foil that would wrap around an actual model, as shown with the UV wireframe overlaid temporarily as you paint.

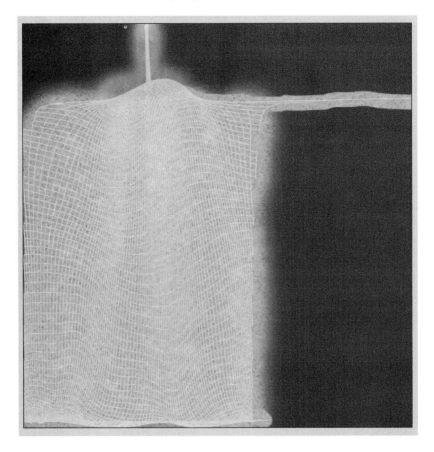

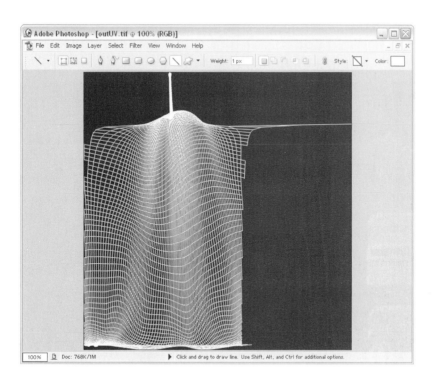

Figure 7.21

The pear's UV coordinates are written out to a TIFF file for reference in an image editor such as Adobe Photoshop.

This ensures that the green part of the pear is painted and mapped to the proper area of the pear surface, while the stem gets its proper color. Just apply the proper shader to the pear, like the Blinn used in the sample file, and import your pear image file for its color attribute as discussed earlier in the chapter. Figure 7.22 shows the pear rendered with an image map painted to its UV coordinates in Photoshop.

Figure 7.22

The pear's painted image texture is applied.

As your polygon models become more complex, UV texture editing will become more complex. You will frequently need to adjust UVs, lay them out again, move particular UVs around on the mesh, and so forth. This is, however, beyond the scope of a beginner's text. Though it is important to at least be exposed to this texturing methodology now, you will more than likely not use UV editing until you are much more experienced with modeling and texturing.

Summary

In this chapter you learned about the types of shaders and how they work. Each shader has a set of attributes that give the material definition and was covered to give you an understanding of how each attribute affects the look of your models. You then textured the axe modeled in Chapter 5 using various shaders, including the Layered shader, to create a wooden handle with a metal tip. We then looked at the methods you can use to project textures onto a surface and how you can bake these projections onto an object to avoid "swimming." You learned about Maya's texture nodes, including PSD networks and the basics of UVs and how they work to place images onto your models by going through an exercise to texture a pear.

Texturing a scene is never an isolated process. Making textures work involves render settings, lighting, and even geometry manipulation and creation. Your work in this chapter will be expanded on in Chapters 10 and 11 with discussions on lighting and rendering.

Just like everything else in Maya, it's all collaboration, and the more experience you gain, the more you'll see how everything intertwines.

But for Maya to be an effective tool for you, it's important to have a clear understanding of the look you want for your CG. This involves plenty of clear research into your project, downloading heaps of images to use as reference, and a good measure of trial and error.

The single best weapon in your arsenal in texturing, and indeed in all aspects of CG art, is your eye, your observations of the world around you, and how they relate to the world you're creating in CG.

CHAPTER 8

Introduction to Animation

The best way to start learning about animation is to start animating, so you'll begin this chapter with the classic exercise of bouncing a ball. You'll then take a closer look at the animation tools Maya software provides and how they work for your scene. You'll do that by throwing the axe you created earlier, and finally you'll tackle animating a more complex system of parts when you bring your locomotive to life.

Topics include:

- Keyframe Animation—Bouncing a Ball
- Throwing an Axe
- Path Animation
- Replacing an Object
- Creating and Deforming Text along a Path
- Rigging the Locomotive, Part One
- Animating a Catapult

Keyframe Animation—Bouncing a Ball

A classic exercise for all animators is creating a bouncing ball. Although it's a straightforward exercise, you can imbue so much character into the ball that the possibilities are almost endless. Animating a bouncing ball is a good exercise in physics, as well as cartoon movement. You'll first create a rubber ball, and then you'll add cartoonish movement to accentuate some principles of the animation techniques discussed in Chapter 1.

Creating a Cartoon Ball

First you need to create the ball, as well as the project for this exercise. Follow these steps:

1. In a new scene, begin with a NURBS sphere, create a poly plane, and scale it up to be the ground plane.

2. Press 5 for shaded mode. Select the ball, and press 3 for a smooth view of the sphere.

3. Move the sphere 1.0 unit up in the Y axis so it's resting on the ground, as shown here, and not halfway through it.

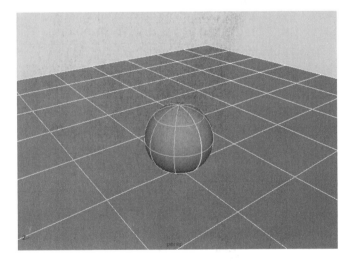

4. Choose **Modify → Freeze Transformations** to set the ball's resting height to 0 as opposed to 1. This action will set the ball's **Translate** attribute back to 0, effectively "resetting" the object. This is called *freezing the transforms*. This is useful when you position, scale, and orient an object and need to set its new location, orientation, and size as the beginning state.

5. Choose **File → Project → New** to create a new project. Call the project bouncing_ball, and place it in the same folder as the solar system project. Click the Use Defaults button to create the necessary folders in your project, and then click Accept. Save the scene file into that project.

Beginners' Gallery

On the following pages, you will find a combination of images from the book and images created by a few artists fairly new to Maya. We hope these images will inspire your own creativity as you become more familiar with 3D in general and Maya specifically.

Some of these artists have been using Maya for only a short period of time and already they've been able to use the tools and techniques they've learned to channel their artistic eye and creativity into some beautiful and interesting imagery.

This still life from Chapter 10 was modeled and textured by Maya students Juan Guitierrez and Robert Jauregui. The fruit still life was modeled by Guitierrez using mostly polygons. The textures were created by Jauregui, who took this opportunity to learn all about UV texture space and mapping polygons since this was his first texturing experience inside Maya. Dariush Derakhshani laid out the scene, lit it, and rendered it to show off Maya's rendering and lighting capabilities.

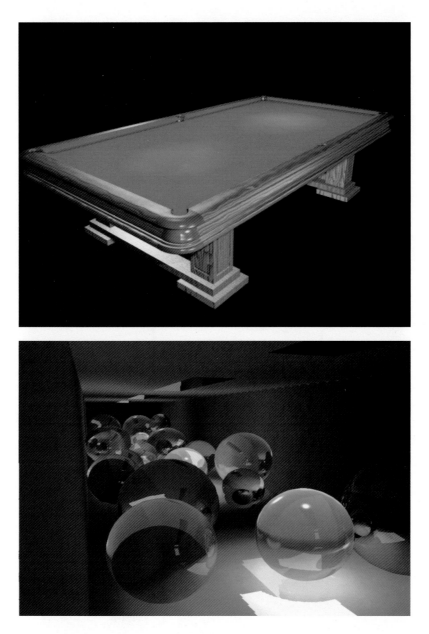

ABOVE: This pool table was modeled by Victor Garza to demonstrate modeling techniques in an introductory Maya class and to show the students how to be creative in putting surfaces together to form a complex object. Once Garza modeled the table, he and Dariush Derakhshani textured and lit the scene. **BELOW:** Dariush Derakhshani created this box full of marbles to test out mental ray for Maya and its capabilities. The scene is made of very simple geometry, with the majority of the work going into lighting and rendering using mental ray for Maya.

ABOVE: A color render of the living room scene. This was modeled by Huyen Dang of The Art Institute of California at Los Angeles for a lighting class and was lighted by Dariush Derakhshani as an example of Global Illumination in mental ray for Maya. The color render will be enhanced with the addition of an Ambient Occlusion pass to add detail and contact shadows. **CENTER:** An Ambient Occlusion render creates contact shadows and some further detail in the dark areas of the image to enhance the look of the color render itself. **BELOW:** This pass is multiplied in a compositing package to add realism to obtain the comp shown.

ABOVE: Benjamin Hendricks created this worm to be composited into the still image. Using careful lighting to match the plate, Benjamin made sure the worm looks like it belongs in the scene. **BELOW:** Daniel George of Piedmont Community College created this abstract monument and used colored lighting to play with the color and contrast of the image. His colorful specular highlights create a nice effect on the contours of the model. The glow is created with a Glow attribute on the sphere's shaders.

Benjamin Hendricks created this plane for his USC thesis film Hircine Airlines. The airplane is inspired by the Titanic and the Spruce Goose and is designed to be massive to make a large impact. Notice how the mental ray lighting creates smooth shadows and gives this mammoth structure good areas of detail.

ABOVE: Yoom Thawilvejakul created this scene for his USC animated film Sunday Party. He created and rigged the strange creatures and rendered them with Maya Software rendering for a stylized cartoon look. He painted the background and composited the scene together using Adobe After Effects.

BELOW: From Daniel George of Piedmont Community College, this abstract tower was built and lit in Maya for class. For the main structure he used a surface extruded along a curve and lattices to create the shape with a Chrome shader applied. The background was created in Photoshop and put onto a plane in Maya. Daniel then used light linking to give the plane a single, even source of illumination. The lights on the ends of the spikes are spheres with a 0.5 intensity glow.

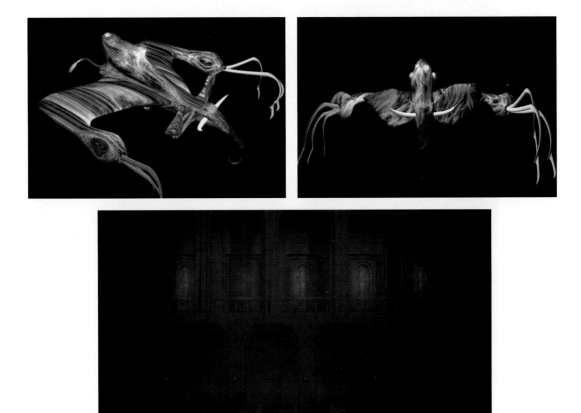

ABOVE: (left and right): This model from Sophie Ohara was made using polygons and the Extrude Faces tool. She began by modeling a simple airplane and then from this framework she extruded faces and successively scaled them down to create elephant ears, tusks, a trunk, squid-like tentacles, and unsquid-like claws. Sophie added a 2D texture projection of rabbit fur to the model, followed by a poly smooth, and finally point lights with a halo glow effect were placed throughout the model. **BELOW**: Jason Martin created this render for a cinematic-style game animation he created for his class at Piedmont Community College. There is a careful use of geometry and texturing to maximize the look without overdoing the geometry, which is perfect for gaming content creation.

Animating the Ball

Your next step is to keyframe the positions of the ball. As introduced in Chapter 1, *keyframing* is the process—borrowed from traditional animation—of setting positions and values at particular frames of the animation. The computer interpolates between these keyframes to fill in the other frames to complete a smooth animation.

You'll start with the "*gross animation*," or the overall movements. This is also widely known as *blocking*. First, move the ball up and down to begin its choreography. Follow these steps to set up the scene and animate the ball:

1. Press W to open the Translate tool, select the sphere, and move it up to the top of the frame, say about 10 units up in the Y axis. Place the camera so that you'll have some room to work in the frame. Next, you'll set keyframes.

2. Instead of selecting the **Translate** attributes in the Channel Box and pressing S as you did in Chapter 3 to set keyframes on the planets, you'll set keyframes for translation in an easier way:

   Press Shift+W to set keyframes on **Translate X**, **Translate Y**, and **Translate Z** at frame 1. To make sure your scene is set up properly, set your animation speed to 30fps by choosing **Window → Settings/Preferences → Preferences** to open the Preferences window or by clicking the Animation Preferences button (🖾) next to the Auto-Key button. In the Settings category of the Preferences window, set **Time** to NTSC (30 fps). A frame range of 1–120 is good for now.

3. Click the Auto Keyframe button (🔳) to turn it on, turning it red. Auto Keyframe automatically sets a keyframe at the current time for any attribute that has changed since its last keyframe for the selected object.

> For the Auto Keyframe feature to work, you have to manually set the initial keyframe for any of the attributes you want to animate.

4. Now you need to set down gross animation keyframes to choreograph the overall movement. Disregarding any specific timing, go to frame 10, and move the ball down in the Y axis until it is about one-quarter through the ground plane. Since you'll be creating squash and stretch (see Chapter 1 for a brief explanation) for this cartoon ball, you'll need to send the ball through the ground a little bit. The Auto Keyframe feature sets a keyframe in the Y axis at frame 10.

5. Move to frame 20, and raise the ball back up to about three-quarters of its original height (about 7.5 units in the Y axis). Auto Keyframe sets a **Y Translation** keyframe at frame 20 and will continue to set keyframes for the ball as you animate.

6. At frame 30, place the ball back down a little bit less than one-quarter of the way through the ground.

7. At frame 40, place the ball back up in the air in the Y axis at about half its original height (5 in Y).

8. Repeat this procedure until you have bounced the ball a few more times. Make sure you are decreasing the ball's height at the crest with each successive bounce and decreasing how much it passes through the ground with every landing. Open the Graph Editor for a peek into the ball's animation curves. (Choose **Window → Animation Editors → Graph Editor**.) You'll pick up this exercise after a look at the Graph Editor.

By holding down Shift as you pressed W in step 2, you set a keyframe for **Translate**; you can also keyframe **Rotation** or **Scale**. Here's a summary of the keystrokes for setting keyframes:

Shift+W	Sets a keyframe for the selection's position in all three axes at the current time
Shift+E	Sets a keyframe for the selection's rotation in all three axes at the current time
Shift+R	Sets a keyframe for the selection's scale in all three axes at the current time

The Graph Editor

The Graph Editor is a critical tool for an animator. You provide most of an animation's finesse through work in this window. As a matter of fact, you can animate a number of objects solely through this window. (See Chapter 2 for an introduction to the Graph Editor.) Using its graph view of where in space and time each keyframe lies, you can conveniently control your animation. Move a keyframe in time to the right, for example, to slow the action. Move the same keyframe to the left in time to speed up the action.

Reading the Curves in the Graph Editor

Understanding what animation curves do in the Graph Editor is crucial to getting your animation right. Using the Graph Editor to read *animation curves*, you can judge an object's direction, speed, acceleration, and timing.

As you will see later in this chapter with the axe-throwing tutorial, you will invariably come across problems and issues with your animation that require a careful review of their curves. Being able to see a curve and translate it into what your object is doing comes with time and practice. Be patient, and don't be afraid to open the Graph Editor and animate through it as much as you can.

First, the curves in the Graph Editor are like the NURBS curves you've modeled with so far. Instead of CVs on a NURBS curve controlling the curvature, points directly on an animation curve represent keyframes and control the curvature with their *tangency handles*. By grabbing one end of a key's handle and dragging it up or down, you adjust the curve.

Second, the graph is a representation of an object attribute's position (vertical) over time (horizontal). Every place on the curve represents where the object is in that axis; there needn't be a keyframe on the curve. Not only does the placement of the keys on the curve make a big difference, so does the shape of the curve itself. Here then is a quick primer on how to read a curve in the Graph Editor and, hence, how to edit it.

In Figure 8.1, the object's **Translate Z** attribute is being animated. At the beginning, the curve begins quickly to move positively (that is, to the right) in the Z axis. The object shoots off to the right and comes to an *ease-out*, where it decelerates to a stop. The stop is signified by the flat part of the curve at the first keyframe at frame 41. The object then quickly accelerates in the negative Z direction (left) and maintains a fairly even speed until it hits frame 62, where it suddenly changes direction and goes back right for about 45 frames. It then slowly decelerates to a full stop in an ease-out.

Consider a single object in motion. The shape of the curve in the Graph Editor defines how the object moves. The object shown animated in Figure 8.2 is moving in a steady manner in one direction.

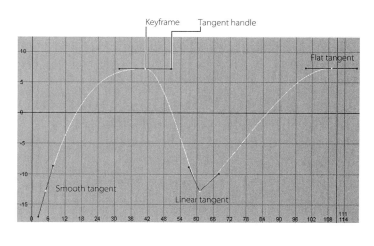

Figure 8.1

An animation curve

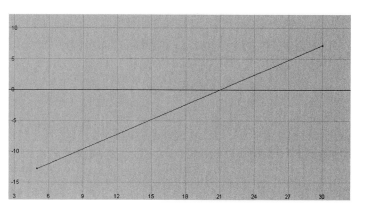

Figure 8.2

Linear movement

Figure 8.3 shows the object slowly accelerating toward frame 30, where it suddenly comes to a stop. If there is nothing beyond the end of the curve, there is no motion. The one exception deals with the *infinity* of curves, which is discussed shortly.

The object in Figure 8.4 begins moving immediately and comes to a slow stop by frame 27, where the curve first becomes flat.

Cartoon Ball

Now let's apply what you've learned about the Graph Editor to the bouncing ball. Follow these steps:

1. Open the Graph Editor and take a look at the ball's animation curves. They should be similar to the curves in Figure 8.5.

2. Notice how only the Y axis translate has a curve, and yet the **Translate X**, **Translate Y**, and **Translate Z** attributes have keyframes in the left column. This is from the initial position keyframe you set at frame 1. And since you've only moved the sphere in the Y axis, Auto-Key has only set Y keys. If you don't have animation on something, it is better not to set keyframes on those attributes. Keep your scene clean.

Figure 8.3

Acceleration (ease-in)

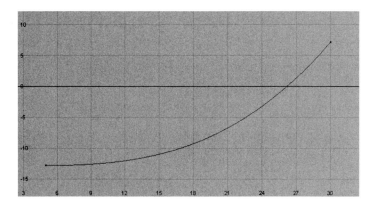

Figure 8.4

Deceleration (ease-out)

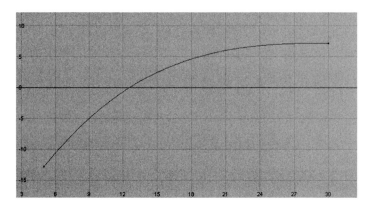

3. Playback the animation and see how it feels. Be sure to open the Animation Preferences window—click the Animation Preferences icon (🖾) to set the playback speed to Real-Time (30fps). You'll find this icon in the Playback section in the Timeline category.

4. Timing is the main issue now, so you're concerned with how fast the ball falls and bounces:

   • The ball is falling too fast initially, although the second and third bounces should look fine.

   • To fix the timing, move the keyframes in the Graph Editor. Select the keyframe at frame 10 and all the others beyond it. Move them all back two frames. (See Figure 8.6.)

   • As the ball's bounce decays over time, it goes up less but still takes the same amount of time (10 frames) to go up the lesser distance. For better timing, adjust the last few bounces to occur faster. Select the keys on the last three bounces and move them, one by one, a frame or two to the left to decrease the time on the last short bounces. (See Figure 8.7.)

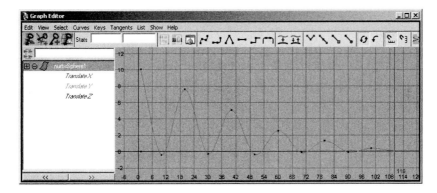

Figure 8.5

The ball's animation curves. Note how the height decays over time.

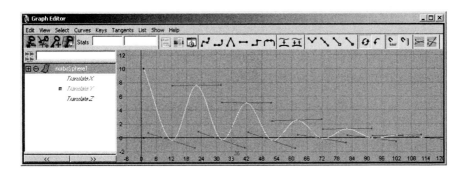

Figure 8.6

Move all the keyframes to the right to slow the initial fall by two frames, but leave the timing the same for the rest.

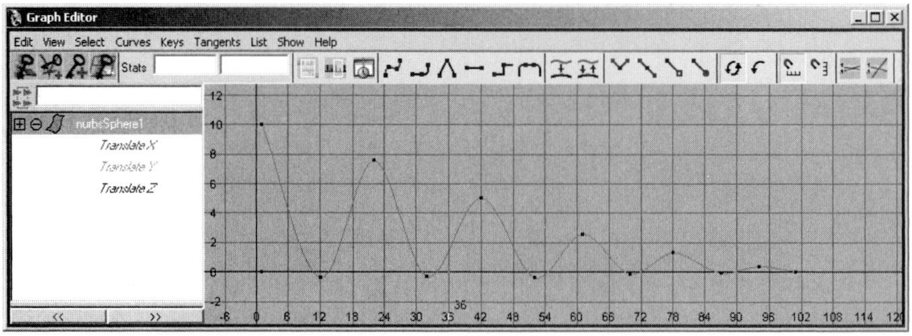

Figure 8.7

Move the keys to the left to make the final short bounces quicker.

To move a key in the Graph Editor, press W to open the Move tool, and MMB move the key as you drag the cursor in the Graph Editor window. Press the Shift key and drag the cursor left and right or up and down to lock the movement to either horizontal or vertical to make it easier to control.

Understanding Timing

In animation, timing is all about getting keyframes in proper order. Judging the speed of an object in animation is critical to getting it to look right, and that comes down to timing. The more you animate, the better your timing, which is why the bouncing ball is such a popular exercise.

Load the file ball_v02.mb from the bouncing_ball project on the CD to get to this point.

When you playback the animation, it should look more natural. But it still looks fake, as if it were rising and falling on a wave as opposed to really bouncing. You still need to edit the timing of the ball. The problem with the animation is that the ball eases in and out as it rises and falls. By default, setting a key in Maya sets the keyframes to have an ease-in and ease-out in their curves, meaning their curves will be smooth like a NURBS curve.

Because of the smooth animation curve, the ball does not look natural in its timing. You need to accelerate the ball as it falls with a sharp valley in the curve, and you need to decelerate it as it rises, with smooth peaks. Follow these steps:

1. In the Graph Editor, select all the landing keyframes (the ones in the valleys of the curve) and change their *interpolation* from smooth to linear by clicking the Linear Tangents button (Λ).

2. Likewise, select all the peak keyframes at the ball's rise, and change their tangents to flat by clicking the Flat Tangents icon (⊢) to make the animation curve like the one shown in Figure 8.8.

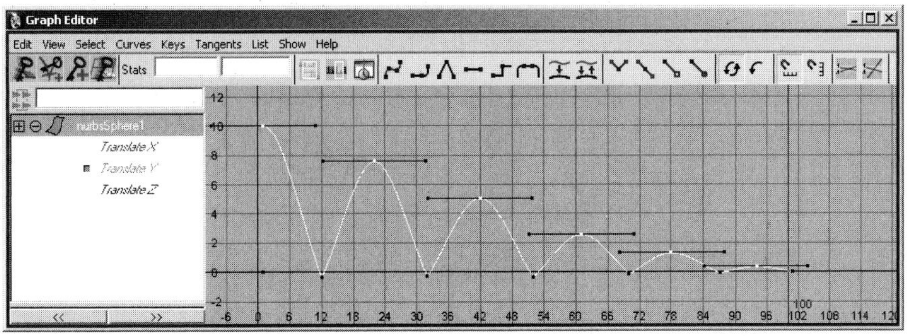

Figure 8.8

The adjusted timing of the bounce

3. When you playback the animation, you'll see that the ball seems like it's moving much more realistically. If you need to, adjust the keys a bit more to get the timing feeling right before you move on to squash and stretch.

Squash and Stretch

The idea of *squash and stretch* has been an animation staple for as long as there has been animation. It is a way to convey the weight of an object by deforming it to react (usually in an exaggerated way) to gravity and motion.

In Maya, you use the Scale tool to squash and stretch your object—in this case, your ball.

Load the file `ball_v03.mb` from the bouncing_ball project on the CD and follow these steps:

1. To initiate squash and stretch, go to frame 12, the first time the ball hits the floor. Press R to open the Scale tool, and scale the ball down in the Y axis until it no longer goes through the floor (about 0.6). Set a keyframe for all the scale axes by pressing Shift+R.

2. Move ahead in the animation about three frames to frame 15, and scale the ball up in the Y axis slightly past normal to stretch it up (about 1.3) right after its bounce. Three frames later at frame 18, set the Y axis scale back to 1.

3. Scrub your animation. The ball stays squashed at the beginning of the animation; that's because you didn't set a key before it hit the ground. Back up to frame 9, and reset the Y axis scale to 1 in the Channel Box. Scrub your animation again, and the ball begins stretching even before it hits the ground. That's a bit too much exaggeration, so open the Graph Editor and move the Y axis scale key from 9 to 11. Now the ball will squash when it hits the floor and stretch as it bounces up.

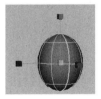

4. Repeat this procedure for the remaining bounces, squashing the ball as it hits the floor and stretching it as it bounces up. Remember to decay the scale factor as the ball's bouncing decays to a stop, as when we decayed the height of the ball's bounce earlier. The final bounce or two should have very little squash and stretch, if any.

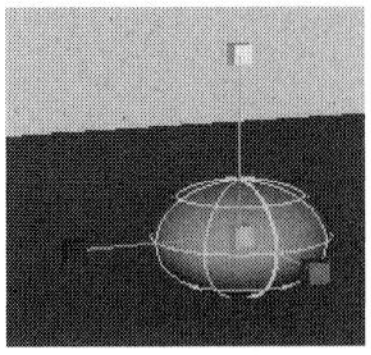

Load the file `ball_v04.mb` from the bouncing_ball project on the CD to see an example. Although the bouncing of this ball looks okay, it could definitely use some finesse, a little timing change, and so on. Open the file, open the Graph Editor, and edit the file to get a feel for how the ball bounces.

Throwing an Axe

This next project will exercise your use of hierarchies and introduce you to creating and refining motion to achieve proper animation for a more complex scene than the bouncing ball. The work flow is simple but standard for properly setting up a scene for animation, also known as *rigging*, especially for more complex objects, as you will see later in this and the next chapter when we rig the locomotive for animation. First, you'll model an axe and a target, and then you'll set up the grouping and pivots for how you want to animate. Then you throw!

Why won't you use the NURBS axe you've already created and textured? Because later in this chapter you'll use that for an exercise on importing and replacing an object in Maya while keeping the animation intact.

The Preproduction Process

To begin the animation right away, you'll create a basic axe, focusing on the animation and the technique. To this end, connect to the Internet if you can, and look up axes and the art of axe throwing to get more familiar with the task at hand. You will also need to create a simple bull's-eye target at which to throw your axe, so look for some references for a target as well.

Create a new project; choose **File → Project → New**. Place this project in the same folder or drive as your other projects, and call it axe_anim so as not to confuse it with your earlier axe_model project. Click the Defaults button to fill in the rest and click Accept. Click the Animation Preferences button, and set the frames per second to 30fps. Later, you'll replace this simple axe with the NURBS axe you modeled in Chapter 5 and textured in Chapter 7 to learn how to properly replace objects and transfer animation in Maya.

Setting Up the Scene

To get started, model the axe and target from primitives and set up their grouping and pivots. Once your scene is set up properly, you will animate. It's important to a healthy work flow that you make sure the scene is set up well before you begin animating.

Making the Axe

The axe will be made of two polygon primitives, a cylinder and a cube. Follow these steps:

1. Choose **Create → Polygon Primitives → Cube ❐**. Set Subdivisions Along Width to 4, and click Create.

2. Call this axe_head.

3. Choose **Create → Polygon Primitives → Cylinder** to create a cylinder to be the handle for your axe, and call it handle.

4. Scale the cylinder so that it's about ½ unit across and about 14 units tall.

5. Move the cube to the top of the cylinder, leaving just a little of the tip showing, and scale it so that it's about 3 units high and 4 units wide in the front view. (See Figure 8.9.)

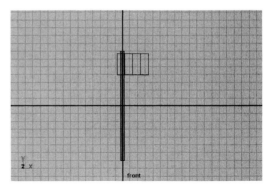

Figure 8.9

Placing the axe's head on the handle

6. Scale the cube in the Z axis so that it's just a little thicker than the handle.

7. To put a sharp edge on the axe, go into component mode (press F8) and select the four vertices on the very end of the cube.

   • Press R to activate the Scale tool.

   • Scale the vertices down in the Z axis to a sharp edge, and scale them slightly up in the Y axis.

   • Select the next four vertices in from the edge. Scale them down in the X axis about halfway, and scale them slightly up in the Y axis. (See Figure 8.10.)

> Most animation work does not depend on precise measurements. The key is using proportions and relative sizes. You can almost always use Maya's generic units (which are set to centimeters by default). The scope of your project will determine if greater precision is necessary.

Figure 8.10

Creating a sharp edge for the axe

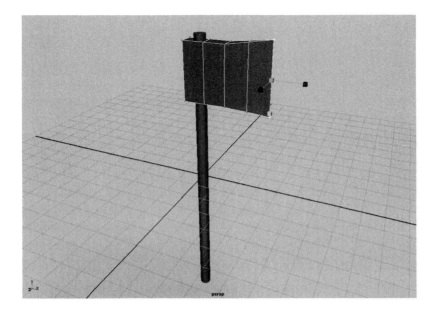

8. Press F8 to get back into object mode, and select both pieces.

9. Choose **Edit → Group** to group the pieces into one hierarchy, and call it axe.

Now, you need to identify the *center of balance* for this axe. Doing so gives you the place for your pivot point. Since the heaviest part of this axe is the head, the center of balance will be toward the top of the handle. In addition, your axe head protrudes in only one direction, so the balance point is a unit or two away from the handle.

10. Press Insert to activate the pivot manipulator, and move the pivot just under the axe head and about 1 unit from the handle, as in Figure 8.11.

Your scene should now look like the file axe_v1.mb in the scenes folder of the axe_anim project on the CD.

Making the Target

Move the axe about 40 units in the negative X axis away from the origin to make some room for the throw, and move it about 15 units up in the Y axis. Now you need to create a simple target for your axe to hit. Follow these steps:

1. Start with a polygonal cylinder.

2. Scale down the cylinder's height to make it squat, and rotate it just a bit past being perpendicular to the ground, facing somewhat toward the sky.

3. Scale the cylinder up about seven times its original size.

Now you need to create a simple stand to put the target on. Follow these steps:

1. Choose **Create → Polygon Primitives → Cube** for the base.

2. Scale the cube so that the target fits on the base with some room to spare.

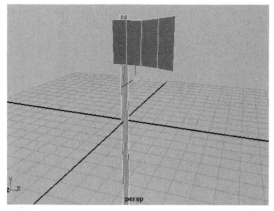

Figure 8.11

Finding the axe's center of balance gives you the proper place for its pivot point.

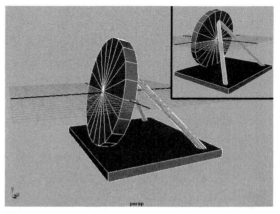

Figure 8.12

Positioning the cross braces for the target

3. Choose **Create → Polygon Primitives → Cylinder** to create two cylinders to make a cross brace for the back of the target.

4. Scale, rotate, and position the cylinders to fit behind the target and into the back of the base. Figure 8.12 shows the positions of the pieces to make up the target.

5. Once you're happy with the target, group the four objects together and name the group Target.

6. Move the target about 40 units in the positive X axis away from the origin, and move it up in the Y axis so its base is basically on the ground plane.

7. Press Insert to move the target's pivot point to the bottom of the base, right where the cross beams connect to it. Figure 8.13 shows the proper pivot placement.

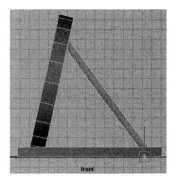

Figure 8.13

The proper placement of the target's pivot point

You're placing the pivot point at that location because the target will jerk up and back a little bit when the axe hits it. This is the best point for you to rotate around to lift the front of the base up a little to make it look like the axe is really hitting it. Save your file as your next version number. The scene is now ready for animation!

Preproduction: Keyframes and Motion Study

What separates good animation from bad animation is the feeling of weight that the audience infers from the animation. Being lifelong observers of natural physics, we all instinctively understand how nature works in motion. We see an object in motion, how it moves, and how it affects its surroundings. From that, we can feel its essence of motion, with its weight making a distinct, albeit subliminal, impression on us. As it pertains to animation, that essence is simply called *weight*, and its observation is called *motion study*.

Unfortunately, merely knowing how something should look while moving is not quite all you'll need to animate it properly. Giving the axe believable weight is your primary job as an animator. You need to make the audience feel as if that CG axe is really moving. Modeling, texturing, and lighting are a small part of it, but motion can make or break the animation. Creating a convincing scene takes compelling motion. And creating compelling motion requires close observation.

A good feeling of weight in animation depends on timing and follow-through, which require practice.

It's a good idea to first try out an action you want to animate. It's not a great idea to grab a real axe and start throwing it around your house. But you can take a pen, remove its cap, and lob it across the room. Notice how it arcs through the air, how it spins around its center of balance, and how it hits its mark. Now put the cap on the pen, lob it again, and notice the subtle yet instrumental differences in motion caused by the cap's mass.

As an animator, this experimentation is part of your preproduction and motion study. It is important to have as thorough an understanding of your subject matter as possible. Just try not to take out anyone's eye with the pen.

According to some Internet research, the perfect axe throw should contain as few spins as possible. This is good information to know, as it will shape your animation and come in handy if you're ever cornered in a hatchet shop.

Animating the Axe: Keyframing Gross Animation

The next step is to keyframe the positions of the axe, starting with the gross animation—the movement from one end of the axe's trajectory to the other.

Setting Initial Keyframes

You can start within your current scene or load the unanimated, premade axe and target from the CD (axe_v2.mb in the scenes folder of the axe_anim project). Follow these steps:

1. Select the axe's top group node—and not just the pieces. To make selecting groups like this easier, display the object's selection handle. To do so, select the axe's top node and choose **Display → Transform Display → Selection Handles**. This will display a small cross at the pivot point of the axe called a *selection handle* (✦). You need only select this handle to select the top node of the axe.

> As you will see later in this chapter's catapult exercise, you can use selection handles to select the children of a group as well as the top node.

Since this node is the parent node of the axe, the selection handle displays as a hollow cross at the node's current pivot point.

> You can turn on selection handles for practically any object in Maya, no matter where it is in a group's hierarchy—whether it is a child or a parent. If it is not the top node, the selection handle appears as a regular cross (+).

2. With the axe selected, go to frame 1, and set a keyframe for the rotation and translation.
3. Hold down Shift and press W for the axe's translation keyframe, and press Shift+E for the axe's rotation keyframe. You won't need to set a scale keyframe on the axe by pressing Shift+R because you won't be changing its size. Once you're done, you have the initial keyframes for the axe at its start position.

Creating Anticipation

Instead of the axe just flying through the air toward the target, you'll animate the axe moving back first to create *anticipation*, as if an invisible arm were pulling the axe back just before throwing it. Follow these steps:

1. Go to frame 15.
2. Move the axe back in the X axis about 8 units, and rotate it counterclockwise about 45 degrees.
3. The Auto Keyframe feature will set keyframes for the position and new rotation at frame 15.

Since you've only moved the axe back in the X axis and made the rotation on the Z axis, Auto Keyframe sets keyframes only for **Translate X** and **Rotate Z**. The other position and rotation axes were not keyframed, since their values did not change.

4. Scrub through the animation, and notice how the axe moves back in anticipation.

> Auto Keyframe inserts a keyframe at the current time for the selected object's changed attributes only.

5. Go to frame 40, and move the axe so that its blade cuts into the center of the target.

Notice that you will have to move the axe in the X and Y axes, whereas before you only had to move it back in the X axis to create anticipation. This is because the axis of motion for the axe rotates along with the axe. This is called the Local Axis. The *Local Axis* for any given object shifts according to the object's orientation. Since you angled the axe back about 45 degrees, its Local Axis rotated back the same amount.

The file axe_v3.mb in the scenes folder of the axe_anim project on the CD will catch you up to this point in the animation.

This last step will reveal a problem with the animation. If you scrub your animation now, you'll notice that the axe's movement back is now different from before, setting a keyframe at frame 40.

This is because of the *Auto Keyframe* feature. At frame 1, you set an initial keyframe for all axes of translation and rotation. Then, at frame 15, you moved the axe back in the X axis only (in addition to rotating it in the Z axis only).

Auto Keyframe set a keyframe for **Translate X** at frame 15. At frame 40, you moved the axe in *both* the X and Y axes to strike the target. Auto Keyframe set a keyframe at 40 for **Translate X** and **Translate Y**. But since the last keyframe for **Translate Y** was set at 1 and not at 15 as **Translate X** was, there is now a bobble in the Y position of the axe between frames 1 and 15.

With the axe selected, open the Graph Editor (choose **Window → Animation Editors → Graph Editor**) to see what's happening here. As you saw in the bouncing ball exercise, using the Graph Editor is crucial, and the more practice you get with it, the better.

When you open the Graph Editor for this scene, you should see red, green, and blue line segments running up and down, left and right. You will probably have to zoom your view to something more intelligible. You can navigate the Graph Editor much as you can any of the modeling windows by using the Alt key (you can use either the Alt key or the Alt/Option key on a Mac) and mouse button combinations.

The hot keys A and F also work in the Graph Editor. Click anywhere in the Graph Editor window to make sure it's the active window, and press A to zoom all your curves into view. Your window should look something like Figure 8.14.

The curves in the Graph Editor represent the values of the axe's position and rotation at any given time. The three axes are in their representative red, green, or blue color, and the specific attributes are listed much as they are in the Outliner in the left column. Selecting an object or an attribute on the left displays its curves on the right.

You should also notice that the curves are all at different scales. The three rotate curves range in value from about –45 to 45, the **Translate Y** curve ranges from about 15 to 5, and the **Translate Z** looks flat in the Graph Editor. You can select the specific attribute and zoom in on its curve to see it better, or now with Maya 7, you can normalize the curves so that you can see them all in one view. Click the N icon in the top icon bar of the Graph Editor. This will *normalize* the view of all the curves within a scale of –1 to 1 to allow you to see the relative movement of all the curves at once. Figure 8.15 shows the Graph Editor from Figure 8.14 once it is normalized. Keep in mind this does not change the animation in the slightest. All it does is allow you to see all the curves and their relative motion. You can denormalize the view by pressing the D icon in the Graph Editor. Normalizing your view is particularly helpful in busy scenes when you want to adjust the smallest scale of values alongside the largest scale of values without having to constantly zoom in and out of the Graph Editor to see the appropriate curves.

Notice that the **Scale** attributes on the axe are not shown in this window; only animated attributes appear here.

Figure 8.14

The Graph Editor displays the axe's animation curves.

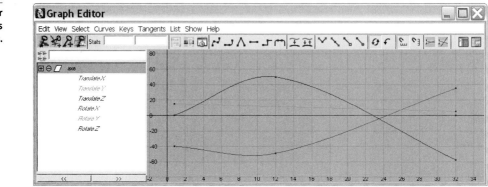

Also notice that the curve for **Translate Y** has keyframes only at frames 1 and 40. The animation dips in the first 15 frames because there is no keyframe at frame 15 as there is for **Translate Z**. That dip was not there before you set the end keyframe at frame 40.

6. Move the first keyframe of **Translate Y** from frame 1 to frame 15 to fix the dip.

   - Press W to activate the Move tool in Maya, or click the Move Nearest Picked Key icon (![icon]) in the Graph Editor.

   - Click the Time Snap icon (![icon]) to toggle it on.

   - Select the offending **Translate Y** keyframe at frame 1, and MMB move it to the right until it's at frame 15.

Scrub your animation, and the backward movement will look as it did before. You might have prevented this problem by manually setting your keyframes for the axe instead of using Auto Keyframe. But the more you work with Maya, the more valuable you'll find Auto Keyframe (although plenty if people get by without it just fine).

The axe now needs an arc on its way to the target.

7. Go to the middle of the axe's flight, frame 27.

8. Move the axe up in the Y axis a bit using the green handle of the tool manipulator.

Auto Keyframe can set a key for both **Translate Y** and **Translate X** if the axe is slightly rotated in frame, though you were perhaps expecting only a key in **Translate Y**. Since the Move tool is on the axe's Local Axis, and since the axe was slightly rotated at frame 27, there is a change in the Y and X position in the World Axis, which is the axis represented in the Graph Editor.

9. Select the **Translate X** key at frame 27, if one was created, and press Delete to delete it.

Now you add a full spin to the axe to give the animation more reality and life. You can spin it in one of two ways:

- Go to frame 40, select the axe, and rotate it clockwise a full 360 degrees positive. Auto Keyframe will enter a new rotation value at frame 40, overwriting the old value. You should see the **Rotate Z** curve angle down steeply as soon as you let go of the rotate manipulator.

- In the Graph Editor, make sure you're at frame 40, grab the last keyframe on the **Rotate Z** curve, and MMB move it down, probably past the lower limit of the window. If you keep the middle mouse button pressed as you move the mouse, the keyframe will keep moving as you move the mouse, even if the keyframe has left the visible bounds of the Graph Editor.

If you hold down Shift as you MMB drag the keyframe to move it in the Graph Editor, the keyframe will move in only one axis (up or down, left or right).

Figure 8.15

The normalized view
in the Graph Editor,
new to Maya 7, lets
you see all the
curves of an anima-
tion together in the
same scale.

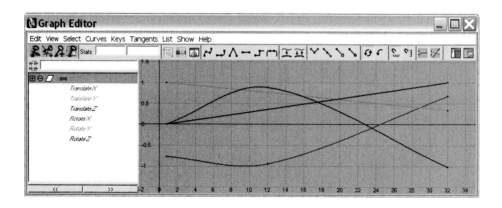

By moving the keyframe down, you're changing the **Rotate Z** value to a lower number, which will spin the axe clockwise. Before you try that, though, move your Graph Editor window so you can see the axe in the perspective window. As you move the **Rotate Z** keyframe down in the Graph Editor, you will see the axe rotate interactively. Move the keyframe down until the axe does a full spin.

Playback the animation. Click the Play button in the playback controls. If your animation looks blazingly fast, Maya's playback speed is probably set to Play Every Frame. Open the Animation Preferences window by clicking its icon (⊠), and set Playback Speed to Real-Time (30 fps).

> Changing the playback speed of an animation through the Animation Preferences window does not alter the timing of your animation. It only changes the speed with which Maya plays the animation back to you in its windows. To change the playback speed, choose **Window →
> Setting/Preferences → Preferences** to open the Preferences window, choose **Settings →
> Working Units**, and select the proper setting.

Now when you playback the animation, it should look slow. Maya is playing the scene back in real time, as long as the options in the Animation Preferences window are set to playback properly at 30fps. Even at 30fps, the scene should playback slowly, and this means that the animation of the axe timing is too slow.

All you need to do is tinker in the Graph Editor a bit to get the right timing. For a good result in timing, move the first set of keyframes from 15 to 13. Then grab the **Translate Y** keyframe at frame 27 and move it to 19. Finally, grab the keyframes at frame 40 and move them all back to frame 25. Playback the scene.

Adding Follow-Through

Load the axe_v4.mb file from the axe_anim project on the CD, or continue with your own file.

The axe is missing weight. Nothing much in this scene indicates that this is a heavy axe. You can add some finesse to the scene using follow-through and secondary motion to give more weight to the scene.

In the axe scene, follow-through motion is the axe blade driving farther into the target a little beyond its initial impact. Secondary motion is the recoil in the target as the momentum of the axe transfers into it. As you increase the amount of follow-through and secondary motion, you increase the axe's implied weight. You must, however, walk a fine line; you don't want to go too far with follow-through or secondary motion. The Graph Editor is great for adding these nuances to the axe. Follow these steps:

1. Select the axe in the scene using its selection handle, and open the Graph Editor.

2. Because you will add three frames to the end of this animation for follow-through, go to frame 28 (25 being the end of the current animation).

3. In the perspective window, rotate the axe another 1.5 degrees in the Z axis.

4. Rotating the axe in step 3 moves the axe's blade down a bit in the Y axis, so move the axe using the **Translate Y** manipulator handle up slightly, to bring the axe back up close to where it was before the extra rotation. This will also dig the axe into the target a little more. You'll see a keyframe for **Translate Y** and most probably for **Translate X**, as well as **Rotate Z**.

If you playback the animation, the follow-through doesn't look good. The axe hits the target and then digs into it as if the action were done in two separate moves by two different animators who never talked to each other. You need to smooth out the transition from the axe strike and its follow-through in the Graph Editor.

5. Highlight the **Rotate Z** attribute in the Graph Editor to get rid of the other curves in the window. Figure 8.16 shows the **Rotate Z** curve of the axe after the follow-through animation is added.

SECONDARY MOTION AND FOLLOW-THROUGH

Secondary motion in animation comprises all the little things in a scene that move because something else in the scene is moving. For example, when a superhero jumps from a tall building and their cape flutters in the wind, the cape's undulation is secondary motion.

Follow-through is the action in animation that immediately follows an object's or a character's main action. For example, once the superhero lands from their jump, their knees buckle a little and the superhero bends at the waist, essentially squashing down a bit. That squashing motion is follow-through. The more follow-throughs, the more cartoon-like the animation appears.

Figure 8.16
The Rotate Z curve of the axe after the follow-through animation

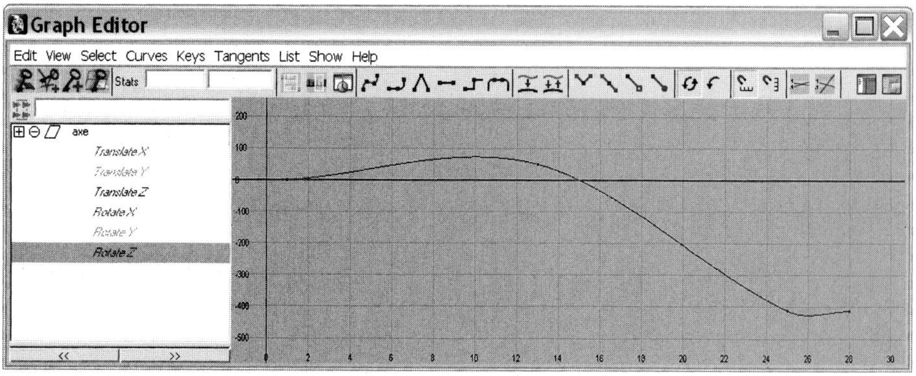

6. Focus in on the last three frames of the curve, and zoom into that range only. The curve, as it is now, dips down past where it should and recoils back up a small amount.

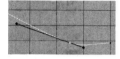

Figure 8.17
The tangent handles of a keyframe. The handle to the left of the keyframe is the *in* tangent, and the handle to the right is its *out* tangent.

When you set keyframes, you create animation curves in the Graph Editor for the axe. These curves are Bezier splines, which stay as smooth as possible from beginning to end. When you set the new keyframe, rotating the axe about 1.5 more degrees for follow-through, the animation curve responds by creating a dip, as seen in Figure 8.16, to keep the whole curve as smooth as possible.

The axe needs to hit the target with force and dig its way into the target, slowly coming to a stop. You need to adjust the curvature of the keyframes at frame 25 by using the keyframe's tangents. *Tangents* are handles that will change the amount of curvature influence that a point on a b-spline (Bezier spline) has. Selecting the keyframe in question reveals its tangents. (See Figure 8.17.)

7. Select the out tangent for the **Rotate Z** attribute's key at frame 25, and MMB move it up to get rid of the dip. Notice that the tangency for the in tangent also changes.
8. Press Z to undo your change. You need to break the tangent handles so that one does not disturb the other.
9. Select the out handle and click the Break Tangents icon ( ) to break the tangent.
10. Move the handle up to get rid of the dip so that the curve segment from frame 25 to frame 28 is a straight line, angled down. Figure 8.18 is zoomed into this segment of the curve after it's been fixed.

Now, to get the axe to slowly stop as it digs into the target, you need to curve that end segment of the **Rotate Z** curve to flatten it out.

11. Grab the last frame to reveal its handles. You can manually move the in handle to make it horizontal, or you can click the Flat Tangents icon ( ) on the left side of the icon bar, under the menus in the Graph Editor.

The curve's final segment for **Rotate Z** should now look like Figure 8.19.

12. Adjust the keyframe tangents similarly for the **Translate Y** and **Translate X** curves for the axe. (See Figure 8.20.)

13. Playback the animation and you should see the axe impact the target and sink into it a bit for its follow-through.

Now you need more polish.

Adding Secondary Motion

Load axe_v5.mb from the axe_anim project on the CD, or continue with your own scene file.

For secondary motion, you will move the target in reaction to the impact from the axe's momentum.

An object in motion has momentum. Momentum is calculated by multiplying the mass of an object by its velocity. So, the heavier and faster an object is, the more momentum it will have. When two objects collide, some or all momentum transfers from one object to the other.

In a game of pool, for example, when the moving cue ball collides with a stationary eight ball, the cue ball transfers some of its momentum into the eight ball, setting it in motion, and uses the rest of its own momentum to ricochet off into another direction.

In the axe scene's impact, the axe lodges into the target and its momentum is almost fully transferred to the target. But, since the target is much more massive than the axe, the target moves only slightly in reaction. The more you make the target recoil, the heavier the axe will seem.

First, group the axe's parent node under the target's parent node. The axe will be left behind to float in midair if you animate the target's parent node without grouping the axe under it. By grouping the axe under the target, you'll move the target to recoil while keeping the axe lodged in it. The animation on the axe will not change when you group the axe and target under a new node.

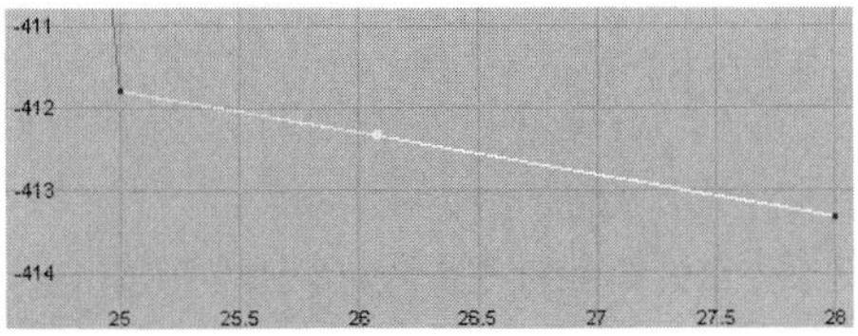

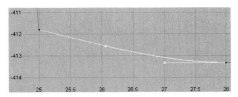

Figure 8.18

Zoomed into the end segment of the Rotate Z animation curve once the dip is fixed

Figure 8.19

Zoomed into the end segment of the Rotate Z animation curve. Notice how the curve now smoothly comes to a stop by flattening out.

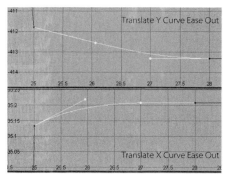

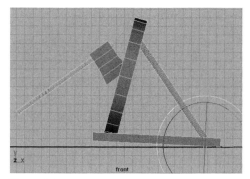

Figure 8.20

Smoothed translate curves to ease out the motion

Figure 8.21

The front panel display of the target reacting to the impact of the axe

Grab the parent node of the target (called Target) and reset its attributes to 0 by freezing its transforms as you did with the ball. This sets the Target node's **Translate** and **Rotate** attributes back to 0 and its **Scale** attributes back to 1.

1. To freeze the transforms, select the Target node, and then choose **Modify → Freeze Transformations**.

2. In the Outliner, MMB drag the Axe node to the Target node to group it under. You could also MMB drag the nodes in the Hypergraph to group the Axe node under the Target node.

3. Go to frame 25, the moment of impact, and set position and rotation keyframes on Target.

4. Go to frame 28, rotate the Target node in the Z axis about –2.5 degrees, and move it up and back slightly in the Y and X axes, as in Figure 8.21.

5. Go to frame 31. Rotate the Target node back to 0 in the Z axis, move it down to 0 in the Y axis, and move it back a bit more in the X axis.

6. Go to frame 35 and repeat step 4, but only move it half as much in **Rotate Z**, **Translate X**, and **Translate Y**.

7. Go to frame 40 and repeat step 5, but move Target back only slightly in the X axis.

If you don't freeze the transforms on the target's parent node before grouping the axe under it, the axe's animation will change and yield undesirable results.

The preceding steps should give you an animation similar to axe_v6.mb in the axe_anim project on the CD.

Motion Trails

You can see a moving object's trajectory, or *motion trail*—its path of motion. Follow these steps:

1. Select the axe through its selection handle, and then choose **Animate → Create Motion Trail** ❐. (See Figure 8.22.)

2. Select Line for Draw Style, and make sure the Show Frame Numbers check box is checked.

3. Click Apply, and then click Close to close the window.

The motion trail will be useful for fine-tuning your motion. Editing the animation curves in the Graph Editor and watching the motion trail adjust in the work panels will show you the precise trajectory of the axe throughout its movement. Playback your animation a few times to get a good sense for how the scene looks.

4. Select the axe and open the Graph Editor.

5. Try adding some more arc to the axe in the middle of its trajectory to the target.

6. In the Graph Editor, focus on the **Translate Y** curve, and select the keyframe at frame 19.

7. Move the keyframe up about 2 units, and watch the motion trail adjust to show you the higher arc.

8. Replay the animation with the higher arc in the middle.

Notice the axe seems a little more solid than before. The extra height in the trajectory really helps give the axe more substance. Figure 8.23 shows the axe and its motion trail after more height is added to its arc.

Figure 8.22
The Motion Trail Options window

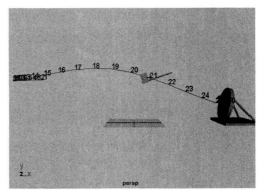

Figure 8.23
The axe and its motion trail

You can toggle the frame number display on/off and change the display type of the motion trail from curve to points or locators through the motion trail's Attribute Editor. To get rid of the motion trail, select it and press Delete.

Path Animation

As an alternative to keyframing the position of the axe, you can animate it *on a path*. *Path animation* allows you to assign an object to move along the course of a curve, called a path.

Load axe_v7.mb from the axe_anim project on the CD. This is the finished axe animation. You'll delete most of your hard work by removing the translation animation on the axe, but you'll keep the rotation and everything else. You will replace the translation keyframes you set up with a motion path instead. Follow these steps:

1. In the front window and with the motion trails turned on, trace the motion trail with a CV curve (choose **Create → CV Curve Tool**) from the beginning of the trail to the end. Make sure the CV Curve tool is set to make cubic (3) curves.

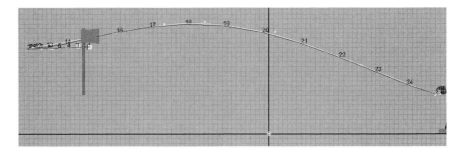

2. Take note of the frames you set important keyframes on for the axe's position (like when it recoils and releases at frame 10 and when it hits the target at frame 25). Select the axe's top node (axe), and delete its translation animation. Select all three **Translate** attributes in the Channel Box, and right-click to display the shortcut menu. Choose Break Connections to delete the animation from those channels. The axe will now spin around, and it and the target will recoil at the moment of impact, but the axe will not actually move.

3. Keep the motion trail in the scene for now to help with the timing you've already created.

4. Select the top axe node, Shift+select the path curve, and click in the Animation menu set. Choose **Animate → Motion Paths → Attach to Motion Path ❒**.

5. In the options window, turn off the Follow check box.

The Follow feature will orient the object on the path so that its front always points in the direction of travel. Because the axe moves backward in anticipation before it's thrown forward, Follow would cause it to turn around twice, so you turn this option off.

Now the axe will follow the curve end to end from frame 1 to frame 60. Of course, you have to adjust the timing to fit it as before.

6. Select the motion trail and move it down in the window to get it out of the way, but do keep it lined up vertically with the path curve so that you can figure out the timing again.

The file `axe_path_v1.mb` in the axe_anim project will bring you up to this point.

7. Select the top axe node, and open the Graph Editor to see the axe's curves. The rotation curve is still intact though the translation curves are missing. Now click motion-Path1 in the Channel Box to highlight it, and a motionPath1.UValue curve that took the place of the translation curves appears in the Graph Editor. On the left side of the Graph Editor, select the motionPath1.UValue curve to display only that. Zoom into it. (Press A for all view.)

8. The curve is an even linear curve from 1 to 60. You need the axe to hit at frame 25, so move the end of the curve to frame 25 from frame 60.

9. Retime the backward movement. Scrub the animation until the axe moves all the way back (frame 4). Using the Insert Keys tool ( ), insert a keyframe at frame 4. Select the animation curve, click the tool, and MMB click the curve to create a key on it. You can MMB drag the cursor to place the key precisely at frame 10 before releasing the mouse button.

10. Move this new keyframe to frame 10 (the frame where backward movement originally ended).

11. Scrub the animation, and the timing is just about right. You'll have to adjust the tangents a bit to make the axe move more like before, but the movement is essentially there with path animation.

The file `axe_path_v2.mb` in the axe_anim project will bring you up to this point.

Path animation is extremely useful for a number of tasks, but particularly for animating an object along a particular course. By adjusting the resulting animation curve in the Graph Editor, you can readjust the timing of the path animation easily.

A good path animation exercise is to create an atom and draw CV curves around the nucleus for the paths of the electrons. Then animate all the electrons orbiting the nucleus with the paths. Also, try reanimating the solar system exercise with paths instead of the keyframes you set on the rotations.

GHOSTING

You can enable *ghosting* in Maya, letting you see the position of an animated object a few frames before and after its current position. For example, select the animated axe in your scene, and open the Animation menu set. Choose **Animate → Ghost Selected**. Maya will now display the axe's three frames before and after the current time. To turn off ghosting, choose **Animate → Unghost Selected**.

Axe Project Summation

In the axe example, you furthered your use of layered animation by beginning with the gross animation to cover the basic movements of the axe. Once those timings were set, you completed most of the rest of the work in the Graph Editor by moving keyframes here and there to add detail to the motion. You added more keyframes to create follow-through and secondary movement to insinuate weight into the axe and target.

Without secondary movement in the target, the axe would seem to weigh nothing. With too much movement, however, the axe would seem too heavy, and the scene would not look right. Subtle nuances can make stunning differences in the simplest of animations. You also went back into the animation and replaced the animation method entirely with path animation. This illustrates the multiple ways to accomplish a task in Maya; finding your own comfort zone with work flow is one of the goals in learning Maya.

Replacing an Object

Aside from the need to model objects and texture them, there is the task of animation setup. Check your pivots, your geometry, and your grouping to make sure your scene will hold up when you animate the scene.

It's also common practice in setup to animate a *proxy* object—a simple stand-in model that you later replace. The next exercise will show you how to replace the simple axe you already animated with the fully textured NURBS from the previous chapter and how to copy an animation from one object to another.

Replacing the Axe

Load your completed keyframed axe animation scene (not the one using path animation), or switch to the axe_anim project and load the scene file axe_v7.mb from the CD. Now, follow these steps:

1. Choose **File → Import**.

2. Locate and import the final textured axe in your project, or use axe_texture_C.mb from the axe_model project on the CD. The new axe appears at the origin in your scene. You will notice that the ambient light is also imported into this scene.

Transferring Animation

To assume all the properties and actions of the original axe requires some setup. Follow these steps:

1. Move the pivot on the new axe to the same relative position as the pivot on the original animated axe (up toward the top and a little out front of the handle, just under the blade). This will ensure that the new axe will have the same spin as the old axe.

2. Rotate the new axe's top node 180 degrees in Y to get it to face the right direction.

3. Use grid snap to place the top node of the new axe at the origin.

4. Freeze transforms on the new axe group to reset all its attributes. However, freezing transforms with the third placement node of the wood grain still grouped in with the axe resets the wood grain. Try it, but make sure to undo the action. As a workaround, MMB drag the wood third placement node momentarily out of the axe group. Choose **Modify → Freeze Transformations** on the new axe group. MMB drag the third placement node back into the axe's hierarchy.

5. Choose **Display → Transform Display → Selection Handles** to turn on the selection handle of the new axe.

6. Go to frame 1. Select the original axe, open the Graph Editor, and choose **Edit → Copy**.

7. Select the new axe to display its curves in the Graph Editor. It has none yet. With the axe_2 node selected in the Graph Editor, choose **Edit → Paste**. As shown in Figure 8.24, the new axe will be slightly offset from the original axe.

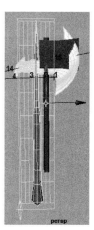

Figure 8.24

The new axe placed next to the original

> When you copy and paste curves in the Graph Editor, make sure you're on the first frame of that animation. Pasting curves will place them at the current frame. Since the animation of the original axe started at frame 1, make sure you're at frame 1 when you paste them to the new axe.

8. Move the new axe to match the original. Since it's already animated, move it using the curves in the Graph Editor as opposed to moving it in the viewport. With the new axe selected, in the Graph Editor select the **Translate Y** curve and move it up to match the height of the original axe.

9. Select the **Translate X** curve and move it to match the axe's X position, as in Figure 8.25. You'll want to line up the axe handle as a guide.

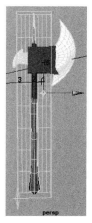

Figure 8.25

Lining up the two axes

Scrub the animation and you'll notice the new axe has the same animation except at the end when it hits the target. It won't have the same follow-through as the original axe. Remember that you grouped the original axe under the Target node for follow-through animation. Place the new axe under this node as well.

The file axe_v8.mb in the axe_anim project on the CD has the new axe imported and all the animation copied. It will get you caught up to this point.

10. Once you scrub the animation and make sure the new axe animates properly, select the original axe and delete it.

Animating Flying Text

It often comes across every animator's path; you're invariably asked to animate a flying logo or some flying text for something or another. As late '80s as that may sound, animating some flying text can teach you a thing or two about path animation and lattice deformers, at least the way we'll do it here. You can always use the following steps to animate pretty much anything that has to twist, wind, and bend along a path, not necessarily text.

First we'll need to create the text itself. To do so, follow these steps:

1. In a new scene, select **Create → Text** ❑. In the option box, type in your text and select a font to use. We'll just stick with Times New Roman. Set the **Type** however, to Bevel.

2. Once you select Bevel, leave the rest of the creation methods at their defaults as shown here. This will create the text as beveled faces to make the 3D text as shown in Figure 8.26.

Setting the **Type** attribute to Poly for your text would create curve outlines for the text and planar faces for the letters for a flat text effect. Setting the **Type** creation option to Curves would give you just the curve outlines. Finally, using Trim to create your text will make the letters out of flat planar NURBS surfaces. There is, however, no surface history created with text. To allow you to edit the text at a later time, you will have to re-create the text and/or font type as needed.

3. Once we have the text, we'll need to create a curve for it to animate along. Using either the CV or EP curve tool, create a winding curve like a roller coaster for the logo as shown.

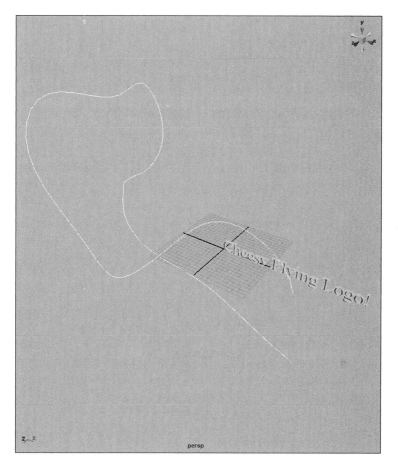

Figure 8.26

Creating the 3D Text for our flying logo

4. Just as you did with the axe exercise, you will assign the text object to this curve. Set your frame range to 1– 00, then select the text, then Shift+select the curve, and in the Animation menu set, choose **Animate → Motion Paths → Attach to Motion Path □**. Set the **Front Axis** to X, the **Up Axis** to Y, and check on **Bank** as shown. Depending on how you create your curve and text, you may need to experiment with the **Front and Up Axis** attributes to get the text to fly the way you wish it to. You will notice there is history created with the path animation, so you may adjust the axes attributes after the fact to see how they will work on the curve you have.

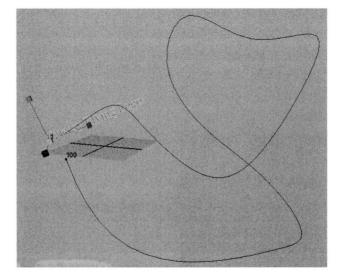

5. Orbit the camera around to the other side, and you can see the text on the path in Figure 8.27. Notice the **U Value** attribute. This is the position of the text along the curve from 0 to 1. Scrub the animation and the text should glide along the curve.

Figure 8.27

The text is on the path.

6. The text is not bending along with the curve at all yet. To accomplish this, we will need to add a lattice that will bend the text to the curvature of the path. And this is simple enough, actually. Select the text object, and choose **Animate → Motion Paths → Flow Path Object** ☐.

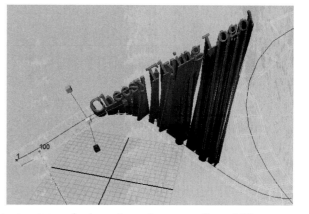

7. In the option box for the Flow Path Object, as seen here, set **Front Divisions** to 120, **Up** to 2, **Side** to 2, and check Curve for **Lattice Around**. Make sure the **Local Effect** box is unchecked. This will create a lattice that will follow the curve, giving it 120 segments along the path. This lattice will deform the text as it travels along the path.

Figure 8.28

The geometry does not fit the lattice well.

8. Scrub your animation and you'll see a fairly strange result, where parts of the text will "explode" out from the lattice, as shown in Figure 8.28.

9. The geometry is simply going outside the influence of the lattice. This is causing the strange behavior. To fix the situation, select the lattice and based node and simply scale up the lattice *and* its base node together to create a larger size of influence around the path as shown.

Scrub your animation to check the frame range and how well the text flies through the lattice, and once the lattice and its base are large enough to handle the text along all your path's corners and turns, viola! Cheesy flying logo! (See Figure 8.29.)

Figure 8.29

Cheesy Flying Logo! makes a nice turn.

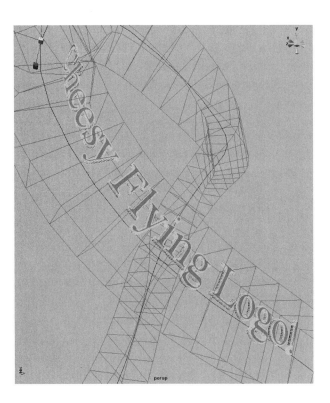

Rigging the Locomotive, Part One

Now you'll return to the locomotive you modeled in Chapter 4 and put your new animation skills to use.

Load the file `locomotve_model_v4.mb`, which is the completed model of the locomotive from the polygon modeling exercise in Chapter 4.

The Scene Setup

It's important to keep animation in mind as you build a model. In particular, making a good scene hierarchy is crucial to getting a smooth animation work flow going. That's why, when you built the locomotive in Chapter 4, you used the Outliner to make sure the objects in your scene were grouped logically. Now, you're going back in there to make sure we have good organization for animation before setting to the task of rigging this thing for animation.

Figure 8.30 shows the organization of the locomotive as it stands now from Chapter 4. Later, we'll use a more finely detailed and prettier locomotive model to rig that will already be grouped properly using the intentions outlined here. This scene is in fairly good shape, but we have to identify the parts of the locomotive that we need to rig, determine how they will move, and decide what is the best hierarchy for the model from there.

The major moving parts of the engine are the wheels and the steam pump drive mechanism. The wheels, of course, will need to rotate, as wheels do, and the steam pump drives the wheel arms back and forth, which is what drives the main wheels to rotate. Aside from animating some steam pumping out of parts of the engine, which we will cover in Chapter 12, this is the basic rigging for the locomotive. First we need to make sure hierarchies are settled well and that pivot points are in their proper places.

The `locomotive_model_v4.mb` scene file has a well-organized hierarchy, but it needs some help to make rigging easier. Make sure that all the individual wheel arms have their pivots at the base as shown. Use Insert (or the Home key on a Mac) to move the pivots as needed. We will be rigging these wheel arms using IK bones in the next chapter.

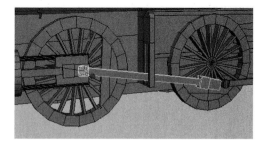

Make sure all the elements that make up a wheel are grouped and that the group's pivot point is centered for all the wheel groups as shown.

Finally, for our simple rig, make sure the steam pump arm elements are properly grouped and that the pivot is placed as shown.

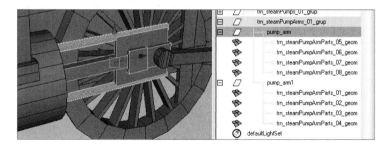

Figure 8.30

The locomotive's Outliner view

If your locomotive is in organizational disarray, identify all the moving parts first, and then begin grouping them logically. Place pivots appropriately and you're all set. The scene file `locomotive_anim_v1.mb` in the Locomotive project on the CD has the locomotive scene file with the pivots and grouping already finished as discussed earlier.

If the pivots and groupings are off, you will notice as soon as you begin to animate; things will just not rotate on the correct axis and pieces will not follow properly. The wheels, for example, may wobble around their axle.

For more practice in grouping and hierarchies, you can load `locomotive_anim_v1.mb` from the CD, ungroup everything in the scene, and piece it all back together. To ungroup everything, select the top node of the locomotive and choose **Edit → Ungroup**. That will ungroup the major parts of the locomotive. With those groups selected, ungroup again to flush out individual geometry. You can also load `locomotive_anim_v1_B.mb` from the CD; it has all major groupings removed. Then regroup and repivot everything.

Selection Handles

Using selection handles makes selection easier and work flow faster, so turn on selection handles for each of the groups you're animating. Select the wheel groups in the Outliner, and then choose **Display → Transform Display → Selection Handles**. Select the wheel arm groups and turn on their selection handles as well. Figure 8.31 shows the selection handles enabled for the wheel, pump arm, and wheel arm.

How selection handles work depends on Maya's selection order. Selection order, which you can customize, sets the priority of one type of object over another when you try to select in a work window. Once the selection handles for the locomotive's wheels and drive arms are turned on, only the handles will be selected (and not the whole locomotive) when you make a marquee selection that covers the entire locomotive. Handles have a high selection priority by default, so they are selected above anything else.

Animating the Locomotive

It's straightforward to animate most of the locomotive. Simple rotations will make the wheels turn. Translating the locomotive's top node will move the entire object. This, however, leaves out the drive mechanism with the steam pump and the wheel and pump arms. These we will rig to automatically animate in the next chapter, using IK handles and connections.

Animating a Catapult

As an exercise in animating a system of parts of a model before we continue to animate the locomotive in the next chapter, we will now animate a catapult. This catapult model is straightforward to animate. We will turn its winch to bend back the catapult arm, which shoots the projectiles, and then we'll fire and watch the arm fly up.

First let's get acquainted with the scene file and make sure its pivots and hierarchies are set up properly. The scene file catapult_anim_v1.mb in the Catapult_Anim project on the CD will have everything in order, though it is always good to make sure. Figure 8.32 shows the catapult with its winch selected and ready to animate.

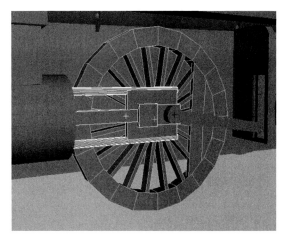

Get a timing put down for the winch first, and use that to pull back the arm to fire. Follow these steps:

1. Select the Winch group with its selection handle, and at frame 1, set a keyframe for rotation. If the selection handle is not turned on, select "Winch" from the Outliner and turn on the selection handle by choosing **Display → Transform Display → Selection Handles.** To keep it clean as you go along, instead of pressing Shift+E to set a key for all three axes of rotation, select only the **Rotate X** attribute in the Channel Box, right-click to open the shortcut menu, and choose **Key Selected**. There only needs to be rotation in X for the winch.

2. Jump to frame 60.

3. Rotate the winch backward a few times. (Or type **–400** or so for the **Rotate X** attribute.)

Figure 8.31

Selection handles make selecting a group of objects much easier.

Figure 8.32

The catapult's winch is ready to animate.

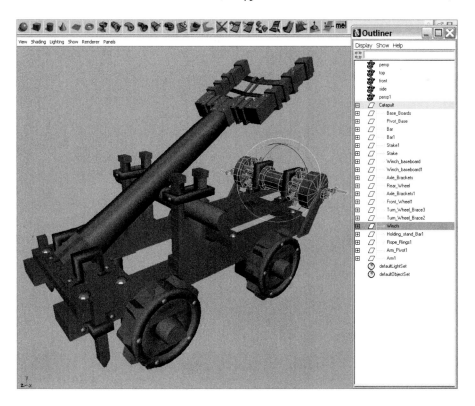

4. Open the Graph Editor, ease in the curve a bit, and ease out the curve a lot so that the rotation starts casually but grinds to a stop as the arm gets more difficult to pull back. Now obviously you're missing the rope between the winch and the arm. Since animating a rope is a fairly advanced task, the catapult will be animated without its rope, but the principle of an imaginary rope pulling the arm down to create tension in the arm will drive the animation.

5. To accentuate the more difficult winding at the end, you'll add a key to the X axis rotation through the Graph Editor. Select the curve, and click the Insert Key Tool icon ( ) in the upper-left corner of the Graph Editor. Your cursor will change to a cross.

6. MMB click frame 42 to add a keyframe already on the curve at frame 42. You can drag the key back and forth on the curve to place it directly at frame 42. It may help to turn on key snapping first. (See Figure 8.33.)

7. Move that keyframe down to create a stronger ease-out for the winch. Be careful not to let the curve dip down so that the winch switches directions. Adjust the handles to smooth the curve. You can also add a little recoil to the winch by inserting a new keyframe through the Graph Editor at frame 70. (See Figure 8.34.)

Figure 8.33

Insert a keyframe at frame 42.

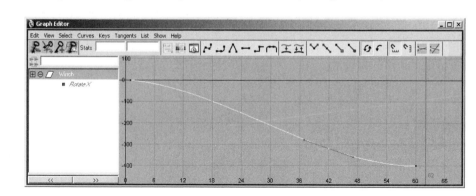

Figure 8.34

Creating a greater ease-out and adding a little recoil at the end

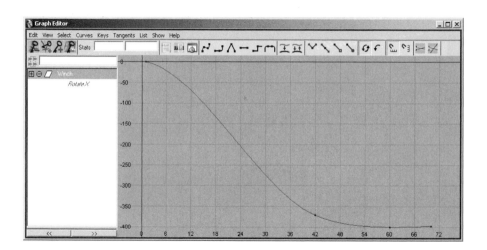

Animating with Deformers

Now's the time to animate the arm coiling back, using the winch's timing as it is driving the arm. Since the catapult's arm is supported by a brace, and the whole idea of a catapult is based on tension, you have to bend the arm back as the winch pulls it.

You'll use a nonlinear deformer just as you did in the axe-modeling exercise in Chapter 5, but you'll be animating it. Follow these steps:

1. Switch to the Animation menu set. Select the Arm1 group, and choose **Deform → Create Nonlinear → Bend** to create a bend deformer perpendicular to your arm. Select the deformer and rotate it to line it up with the arm.

2. With the bend deformer selected, look in the Channel Box for bend1 under the INPUTS section, and click it to expand its attributes. Try entering **0.5** for **Curvature**. More than likely, the catapult arm bends sideways. Rotate the deformer so that the arm is bending back instead.

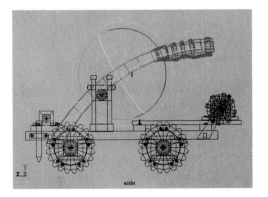

3. You don't want the arm's base to bend back, just the basket side. And you want it to bend at the brace point, not in the middle where it is now. Move the deformer down the length of the arm until the middle lines up with the support brace of the arm.

4. To prevent the bottom of the arm from bending, change the **Low Bound** attribute to 0. To keep the basket from bending, set the **High Bound** attribute to 0.9.

> The **Low Bound** and **High Bound** attributes control how far up and down the deformer the object is affected. The **Envelope** attribute for a deformer governs how much the object is affected *overall*, with 0 not affecting the geometry at all.

5. Instead of trying to match the speed, ease in and out of the winch and set the gross keyframes for the arm pulling back first. Reset **Curvature** to 0, and set a key for **Curvature** at frame 1. (Select bend1's **Curvature** in the Channel Box, right-click, and choose **Key Selected** from the shortcut menu.)

6. Go to frame 60, and set **Curvature** to 0.8. If Auto Key is turned on, this sets a keyframe; otherwise, set a key manually. (See Figure 8.35.)

7. If you playback the animation, you'll notice that the way the winch winds back and the way the arm bends don't match. In the Graph Editor, you can adjust the animation curve on the bend deformer to match the winch's curve.

8. Insert a key on the **Curvature** curve at frame 42, and move it up to match the curvature you created for the winch.

Figure 8.35

Bend the arm back at frame 60.

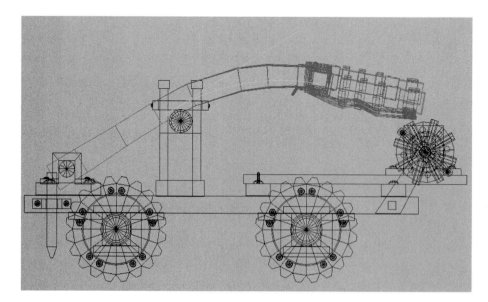

9. Insert a new key at frame 70, and make the arm bend back up a bit as the winch recoils. Set **Curvature** to about 0.79 from 0.8. (See Figure 8.36.)

10. Go to frame 90 and set a key again at **Curvature** of 0, set a key at 0.82 for frame 97 to create anticipation, and then keyframe at frame 103 to release the arm and fire its imaginary payload with a **Curvature** of –0.8.

11. Now you'll add some rotation to the arm for dramatic effect. At about frame 100, during the release, the arm is almost straight. Select the Arm1 group, and set a rotation key on the X axis. Go to frame 105, and rotate the arm 45 degrees to the left in the X axis. If the starting rotation of the arm is at 30 (as it is in the sample file), set an X axis rotation key of 75 at frame 105.

12. Notice that the arm is bending strangely now that it's being rotated. It is moving off the deformer, so its influence is changing for the worse. To fix this, go back to frame 100, and group the deformer node under the Arm1 group. Now it will rotate along with the arm, adding its own bending influence.

13. Work on setting keyframes on the deformer and the arm's rotation so that the arm falls back down onto the support brace and quivers a bit until it becomes straight again. The animation curve for the bend deformer should look like Figure 8.37. The rotation of the arm should look like Figure 8.38. Remember to make the tangents flat on the keys where the arm bounces off the brace linear and the peaks, like the ball's bounce from before.

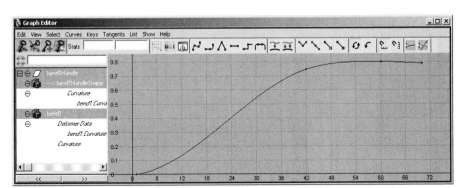

Figure 8.36

Try to match the relative curvature of the winch's animation curve with the bend deformer's animation curve.

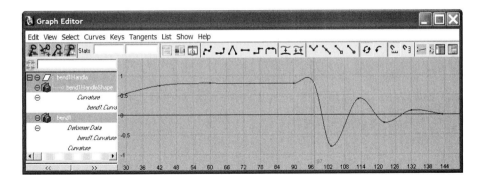

Figure 8.37

The animation curve for the arm's vibration back and forth as it comes to a rest

Figure 8.38

The animation curve for the arm's rotation as it heaves up and falls back down, coming to an easy rest on the brace

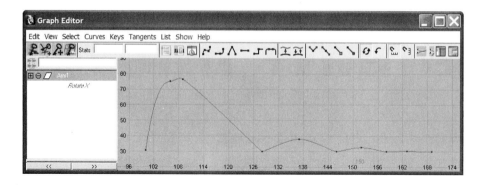

 The file `catapult_anim_v2.mb` will give you a good reference to check out timing of the arm bend and rotation.

Without getting into a lot more detail here, try your hand at animating the catapult on your own. Here are some items you'll want to animate to make this a complete animation:

- Spin the winch around as the arm releases, as if its rope is being yanked away from it.

- Animate the entire catapult rocking forward and backward as the arm releases, sort of like a car would rock when you jump onto the hood.

- Move the catapult forward on a road, spinning its wheels as best you can to match the distance it travels.

- Design and build your own catapult and animate it along the same lines.

Summary

In this chapter, you began to learn the fundamentals of animating a scene. Starting with a bouncing ball, you learned how to work in the Graph Editor to set up and adjust timing as well as how to add squash and stretch to the animation. The next exercise of throwing an axe showed you how to set up a scene for animation, expanded on your experience in creating timing in the Graph Editor, and showed you how to add anticipation, follow-through, and secondary motion to your scene. You then learned how to adjust animation using motion trails and how to animate the axe throw using path animation. And then you went on to learn how to replace a proxy object that is already animated with a finished model and how to transfer the animation. Back to our locomotive from Chapter 4, we began to set up the scene for rigging in the next chapter by setting proper pivots and hierarchy. Finally, you used a catapult to animate with deformers and further your experience in the Graph Editor.

Animating a complex system such as a catapult or a locomotive involves creating layers of animation based on facets of the mechanics of the system's movement. With the catapult, you tackled the individual parts separately and then worked to unify the animations.

We will use rigging concepts in the next chapter to automate some of that process for the locomotive.

The same is true of the bouncing ball and axe-throwing exercises. The different needs of the animation were addressed one by one, starting with the gross animation and ending with finishing touches to add weight. Finally, the art of timing brings the entire effort into a cohesive whole.

Even when animation is already applied, it is simple to change *how* the animation is accomplished as you did with path animation or even to replace the animated object entirely.

Animation is the art of observation, interpretation, and implementation. Learning to see how things move, deciphering why they move as they do, and then applying all that to your Maya scene is what animation is all about.

CHAPTER 9

Further Animation Practices

Now that you have a little more animation experience, you'll get into some more involved animation practices and toolsets. Take the principles covered in this book and its examples further. Animation is a growing exploration, and you should use this text as a stepping-off point. For everything you're being exposed to here, there are many more techniques to discover.

Topics include:

- **Skeletons and Kinematics**

- **Skeletons: The Hand**

- **Inverse Kinematics**

- **Basic Relationships: Constraints**

- **Basic Relationships: Set Driven Keys**

- **Application: Rigging the Locomotive**

Skeletons and Kinematics

In your physical body, your muscles move your bones, and as your bones move, parts of your body move. Bones are your internal framework.

In CG animation, a *skeleton* is an armature built into a 3D model that drives the geometry. You insert a skeleton into a CG model and attach or bind it to the geometry. The skeleton's bones are animated (typically with rotations), which in turn move the parts of the geometry to which they are attached. Using a skeleton allows for bending and deformation of the attached geometry at *joints* of the skeleton. A skeleton is, of course, useful for character work, but skeletons have many other uses. Any time you need to drive the geometry of a model with an internal system, such as a whip or a tree bending in the wind, you can use skeletons. We will use them to drive the locomotive later in this chapter.

Skeletons and Hierarchy

Skeletons rely on hierarchies. Bones are created in a hierarchical manner, resulting in a *root joint* that is the parent of all the joints beneath it in the hierarchy. For example, a hip joint can be the root joint of a leg skeleton system in which the *knee joint* is the leg's child, the *ankle joint* belongs to the knee, and the five *toe joints* are the ankle's children. (See Figure 9.1.)

Using skeletons, you can easily create an immediate hierarchical system with which to animate. Furthermore, pieces of geometry need not deform to be attached to a bone system. Objects can be grouped with or under joints. They move under their parent joint and rotate around that joint's pivot as opposed to their own pivot point.

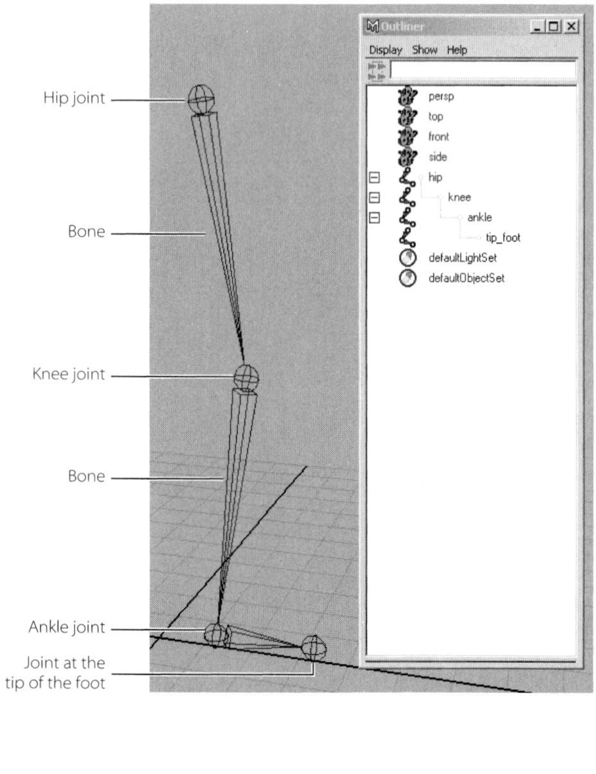

A skeleton is really just a collection of grouped and properly positioned pivot points called joints that you use to move your geometry, whether it deforms or not. A *bone* is the length between each joint; bones only show you the skeletal system.

Inverse Kinematics (IK) and *Forward Kinematics (FK)* are the methods you use to animate a skeletal system. FK rotates the bones directly at their top joint to assume poses. This method resembles stop-motion animation in which a puppet, along with its underlying armature, is posed frame by frame. With FK, the animator moves the character into position by rotating the joints that run the geometry.

Figure 9.1

A leg skeleton and its hierarchy

Hip joint

Bone

Knee joint

Bone

Ankle joint

Joint at the tip of the foot

The rotation of a joint affects the position of the bones and joints beneath it in the hierarchy (see Figure 9.2). If you rotate the hip up, the knee and ankle will swing up as if the character is kicking. If you rotate the knee down, the ankle pivots down as if this character is seated. The form of motion moves the way you would expect it in hierarchies and is therefore called Forward Kinematics.

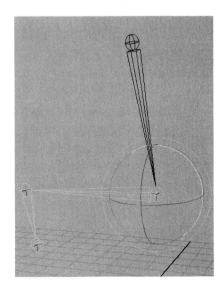

Figure 9.2

In Forward Kinematics, the joints are rotated directly.

IK uses a more complex, but often easier, system of *IK handles* that are attached to the tip of a joint system. The corresponding base of the IK system is attached farther up the skeleton hierarchy to a joint determined to be the root of that IK segment. It need not be the root joint of the entire skeleton, though.

The bones and joints in the IK chain are affected only by movement of the IK handle. When the handle moves, an *IK solver* figures out how to rotate all the joints to accommodate the new position of the IK handle. Moving an IK handle will cause the bones to rotate around their joints to accommodate a new position.

Figure 9.3

In Inverse Kinematics, the joints rotate in response to the IK handle's position.

The effect is as if someone grabbed your hand and moved it. The person holding your hand is similar to an IK handle. Moving your hand causes the bones in your arm to rotate around the shoulder, elbow, and wrist. As you can see in Figure 9.3, the animation flows up the hierarchy and is therefore called Inverse Kinematics.

Forward Kinematics: The Block Man

To understand skeletal hierarchy, take a look at a simple biped (two-legged) character made of primitive blocks called *block man*. In Figure 9.4, each block represents a part of the body, with gaps in between the blocks representing points where the body pivots.

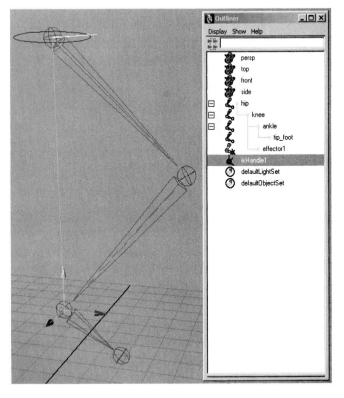

The pivot of each block is placed to represent the appropriate joint location. For example, the shin's pivot is located at the knee. Each block is grouped up the chain so

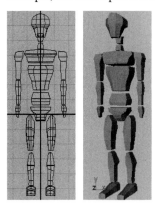

Figure 9.4

The block man's cubes arranged

that the foot moves with the shin, which moves with the thigh, which moves with the pelvis.

The hands are grouped under the arms, which group under the shoulders, and so forth down the spine to the pelvis. The head groups under the first neck block, and so on down the spine to the pelvis. The pelvis is the center of the body, which is known as the root of the figure.

The way this figure is grouped (see Figure 9.5) represents how the hierarchy of a character works for the most part. Each body part is attached and becomes the child of the part "above" it in the chain.

Load the file `block_man_v02.mb` from the Block_Man project on the CD for a good reference of the grouping structure. This file shows you what a skeleton hierarchy does.

In the Hypergraph, choose **Options → Layout → Freeform Layout** to position the nodes in any way you want. To make selections easier, you can arrange the nodes as if they were on a body (see Figure 9.6). You can toggle between freeform and automatic and your freeform layout will be retained.

Creating the Skeleton

The basis of how the block man is laid out and grouped is what skeletons are all about. Skeletons make character animation easier by automating, at the very least, the hierarchy and pivot placement described earlier.

THE PELVIS AS ROOT

Traditionally, the pelvis is the basis of all biped setups. The root of any skeletal system (whether using bones or geometry as the example) is the character's pivot point, the center of balance. Since biped characters center themselves on two feet, their pelvis becomes the root of their skeletal system. In CG, the pelvis becomes the parent node of the whole system and is the node used to move or orient the entire character. In a skeleton system, this would be the root joint.

The root is then the top parent of the system below it and runs the entire chain. Thus, selecting character parts straight from the Outliner or the Hypergraph is sometimes easier. You can, therefore, see that a good naming convention is always important with character setups.

You'll use the block man to create a skeleton. Load `block_man_v01.mb` from the Block_Man project. This is the same as `block_man_v02.mb`, but this version is not grouped.

1. Maximize the front view window. Switch to the Animation menu set by using the drop-down menu or by pressing F2.

2. Activate the Joint tool by choosing **Skeleton → Joint Tool**. Your cursor will turn into a cross.

3. Click in the middle of the pelvis to place the first joint, the root joint of the skeleton.

4. Shift+LMB click up to the space between the pelvis and the waist.

By pressing Shift as you click, you create a joint in a straight line from the last joint placement. A bone is created between the two joints, as a visual guide to the skeleton. The placement of the joints does depend on the active view, so placing a second joint in a different view may place the joint in an awkward location.

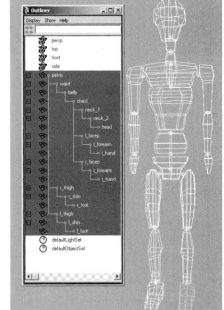

Figure 9.5
Pivot placements and grouping

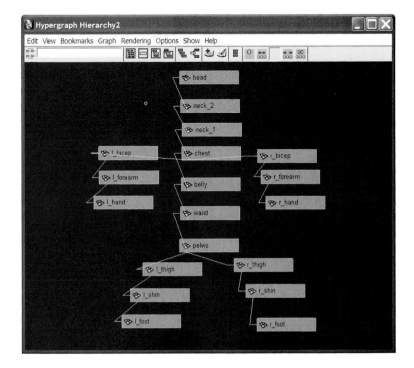

Figure 9.6
A freeform layout in the Hypergraph Hierarchy window

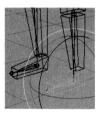

5. Click more joints up the spine at the gaps between the body parts as shown (top left).

6. You need to start a new branch of joints leading into the legs and arms. You'll begin with the arms. With the Joint tool still active, press the Up arrow key three times to move up the hierarchy of joints to the one between the neck and chest parts.

> Pressing the Up arrow key takes you up one node in a hierarchy; pressing the Down arrow key takes you down one node in a hierarchy. This approach also applies to skeletons, since they are hierarchies.

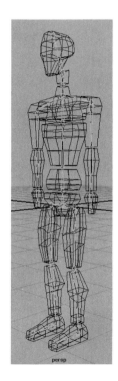

7. From this joint, click to place the right joint at the top of the right bicep. Click down to create joints at the elbow, the wrist, and the tip of the hand.

8. Press the Up arrow to *pick walk up* the chain to the neck/chest joint, and repeat step 7 to create the joints for the left arm as shown (left).

9. To start another string of joints in the first leg, pick walk back up the skeleton until you're at the pelvis root joint.

10. From the root joint at the pelvis, click to create a joint at the tip of the right thigh and work down to the knee and ankle. Place the ankle joint at the middle of the foot, as shown, as opposed to the gap between the shin and the foot. Press the spacebar to return to the four-way view, and maximize the side view. Click to create a joint at the tip of the foot. This allows you to place a joint in the proper axis.

11. Return to the front view, and press the Up arrow to get back to the pelvis joint. Repeat step 10 to create joints for the left leg. After you place your joints, press Enter (right).

Attaching to the Skeleton

You now have a full skeleton for your character. To attach the geometry, all you need to do is parent the body parts under their appropriate joints. Before you get to that, take a few minutes and name all the joints in the Outliner to make the scene easier to manage. Figure 9.7 shows the names used in the project on the CD.

You can also load the `block_man_skeleton_v01.mb` file from the Block_Man project to get to this point.

To parent the block man's geometry to the skeleton, follow these steps:

1. Starting with the right foot, parent it under the right ankle joint (rt_ankle) by MMB dragging it to rt_ankle in the Outliner or the Hypergraph. You don't want to parent it under the right foot joint (rt_foot) because you need the foot geometry to pivot with that foot bone and inherit the rotations from the ankle above it. Parent the left foot under the left ankle (lt_ankle).

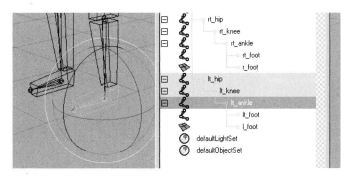

2. Parent the rest of the body parts under their respective joints as shown in Figure 9.8.

    *   Shins under the knees and thighs under the hips

    *   Hands under the wrists and forearms under the elbows

    *   Biceps under the shoulders

    *   Head under the head joint (the joint between the head and the top neck geometry)

    *   The top neck geometry under the joint between the two neck pieces

    *   The bottom neck geometry under the joint between the chest and the neck

    *   The chest under the joint between the chest and belly pieces

    *   The belly under the joint between the belly and waist

    *   The pelvis with the root joint

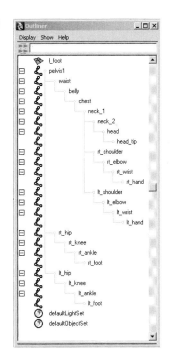

Figure 9.7

A consistent naming scheme for joints makes it easy to keep track of them.

Figure 9.8

Views of the skeleton and geometry hierarchy in the Outliner and the Hypergraph

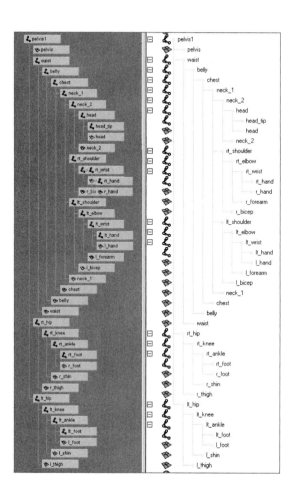

The Block Man: Walk Cycle

A *walk cycle* is an animation that takes the character through a few steps that can be repeated many times so that the character seems to be taking numerous steps. In a cycle, make sure the position of the first frame matches the position of the last frame so that when the animation sequence is cycled, no "pop" occurs in the motion at that point.

Now try animating this character's walk cycle using FK on the skeleton. You'll find the work flow straightforward, as if you were adjusting positions on a doll.

 Load the `block_man_skeleton_v02.mb` file from the Block_Man project on the CD for the properly grouped model and skeleton.

Use the key poses in the following figures to guide you in animating the body as it walks. You'll key at 5-frame intervals to lay down the gross animation. You can go back and adjust the timing of the joint rotations in the Graph Editor to make the animation better. The white leg and arm are behind the body, farther from the camera.

This animation is also called *pose animation* because you are posing the character from keyframe to keyframe.

Starting Out: Frames 1 and 5

Figure 9.9 shows the character's starting position. Here you'll set a key for this position and then begin the walk cycle by moving the joints into their second position and key-framing that.

1. At frame 1, set a key for the rotation of all the joints. It's easiest to select all the joints in the Outliner or the Hypergraph. With this pose animation, make sure all the joints are keyframed at every step, even if Auto Keyframe is turned on. Also set a position keyframe for just the pelvis joint.

A quick way to select all the joints and only the joints is to filter the Outliner view to show only joints. In the Outliner, choose **Show → Objects → Joints**. To reset the Outliner, choose **Show → Show All**.

2. Go to frame 5. Rotate the back leg (the block man's right, white leg) back, and rotate the foot to make it level again. Lower the body (select and move the pelvis joint) to line up the back heel with the ground. This will keep the man on the ground as he goes through the walk cycle, though he won't actually move forward yet.

3. Rotate the near leg (the man's left leg) forward, bend the knee, and pivot the foot up a bit.

4. Rotate the back arm forward, and rotate the near arm back (opposite from the legs). Bend the arms at the elbows.

5. Bend the man forward at the waist, bend neck_1 forward, and tilt the head back up to compensate a little. Figure 9.10 shows the pose at this point.

6. Select everything in the Outliner, and set a rotation key. You're setting a pose for all the joints, which will ensure that all body parts are in synch.

If you don't key everything every step of the way, some parts of the body will not key with Auto Keyframe properly because the last time they moved may have been two steps previous.

Frame 10

Figure 9.11 shows the position you'll keyframe at frame 10; it's approximately midstride for the first leg.

1. Go to frame 10. Rotate the back leg out farther, and level the foot. Lower the body to place the man on the ground.

2. Rotate the front leg out, straighten the knee, and flatten the foot to place it on the ground. This is midstride. Swing the arms in their current direction a touch more. Bend the torso forward some more. Make sure you set a key for all the joints.

Frame 15

Figure 9.12 shows the position you'll keyframe at frame 15. At this point, the character begins to shift his weight to the front leg as it plants on the ground, and the character also begins lifting the back leg.

1. Go to frame 15. Rotate the front leg back toward the body, and raise the body as the man steps to keep the front foot flat on the ground. Rotate the back knee up to lift the foot, and rotate the foot down to make him push off the toe.

2. Start swinging the arms in the opposite direction. Start straightening the torso back up, but bend the head forward a bit.

Frame 20

At frame 20, the man will shift all his weight on the front leg and move his body over that leg, lifting his rear leg to begin its swing out front to finish the stride. Figure 9.13 shows the pose.

1. Rotate the front leg almost straight under the man, and lift up the body to keep the front foot on the ground. Lift the rear leg and swing it forward.

2. Straighten the torso and keep the arms swinging in their new direction. Key all the joints.

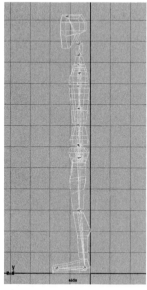

Figure 9.9

The character's starting position

Figure 9.10

The second pose (frame 5)

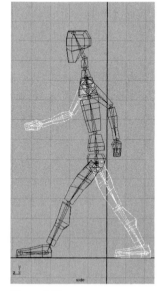

Figure 9.11

The third pose (frame 10)

Frame 25

Now the man will swing his whole body forward, pivoting on the left leg (the dark one) to put himself off center and ready to fall forward into the next step. Figure 9.14 shows the pose.

1. Go to frame 25.

2. Rotate the front (dark) leg back behind the man, and swing the white leg up and ready to take the next step. Lower the body to keep the now rear foot (the dark one) on the ground.

Frame 30

Use Figure 9.15 as a guide for creating the next pose. Notice that it is similar to the pose at frame 10 (in Figure 9.11). As a matter of fact, the only major difference is really which leg and arm are out in front. Everything else should be about the same. You'll want some variety in the exact positions to make the animation more interesting, but the poses are much the same.

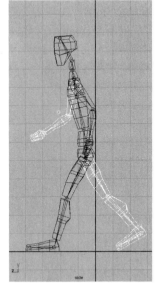

Figure 9.12

The fourth pose (frame 15)

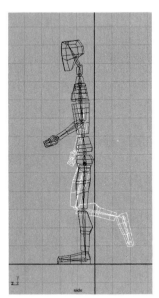

Figure 9.13

The fifth pose (frame 20)

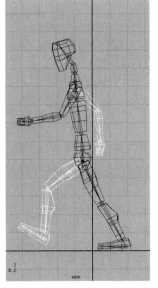

Figure 9.14

The sixth pose (frame 25)

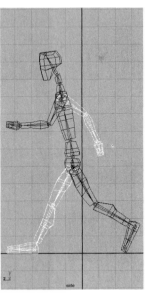

Figure 9.15

The seventh pose (frame 30)

Completing the Cycle

You've finished a set of poses for the character's first step. The next set of poses for your walk cycle will correspond to the first set, but now the other leg and arm corresponds to these positions. For example, you animated the left leg taking a step forward in the first series of poses. The next series of poses will have to do with the right leg. The pose at frame 35 corresponds to the pose at frame 15. Frame 40 matches frame 20. You can start a new series of poses with the left leg.

Once a 30-frame section is complete, you will need to return to the animation through the Graph Editor. Adjust all the keyframes that you set at five-frame intervals to make the animation more realistic. Right now you have only the gross keyframes in place, so the timing is off. Your next step is to time the frames properly. This is ultimately a matter of how the animation looks to you.

Logistically speaking, some poses take a little less time to achieve than the evenly spaced five frames you used. For example, achieving the second pose from the start position should take four frames. The third pose (see Figure 9.11 earlier in the chapter) from frame 5 to frame 10 should take four frames. The next frame section originally from frame 10 to 15 (the fourth pose; see Figure 9.12 earlier in the chapter) should also take only three frames. To accomplish this easily, follow these steps:

1. Select the top node of the skeleton (the pelvis), and open the Graph Editor. On the pelvis node in the left side of the Graph Editor, Shift+click the plus sign to open the entire tree of nodes beneath the pelvis. All the animated channels will show their curves to the right.

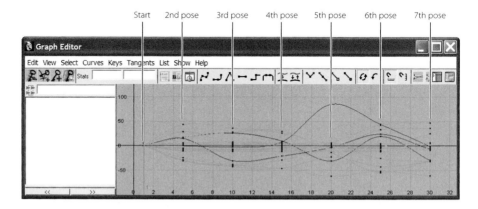

2. Marquee-select all the keyframes beyond frame 1, not including frame 1. Press the W key to active the Translate tool. Shift+MMB click in the Graph Editor, and drag the keys horizontally to move them all one unit (frame) to the left. The second pose now goes from frame 1 to frame 4.

3. Deselect the keys at frame 4 by holding down the Ctrl key (you will also use the Ctrl key on a Mac) and marquee-selecting all the keys at frame 4. Shift+drag the remaining selected keys one unit to the left. The third pose now goes from frame 4 to frame 8.

4. Deselect the keys at frame 8 and Shift+drag the selected keys to the left two frames so that the fourth pose animates from frame 8 to frame 9. Deselect the frame 11 keys, and move the rest over two frames to the left so that the section runs from frame 11 to frame 14. The next section should go from frame 14 to frame 18. The final section should go from frame 18 to frame 22.

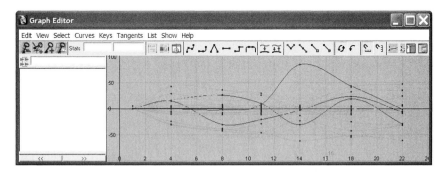

5. Continue to set and adjust keys for another cycle or two of the walk. The majority of time spent in animating something like this involves using the Graph Editor to time out the keyframes to make the animation look believable. Also try offsetting some of the arm rotations a frame to the left or right to break up the monotony that arises from having everything keyed on the same frame.

Load the file block_walk_v01.mov or block_walk_v01.avi of this walk cycle from the images folder of the Block_Man project on the CD to see the animation in motion. It's a rough cycle, and you have to keep adjusting the character's height to keep the feet on the ground. This is where IK comes in handy, as you'll see later in this chapter. Also, the file block_man_skeleton_walk_v01.mb in the Block_Man project has the keyframed cycle for you to play with and continue animating.

Walk Cycle Wrap-Up

This walk cycle animation is more about getting comfortable with keyframing and skeletons than it is with creating great walk cycles, so take some time to practice and get better. Animating walk cycles is a good way to hone your animation skills. Several great books are devoted to character rigging and animation alone, and you can research the field for ways to become more proficient. But keep in mind that movement and timing are what make animation good, not the setup or the model.

Skeletons: The Hand

For another foray into a skeletal system, you can give yourself a hand—literally. You'll use a skeleton to deform the geometry to animate it as a hand would move.

Load the file `poly_hand_skeleton_v01.ma` from the Poly_Hand_Anim project on the CD. The hand initially looks like this:

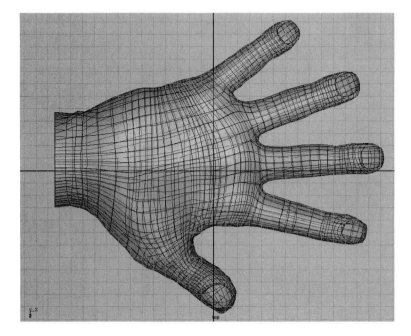

You'll use it to create a bone structure to make the hand animate. This is called *rigging*.

Rigging the Hand

To create the first bones of the hand, follow these steps:

1. Maximize the top view window. Switch to the Animation menu set by using the drop-down menu or by pressing F2.

2. Activate the Joint tool by choosing **Skeleton → Joint Tool**. Your cursor will turn into a cross.

3. Click at the base of the wrist to place the first joint. This will be the root joint of the hand.

4. Shift+LMB click the bottom part of the palm.

5. Place joints down through the thumb from this second joint according to the corresponding bones in Figure 9.16.

6. To start another string of joints into the palm, press the Up arrow key four times until you're at the second joint at the base of the palm.

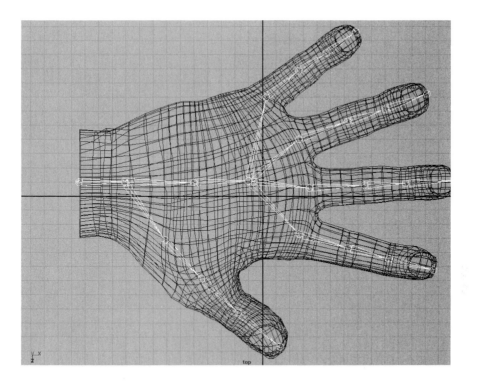

Figure 9.16

The joints in the hand

7. The next joint you place will be a branch from this joint. Place that joint in the middle of the palm. Place another joint up farther along the palm, and then branch it out to the index finger. Press the Up arrow key to return to that upper palm joint, and start a new branch into the middle finger. Repeat to place joints for the remaining fingers as shown in Figure 9.16. With these joints placed, you have a simple skeleton rig for the hand. This rig allows you quite a bit of hand and finger movement.

Check the other views (see Figure 9.17) to see where you need to tweak your joint positions to fit the hand. Ideally you want the joints to be set inside your intended geometry in the same way that real bones are laid out.

To position the joints, you can use either of two Maya tools: Move or Move Pivot. First you'll try the Move tool. Select the tip joint for the pinkie. It needs to be lowered into the pinkie itself. Select the Move tool (press W), and move it down into the tip of the pinkie. Now move on to the top pinkie knuckle. Notice that if you move the knuckle, the tip will move as well.

It's best to move joints as pivots. Since joints are nothing more than pivots, go into the move pivot mode (press the Ins key) to move joints. Select the top pinkie knuckle joint, and move it with Move Pivot (press Ins) instead. Only the joint moves, and the bones adjust to the new positioning. Set the positions on the remaining joints as shown in Figures 9.18 and 9.19.

Figure 9.17

Four views of the hand with initial placement of the joints

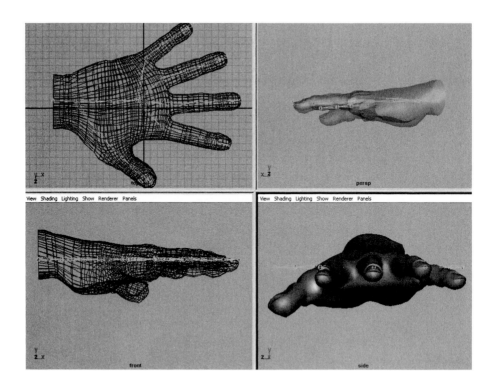

Figure 9.18

The joints of the hand placed properly in the geometry

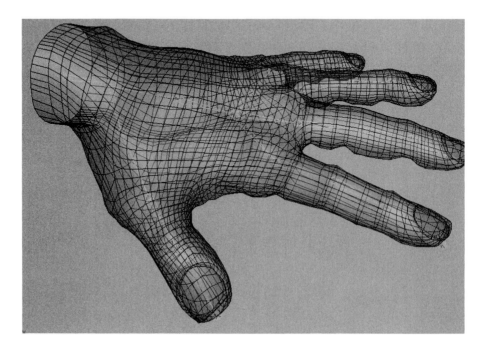

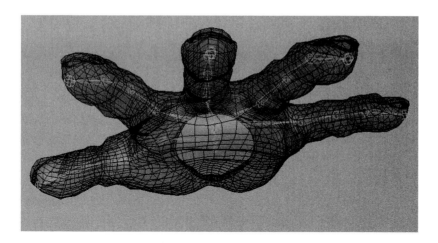

Figure 9.19

Second view of the hand's skeleton

Binding to Geometry

An integral part of rigging a character or an object with a skeleton is *binding*, also known as *skinning*. Binding is another way to attach geometry to a skeletal system. Whereas with the block man you directly attached the whole pieces of geometry to the bones through parenting, binding involves attaching *clusters*, or groups of vertices or CVs, of the geometry to the skeleton to allow it to deform the model. This is typically how skeletons are used in character animation work. (For more on grouping and parenting, refer to Chapter 3's exercise on the nine planets.)

The basic technique of binding a character is easy. However, Maya gives you tremendous control over how your geometry deforms.

Binding Overview

Binding is, in theory, identical to the lattice deformer you saw in Chapter 6. A lattice attached to an object exerts influence on parts of the model according to the sections of the lattice. Each section affects a NURBS surface's CVs or a polygon surface's vertices within its borders, and as a section of the lattice moves, it takes those points of the model with it.

Skeletal binding does much the same thing. It attaches the model's points to the bones, and as the bones pivot around their joints, the section of the model that is attached follows.

By attaching vertices or CVs (depending on your geometry) to a skeleton, you can bend or distort the geometry. When a bone moves or rotates about its joint, it pulls with it the points that are attached to it. The geometry then deforms to fit the new configuration of the bones bound to it.

Figure 9.20

Rigid Bind of a cylinder. The crease is pronounced.

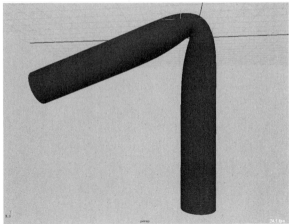

Figure 9.21

Smooth Bind of the cylinder shown in Figure 9.20. The crease is smoother, yet less defined.

You can directly bind geometry to a skeleton in two ways: using Smooth Bind and using Rigid Bind. You can indirectly deform geometry using deformers and lattices attached to skeletons, but here you'll use the direct methods. Figure 9.20 shows a Rigid Bind, and Figure 9.21 shows a Smooth Bind.

Create a tall NURBS cylinder, with a span of 16 or more. The more spans you have in the deformable model, the better it will bend. Duplicate the cylinder, and move it over in your window. Now in the front view, create a four-bone (five-joint) skeleton that starts at the bottom of the first cylinder and goes straight up the middle, ending at the tip. Duplicate the skeleton, and move it to the center of the second cylinder.

CREATING A RIGID BIND

A Rigid Bind is the simpler of the two, because only one surface point (vertex or CV) is affected by a joint at a time. A *Rigid Bind* groups the CVs of a NURBS or the vertices of a polygon into *joint clusters* that are then attached to the bones. No one surface point is influenced by more than one joint.

Thus, bending a model about a joint with a Rigid Bind yields a more articulate crease than a Smooth Bind, which allows more than one joint to affect the CV or vertex, resulting in a more rounded and smooth bend.

To create a Rigid Bind, select the first skeleton and Shift+select its cylinder. In the Animation menu set, choose **Skin → Bind Skin → Rigid Bind** ❐.

In the option box, you'll find almost everything you need is already the default. The Bind To parameter lets you Rigid Bind the entire skeleton to the geometry or just the joints selected. Using Selected Joints gives you the option of using just part of a skeleton system to Rigid Bind, giving you flexibility in how your rig affects the model. You'll leave that option on Complete Skeleton to attach the whole thing.

Click the Color Joints check box to set a different color for each joint in the bind, which can make for an easier work flow. The Bind Method parameter deals with how the points in the model will be attached. The default, Closest Point, organizes the points into skin point sets according to which joint they are closest to. They are then assigned to be influenced by that joint only.

The Partition Set option lets you define your own points before you bind and select which points are set to which joints. If you define a partition set for each joint you have, Maya then assigns each set to the nearest joint. For example, you can define some points at the top of the surface to be a part of a set controlled by a joint in the bottom part. Closest Point is the best option for most work.

Using the defaults and turning on Color Joints, click the Bind Skin button in the option box. The root of the skeleton is now selected and the cylinder turns magenta, signifying it has input connections (such as history).

CREATING A SMOOTH BIND

A *Smooth Bind* allows a joint to influence more than one skin point on the model. This allows for areas of the model farther from the joint to bend when that joint rotates. Joints influence points to varying degrees between 0 and 1 across the surface, decreasing in influence the farther the point is from the joint. The multiple influences on a point all need to add up to 1 across all the joints that influence it. Maya automatically generates the proper influence amounts upon binding, although the animator can change these values later.

To create a Smooth Bind, select the second skeleton and its cylinder, and choose **Skin → Bind Skin → Smooth Bind ❑**.

In the option box, you'll find the familiar Bind To parameter. You will also find, under the Bind Method drop-down menu, the options Closest in Hierarchy and Closest Distance. Choosing Closest in Hierarchy assigns the skin points to the nearest joint in the hierarchy. This is most commonly used for character work, because it pays attention to the way the skeleton is laid out.

For example, a surface point on the right leg would not be affected by the thigh joint on the left leg simply because it is near it on the model. Closest Distance, on the other hand, disregards a joint's position in the hierarchy of the skeleton and simply assigns influences according to how far the point is from the joint.

Max Influences sets a limit on how many joints can affect a single point. Dropoff Rate determines how a joint's influence diminishes on points farther from it. For example, with Smooth Bind, one shoulder joint can influence, to varying degrees, points stretching down the arm and into the chest and belly. By limiting these two parameters, you can control how much of your model is pulled along by a particular joint.

Using all the defaults is typically best. So click Bind Skin in the option box to smooth bind your second cylinder to the bones.

Bend both cylinders to get a feel for how each creases at the bending joints. Figure 9.22 shows the difference.

DETACHING A SKELETON

If you want to do away with your binding, select the skeleton and its geometry and choose **Skin → Detach Skin**. The model will snap to its original shape before the bind was applied and the joints rotated. It's common to bind and detach skeletons several times on the same model as you try to figure out the exact configuration that works best for you and your animation.

If you need to go back to the initial position of the skeleton at the point of binding it to the model, you can automatically set the skeleton back to the bind pose after any rotations have been applied to any of its joints. Simply select the skeleton and choose **Skin → Go to Bind Pose** to snap the skeleton and model into the position they were when you bound them together. It is also best to set your skeleton to bind the pose whenever you edit your binding weights.

Figure 9.22

Rigid and smooth bound cylinders. The smaller cylinder is rigid bound, and the larger is smooth bound.

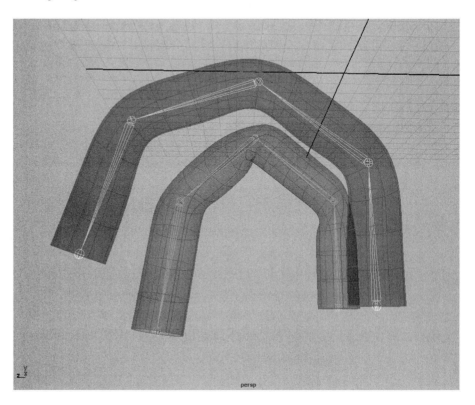

A MODELING TRICK USING A SKELETON

An easy way to create bends and creases in a model is to create the surface without the bend and use a skeleton to deform it the way you want. You can then detach the skin and *bake* the history so that the surface retains its deformation but loses its connection to the skeleton. Bind your geometry to the skeleton chain using Smooth Bind or Rigid Bind. Bend the skeleton to deform the geometry, and then choose **Skin → Detach Skin** ❐. In the option box, set the History parameter to Bake History and click Detach. The model will retain its deformed state but will lose all connections to the skeleton. This is just like using a nonlinear or lattice deformer on an object and then deleting the object's history to rid it of the deformer. With a detached skin, however, you won't lose any other history already applied to that object as you would if you deleted history through the Edit menu.

Binding the Hand: Rigid

Since you'll want definitive creases at the finger joints, you'll use Rigid Bind for the hand.

Load your hand and positioned skeleton, or use the file `poly_hand_skeleton_v02.ma` from the Poly_Hand_Anim project on the CD. Now follow these steps to Rigid Bind the hand:

1. Select the skeleton's root at the wrist, and Shift+select the top node of the hand. Select the hand's top node (polysurface2) using the CD file, to make sure you select the fingernails as well.

2. Choose **Skin → Bind Skin → Rigid Bind** ❐. Turn on Color Joints, and click the Bind Skin button in the option box. You're bound and ready to animate the hand.

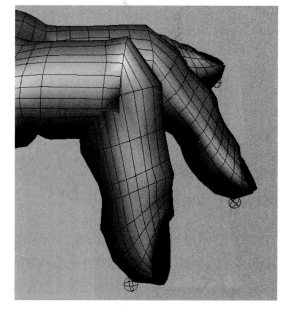

3. Select some of the finger joints and rotate them. Notice how the model creases at the knuckles. If you rotate far enough, the model will fold in over itself, especially since this model is polygonal.

Editing a Rigid Bind

Having a Rigid Bind doesn't mean your creases always have to be this hard. With *flexors* (basically a lattice, as seen in Chapter 6), you can smooth out specific areas of a joint for a better look. This is useful at shoulder joints or hip joints where a crease like an elbow is not desired. In this case, it will help smooth out the knuckles so the geometry doesn't fold over itself, as in the previous graphic.

1. Choose **Skin → Go to Bind Pose** to reset your skeleton.

2. Select the middle knuckle of the index finger, and choose **Skin → Edit Rigid Skin → Create Flexor** to open the option box for Create Flexor.

3. You'll notice that these options are similar to the lattice you created in Chapter 6 to edit the model. You can adjust the number of divisions later through the Attribute Editor, so you don't need to know exactly what you require before you create the flexor. Click Create to display a lattice at the joint position, as shown in Figure 9.23.

4. In the Outliner, drill down to the jointFfd1LatticeGroup node now attached under that knuckle joint in the hierarchy. Select the lattice as well as its base so you can adjust the size, and if need be, position of the flexor, just as you did on the lattice work earlier. Resize the flexor so that it better conforms to the knuckle, and elongate it so that it covers more of the finger, as shown in Figure 9.24.

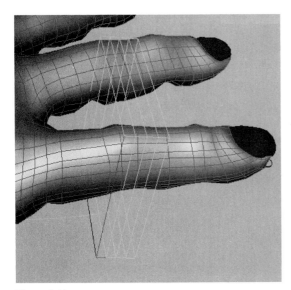

Figure 9.23

Creating a flexor at the middle knuckle

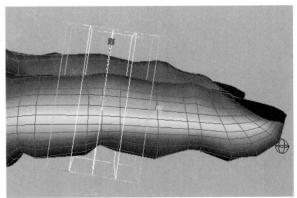

Figure 9.24

Scaling the flexor to fit better on the knuckle

5. Scaling and positioning the flexor (when both lattice and base nodes are selected) will make the joint bend smoother, without affecting more than is necessary. By elongating the flexor here, you smooth out the knuckle's bend and prevent the polygons from bending over each other and still maintain a crisp crease, as shown in Figure 9.25.

6. Create flexors for the other knuckles that will need them. Be sure to scale the flexors to make the most efficient use of them and fit them only where they need to be. Figure 9.26 shows how the finger reacts when bending with flexors at each joint.

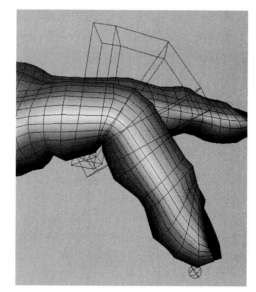

Figure 9.25

The knuckle's crease is now sharp, but the geometry does not fold over itself as before.

The scene `poly_hand_skeleton_v03.ma` from the Poly_Hand_Anim project on the CD has the hand rigid bound with flexors on one finger for your reference. Start with it to create flexors for the rest of the fingers, and animate the hand making some sign language positions, grabbing a pencil, or pressing a button.

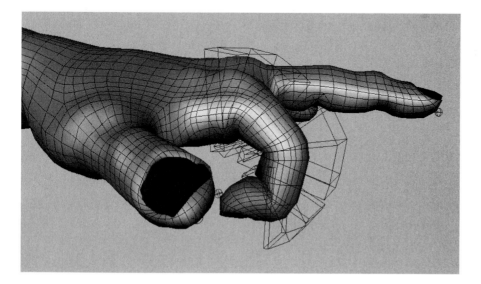

Figure 9.26

Flexors along the index finger

Binding the Hand: Smooth

Now try skinning the hand with Smooth Bind.

Load your prebound hand or `poly_hand_skeleton_v02.ma` from the Poly_Hand_Anim project on the CD. Now follow these steps to Smooth Bind the hand:

1. Select the root at the wrist and the top node of the hand. Choose **Skin → Bind Skin → Smooth Bind**.

2. Try rotating some of the knuckle joints to see how the fingers respond. Go back to the bind pose when you're done.

3. Rotate the middle knuckle of the index finger down. Notice how the knuckle gets thinner the more you bend the finger there. Go to the top knuckle of the index finger and rotate that joint. Notice that part of the hand moves with the finger. This is again exaggerated because the hand is polygonal, so its deformations seem more severe than a NURBS model of the same hand. Figure 9.27 shows the result of bending at the index finger.

Editing a Smooth Bind

You usually edit a Smooth Bind by *painting skin weights*. Since points on the model are influenced by multiple joints in a Smooth Bind, you will need to adjust just how much influence is exerted by these joints on the same points.

1. Make sure you are in shaded mode (press 5). Select the hand, and then choose **Skin → Edit Smooth Skin → Paint Skin Weights Tool □**.

> You paint skin weights on the affected geometry and not on the joints themselves, so you need to select the model and not the skeleton before invoking this tool.

Figure 9.27

Bending at the index finger causes some unwanted deformation.

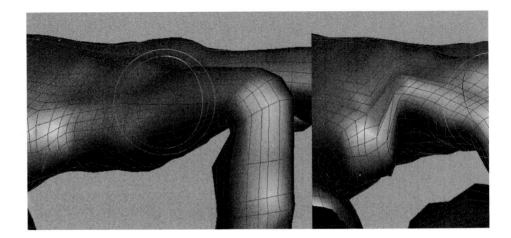

2. Your hand should now turn black, with a bit of light gray at the wrist. The option box will appear, listing the joints that are connected to the hand.

3. The color value (between white and black) determines how much the selected joint in the option box is exerting on that part of the geometry. It's best to name your joints properly so that selecting from this window is easier and more intuitive. If you loaded the file from the CD, you'll need to name the joints yourself to make the scene organized and easier to work with.

4. In the option box, make sure the Paint Operation button under the Paint Weights section is set to Replace. Change the Value slider to 0. In the Brush section, the Radius(U) and Radius(L) govern the size of your brush. Make sure the Opacity slider is set to 1.

5. Using the LMB, paint the black value around parts of the hand and palm that should not be affected by the index finger bending at its top knuckle, as shown in Figure 9.28.

Skin weights must always be *normalized* in a Smooth Bind, meaning the values have to add up to 1. When you reduce the influence of a joint on an area of the surface, it is automatically shifted to other joints in the hierarchy that have influence over that area, so those joints are now more responsible for its movement.

6. Smooth out the area where it goes from white to black. In the Tool Options window, set Paint Operation to Smooth. RMB to smooth the area around the knuckle for a cleaner deformation. Your index knuckle should now bend beautifully.

You can exit the Paint Skin Weights tool by selecting another tool (press W for Translate, for example) and your view will return to regular shaded mode. Try bending the rest of the fingers and painting their influences, and then animate the hand making gestures or grabbing an object using FK animation to set keys on the rotations.

Figure 9.28

Paint the new weights to avoid unwanted deformations in the hand.

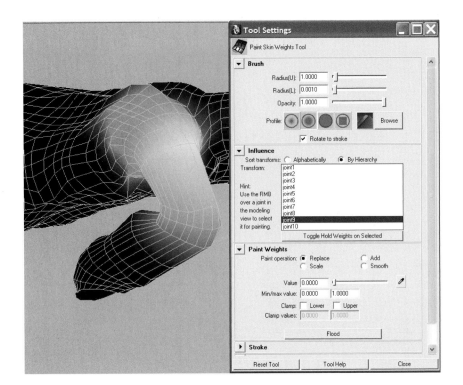

When you paint weights on polygons, keep in mind that you will be painting using the UVs. You might need to re-create the UVs of a polygonal mesh with a UV projection map for the Paint Weights tool to function properly, especially when importing and exporting the weight maps from one mesh to another (a procedure you won't encounter until later in your Maya experience).

The scene `poly_hand_skeleton_v04.ma` from the Poly_Hand_Anim project on the CD has the hand smooth bound with painted weights on the index finger for your reference. Try painting the other knuckles as needed for your animation.

Rigging work is essential for getting a good animation from your model. In a professional shop, it usually falls under the domain of a technical director who oversees the setup of characters and may also model their geometry. Time spent on rigging pays off in easier animation.

Inverse Kinematics

With IK, you have tools that let you plant a foot where it needs to be so you're not always moving the skeleton or model to compensate and keep the heel in place.

For legs, IK is nothing short of a blessing. There is no clearly preferable work flow to suggest when dealing with rigging arms and hands, however. Many people use IK on hands as well, but it can be better to animate the legs with IK and animate every other part of the body with FK. IK is best used when parts of the body (such as the feet) need to be planted at times. Planting the hands is not necessary for a walk cycle, and having IK handles on the arms may create additional work while animating them.

Rigging the IK legs

Now it's back to the block man. Switch to that project and load your version or the `block_man_skeleton_v02.mb` file from the Block_Man project on the CD.

You will create an IK chain from the hip to the ankle on each foot. Creating the IK from the hip to the toe will not work as well.

Since IK automatically bends the joints in its chain according to where its end-effector, or IK handle, is located, it has to choose which way to bend at a particular joint. To prevent IK from choosing the wrong way, you will first nudge the knees slightly to let the IK solver know which way that joint is supposed to go. Follow these steps:

Figure 9.29

IK handles on both ankles with the roots at the hip joints

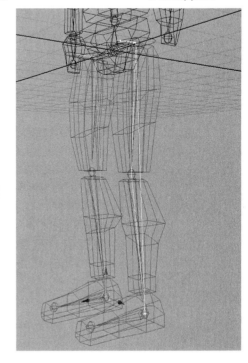

1. Select the two knee joints. In pivot mode (press Ins), move the knees a little bit forward to create a slight crook in the leg.

2. Open the IK Handle tool by choosing **Skeleton → IK Handle Tool**. Your cursor will change to a cross.

3. Select the start joint for the IK chain. This will be the root of this chain. Click the left thigh joint, and then pick your end-effector at the heel joint. Repeat for the other leg. Figure 9.29 shows handles on both ankles.

   If for some reason you can't manage to pick a joint for the IK tool, make sure in your viewport that **Show → Pivots** is turned on. Also, if you have difficulty seeing the handles, you can increase their size by choosing **Display → Animation ⊕ IK Handle Size**.

4. Move the IK handles around and see how the legs react. When you're done, reset the IK handle positions.

5. Grab the top joint of the skeleton, the pelvis joint. Move the joint and the entire body moves with it. Select both ankle IK handles, and set a translation key for them (press Shift+W).

Grab the pelvis joint again and move it. The feet will stick to their positions on the ground. Move the pelvis down and the legs bend at the knees. Notice how the feet bend into the ground, though (below left).

6. Move the pelvis back to the origin. You'll now create an IK handle for the foot so that the foot stays flat on the ground. Open the IK Handle tool. For the start joint, select the ankle; for the end-effector, select the joint at the tip of the foot. Repeat for the other foot.

You can invoke the last tool you used by pressing Y.

7. Set a translate key for the foot IK handles. Move the pelvis down and the legs bend at the knees and the ankle, keeping the feet flush on the ground (below right).

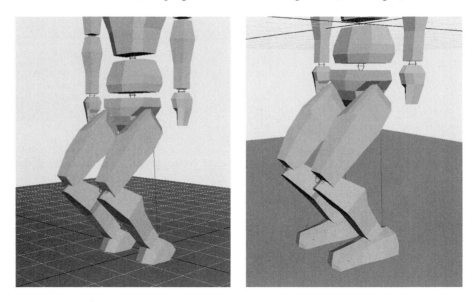

Creating an IK Walk Cycle

Because the feet will stick to the ground, creating a walk cycle with IK animation will be far easier than using FK. Making the animation look good is still a tough job that requires a lot of practice.

Load `block_man_IK_v01.mb` from the Block_Man project on the CD, or use your own IK-rigged block man with handles at the ankles and feet. The white leg and arm are again on the far side of the character. You'll set keys at every five frames again for the gross animation. To keep this short, you'll just go over setting poses with the feet. You can always return to the scene to add animation to the upper body with FK as you did earlier in this chapter.

1. On frame 1, set translate keys on the pelvis joint and all four IK handles for their start position.

2. Go to frame 5, and move the pelvis forward about one unit. The legs and feet will lift up off the ground a bit and strain to keep their position. Lower the pelvis to get the feet flat on the ground again. Set a key for the pelvis. Because Auto Keyframe is turned on, all keys are set for this animation. (With the FK animation, you set keys for everything at every pose.)

3. Grab the near IK handles for the ankle and foot, and move them forward and up to match the pose shown below left.

4. Go to frame 10. Move the front foot forward and plant it on the ground. Move the pelvis another three-fourths of a unit. Set translation keys for the rear ankle and foot handles where they are. Make sure to place the pelvis so that the rear foot is almost flat on the ground. Match the pose shown below middle.

5. Go to frame 15. Move the pelvis another two units to center the body over the front foot. Lift the rear ankle and foot IK handles up to bend the knee, and bring the knee up a bit. Match the pose shown below right.

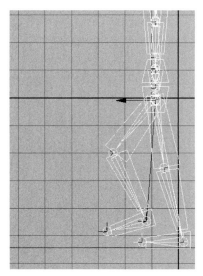 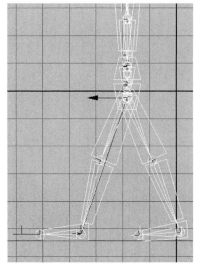 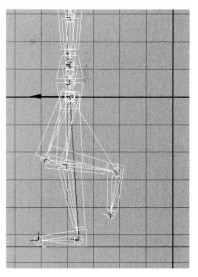

6. Go to frame 20. Move the pelvis forward one unit, and swing the white leg forward as in the pose shown below left.

7. Move the pelvis three-fourths of a unit forward, and plant the front leg down. Set keys for the rear leg and foot where they stand. Match the pose shown below right.

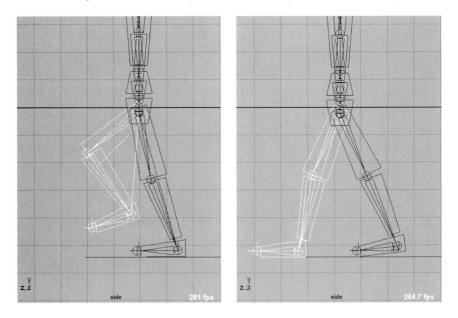

The next pose should match the pose in frame 10, though with the other leg. Continue the cycle, with each successive pose matching the one 15 frames before it on the opposite side. And don't forget to add FK animation to the top of the body to give your character some weight.

Further Uses for IK Chains

Many animators use IK chains more often in effects animation than in character work. IK chains can drive whips and ropes, flutter flags, bounce ponytails, and pump pistons as well as move legs and arms. For example, you can use a different type of IK chain, the *spline IK chain,* to control the shape of your bone chain with a NURBS spline. This is great for snakes and other long, deforming objects.

To create a spline IK chain, choose **Skeleton → IK Spline Handle Tool**, and then select your top joint and end-effector. Maya will create a spline running the length of the bone chain. Adjusting the curvature of the spline will in turn drive the bones, which in turn drive the geometry bound to them. Figure 9.30 shows a spline curve affecting the curvature of the bones in its spline IK chain.

Basic Relationships: Constraints

As you know, Maya is all about relationships between object nodes. You can create animation on one object based on the animation of another object by setting up a relationship between the objects. The simplest way to do that (outside of grouping) is to create a *constraint*. For example, you can "glue" one object to another's position or rotation through a constraint.

A constraint creates a direct relationship between the source and the target object's **Translate** or **Rotate** attributes. This section explores six types of constraints: point, orient, scale, aim, geometry, and normal.

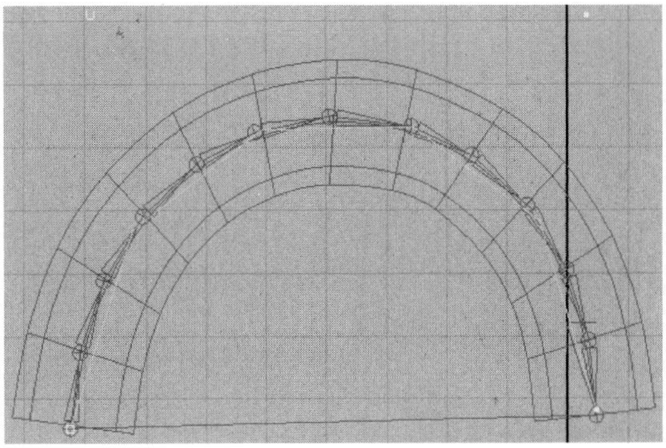

The Point Constraint

To attach a source object to a target object but have the source follow only the position of the target, use a point constraint. A *point constraint* will connect only the **Translate** attributes of the source to the target. To use this method, select the target object(s), and then Shift+select the source object. In the Animation menu set, choose **Constrain → Point ☐**.

The options allow you to set an offset that will create a gap between the source and the target. Constraints are based on the pivots of the objects, so a point constraint will snap the source at its pivot point to the pivot point of the target. Offset would dictate the distance between their pivots in any of the axes.

You can constrain the same source to more than one target object. The source will then take up the average position between the multiple targets. By setting the Weight slider in the option box, you can create more of an influence on the source by any of the targets.

In Figure 9.31, a cone has been point constrained to a sphere. Wherever the sphere goes, the cone follows. This is different from parenting the cone to the sphere in that only its translations are affected by the sphere. If you rotate or scale the sphere, the cone will not rotate or scale with it.

Although you can blend keyframe animation with constraint animation, as a beginner to Maya, consider that once you set a point constraint, you will be unable to control the cone's **Translate** attributes since they are being driven by the sphere's translations.

Figure 9.30

A spline IK chain is driven by the curvature of a NURBS spline. Adjusting the curve's CVs moves the joints.

Figure 9.31

A cone point constrained to a sphere follows the sphere's position.

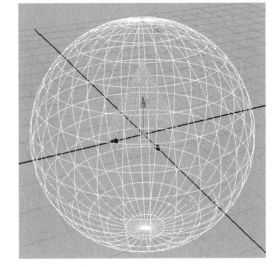

Point constraints are perfect to animate a character carrying a cane or a sword, for example. The rotations on the sword are still free to animate, but the sword is attached to the character's belt and will follow the character throughout the scene.

The Orient Constraint

An *orient constraint* will attach the source's **Rotation** attributes to the target's **Rotation** attributes. Select the target object(s) first, and then Shift+select the source object. In the Animation menu set, choose **Constrain → Orient** ❑.

The Offset parameter allows you to set an offset in any axis. Otherwise, the source will assume the exact orientation of the target. In the case of multiple targets, the source will use the average of their orientations. Figure 9.32 shows the cone's orientation following an elongated sphere (the target).

A rotation constraint saves a lot of hassle when you have to animate an object to keep rotating in the same direction as another object. For example, if two speedboats are cruising along neck and neck and one turns, the other could turn to match, keeping them both on course. You could also set offsets and animate them to make the second boat look as if it's reacting to the other so that the animation doesn't look too perfect.

The Scale Constraint

A *scale constraint* will attach the source's **Scale** attributes to the target's **Scale** attributes. Select the target object(s) first, and then Shift+select the source object. In the Animation menu set, choose **Constrain → Scale** ❑.

Figure 9.32

The cone's rotations will match the sphere's rotations.

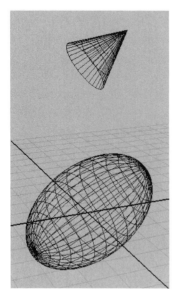

The Offset parameter allows you to set a scale offset in any axis. Otherwise, the source will assume the exact scale of the target. The source will use the average of the scales of multiple targets. Figure 9.33 shows the cone's scale matching the target sphere.

The scale constraint is good for matching the sizes of objects. For example, if an air hose is inflating a string of balloons, constraining the balloons to one target saves you the hassle of animating all their **Scale** attributes in unison. Or if a cartoon character's eyes are bugging out at something, you can scale constrain one to the other so that both bug out in the same time and proportion.

The Aim Constraint

The *aim constraint* adjusts the source's rotations so that the source always points to the target object. Select the target object(s) first, and then Shift+select the source object. In the Animation menu set, choose **Constrain → Aim** ❐.

The aim constraint has more options than the other constraints because you need to specify which axis of the source is to point to the target. You do so using the Aim Vector and Up Vector settings.

The Aim Vector setting specifies which axis of the source is the "front" and will point to the target. In the cone and sphere examples, you would set the Aim Vector of the cone to 0,1,0 to make the Y axis the "front" so that the cone's point aims at the sphere. If Aim Vector is set to 1,0,0, for example, the cone's side points to the sphere. Figure 9.34 shows the cone pointing to the sphere with an Aim Vector setting of 0,1,0.

The Offset values will create an offset on the source's **Rotation** attributes, tilting it one way or another. The Up Vector setting specifies which way the cone will face when it's pointing to the sphere.

Aim constraints are perfect for animating cameras to follow a subject, such as a car at a racetrack.

Geometry and Normal Constraints

The geometry and normal constraints will constrain the source object to the surface of the target object (as long as it's a NURBS or poly mesh).

With a geometry constraint, the source object attaches at its pivot point to the surface of the target. It will try to keep its own position as best it can, shifting as its target surface changes beneath it. Again, select the target, select the source object, and choose **Constrain → Geometry**.

Figure 9.33

The cone will now match the sphere's scale.

Figure 9.34

The cone aiming at the sphere

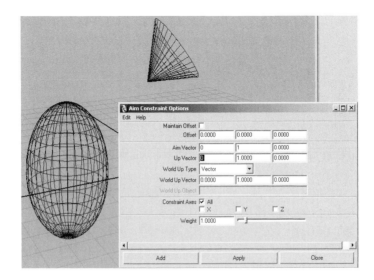

Using a geometry constraint is useful when you want to keep an object on a deforming surface, such as a floating boat on a lake. Figure 9.35 shows the cone after it has been geometry constrained to a NURBS plane that is being deformed by a wave deformer (choose **Deform → Create Nonlinear → Wave**). The cone will sit on the surface as the waves ripple through, but it will not rock back and forth to stay oriented with the surface.

To get the cone to orient itself so that it truly floats on the surface, you need to use a normal constraint. Using a normal constraint rotates the cone to follow the surface's normals, keeping it perpendicular to the surface.

A surface normal is an imaginary perpendicular tangent line that emanates from all surfaces to give the surface direction.

The normal constraint is similar to the aim constraint, and its options are similar. Using the Aim Vector setting, you specify which way is "up" for the object to define the orientation that the source should maintain. This setting will not, however, constrain the location of the source to the target. If you want a floating effect, use a geometry and a normal constraint to get the cone to bob up and down and roll back and forth as the waves ripple along (see Figure 9.36).

Parent, Tangent, and Pole Vector Constraints

Three more constraints are possible in Maya: the parent, tangent, and pole vector constraints. A *parent constraint* constrains an object's translation and rotation to another object by mimicking a parent-child relationship without actually parenting the objects. This keeps objects aligned without worrying about any grouping issues. A *tangent constraint* keeps an object's orientation so that the object always points along a curve's direction. This constraint is usually used with a geometry constraint or path animation to keep the object traveling along a curve pointed in the right direction, no matter the direction of the curve. *Pole vector* constraints are used extensively in character animation rigs to keep IK joints from flipping beyond 180 degrees of motion.

Basic Relationships: Set Driven Keys

A favorite feature for character riggers is the set driven key (SDK). A *set driven key* establishes a relationship for objects that lets you create controls that drive certain features of a character or an object in a scene.

Before you can use an SDK, you must create extra attributes and attach them to the top node of a character. These new attributes drive part of the character's animation. The term *character* is used broadly here. For example, you can set up a vehicle so that an SDK turns its wheels.

Let's start with a simple SDK relationship between two objects. You will create a relationship between a ball and a cone. As the ball moves up in the Y axis, the cone spins in the X axis. As the ball descends, the cone spins back. You will then revisit the hand and set up SDK on the skeleton that animates the model.

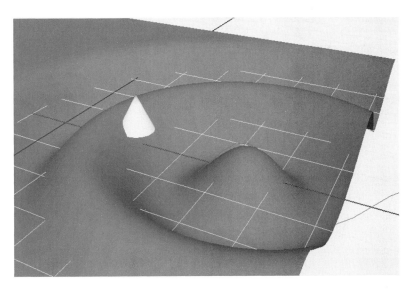

Figure 9.35

With a geometry constraint, the cone sits on the deforming surface.

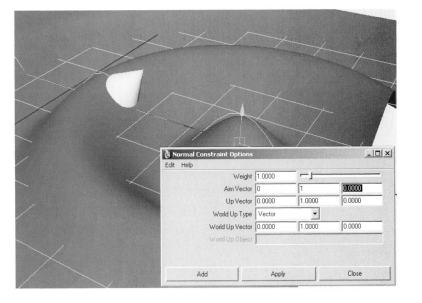

Figure 9.36

The cone now animates to float on the water surface, using both geometry and normal constraints.

Creating a Set Driven Key

To create a simple SDK to make a sphere control the animation of a cone's rotation, follow these steps:

1. Create a NURBS sphere and a cone in a new scene. Move the cone to the side of the sphere, and lay it on its side.

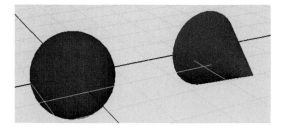

2. Select the sphere, and in the Animation menu set, choose **Animate → Set Driven Key → Set…**. The Set Driven Key window opens with the nurbsSphere1 object selected in the lower half of the window (the Driven section). Its attributes are listed on the right, as you can see in Figure 9.37.

3. You want the sphere to drive the animation of the cone, so you need to switch the sphere to be the driver and not what's driven. Click the Load Driver button to list the sphere in the top half of the window.

4. Select the cone, and click the Load Driven button to display the cone's attributes in the bottom half of the window.

5. In the Driver section, select the sphere's **translateY** attribute. In the Driven section, select the cone's **rotateX** attribute. Click the Key button to set an SDK that essentially says that when the sphere is on the ground (Y = 0), the cone's X rotation is 0 since both attributes are currently 0. The cone's **rotateX** attribute turns orange in the Channel Box, meaning a driven key has been set.

6. Select the sphere and raise it up in Y to a height of 5. Select the cone and rotate it in X to 1800 to make it spin properly. Click the Key button in the Set Driven Key window to specify that when the sphere is at a height of 5, the cone's **rotateX** attribute will be 1800 degrees. As the sphere's height increases from 0 to 5, the cone spins from 0 to 1800 in X.

An Advanced Set Driven Key: The Hand

Automating some animations on a character is indispensable to an animator. This can't be truer than setting up an SDK for hand control. After you model and bind a hand to a skeleton, you're ready for an SDK.

Open the scene `poly_hand_skeleton_v05.ma` from the Poly_Hand_Anim project on the CD, or use your own file that has the hand and its skeleton and is bound (either smooth or rigid) to the skin. Your file should not have animation, though. Set your hand to the bind pose before you begin.

Creating a New Attribute

First, you'll create a new attribute called **index_pull** to control a contracting finger.

1. Select the hand. (It's best to select the top node polySurface2 instead of just the poly mesh of the hand.) In the polySurface2 tab of the Attribute Editor, click the Extra Attributes section. For now, at least, this section is empty.

2. In the Attribute Editor menu, choose **Attributes → Add Attributes** to open the Add Attribute window, which is shown in Figure 9.38. In the Attribute Name field, enter **index_pull**. Be sure that the Make Attribute Keyable check box is checked and that the Float option is selected in the Data Type section. In the Numeric Attribute Properties section, set Minimum to 0, set Maximum to 10, and set Default to 0. Click OK.

After you click OK, the Index_pull slider appears in the Attribute Editor and the Channel Box. This attribute alone will control the entire index finger.

Assigning the Set Driven Key

To set up the relationships with the SDK, follow these steps:

1. With the top hand node selected, open the Set Driven Key window (choose **Animate → Set Driven Key → Set**). Click Load Driver to specify that the hand should drive the animation.

2. Since you're animating the index finger pulling back, you'll want to drive the rotations of the top three knuckles. Shift+select all three knuckles on the index finger. Click the Load Driven button. All three knuckles will appear on the bottom.

3. Select the hand's **index_pull** attribute and the three knuckles' **rotateY** attributes, as shown in Figure 9.39.

4. With the rotations of the knuckles at 0 and the **index_pull** attribute at 0 as well, click the Key button to set the first relationship. When **index_pull** is at 0, the finger will be extended.

Figure 9.37

The Set Driven Key window

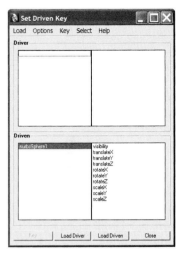

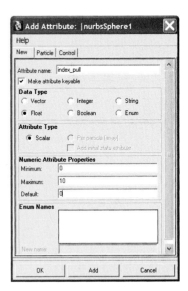

Figure 9.38

The Add Attribute window

5. Select the top hand node, and set the **index_pull** attribute to 5.

6. Select the fingertip's knuckle (joint11 in the CD file), and rotate it in Y to 20. Select the next joint up the chain (the middle knuckle, joint10), and rotate it to 35 in the Y axis. Select the final index knuckle (joint9), and rotate it in the Y axis to 5. Click the Key button. When the **index_pull** attribute is at 5, the finger will assume this bent position.

7. Select the top hand node, and set **index_pull** to 10.

8. Select each of the three knuckles. Set the tip to rotate to 65 in Y. Set the middle knuckle to 60. Set the last knuckle to 50. Click the Key button to see the result shown in Figure 9.40.

Select the top hand node, and change the value of the **index_pull** attribute to animate your finger. All you need to do to pull the finger is to set keys on that attribute, without having to constantly rotate the knuckles. Furthermore, you can set up a single SDK to control the bending of all the fingers at once, or you can set up one SDK for each finger for more control.

 Open the scene `poly_hand_skeleton_v06.ma` from the Poly_Hand_Anim project on the CD to see the hand with the SDK setup on the index finger.

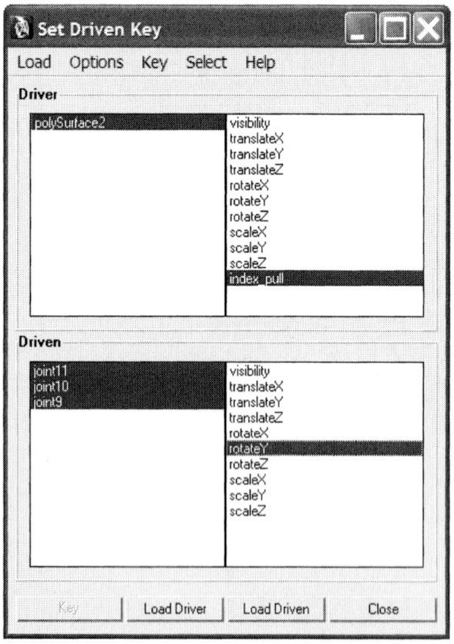

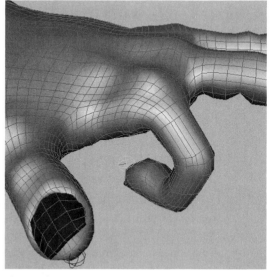

Figure 9.39
The Set Driven Key window for the hand

Figure 9.40
The bent index finger

Application: Rigging the Locomotive

Back to our locomotive. In the previous chapter, you made sure the hierarchy and pivot placements were proper. In this exercise, you can use your own locomotive scene or the `locomotive_anim_v1.mb` file from the previous chapter. You can also use a fancy version of the locomotive, called `fancy_locomotive_anim_v1.mb`, that is set up similarly to `locomotive_anim_v1.mb` for the exercise. This scene is shown in Figure 9.41.

Familiarize yourself with the scene file first. You can use this scene file to remodel your own fancy locomotive if you like, to give you more modeling practice. All the parts of this fancy locomotive were made using the basic tools and procedures laid out in Chapter 4.

Setting Up Wheel Control

Our goal here is to rig the scene to automatically animate all the secondary movements based on some simple controls, such as we did for the hand earlier this chapter. In reality, the locomotive's steam pump drives the arms that then turn the wheels on the locomotive. We will work backward, however, and use one wheel to drive the animation of everything else.

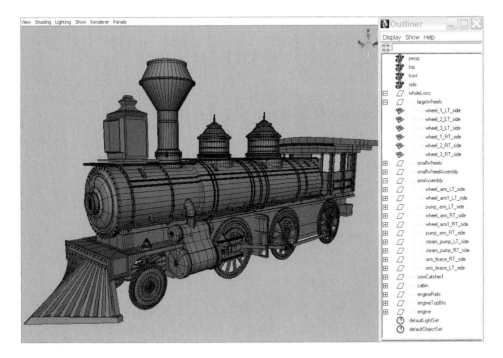

Figure 9.41

The fancier loco-motive model

Since all the large wheels have the same diameter, they will rotate the same as the locomotive moves. In this case, we will use the Connection Editor to attach the X Rotation on all the wheels to our main control wheel. We will pick the middle wheel to be the control. To set up the locomotive, follow these steps:

1. Select the middle wheel on the left side of the locomotive (node wheel_2_LT_side) as shown. Open the Connection Editor (choose **Window → General Editors → Connection Editor**). Click the Reload Left button to load the attributes of the selected middle wheel. Now select the front wheel on the left side, and click the Reload Right button.

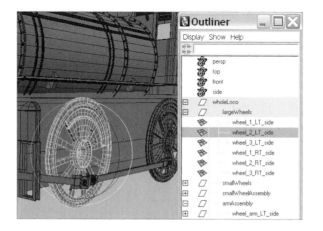

Figure 9.42

Connect the rotations of the two wheels.

2. Scroll down in the Connection Editor until you find Rotate in both columns. First, click to highlight Rotate in the left column, and then click to highlight Rotate in the right column. This connects the two rotations so that they will both rotate at the same time, effectively letting you drive the animation of both wheels from just the center wheel. Figure 9.42 shows the Connection Editor.

3. Select the back wheel on the left side (wheel_3_LT_side). Click the Reload Right button in the Connection Editor. Connect the **Rotate** attribute for the middle and the back wheels. Close the Connection Editor, and select just the middle wheel. When you rotate the wheel, all three wheels rotate together.

4. Repeat this procedure to connect the rotations of the three wheels on the other side to this middle wheel as well. Now all six wheels rotate in synch with the one control wheel. As a matter of fact, when you select that left side middle wheel (the control wheel), the other five wheels turn magenta, signifying a connection between these objects.

If connecting the rotations of objects such as these wheels gives you strange results, such as the wheels flipping over or rotating the opposite direction of the control wheel, try disconnecting all the connections, freezing transforms, and reconnecting the attributes.

Controlling the Wheel Arms

We've now automated the animation of the wheels. Next we will figure out how to connect the wheel arms to the wheels and drive their motion as well. To do so, follow these steps:

1. Create a single joint that lines up with the first wheel arm. The root joint will be placed where the wheel arm meets the middle wheel (control wheel), and the end joint will be placed where the wheel arm meets the pump arm, as shown here. The pump arm has been templated in this graphic to show you the entire wheel arm and joint.

2. Group the joint under the control wheel's node, as shown in the Outliner in Figure 9.43. Then group the wheel arm under the top joint. This way the joint will rotate with the control wheel, also shown in Figure 9.43.

3. As you can see in Figure 9.43, the joint is not rotating properly. The other end of it needs to attach to the pump arm in front of the front wheel. We'll use an IK handle for this. Make sure the rotation of the control wheel and the joint/wheel arm are set back to 0 to

place them back in position. In the Animation menu set, choose **Skeleton → IK Handle Tool**. Make sure the settings are reset for the tool. Select the root joint as the start joint for the IK Handle. Select the other tip of the bone as the end effector. You now have an IK handle at the tip where the wheel arm connects to the pump arm as shown.

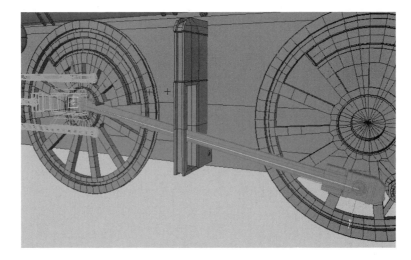

4. If you rotate the control wheel now, the wheel arm still separates from the pump arm as before. This is because the IK handle we just created needs a keyframe to keep it in position, that is, attached to the pump arm. Select the IK handle, and at frame 1, set a position keyframe. Now if you rotate the control wheel, the joint and wheel arm will pump back and forth.

Figure 9.43

Group the top joint under the wheel, and then group the wheel arm under the top joint.

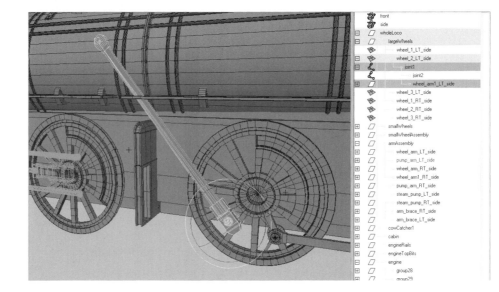

Controlling the Pump Arm

Now we need to attach the pump arm to the wheel arm so it pumps back and forth as the control wheel turns. If we simply group the pump arm in with the end joint of the wheel arm's bone, the pump arm would float up and down as it pumps back and forth. We will need to use a constraint to force the pump arm to move back and forth only in the Z axis.

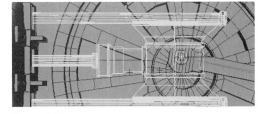

Figure 9.44

Line up the pivot of the pump arm with the end joint of the wheel arm joint.

1. Select the pump arm, shown in Figure 9.44 templated so that you can see through to the wheel arm and joint, and line up its pivot with the end joint of the wheel arm bone. Make sure the control wheel is set back to 0 rotation first, however.

2. Select the end joint (called joint2), Shift+select the pump arm group (called pump_arm_LT_side), and in the Animation menu set choose **Constrain → Point** ❑. In the option box, uncheck All under Constraint Axes, and select only Z to constrain the pump arm only in the Z axis and hit the Add button. Now if you rotate the control wheel, you will see the pump arm and wheel arm connected. The pump arm will pump back and forth, though you'll immediately notice a need to adjust the model to make the piece fit when it animates. Figure 9.45 shows the pump arm's geometry is not quite right yet for animation. This is quite normal in this process and luckily needs only a quick fix.

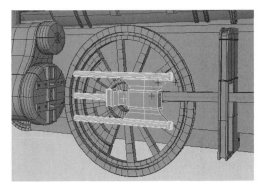

Figure 9.45

The pump arm is too short!

3. To fix the pump arm, simply select the vertices on the ends of the cylinders and extend them to make them longer, as shown in Figure 9.46. Now the pump arm will not pull out of the steam pump assembly.

4. You will also have to adjust the pump arm so that the geometry fits when the pump pushes in as well.

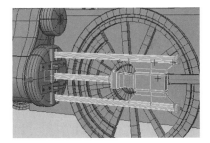

Figure 9.46

Use vertices to extend the pump arm.

The scene file fancy_locomotive_anim_v2.mb will catch you up to this point. Use it to compare you work.

Controlling the Back Wheel

Now, all that remains is to control the animation of the back wheel and its wheel arm. To set up the wheel arm animation, follow these steps:

1. Using the methods described previously, create a joint to follow along the wheel arm between the middle control wheel and the back wheel. The root of the joint will be set at the control wheel.

2. Create an IK handle as before for the end joint of this new bone, where it meets the back wheel, as shown in Figure 9.47.

3. Group the wheel arm under this new joint. Now if you rotate the control wheel, the wheel arm rotates with the joint and wheel, but does not connect to the back wheel just yet. We need to attach the IK handle we just created for that joint to the back wheel. If you simply group the IK handle, as shown in Figure 9.48, you will run into a problem when you animate. Let's check it out. Group the IK under the end back wheel as shown in Figure 9.48, and then rotate the control wheel. The wheel arm pumps back and forth along with the back wheel, but every now and then, the wheel arm flips over backward. This is not good.

Fixing this is terribly easy. What is causing the issue is the grouping of the IK handle to the back wheel. Though that is much what we want to do, parenting the IK handle under the wheel is problematic. Here is where the parent constraint becomes extremely helpful. It will give us the desired result without the flipping.

4. Use the MMB in the Outliner to remove the IK handle from under the back wheel's node. Make sure your control wheel is back to 0 rotation first!

5. Select the back wheel, Shift+select the IK handle, and choose **Constrain → Parent**. Now if you rotate the control wheel, everything works great!

Figure 9.47

Create a joint and an IK handle to attach the wheel arm and the back wheel to the control wheel.

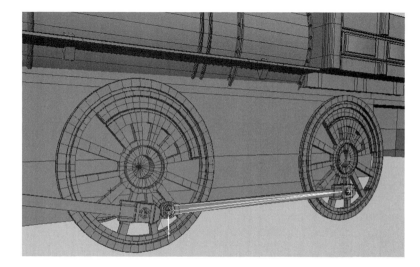

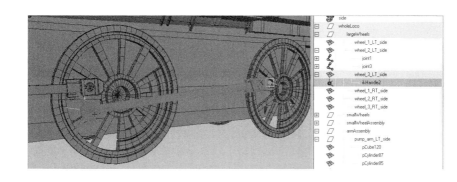

Figure 9.48

The wheel arm flips over!

Finishing the Rig

We're almost home free with the locomotive wheel rigging. Even though everything works great now when you rotate the control wheel, we have left out one small detail. If you select the top node of the train, here called wholeLoco, and translate the train back and forth, the front wheel arm snaps out of place. This is because of the first IK handle we created for that wheel arm. Simply group that IK handle under the top wholeLoco node when the train is in its initial place in the scene, and you're all done.

But why not group the other IK handle we created for the back wheel arm? This IK handle already has a parent constraint attaching it to the back wheel, so grouping that IK handle is not necessary. You can use fancy_locomotive_anim_v3.mb to compare your work (see Figure 9.49).

Repeat these procedures to connect the wheel arms and wheels on the other side of the locomotive, and you're really all done.

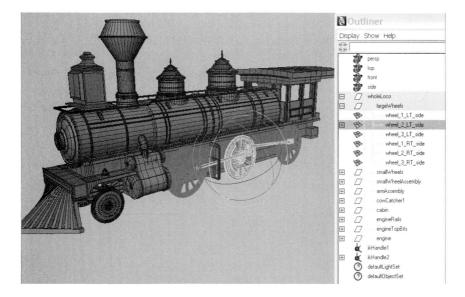

Figure 9.49

The rigged fancy locomotive

Summary

In this chapter, you extended your experience with animation and learned about rigging techniques and automation. Starting with a simple block man, you learned how to set up a hierarchy for Forward Kinematics animation to create a walk cycle. Then you revisited the hand model and used a skeleton to rig the hand for animation. You then learned how to bind the geometry of the hand to the skeleton using rigid and smooth binds and how to edit the binding. You also learned how to create an IK system to drive the joints in the block man for an IK walk cycle animation. Next you learned how constraints can be used in rigging and how to set up set driven keys to create easy controls to animate the hand. Last, you put all these rigging tricks together to rig the wheels of the locomotive to automate the animation of that complex system with a single control.

The true work in animation comes from recognizing what to do in the face of certain tasks and how to approach their solutions. Maya offers a large animation toolset, and the more you become familiar with the tools, the better you'll be able to judge which tools to use in your work. Don't stop where this chapter does; experiment with the rest of the features not covered here and see what happens.

Animation is about observation and interpretation. The animator's duty is to understand how and why something moves and to translate that into their medium without losing the movement's fidelity, tenacity, or honesty.

CHAPTER 10

Maya Lighting

Light shapes the world by showing us what we see. It creates a sense of depth, it initiates the perception of color, and it allows us to distinguish shape and form. This reality of light needs to be as faithfully reproduced in CG as possible for a successful scene. The trick is learning to see light and its astonishing effects on the world around us.

Topics include:

- **Basic Lighting Concepts**
- **Maya Lights**
- **Light Linking**
- **Adding Shadows**
- **Soft Shadows with mental ray**
- **Lighting with mental ray Global Illumination**
- **Lighting Effects**
- **Tips for Using and Animating Lights**

Basic Lighting Concepts

It is no surprise that Maya's lighting resembles actual direct-lighting techniques used in photography and filmmaking. Lights of various types are placed around the scene to illuminate the subjects as they would for a still life or a portrait. Your scene and what's in it dictate, to some degree at least, which lights you put where. Choosing the *type* of lights to be used depends on the desired effect.

At the basic level, you want your lights to illuminate the scene. Without lights, your cameras have nothing to capture. Although it seems rather easy to throw your lights in, turn them all on, and render the scene, that couldn't be further from the truth.

Lighting is the backbone of CG. Although it is technically easy to insert and configure lights, it is *how* you light that will make or break your scene. And that really only comes with a good deal of experience and experimentation, as well as a good eye and some patience.

This chapter will familiarize you with the basic techniques of lighting a scene in Maya and start you on the road to finding more.

Learning to See

There are so many nuances to the real-world lighting around us that we take them for granted. We intuitively understand what we see and how it's lit and infer a tremendous amount of visual information without much consideration. With CG lighting, you must re-create these nuances for your scene. That amounts to all the *work* of lighting.

The most valuable thing you can do to improve your lighting technique is to relearn how you see your environment. Simply put, refuse to take for granted what you see. Question why things look the way they do and you'll find that the answers almost always come around to lighting.

Take note of the distinction between light and dark in the room you're in now. Notice the difference in the brightness of highlights and how they dissipate into diffused light and then into shadow.

When you start understanding how real light affects objects, you'll be much better equipped to generate your own light. After all, the key to good lighting starts with the desire to simply create an interesting image.

What Your Scene Needs

Ideally, your scene needs areas of highlight and shadow. Overlighting a scene flattens everything and diminishes details. This is perhaps the number one mistake of beginners. Figure 10.1 shows a still life with too many bright lights, which only flatten the image and remove any sense of color and depth.

Similarly, underlighting your scene makes it *muddy*, gray, and rather lifeless, as well as covering your details in darkness and flattening the entire frame. Figure 10.2 shows the still life underlit. The bumps and curves of the mesh are hardly noticeable.

Figure 10.1
An over-lit still life

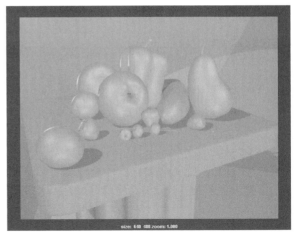

Figure 10.2
An under-lit still life

Finding a good middle ground to lighting your scene is key. Like a photographer, you want your image to have the full range of exposure. You want the richest blacks to the brightest whites in your frame to create a deep sense of detail. Even though you may not have an absolute black to white in the rendered image, the concept is appealing. As in Figure 10.3, light and shadow complement each other and work to show the features of your surface.

Three-Point Lighting

Since your scene needs to be rendered, and lighting can be a fairly heavy computational process when it comes to rendering, your lighting needs to be efficient. That means not using dozens of lights for every part of the scene.

Figure 10.3
Balanced lighting creates a more interesting picture.

The traditional approach to efficiently lighting an object, culled from filmmaking and television, starts with *three-point lighting*. In this setup, three distinct roles are used to light the subject of a shot. More than one light can be used for each of the three roles, but the scene should in effect seem to have only one primary, or key, light, a softer light to fill the scene, and a back light to pop the subject out from the background.

Three-point lighting ensures that the primary subject's features are not just illuminated, but featured with highlights and shadow. Using three directions and qualities of light creates the best level of depth. Figure 10.4 shows a schematic of a basic three-point setup.

Figure 10.4

**A three-point light-
ing schematic**

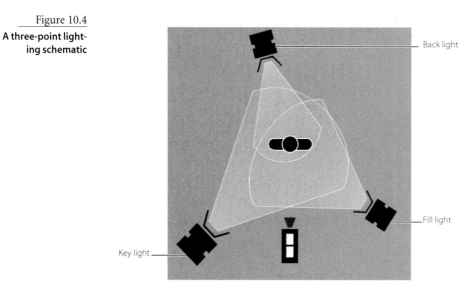

Back light

Fill light

Key light

Key Light

A *key light* is placed in front of the subject and off to the side to provide the principal light on the subject. Since it is usually off center, the key light creates one side of brighter light, increasing the depth of the shot. This light also provides the primary shadows and gives the important sense of lighting direction in the shot.

Although it is possible for several lights to fulfill the role of key light in a scene—for example, three ceiling lights overhead—one light should dominate, creating a definitive direction. Figure 10.5 shows the subject being lit by only a key light, although it is physically composed of two lights.

The direction of the two lights remains the same, and one takes intensity precedence over the other and casts shadows. The effect creates a single key light, which produces a moody still life.

Fill Light

A more diffused light than the key light, the *fill light* seems directionless and evenly spread across the subject's dark side. This fills the rest of the subject with light and decreases the dark area caused by the key light.

The fill light is not meant to cast any shadows onto the subject or background itself and is actually used to help soften the shadows created by the key light. Figure 10.6 shows the still life with an added fill light. Notice how it softens the shadows and illuminates the dark areas the key light misses.

Figure 10.5
Key light only

Figure 10.6
A fill light is now included.

Typically, you place the fill light in front of the subject and aim it so that it comes from the opposite side of the key light to target the dark side of the subject. Even though the still life in Figure 10.6 is still a fairly moody composition, there is much more visible than with only the key light in Figure 10.5.

Back Light

The *back light*, or *rim light*, is placed behind the subject to create a bit of a halo, which helps to pop the subject out in the shot. Thus, the subject has more presence against its background. Figure 10.7 shows how helpful a back light can be.

The back light brings the fruit in this still life out from the background and adds some highlights to the edges, giving the composition more focus on the fruit.

Don't confuse the back light with the background light, which lights the environment behind the subject.

Figure 10.7
A back light pops the subject right out.

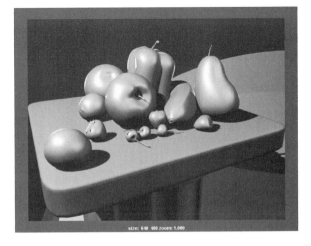

Using Three-Point Lighting

The three-point lighting system is used for the primary subject of the scene. Since it is based on position and angle of the subject to the camera, a new setup is needed when the camera is moved for a different shot in the same scene. Three-point lighting is therefore not scene specific but shot specific.

Once the lighting is set up for the subject of a shot, the background must be lit. Use a directed primary light source that matches the direction of the key light for the main light, and use a softer fill light to illuminate the rest of the scene and soften the primary shadows.

Practical Lighting

Practical lighting is a theatrical term describing any lights in a scene that are cast from lighting objects within the scene. For example, a desk lamp on a table in the background of a scene would need practical lighting when it's on. You never want the practical lighting to interfere with the main lighting of the scene, unless the scene's lighting is explicitly coming from such a source.

Each light-emitting object in your CG scene doesn't necessarily need its own Maya light. Rendering tricks such as *glow* (for glow effects, see "Lighting Effects" later in this chapter) can simulate the effect that a light is turned on without actually having to use a Maya light. Of course, if you need the practical light to illuminate something in the scene, you need to create a light for it.

Maya Lights

Six types of light are available in Maya: Ambient, Directional, Point, Spot, Area, and Volume. How you use each dictates whether they become key, fill, or rim lights. Each light can fill any of those roles, although some are better for certain jobs than others. The most commonly used light types for most scenes are Spot, Directional, and Ambient.

To create each light, choose **Create → Lights** and click the light type.

Figure 10.8

A typical light's Attribute Editor

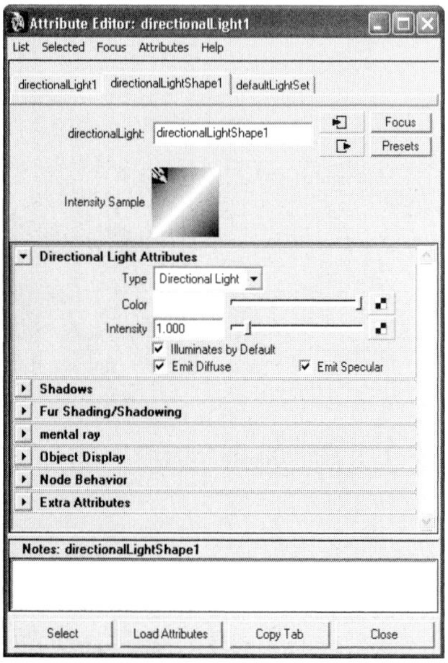

Common Light Attributes

Lights in Maya are treated as any other object nodes. They can be transformed, rotated, scaled, duplicated, deleted, and so forth and are visible as nodes in the Hypergraph and Outliner alongside other objects in the scene. Like any other node, lights have attributes that govern how they function. Figure 10.8 shows the Attribute Editor for a typical light.

When you select any light type and then open the Attribute Editor, you'll see the following attributes and options:

Type This drop-down menu sets the type of light. You can change from one light type to another (for instance, from Spot to Point) at any time.

Color This attribute controls the color cast by the light. The darker the color, the dimmer the light. You can use **Color** in conjunction with **Intensity** to govern brightness, although it's best to leave that to **Intensity** only.

Figure 10.9

Full render   Diffuse only render   Specular only render

Figure 10.9

Lighting renders can be separated for greater control later.

Intensity This attribute specifies how much light is cast. The higher the intensity, the brighter the illumination.

Illuminates By Default This check box deals with light linking, or the ability to illuminate specific objects with specific lights. Clearing this check box causes the light to not illuminate all objects by default. Keep this check box checked unless you are linking lights to specific objects. This chapter will touch on light linking briefly later.

Emit Diffuse and Emit Specular These two check boxes are not available with the Ambient light type. For all other light types, they toggle on or off the ability to cast diffuse lighting or specular highlights on an object. This is useful for creating specific render passes to give you precise control of your final image. For example, turning off Emit Diffuse will cast only specular highlights in your scene. This, once rendered, would be a highlight pass that can be separately adjusted and then composited onto your final image. You'll find more on this later in this chapter. Figure 10.9 shows how you can separate renders to better control lighting details when the image is composited back together.

Light Types

Beyond the common light attributes, each light type carries its own attributes that govern its particular settings.

Ambient Lights

Ambient lights cast an even light across the entire scene. These lights are great for creating a quick, even illumination in a scene, but as you can see in Figure 10.10, they run the risk of flattening the composition. They are perhaps best used sparingly and at low intensities as fill lights or background lights.

Figure 10.10

Ambient light

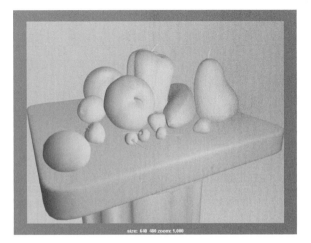

Figure 10.11

A low Ambient Shade setting flattens the image.

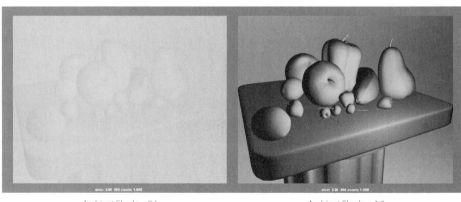

Ambient Shade = 0.1   Ambient Shade = 1.0

The **Ambient Shade** slider in the Attribute Editor governs how flat the lighting will be. The lower the value, the flatter the lighting. Figure 10.11 shows the effect of two contrasting Ambient Shade settings.

Directional Lights

Directional lights cast a light in a general direction evenly across the scene (see Figure 10.12). These lights are perhaps second to Spot lights as the most commonly used light type. They are perfect for sunlight or general indoor lighting, for key lights, and for fill and back lights. They give a perfect sense of direction without having to come from a specific source.

Point Lights

A *Point light* casts light from a single specific point in space, similar to a bare lightbulb. Its light is spread evenly from the emission point (see Figure 10.13).

Figure 10.12

Directional light

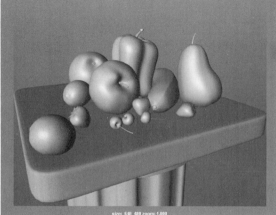

Using the **Decay Rate** drop-down menu in the Attribute Editor, you can set how a Point light's intensity diminishes over distance. With No Decay, the Point light will illuminate an object far away as evenly as it does up close. This is the most common setting for most applications.

Setting the **Decay Rate** to Linear, Quadratic, or Cubic will require you to exponentially increase the intensity level to compensate for the decay. You can use decay rate settings to illuminate nearby objects and to leave distant ones unaffected. In reality, lights have decay rates. But in CG, they don't really need to unless the falloff effect is called for (as in Figure 10.14). Clever lighting can easily avoid this cumbersome calculation.

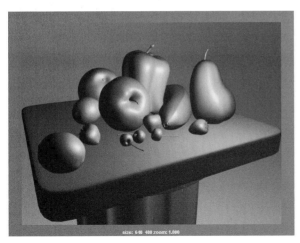

Figure 10.13

A Point light placed in the front right of frame

Figure 10.14

A Point light with a decay rate set

Point lights are good for effects such as candlelight or mood setting.

Spot Lights

Spot lights are arguably the most often used lights in Maya because they can be used for keys, fills, or rims and they are highly efficient, casting light in specific areas, just like a real spotlight.

Similar to a Directional light, Spot lights emphasize direction. But these lights, unlike Directionals, emit from a specific point and radiate out in a cone shape, whereas a Directional emits from an infinite source from a certain direction. As such, Spot lights can create a circular focus of light on the geometry much like a flashlight on a wall; Directionals spread the light evenly. Figure 10.15 shows a Spot light on the still life.

The following attributes govern the behavior of Spot lights:

Decay Rate Specifies that the light's intensity falls off with distance, as with the Point light. Again, the intensity needs to increase exponentially to account for any decay.

Cone Angle Sets the width of the cone of light emitted by the Spot light. The wider a cone, the more calculation intensive it becomes.

Penumbra Angle Specifies how much the intensity at the edges of the cone and hence the circular focus dissipates. (See Figure 10.16.) A negative value softens the light into the width of the cone, decreasing the size of the focus; a positive value softens away from the cone.

Figure 10.15

Using a Spot light

Penumbra = 0   Penumbra = –10   Penumbra = 10

Dropoff Specifies how much light is decayed along the distance of the cone. The higher the dropoff, the dimmer the light gets farther along the length of the cone. This effect is much better to use than a decay rate and gives similar results.

Most practical lights are created with Spot lights. For example, a desk lamp's light is best simulated with a Spot light. Spot lights are also the lights of choice to cast shadows. You'll find more on shadows later in the chapter.

Area Lights

Area lights emit light from a flat rectangular shape only (see Figure 10.17). They behave similarly to Point lights except that they emit from an area and not from a single point. You can still set a decay rate, just as you can with Point lights. Area lights are the only lights whose scale affects their intensity. The larger an Area light, the brighter the light.

Since you can control the size of the area of light being emitted, these lights are good for creating effects such as a sliver of light falling onto an object from a crack in a door, as in Figure 10.18, overhead skylights, or the simulation of large diffused lighting fixtures such as some overhead office lights. Use Area lights when you need to light a specific area of an object.

Figure 10.17

An Area light and its placement

Volume Lights

Volume lights (see Figure 10.19) emit light from a specific 3D volumetric area as opposed to an Area light's flat rectangle. Proximity is important for a Volume light, as is its scale.

A Volume light can have the following attributes:

Light Shape A Volume light can be in the shape of a sphere, a box, a cylinder, or a cone. You select a shape from the Light Shape drop-down menu.

Color Range This section of attributes sets the color of the light using a built-in ramp. The ramp (from right to left) specifies the color from inside to outside. For instance, a white to black ramp from right to left creates a white light at the center of the Volume light that grades down to black toward the outer edge.

Volume Light Dir This attribute sets the direction for the light's color range. Outward lights from inside out, Inward lights from the volume's edge into the center, and Down Axis lights as a gradient in an axis of the light.

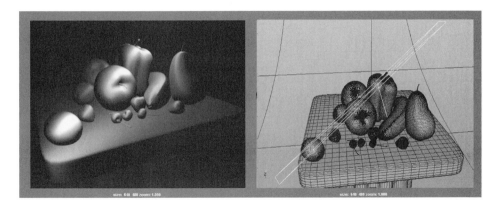

Figure 10.18

An Area light as a sliver and its placement

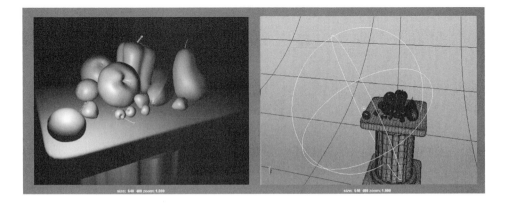

Figure 10.19

A Volume light and placement

Arc and Cone End Radius This attribute defines the shape for the volume.

Penumbra For cylinder and cone shapes, this attribute adjusts how much the light dims along the edge of its length.

Use Volume lights when you need to control the specific area in which light is cast or when you need an object to move into and out of a particular area of light. Volume lights are also great for creating volumetric lighting effects such as areas of lit fog. For volumetric effects, see the section "Volumetric Lighting" later in this chapter.

Lighting a Scene

It's best to start with just a couple of light types such as Directional and Spot before turning to the more sophisticated types such as Area and Volume.

Getting the essence of lighting is far more important in the beginning than understanding the nuances of all the attributes of a light. At first, limit yourself to Spots and Directionals with the occasional Ambient use.

Light Linking

You can control which lights illuminate which objects by using Maya's *light linking*. Inevitably, a time will come when you want to create a special light for a part of your scene but not for all of it. You will need to create a special relationship, a connection from a special light or lights to specific objects and not the others.

By default, lights created in your scene illuminate all objects in the scene. The easiest way to create an exclusive lighting relationship is first to create a light and turn off Illuminates By Default in the light's Attribute Editor. This ensures that this light will not cast light on any object unless made specifically to do so through light linking.

To assign your new light to the object(s) you want to exclusively illuminate, choose **Window → Relationship Editors → Light Linking → Light-Centric**. This will open the Relationship Editor and set it for light linking. Light-Centric means the lights will be featured in the left side of the panel as shown here and the objects in your scene will be lit on the right.

As you can see in Figure 10.20, the still life is lit evenly, and adding a new light with Illuminate By Default disabled will not increase the light level in the scene. Now simply select the light you want to link, in this case directionalLight2 we just created, and the objects in the scene

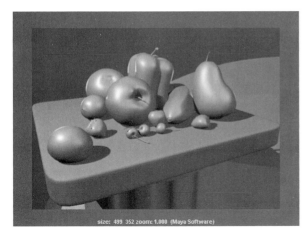

Figure 10.20

All the scene's lights illuminate the scene.

Figure 10.21

A linked light creates extra light for only the apple and the pepper behind it. The other objects are not illuminated by that light.

you'd like to link to, in this case the apple and the pepper. Notice that no other objects in the right side of the Relationship Editor are selected; that means they will receive no illumination from this light source. When you render your scene, the objects you linked will be lit by the new light. In this case, the apple and the pepper are brighter than the other fruit in the still life. (See Figure 10.21.)

Keep in mind, however, that linked lights are not taken into account in the view panel displays when you are in lighted mode (when you press 7 in the shaded panel). The linking comes through in the render.

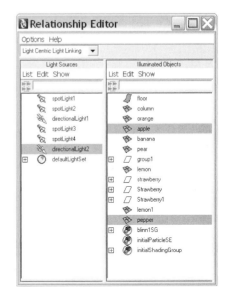

Adding Shadows

Don't be too quick to create an abundance of light in your scene, eager to show off your models and textures. Shrouding objects in darkness and shadow is just as important as revealing them in light. You can say a lot visually by not showing parts of a whole, leaving some interpretation to the audience.

A careful balance of light and dark is important for a composition. As Figure 10.22 shows, the reality of a scene is greatly increased with the simple addition of well-placed shadows. Don't be afraid of the dark. Use it liberally, but in balance.

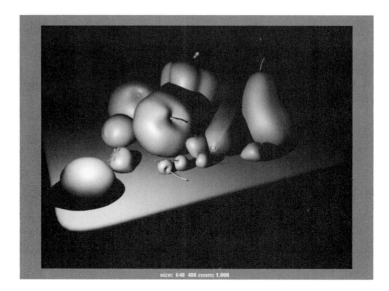

size: 640 480 zoom: 1.000

Creating Shadows in Maya

Maya lights do not cast shadows by default; you need to enable this feature in the light's Attribute Editor. When you do that, however, lights can cast shadows in one of two ways, depending on how the scene is rendered.

The more common way of the two methods to create shadows is by using Depth Map shadows. Once you enable *shadow maps* (by clicking the **Use Depth Map Shadows** check box in the Shadows area of a light's Attribute Editor), Maya generates shadow maps that locate where shadows fall by following the path of the light backward from the lighted object to the light itself. Shadow maps create fast, accurate shadows through Maya's renderer. See the next section on how to create shadow map shadows.

The second method for casting shadows is achieved by *raytracing* with Maya's software renderer. With raytracing enabled in the Render Settings window and raytracing shadows enabled for each light, you can create *raytraced shadows*. See Chapter 11 for more on rendering.

Raytracing involves tracing a ray of light from every light source in all directions and tracing their reflection to the camera lens. Thus, you can create more accurate shadows with raytracing. However, this render takes significantly longer to calculate. Later in this chapter you'll learn how to create raytraced shadows.

Only when you want either a soft and diffused shadow or a very sharp and crisp-edged shadow will you need to turn on raytraced shadows. See Figures 10.23 and 10.24.

Figure 10.23

Directional light with Depth Map shadows render faster and usually are detailed enough.

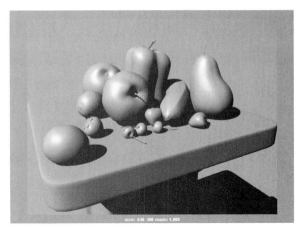

Figure 10.24

Directional light with raytraced shadows produces more detailed shadows but slower renders.

Shadow Map Shadows

You can turn on shadow maps for every light type except Ambient through the light type's Attribute Editor, as shown in Figure 10.25.

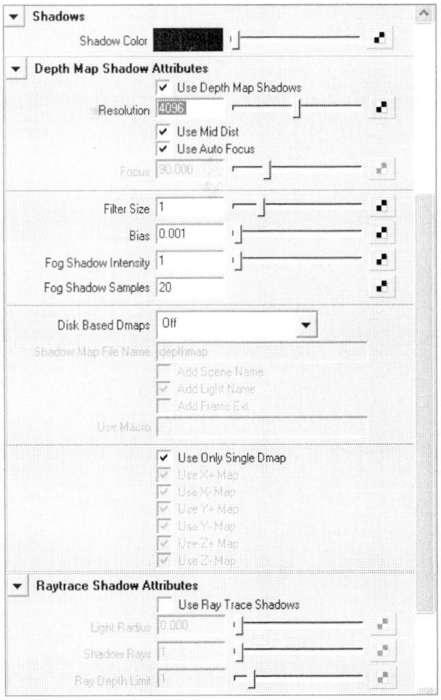

The depth map **Resolution** defaults at 512. The higher this resolution, the better defined the shadows. Figure 10.23 was rendered with a depth map **Resolution** of 4096, a very high value. Figure 10.26 is the same render with a depth map **Resolution** of 768. Most shadows will be detailed enough with a depth map **Resolution** of 1024.

Now, Directional lights are not the best lights to use for detailed shadow map shadows because they require a high resolution for the maps; however, their raytraced shadows are extremely well done, as shown in Figure 10.24 earlier in this chapter.

Spot lights create shadow maps with greater accuracy at lower depth map **Resolution** settings and faster render times. As such, Spots are preferred to Directionals for shadow-casting lights. Figure 10.27 shows the same render with a Spot light and a depth map **Resolution** setting of only 1024, one-fourth the size of the Directional light's depth map **Resolution**.

Figure 10.25

Turning on shadow maps in the Attribute Editor for a Directional light

Figure 10.26

The depth map Resolution setting affects shadow quality for shadow maps.

Figure 10.27

Spot lights cast faster and more detailed shadow map shadows.

Trying to squeeze a detailed shadow map from a Directional light with an absurdly high depth map **Resolution** setting can even crash your system. In these cases, it is wiser to use a Spot light. If a Spot light cannot be used (for example, when an even Directional light is needed instead), use raytraced shadows.

Raytraced Shadows

Figure 10.28

The Spot light shown in Figure 10.27 but now with ray-traced shadows

To enable raytraced shadows, turn on the light's **Use Ray Trace Shadows** setting in the Attribute Editor (see Figure 10.25 earlier in this chapter) and enable raytracing in the Render Settings window. Choose **Window → Rendering Editors → Render Settings** or click the Render Settings icon (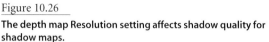) in the Status line.

Figure 10.28 shows the Spot light from Figure 10.27, this time rendered with a raytraced shadow. Notice that there is not much difference in the renders. This shows how well you can detail spot shadow maps, and again, the rendering time is less than with raytraced shadows.

For an object that has a transparency map applied to its shader, however, only raytraced shadows can cast proper shadows. On the left in Figure 10.29 is a plane with a mapped checkerboard transparency casting a raytraced shadow over the still life. On the right is the same light using shadow maps instead of raytraced shadows.

Figure 10.29

Only raytraced shadows work with transparencies.

Raytraced Shadow   Shadow Map Shadow

Controlling Shadows per Object

You can specify whether an object can cast and receive shadows in Maya to better control your lighting. For example, if you have geometry casting light in front of a shadow but you do not want it to cast a shadow, you can manually turn that feature off for that object only.

To turn off shadow casting for an object, select the object and open its Attribute Editor. In the Render Stats section is a group of check boxes that control the render properties of the object. Clear the **Casts Shadows** check box. If you do not want the object to receive shadows, clear the **Receive Shadows** check box.

Soft Shadow Maps with mental ray

Maya lights can generate either Maya shadow maps or mental ray's own shadow maps. mental ray's shadows can be more detailed than Maya shadow maps and, more important, can be easily and very nicely softened to create a more natural look, especially in some outdoor scenes. To enable mental ray shadow maps, select the light and in its Attribute Editor, check on **Shadow Map** under the mental ray Shadow Map Attributes heading. Of course, these shadows can work only with mental ray renders, but you do not have to enable GI or Caustics or Final Gather for them to work.

The primary shadow attributes are as follows:

Resolution Since Shadow Map shadows are created by using maps, the resolution sets the quality level of the shadow map used. The higher the resolution of the map, the more detailed the shadow for that object.

Samples The higher the samples for a shadow map, the smoother the shadows will render. You will need higher samples for detailed shadows and especially soft shadows.

Softness mental ray shadow maps can render soft, for a more natural look, especially for external scenes.

Try This Open the file still_life_v01.mb in the scenes folder of the Lighting project on the CD. Create a spotlight and place it to point down at an angle at the still life arrangement as shown. Place the *persp* camera to show the fruit arrangement as well as the column stand.

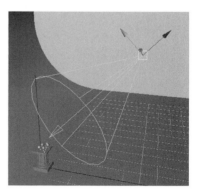

1. Select the light, open the Attribute Editor, and set a **Penumbra Angle** of 5 to soften the edge of the spotlight, just in case it falls into frame (or widen the spotlight's **Cone Angle** to 60 or so).

2. Under the mental ray heading for the light, enable the **Shadow Map** check box and set the **Resolution** value to 2048. You can leave **Samples** and **Softness** to their defaults of 1 and 0 respectively for now.

3. In the Render Settings window, switch to **Render Using** mental ray with a **Quality Preset** of Draft. Render a frame and you should have something similar to what is shown here. If your render is quite jaggy, you can set the **Min Sample Level** and **Max Sample Level** to 1 and 2 respectively in the Render Settings window. We'll cover these settings in the next chapter (below left).

4. Select the light, and in the Attribute Editor, set a **Softness** value of 0.05 in the Shadow Map Attributes of the mental ray section. Render a frame and compare it to the following image. You should see a softer shadow but at a fairly dithered, jagged quality (below right).

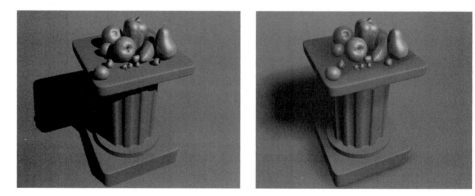

5. To increase the smoothness of the soft shadow, increase the **Samples** value to 50. Render the frame and compare to the image here. You should notice a big difference in the quality of the soft shadow.

You should have noticed that the softer shadow and the higher Samples rate increased your render times, but close to twice the time. Also keep in mind, the softer your shadow, the less it will appear around your object. Small **Softness** values go a long way. It's also wise to find the lowest possible **Samples** value to use for the best result.

mental ray Lighting

mental ray lighting and rendering opens up a large range of possibilities within Maya. As with all rendering, lighting plays the primary role. We will cover mental ray rendering more in the next chapter, but since rendering and lighting go hand in hand, it's tough to ignore in this chapter. This section is a primer on mental ray light functionality.

Open the Render Settings window by choosing **Window → Rendering Editors → Render Settings**. If you don't see the mental ray for Maya (or any other, such as the Vector) option in the **Render Using** drop-down menu, you will need to load the plug-in. Choose **Window → Settings/Preferences → Plug-in Manager** to open the Plug-in Manager. Make sure **Mayatomr.mll** is checked for **Loaded** as well as for **Auto Load** to ensure that it loads by default.

Two important functions that mental ray brings to the Maya table are called Caustics and Global Illumination (a.k.a. GI). *Caustics* is the scattering of light reflections off and through semitransparent objects, such as the light that shines on the ceiling of an indoor pool or the sunshine at the bottom of an outdoor pool. *Global illumination* is the effect of light reflected from one object to another. For example, if you place colored spheres inside a gray box and shine a light into the box, the walls and floor of that box pick up the color of the spheres. The light from the spheres reflects onto the walls and tints them with their color. Furthermore, the light from the floor of the box bounces and helps illuminate the underside of the balls.

For example, Figures 10.30 and 10.31 show a scene file that has a dozen or so glass spheres inside an enclosed box. The box has four holes in the top, and two spotlights with shadows turned on are positioned outside the box, shining in through the holes. Figure 10.30 shows a typical software render. The spheres under the holes are visible, and the rest of the box is in shadow.

However, rendering through mental ray for Maya (see Figure 10.31), the light that enters the box bounces around the scene and illuminates the other spheres. The color of the spheres also colors the area immediately around them due to global illumination. Additionally, the light shines through the semitransparent spheres and casts caustic highlights on the floor. (You'll see the full effect in the color section of this book.)

mental ray Light Attributes

Every light in Maya has a section of attributes that define its mental ray capabilities. Since rendering with mental ray is becoming much more popular with Maya, it is a good idea to have an idea of how mental ray treats Maya lights.

Figure 10.30
The Maya Software render of the box of spheres scene

Figure 10.31
The mental ray for Maya render of the scene in Figure 10.30

For Caustics or GI to work, mental ray lights need to emit photons. These photons are emitted from enabled lights to bounce in the scene and create *indirect lighting* that leads to the caustic and GI effects. In reality, light photons are reflected from surfaces many times over, so a single light can light an entire room; that is, the light bounces off all the surfaces in that room to help light it indirectly. mental ray attempts to simulate this effect by tracing photons from your scene lights as they bounce from surface to surface, all within reason of course. Computationally, you would want to use the least amount of bounces to best light your room. Indirect lighting can sometimes lead to extraordinary photo-realistic results. But as anything in life, getting to a point of mastery takes tremendous time and effort.

Caustic and Global Illumination

Each light in Maya allows you to enable mental ray attributes. By checking on the box for **Emit Photons** in the Caustic and Global Illumination section in the light's Attribute Editor, you allow the light to participate in either the caustic or GI effect. Photons in Global Illumination, in short, are traced around in the scene. As they bounce from one surface to another, they indirectly add to the lighting on that surface. We will experiment with these values in a GI exercise later in this section.

Photon Color Defines the color of the photons. This color is added to the direct lighting (if any) that the surface receives from any lights in the scene. Typically, this color is left to white, but you can change the color to cast a different hue effect on the affected surface(s).

Photon Intensity Each photon will affect the scene by a certain amount. The greater the intensity, the greater the GI or Caustic effect. For example, a high **Intensity** value in a GI scene will create a large amount of bright indirect light, such as a bright morning sun lighting a room through a large window.

Exponent This value basically adjusts the intensity of the photons according to distance from the light source to the surface.

Caustic Photons The number of photons used in the photon map to generate a caustic effect. The greater the number, the greater the accuracy and quality of the render. However, a higher photon number will increase render times.

Global Illum Photons The number of photons used in the photon map to generate the GI effect. Again, the greater the number of photons used, the greater the accuracy and quality of the render. However, more photons will increase render times.

Lighting with Global Illumination

Global Illumination creates a natural soft look for a scene by providing for the influence of indirect light. This indirect light is influenced by the color of the objects in the room, so red walls will cast a red tint on the objects next to them. This allows for a more realistic lighting for your scene. GI can be fairly deep and complex, so getting too deep into it is way beyond the scope of this text; however, in keeping with the purpose of this book, here is a primer, a push into the usage of GI to get you going with at least a little place to start your experience.

In this exercise, we will light a living room scene to simulate sunlight coming through the window. For this we'll need a nice soft look to the room, depending mostly on indirect light for the primary illumination, eschewing the traditional three-point lighting system for the magic of GI.

The Living Room

This scene, a nicely modeled living room by student Huyen Dang, is perfect for a GI setup and can be seen in Figure 10.32. In this scene, there are two windows that will provide for the actual light. There is a single Directional light setup to run light through the window. Figure 10.33 shows a regular non-GI render of the room through mental ray. To begin lighting with GI, make sure mental ray is loaded (see the note in this chapter on how to check on and enable mental ray) and follow these steps:

1. Start with the livingRoom_v1.mb file from the scenes folder of the Livingroom project on the CD. Make sure to set your project to Livingroom project to make sure all the texture files load properly.

2. Using the view from camera1, render a frame of the scene file with the file's current mental ray settings and you should have a frame that looks like Figure 10.33. As you can see, because shadows are enabled on the one light, much of the room is dark, save for the area in front of the window.

3. Select the directionalLight1 node and open the Attribute Editor. Under the mental ray heading, enable **Emit Photons** under the Caustic And Global Illumination subheading. For now, leave everything at their default settings here.

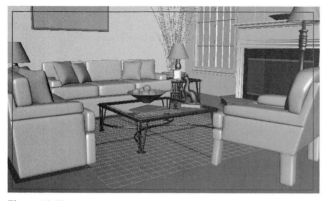

Figure 10.32

The living room setup

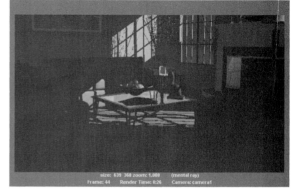

Figure 10.33

A mental ray render of the living room with no Global Illumination

4. Open the Render Settings window, and make sure the **Render Using** drop-down menu is set to mental ray as it should be. In the mental ray tab, set the **Quality Presets** to PreviewGlobalIllum. Scroll down the Render Settings window and take a gander at some of the settings. **Ray Tracing** is enabled; mental ray requires raytracing for GI. Also notice under the Caustics And Global Illumination heading that **Global Illumination** is enabled with a **Global Illum Accuracy** of 500. We will cover what's what and who's who in the next chapter on rendering, so don't get too antsy just yet. Figure 10.34 shows the Render Settings window.

5. Now render the same frame from camera1. This will take a little bit longer than before; mental ray has to calculate its photon emissions in addition to the actual render. Whoa! Now the scene is drowning in light. Figure 10.35 shows the overly bright render. Get your sunglasses.

6. Now, just as you had to enable GI in the light by emitting photons and by checking the box in the Render Settings window, you will need to control the GI effect through both the light and the Render Settings window. Select your light, and adjust the **Exponent** value from 2.0 to 3.1. You will find **Exponent** under the mental ray Caustic And Global Illumination heading as shown. Render.

7. Figure 10.36 shows a render with **Exponent** set to 3.1. The indirect lighting lights up the room much better than before, without blowing it way out. Increasing the **Exponent** value will decrease the intensity of the GI effect, in simple terms at least. Play around with **Exponent** and you'll see pretty quickly how touchy it is; small value changes create large changes in the render.

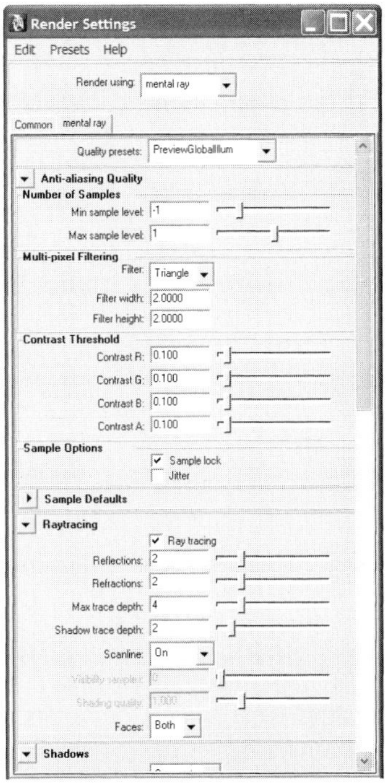

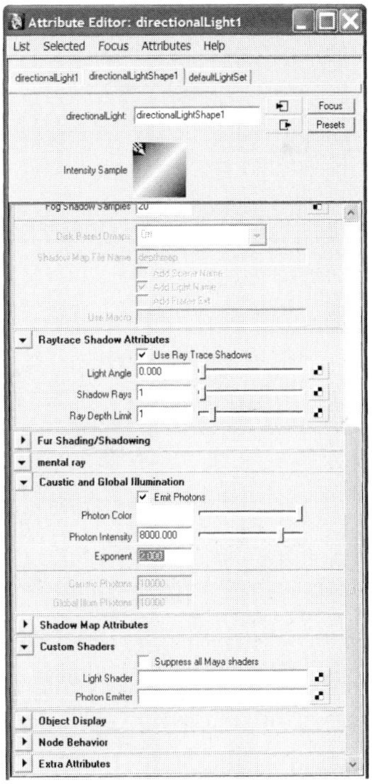

Figure 10.34

The Render Settings setup

Figure 10.35

Umm, yeah, a little bright

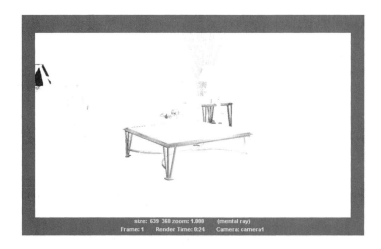

Figure 10.36

Ah see…much better now; indirect lighting shows us the rest of the room nicely.

8. But still, this render has a little way to go. Notice how the fruit bowl on the coffee table blows out bright to white. This is called *clipping*. When color values get too bright, they stop at a white value of 1; hence they clip to white.

In this scene, this fruit basket piece of geometry seems to be receiving an inordinate amount of bounce light from the floor and the glass tabletop and its shader is basically exploding directly to white. A lot of lighting and rendering relies on troubleshooting elements of a scene. The simplest way to go from here is to address the fruit bowl directly and reduce the amount of light it receives and reflects. Since there is only one light in the scene, it does not make sense to use light linking to detach it from any lights in the scene. Also, its shader is a Lambert and has no specular value, so it is not a blown-out highlight that we can reduce with a darker **Specular Color** (see Chapter 7 on texturing for more on shaders and specular highlights). Instead, we will deal with its diffuse value. To reduce the clipping of the fruit bowl, continue with these steps:

9. Select the bowl and open the Hypershade window to examine its Lambert shader, called *basket*. Reduce the **Diffuse** value on this shader from 0.8 to 0.25.

10. Render and you will see the fruit basket is now much less bright and does not clip. See Figure 10.37.

There is still some work to be done here on the fruit bowl, but the intention is clear. You have to engage the shader as well as the light settings when lighting and rendering a scene. Don't fret; we're not done yet with this scene.

Figure 10.37

Fixing the fruit basket clipping

To automatically bring up the shader for a particular object, remember you can select the geometry in a view panel, and then in the Hypershade window, click the icon for Graph Materials On Select Objects (⚏).

Now that we have tackled the primary issue with the basket, let's address the splotchy nature of the render. You can easily see circles of light and dark all over the living room. This is from the photon emission and can be made better by increasing the emission number of photons in the light and the radius of each photon influence in the Render Settings window.

1. In the Render Settings window, increase the **Global Illum Accuracy** to 2400 as shown below and the **Global Illum Radius** to 24.0. A larger radius attribute and higher accuracy value allows mental ray to better smooth the photons together to get rid of the splotches of light you can see in Figure 10.37.

2. Select the light and increase the **Global Illum Photons** value to 100,000 from the current 10,000. The more photons that are emitted, the smoother the indirect light will render. Of course, it will increase processing time as well. Part of the trick is to find just the right balance between radius, accuracy, and number of photons. Figure 10.38 shows a frame rendered with these better GI settings.

You can load the scene file `livingRoom_v2.mb` from the CD to check your work.

As you can see, there are a lot of switches to play with among the shader, Render Settings, and light attributes to influence your render. GI is a powerful lighting solution, but it's a bit touchy, so it's a tough nut to crack. What will work in one scene probably will not in others. It's important to get the feel for it, so try changing some of the values such as **Exponent**, **Photon Intensity**, and so on to see how you can alter the lighting of this scene. There's quite a bit more one can do with this room, so have at it. Just don't expect yourself to get good right away; get some more experience with lighting and GI will come more naturally over time.

We will see some other rendering options with this scene in the next chapter, including how to increase the mental ray quality settings as well as creating the image in passes to heighten the realism of the final composited result.

Lighting Effects

In CG, you must fake certain traits of light in the real world. Using certain methods, you can create smoky light beams, glowing lights, and lens flares. Although some of these effects fall under the domain of rendering and shader tricks, they are best explored in the context of lighting, as they are indeed created by light in the real world.

Volumetric Lighting

How do you create an effect such as a flashlight beam shining through fog? This lighting effect is called *volumetric lighting,* and you can use it to create some stunning results, which can sometimes be time consuming to render.

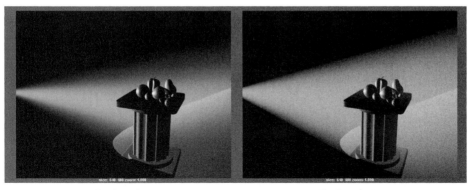

Fog Spread = 0.5   Fog Spread = 2.0

You cannot apply volumetric effects to Ambient and Directional light types. To add a volumetric effect to any of the other types of lights, select the light, and in the Attribute Editor under the Light Effects section, click the checkered Map button to the right of the **Light Fog** attribute. This will create a new render node that will appear in the Hypershade and Multilister windows. Once you click the Map button, the Attribute Editor will take you to the lightFog node.

The way Maya handles volumetric lights is to attach a lightFog node to the light. The **Color** and **Density** attributes under this node control the brightness, thickness, and color of the fog attached to that light. Furthermore, in the light's Attribute Editor, you can control the fog with the **Fog Spread** and **Fog Intensity** settings. **Fog Intensity** increases the brightness of the fog, and **Fog Spread** controls how well the fog is defined within its confines. For example, a Spot light with a fog will show the fog in its cone. Figure 10.39 shows how spread affects the conical fog shape.

> To remove a fog effect, right-click the Light Fog label in the light's Attribute Editor and choose **Break Connection** from the shortcut menu.

If you want the light fog-cast shadows to make rays of light within the fog, simply check on **Use Depth Map Shadows** for the light. You will have to increase the depth map **Resolution** for a higher-quality image.

Lens Flare

Lens flare and *light glow,* illustrated in Figure 10.40, mimic the real-world effect created when light strikes a lens or when the light source is visible in the frame. The flare is created when the light hits the lens at a particular angle and causes a reflection of itself in the optics of the lens.

To enable a light glow, under the Light Effects section in the light's Attribute Editor, click the checkered Map button next to the **Light Glow** attribute to create an OpticalFX node that will appear in the Hypershade and Multi-lister. The Attribute Editor will shift focus to that new node, which will control the behavior of the light glow and lens flare. The OpticalFX node will contain the following attributes and settings:

Glow Type Setting this attribute specifies the kind of glow: Linear, Exponential, Ball, Lens Flare, and Rim Halo. These define the size and shape of the glow from the light.

Halo Type Specifying a halo will create a foggy halo around the light in addition to the glow. Controls for the halo can be found under the Halo section in the Attribute Editor.

Figure 10.40

Light glow and lens flare turned on for the back light

Star Points Setting this attribute specifies the number of star points the glow generates.

Rotation Setting this attribute rotates the orientation of the star points.

Radial Frequency Used in conjunction with the **Glow Radial Noise** attribute (see the next item) in the Glow section, this attribute defines the smoothness of any added glow noise.

Glow Radial Noise Setting this attribute adds noise to the glow effect, creating light and dark patches within the glow for a more random look.

Glow Color Setting this attribute specifies the color of the glow.

Glow Intensity and Spread Setting these attributes specifies the brightness and thickness of the glow and how well it fades away.

Glow Radial Noise = 0   Glow Radial Noise = 0.5

To turn on a lens flare along with the light glow, simply click the **Lens Flare** check box at the top right in the Attribute Editor for OpticalFX. The attributes under the Lens Flare section will control the look of the flare.

Light glows and flares can be highly effective in scenes, adding credibility to the lighting, but they are often misused or, worse, overused in CG. Used sparingly and with subtlety, lens flares can go a long way toward adding a nice touch to your scene.

Shader Glow Effects

To create a glowing effect, it is sometimes better to place a glow on a geometry's shader instead of the light itself. Since a light must be seen in the shot and pointed at the camera to see any light glow and flare, a shader glow is sometimes more desirable. This process will composite a glow on the object assigned the glow shader to simulate a volumetric light such as a street lamp on a foggy night. Shader glows have far less render cost than true volumetric lights.

Try This To light a still-life scene, follow these steps:

1. Open the `still_life_v03.mb` file in the Lighting project on the CD. Create a Spot light, place it over the still life, and aim it directly down onto the fruit. Turn on **Use Depth Map Shadows** for the light, and set **Resolution** to 1024. Set **Penumbra Angle** to 10 and **Intensity** to 1.5. Press 7 for lighted mode in the camera1 view panel to see how the light is being cast.

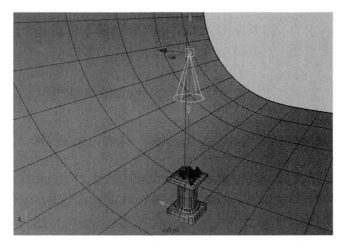

2. The Spot light will provide the practical light in the scene. You will place a bare bulb on a wire directly above the fruit. Create a NURBS sphere and position it right over the fruit but in the frame for camera1 to see. In the Render Stats section of the Attribute Editor for the sphere, turn off **Casts Shadows**.

3. Create a long, thin cylinder for the lightbulb's wire, and position it as if the bulb were hanging from it. Turn off **Casts Shadows** for it as well.

4. Create a black Phong E shader to assign to the cylinder.

5. Create a Phong shader for the bulb and assign it to the NURBS sphere. Set its **Color** to a pale, light yellow, and make it about 50 percent transparent.

6. Select the Spot light and set its **Color** to the same yellow. You can do this easily through the Color Chooser. With the shader for the bulb selected, open the Color Chooser by clicking the pale yellow color you just made. Click the right arrow to place the yellow color in the swatches to the right of the main color swatch, or RMB click any of the swatches.

7. Pick the Spot light, and click its **Color** attribute to set the Color Chooser to that color. Simply LMB click the yellow swatch you created to get the same color on the light. For detail's sake, make the light's color less saturated. Click Accept to close the Color Chooser window.

8. To make the shader glow for the bulb, open the Hypershade and select the bulb's Phong material. In the Attribute Editor, in the Special Effects section, drag the **Glow Intensity** slider from 0 to 1.0. If you render the frame, you'll see the glow not quite enough to make it a convincing lightbulb yet. In the Hypershade, select the shaderGlow1 node. This node controls all the glows in the scene.

9. Set **Quality** to 0.1. In the Glow Attributes section, set **Glow Intensity** to 6.0, set **Glow Spread** to 0.5, and set **Glow Radial Noise** to 0.2.

The scene file still_life_v04.mb on the CD contains the full scene for your reference. See Figure 10.41 for the final result.

Further Practice

The best way to learn about lighting is to light some scenes.

The file `still_life_v01.mb` in the Lighting project on the CD contains the scene of the still life with no lights so you can play with lighting and shadow methods as well as light linking to create some extra focus on some parts of the frame. The file `still_life_v02.mb` contains the same scene, but with three-point lighting already set up.

Notice in the `still_life_v02.mb` file that two lights make up the key light (spotLight1 and spot-Light2). One light makes up the fill light (directionalLight1), and two lights (spotLight3 and spotLight4) make up the back light.

For practice, download some models from the Internet and arrange them into your own still-life scenes to gain more lighting experience. Set up scenes, time the rendering process, and try to achieve the same lighting look using faster lighting setups that may not be as taxing on the renderer. Lighting professionals in the CG field are called on to find the most efficient way to light a scene and have it look at the peak of its beauty. Again, this only comes from experience.

Try setting up simple scenes, first for an indoor location that is lit by a single lightbulb, for example. Then try the same scene in the following locations to expand your lighting repertoire:

Figure 10.41

The bare lightbulb over the still life is created with a shader glow.

1. A photography studio
2. Outside in the morning on a bright summer day
3. Outside at dusk in the fall
4. Outside at night under a street lamp
5. Inside on a window ledge
6. At the bottom of a closet lit by a nearby hallway light

Tips for Using and Animating Lights

When lighting a scene, invoking a lighting mode in your perspective or camera view panel will give you great feedback on the relative brightness and direction of your lights. Most computer system's graphics cards can handle a maximum of eight lights in lighted mode, with some professional cards increasing this capability.

You invoke lighted mode by pressing the number 7 on your keyboard (not through the number pad on the side). You must first be in shaded mode (press 5) or texture mode (press 6) for lighted mode. Remember that lighted mode will display linked lights as if they are lighting the entire scene. This can cause some confusion, so it's wise to take notes on any light linking in your scene.

Maya's IPR renderer is also useful when lighting a scene. This almost real-time updating renderer will give you a high-quality render of your scene as you adjust your lights. Chapter 11 will explore the IPR renderer.

Animating a Light

Any attributes of a light can be animated in the same way that you animate any other object attribute. You cannot, however, animate a light's type. To edit a light's animation, you need only select the light and open the Graph Editor to access its keyframes. You can set keyframes on **Intensity**, **Penumbra Angle**, **Color**, and so on within the Channel Box or the Attribute Editor. Right-click the name of the attribute, and choose **Key Selected** from the shortcut menu.

> By animating a light's intensity, you can simulate the real-world appearance of a light turning on or off. To turn on a light, create a quickly increasing curve so that its brightness arcs up slowly at first before climbing to full brightness. This animation better mimics the way real lights turn on and off than simply enabling or disabling them in your scene.

Animating the color of a light, as well as the color for a shader, will set keyframes for the color's RGB values as three separate keyframes. The Graph Editor will show a separate curve for the red, green, and blue channels of color when you animate a light's color. You can set all three keys at once by right-clicking the color attribute in the Attribute Editor and choosing **Set Key** from the shortcut menu.

In addition, lights can be animated to be moved, scaled, and rotated like any other object. For further study, try animating the lighting for the simple scene(s) you set up to practice lighting from the previous section. Try creating animated lights to simulate a candle illuminating your scene, or a camp fire, or perhaps even flashing emergency lights you would find in your average space station airlock. Who doesn't have one of those?

Using the Show Manipulator Tool for Lights

An easy way to manipulate lights is to use their special manipulator (invoked by pressing T). For example, pressing T—or clicking the Show Manipulator icon (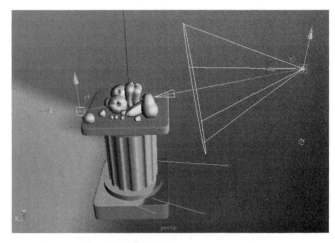) in the Tool Box— to select the Show Manipulator tool with a Spot light selected will give you two translate manipulators in the view panel.

This will allow you to move the source or target of the light to better aim it. By clicking the cyan circle that appears below the source's translate manipulator, you can toggle through a number of manipulators to adjust the Spot light's settings, such as cone angle (two clicks clockwise) and penumbra angle (three clicks clockwise). The manipulator for cone angle is shown here.

A source and target translate manipulator is available for all light types through the Show Manipulator tool as well.

Summary

This chapter explored lighting in Maya, begin-ning with basic concepts that included the three-point lighting technique. You then learned about the different lights in Maya, how they work, and how you can use light linking to better control your scene. Shadows are an important part of lighting and were covered next in this chapter, followed by a quick exploration of Global Illumi-nation with mental ray and then lighting effects such as lens flare and light glows. Finally, you learned how to begin animating lights for use in your scenes.

Lighting is truly the linchpin of CG. It can make or break a scene with the flick of a switch. Lighting goes hand in hand with rendering and shading, and the more you under-stand about all three functions, the better your scenes will look.

As mentioned, the trick to lighting is understanding how light works in reality and how to approximate its effects in Maya. That comes with practice, so don't be afraid to experi-ment with lighting and shading schemes on all your projects.

CHAPTER 11

Maya Rendering

Rendering is the last step in creating your CG work. It is the process by which the computer calculates the surface properties, lighting and shadows, and movement and shape of objects and saves a sequence of images. Although the computer does all the thinking at this point, you still need to set up your cameras and the render to get exactly what you want.

This chapter will show you how to render out your scene using Maya's software renderer and how to create reflections and refractions. It will also introduce you to Maya's other rendering methods. In this chapter, you will use a wine bottle and still life from previous chapters and animate a camera to render out a sequence.

- **The Rendering Setup**
- **Previewing Your Render**
- **Reflections and Refractions**
- **Using Cameras**
- **Motion Blur**
- **Batch Rendering**
- **Rendering the Wine Bottle**
- **mental ray for Maya**
- **Final Gather Rendering with mental ray**
- **Render Layers**
- **Ambient Occlusion**

The Rendering Setup

When your scene is complete, you've already had a celebration smoothie for your hard work, and you're ready to start a render, you need to set up how you want it rendered. Although this is the last part of the CG process, in many ways rendering should be in your thinking all along. If you create models and textures with the final image in mind and gear the lighting toward elegantly showing off the scene, the final touches are relatively easy to set up.

First, you decide which render engine you will use: Maya Software, Maya Hardware, mental ray for Maya (increasing in popularity by far), or Maya Vector. Each engine renders differently and can yield different results entirely, though mental ray and Maya Software are close in look if you don't use the special features of mental ray. The choice of a rendering method depends on your final look and sometimes on the number of machines and licenses you have to render with. Maya comes with an unlimited number of rendering licenses, which means you can render on any machine you have, though you can use Maya

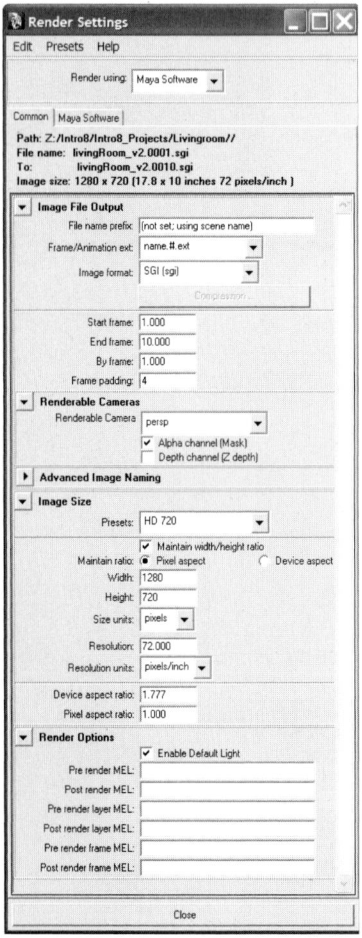

Figure 11.1

The Render Settings window

only on as many as you have licenses for. There are also third-party developers in the CG field who have created other render engines that plug right into Maya, such as Maxwell or RenderMan for Maya from Pixar. No matter the renderer, the lighting and general setup is fairly common across the board, though it is true that some steps in the creation of your scene, from modeling to lighting, will depend on which render engine you plan to use. It is therefore best to choose your render engine as you begin creating your scene. All in all, it's best to begin with Maya Software or the basics of mental ray (without the use of GI as shown in the Chapter 10) to pick up the basics of lighting, texturing, and rendering before you venture into mental ray's special features or other renderers altogether.

Regardless of the type of render, you need to specify a set of common attributes in the Render Settings window, previously and sometimes still known as the Render Global Settings or Render Globals window. As Figure 11.1 shows, you use the options in this window to set up all your rendering preferences, including the resolution, file type, frame range, and so forth. Choose **Window → Rendering Editors → Render Settings** to open the Render Settings window.

The *Render Settings* window has two tabs: the Common tab and a tab for the rendering method being used (Maya Software, Maya Hardware, mental ray, or Maya Vector). The Common tab contains the settings common to all the rendering methods. You may notice that some of the render engines do not show up in this window right away. In this case, the renderers' respective plug-ins must be loaded first. More on this in the section on mental ray for Maya in this chapter.

You will render most scenes using the Maya Software renderer. All illustrations and examples in the previous chapters were rendered using Maya Software except where noted.

Choosing a Filename

Rendered images are identified by a filename, a frame number, and an extension, in the form *filename.####.ext*, for example, stillife.0234.tif.

In the **File Name Prefix** text box, enter the image sequence name. If you don't enter anything in this text box, Maya automatically names your rendered images after your scene file (stillife in the example). When dealing with numerous scene files, this is the preferred naming convention; using it, you can immediately identify the scene file from which a particular image file was rendered. This is the preferred naming convention for most production houses and is a good habit to establish.

The frame number portion of an image sequence name (0234 in the example) identifies which frame in the sequence the image represents. In the **Frame/Animation Ext** drop-down list box, select name.#.ext to render out a sequence of files. If you leave this setting at the default of name.ext, only a single frame will render, no matter what the animation range is in the Time Slider.

Name.#.ext is perhaps the most commonly used convention, as opposed to name.ext.# or name.#, because it allows you to identify the file type easily in Windows. Although Macintosh OS X is not as picky about the order of number and extension, most Mac compositing software (such as After Effects and Shake) wants filenames that end in the three-letter extension. Therefore, it is best for both Mac and Windows to use the name.#.ext format.

The extension portion of the image name is a three-letter abbreviation for the type of file you are writing to disk. By specifying in the **Frame/Animation Ext** drop-down list box that you want an extension appended to each image filename, you ensure that you can identify the file type.

Image Format

In the **Image Format** drop-down list box, select the type of image file you want to render. Maya then adds the appropriate extension to the filename.

You can save your images in a wide range of formats. The format you choose depends on your own preference and your output needs. For example, JPEG (Joint Photographic Experts Group) files may be great for the small file sizes preferred on the Internet, but their color compression and lack of alpha channel (a feature discussed later in this chapter) make them undesirable for professional film or television production work beyond test renders and *dailies*, a meeting in which the day's (or week's) work on a production is looked at and discussed for direction.

Furthermore, it's best to render a sequence of images rather than a movie file for two reasons. First, you want your renders to be their best quality with little to no image compression. Second, if a render fails during a movie render, you must rerender the entire sequence. With an image sequence, however, you can pick up where the last frame left off. The best file type format to render to is TIFF (Tagged Image File Format). This format enjoys universal support, has little to no compression, and supports an alpha channel. Almost all image-editing and compositing packages can read Targa and TIFF formatted files, so either is a safe choice most of the time. Also, the SGI (Silicon Graphics Image) and Maya IFF (Maya Image File Format) formats are good, though some older versions of image editors may not be able to load them without a plug-in. For more on image formats, see Chapter 1.

Frame Range

Choosing the frame range ensures that your entire animation is rendered out. Maya defaults to the range 1–10, which you may often need to change to render your entire sequence. If you still have the **Frame/Animation Ext** attribute set to name (Single Frame), the frame range text boxes will be grayed out. You must choose a naming convention other than name (Single Frame) first. This is a common oversight when people first try to render their animations and see that only a single frame is rendering.

Once you have selected a naming convention other than name (Single Frame), enter the **Start Frame** and **End Frame** attributes for part of the sequence or the entire sequence. These attributes are also helpful if you need to render parts of the sequence at different times. By specifying new start and end frames, you can render different portions of a sequence or pick up where a previous render left off.

The **By Frame** attribute specifies the intervals at which the sequence will render. For example, if you want to render only the odd-numbered frames, set the **Start Frame** attribute to 1 and set the **By Frame** attribute to 2. If you want to render only even-numbered frames, set the **Start Frame** attribute to 2 and set the **By Frame** attribute to 2. And so on. Typically, you leave the **By Frame** attribute set to 1 so that Maya renders each frame. In certain cases, such as in previsualization work or in rendering tests of a scene, it may be necessary to render only every 2nd, 3rd, or even 10th frame instead.

The **Frame Padding** attribute has to do with the way an operating system, such as Windows or Mac OS X, orders its files by inserting leading zeros in the frame number. If the **Frame Padding** attribute is set to 2, for example, a single zero precedes every single-digit frame number in the filename. In this case, frame 8 is `name.08.tif` as opposed to `name.8.tif` (which is set to a padding of 1). If the **Frame Padding** attribute is set to 4, the filename contains three leading zeros, and thus frame 8 is `name.0008.tif`.

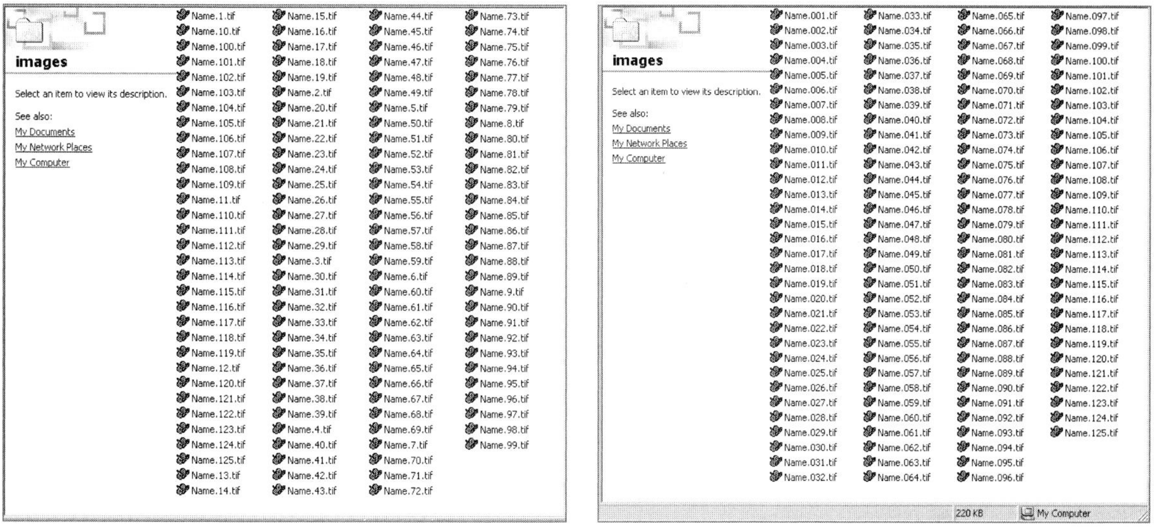

Large sequences of files are easier to organize if they all have a frame padding of at least 3. Figure 11.2 shows an image sequence without padding (left) and the same sequence with padding (right). The files without padding are not in numeric order. Because rendering can generate a large number of files, it's important to be able to manage them efficiently.

Figure 11.2

Images rendered without frame padding (left). Frame padding makes file sequences easier to organize (right).

Camera

Under the Renderable Cameras heading, you can choose the camera to render as well as the *image channels* to output.

Image files are composed of red, green, and blue channels. Each channel specifies the amount of the primary additive color (red, green, or blue, respectively) in the image. (See Chapter 1 for more on how computers define color.) In addition, some file formats can also save a fourth channel, called the alpha channel. This channel defines the transparency level of the image. Just as the red channel defines how much red is in an area of the image, the *alpha channel* defines how transparent the image is when layered or composited on another image. If the alpha channel is black, the image is perfectly see-through. If the alpha channel is white, the image is opaque. The alpha channel is also known as the *matte*. An object with a transparency will render with a gray alpha channel, as shown in Figure 11.3.

Figure 11.3

This wine bottle's transparency renders with a gray alpha channel.

The alpha channel can be displayed in the Render View window. As discussed later in this chapter, your test renders also display in this window.

> To view an image's alpha channel in the Render View window, click the Display Alpha Channel icon (⬭). To reset the view to RGB (full-color view), click the Display RGB Channels icon (▦).

Most renders will have RGB as well as alpha channels selected, so leave the **Alpha Channel (Mask)** check box checked at all times. Note, however, that JPEG, GIF (Graphics Interchange Format), and Windows bitmap files do not support alpha channels, regardless of whether the Alpha Channel (Mask) check box is checked.

> Only a few file formats, such as Maya IFF, support the depth channel. This grayscale channel resembles the alpha channel but conveys depth information, that is, the distance of an object from the camera. The Depth Channel (Z Depth) setting is typically used when compositing images.

Setting Resolution

The **Width** and **Height** attributes set the pixel size of the image to be rendered, a.k.a. the image resolution. In the Image Size section of the Render Settings window, you can select a resolution from the **Presets** drop-down list box. The commonly used resolution for professional broadcast is 720×486 NTSC (National Television Standards Committee), which appears as CCIR 601/Quantel NTSC in the **Presets** list. To composite Maya CG into a home shot DV (digital video) movie, you use the standard DV resolution of 720×480 to render your scene, but you must enter that resolution manually in the **Width** and **Height** fields. (For more on resolutions, see Chapter 1.)

The **Device Aspect Ratio** and **Pixel Aspect Ratio** attributes adjust the width of the image to accommodate certain professional output needs; you need not adjust them here.

> Make sure your **Pixel Aspect Ratio** attribute is set to 1 before you render, unless you need to render CCIR 601/Quantel NTSC or DV for television needs; otherwise, your image may look squeezed or widened in comparison with any live-action footage you composite into.

The higher your resolution, the longer the scene will take to render. Doubling the resolution may quadruple the render time. With large frame sequences, it's advisable to render tests at half the resolution of the final output or less to save time.

Besides the image resolution, the image quality of a render also dictates how long a render will take. In addition to turning down the resolution for a test, you can use a lower-quality render. Each rendering method has its own set of quality settings, which are explained in the following sections.

Selecting a Render Engine

Maya allows you to select a render engine in the Render Settings window. Although Maya Software is commonly used for most applications, the other rendering methods give you flexibility in choosing a final look for your project.

Maya Software

Maya Software, the default software rendering method, can capture just about everything you would want in your scene, from reflections to motion blur and transparencies. You can use the software rendering method in a couple of ways.

USING RAYTRACING

Raytracing, a topic introduced in Chapter 10, is used to incorporate two optical effects into a rendering that the default software rendering method cannot handle. *Raytracing* traces rays of light from each light source to every object in the shot and then traces the light's reflection from the object to the camera's lens. This allows true *reflections* and *refractions* to appear in the render, as well as highly defined shadows. (For more on shadows, see Chapter 10.) You saw in the previous chapter that raytracing is also a vital component of mental ray for Maya as well as Maya's software renderer.

Since the default software renderer renders the same image without true reflections or refractions and can generate detailed shadows with shadow maps, the only reason to use raytracing is for reflective and refractive surfaces (as well as raytraced shadows) or to enable some of mental ray's features such as Global Illumination.

True Reflections True reflections occur when every object in the scene is seen in a reflective surface, as a reflection of course. You can also have objects with reflections explicitly turned off through the Render Stats section in the Attribute Editor in case you don't want a particular reflection, which is common. Although it is possible to simulate reflections in Maya Software using *reflection maps*, true reflections can only be generated through raytracing. (In Chapter 7, the axe project shows how to apply reflection maps.)

As with raytraced shadows, raytraced reflections need to be enabled. To do so, click Raytracing in the Raytracing Quality section of the Maya Software tab in the Render Settings window. Unlike raytraced shadows, however, raytraced reflections need not be explicitly turned on through the lights.

As soon as raytracing is enabled, any reflective surface will receive a true reflection of the objects and environment in the scene. Even objects with reflection maps will reflect other objects in addition to their reflection maps. For more on reflection maps, see the section "Reflections and Refractions" later in this chapter.

Refractions *Refractions* occur when light bends as it passes through one medium into another medium of different density. For example, a pencil in a glass of water will appear to be broken. The light bouncing off the pencil refracts as it travels from the water into the air, bending a bit during the transition. That displaces the view of the pencil under the water, making it seem broken.

RENDER QUALITY

With software rendering, the render quality depends most noticeably on *anti-aliasing*. Anti-aliasing is the effect when pixels appear to blur together to soften a jagged edge on an angled line. Increasing the anti-aliasing level of a render produces an image that has smoother angles and curves. The Render Settings window contains presets that specify this level and a few others to set the quality of your render.

1. In the Render Settings window, make sure Maya Software is selected in the **Render Using** drop-down list box, and click the Maya Software tab.

2. In the Anti-aliasing Quality section, select either Preview Quality or Production Quality from the Quality preset drop-down list box.

Figure 11.4 shows the fruit still life from Chapter 10 rendered with the Preview Quality preset and the same image with the Production Quality preset.

Of course, the higher the quality, the longer the render time. As you become more experienced, you will be better able to balance uncompromised quality with efficient render times.

Maya Hardware

The hardware rendering method uses your graphic card's processor to render the scene. Hardware renders are similar to what you see when you play a 3D video game. The data output by the game is fed directly into the graphics pipeline of your hardware setup and is rendered on-the-fly as you play.

This method results in faster render times but lacks some of the features and quality you get from a software render. In Figure 11.5, the first image shows a wine bottle as rendered through hardware. The render time is blazingly fast, but the quality suffers. The second image shows the software render of the same frame. Hardware rendering becomes a good way to test-render a scene, although only a few professional video cards fully support Maya's hardware rendering.

To use the Maya Hardware renderer, in the Render Settings window, make sure Maya Hardware is selected in the **Render Using** drop-down list box. To specify hardware quality, select a level from the **Number Of Samples** drop-down list box under the Maya Hardware tab.

Figure 11.4

With Preview Quality (left) the edges of the fruit are jagged. With Production Quality (right) the jaggedness is gone.

Figure 11.5

The hardware-rendered wine bottle (left) lacks some subtleties. The software-rendered wine bottle shows better specularity and surface detail (right).

mental ray for Maya

The mental ray for Maya rendering method lets you emulate the behavior of light even more realistically than the other rendering methods, as you saw in the previous chapter on lighting. Based on raytracing, mental ray takes the concept further by adding photon maps to the light traces. That is, it projects photon particles from lights and records their behavior and trajectory. The end result allows the phenomena of light *caustics* and *bounce,* also known as *radiosity* and *global illumination.*

The mental ray for Maya renderer is an advanced and intricate rendering language with shaders and procedures all its own. This chapter briefly covers one of the popular mental ray methods called Final Gather at the end and should, in addition to the the previous chapter's Global Illumination lighting exercise, give you a primer on rendering with mental ray for Maya. More and more, mental ray is becoming an overall rendering solution as well as being used for renders that require a highly sophisticated lighting look. To use it, you need to be experienced with the basics of lighting and rendering. At its base, mental ray will give you results similar to that of Maya Software, without any of the mental ray

Figure 11.6

The fruit still life as a vector render

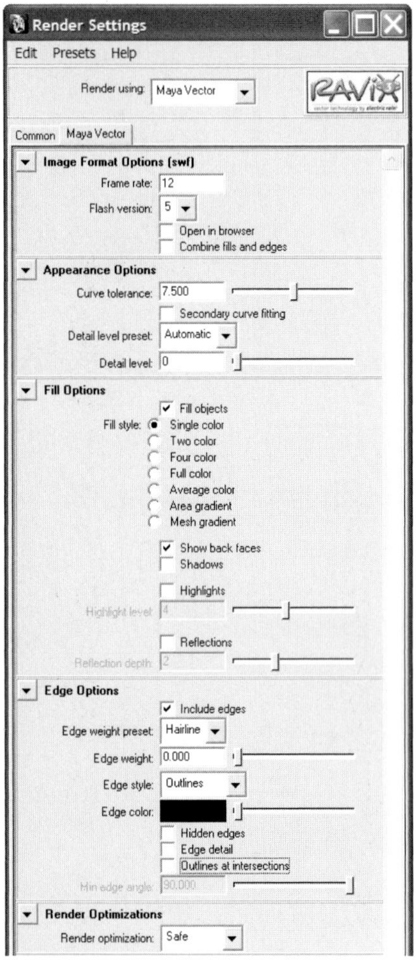

Figure 11.7

The Maya Vector rendering settings

bells and whistles enabled. A scene lighted and set up for Maya Software will render out pretty much the same through a base mental ray render, though some of the quality settings are slightly different (and covered later in this chapter).

Maya Vector

Vector rendering lets you render your objects with an illustrated or cartoon look. You can render "ink" outlines of your characters to composite over flat-color passes. Figure 11.6 shows the fruit still-life scene rendered with Maya Vector.

Maya Vector can output animated files in Macromedia Flash format for direct use in web pages and animations, as well as Adobe Illustrator files and the usual list of image formats. To specify the attribute settings for Maya Vector, you use the Maya Vector tab in the Render Settings window (see Figure 11.7).

In the Fill Options section, click the Fill Objects check box and select the number of colors for each object to set the look of the render. If you want the renderer to include an outline of the edges of your geometry, in the Edge Options section click the Include Edges check box and set the line weights.

Previewing Your Render: The Render View Window

The Render View window automatically opens when you test-render a frame. To open it manually, choose **Window → Rendering Editors → Render View**. Your current scene renders in the Render View window. Figure 11.8 shows the important icons in this window.

Redo Previous Render Renders the last-rendered view panel.

Render Region Renders only the selected portion of an image. To select a portion of an image, click within the image in the Render View window and drag a red box around a region.

Open Render Settings Window Opens the Render Settings window (also known as the Render Globals window in previous versions of Maya).

Display RGB Channels Displays the full color of the image.

Display Alpha Channel Displays only the alpha matte of the render as a black-and-white image.

Display Real Size Resets the image size to 100 percent to make sure the image displays properly. When the Render View window is resized or you select a new render resolution, the image renders to fit the window and the image is resized if need be. If your render looks blocky, make sure the Render View window is displaying at real size before adjusting the options in the Render Settings window.

Select a Renderer Lets you select the rendering method. This is the same as selecting it in the Render Settings window.

Information Readout At the bottom of the Render View is a readout of information about the frame rendered. This information will tell you the resolution, renderer used, frame number, render time, and the camera used to render. This readout is a huge help in comparing different render settings and different frames as you progress in your work, especially when you keep images in the buffer (explained later).

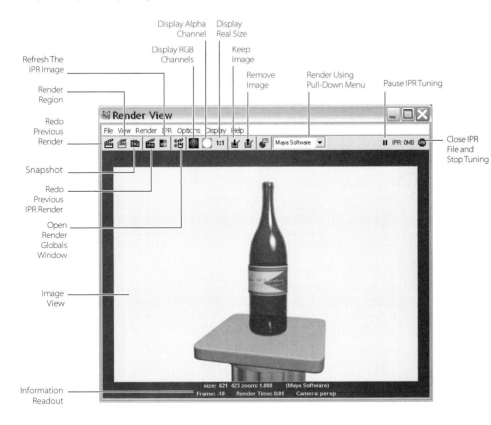

Figure 11.8

The Render View window

Saving/Loading an Image

Although you typically use the Render View window to test a scene, you can also use it to save single frames by choosing **File → Save Image** to save in all Maya's supported image formats. Likewise, choose **File → Open Image** to display any previously rendered image file in this window. If your task in Maya is to create a single frame, this is the best way to render and save it.

Keep/Remove Image

The Render View window is a prime place to see adjustments to various parts of your scene. You can store images in its buffer by clicking the Keep Image icon. When you do, a scroll bar appears at the bottom of the window, and you can scroll through any saved images. This is handy for making a change, rendering it, and scrolling back and forth between the old saved image and the new render to make sure the change is to your liking. You can store a number of images in the buffer. For a faster way to preview changes, use IPR rendering, as discussed next.

IPR Rendering

As you saw in Chapter 7, a fast way to preview changes to your scene is to use Maya's IPR (Interactive Photorealistic Rendering). After you IPR-render a view panel, specify the region you want to tune by dragging a box around that area of the image in the Render View window. Maya updates that region every time you make a shader or lighting change to the scene. Figure 11.9 shows the fruit still life as an IPR render as the color and specular levels are being fine-tuned.

Figure 11.9

IPR rendering lets you fine-tune your textures and lighting with near real-time feedback.

IPR is perfect for finding just the right lighting and specular levels. It will not, however, register any raytracing elements such as refractions or true reflections. But overall, IPR quality is close to that of a full software render while still allowing you to watch your tuning in real time. IPR will not register shifts in the Timeline or changes to the geometry.

Reflections and Refractions

You can either map or raytrace reflections. As you saw in Chapter 7, it is pretty simple to create a reflection map for an object. Simply assign a Phong, PhongE, Blinn, or Anisotropic material to your object and make sure the **Reflectivity** attribute is greater than zero. Then click the Reflected Color map button to add a texture or a file as a map to create the reflection. (See the axe project in Chapter 7 for more on reflection maps and shaders.)

To generate true reflections, however, you will need to enable raytracing. Mapping textures to the reflected color is not necessary when raytracing is enabled, as Maya will simply reflect any objects in the scene that fall in the proper line of sight.

Raytraced Reflections

To enable raytraced reflections, use a material with a **Reflections** attribute such as a Phong, and open the Render Settings window. Choose Maya Software, and in the Maya Software tab, click the Raytracing check box in the Raytracing Quality section.

The sliders control the quality of the render by specifying how many times to reflect or refract for any given object. Setting Reflections to 2, for example, enables an object's reflection in a second object to appear as part of its reflection in a third object.

The first image in Figure 11.10 shows the still life reflecting onto the surface of its table. In this case, **Reflections** is set to 1. If you increase **Reflections** to 2, however, you'll see the reflections of the pieces of fruit in each other also reflecting in the surface of the table.

Figure 11.10

(Left) Reflections set to 1. (Right) Reflections set to 2.

Notice the difference in the reflections of the fruit in the table between the two renders. Raytraced reflections can consume valuable render resources and time, so it's a good idea to make your scene efficient. You don't want to reflect more than necessary.

You can control the number of reflections on a per-object basis as opposed to setting limits on the entire scene through the Render Settings window. To access a shader's reflection limits, select the shader in the Hypershade and open the Attribute Editor. In the Raytrace Options section, drag the Reflection Limit slider to set the maximum number of reflections for that shader. The lower of this value or the **Reflections** value in the Render Settings window will dictate how many reflections are rendered for every object attached to that shader. The default shader reflection limit is 1, so make sure you change the **Reflections** value as well as each shader's value if you want more than one level of reflection.

Furthermore, you might want some objects not to cast reflections in a scene with raytraced reflections. To specify that an object does not cast reflections, select the object in a Maya panel and open the Attribute Editor. In the Render Stats section, clear the Visible in Reflections check box.

Rendering Refractions

Refractions are also a raytraced-only ability. Refractions require that an object be semi-transparent so that you can see through it to the object (or objects) behind it that is being refracted. To control refractions, use the shader.

To enable refractions, select the appropriate shader in the Hypershade and open the Attribute Editor. In the Raytrace Options section, click the Refractions check box. Now you need to set a refractive index for the shader and a refraction limit, similar to the reflection limit.

The refractive index must be greater or less than 1 to cause a refraction. Typically, a number within 0.2 of 1 is perfect for most refraction effects. The first image in Figure 11.11 is raytraced with a refractive index of 1.2 on the wine bottle and glasses; the second image has a refractive index of 0.8 on both bottle and glasses.

You can specify whether an object is visible in a refracting object by clicking or clearing the Visible in Refractions check box in the Render Stats section of the object's Attribute Editor.

Using Cameras

Cameras capture all the animation fun in the scene. In theory, Maya's cameras work in the same way as real cameras. The more you know about photography, the easier these concepts are to understand.

The term *camera*, in essence, refers to the perspective view. You can have as many cameras in the scene as you want, but it's wise to have a camera you're planning to render with

Figure 11.11

(Left) Refractive index of 1.2. (Right) Refractive index of 0.8.

placed to frame the shot and another camera acting as the perspective work view so you can move around your scene as you work. The original *persp* panel fits that latter role well, though it can be used as a render camera just as easily.

You can also render any of your work windows to test-render orthogonal views of your model the same way you render a perspective view.

Creating a Camera

The simplest way to create a new camera is to choose **Panels → Perspective → New**. This creates a new camera node in Maya and sets that active panel to its view.

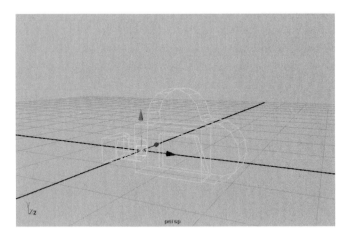

You can select a camera and transform it (move it, rotate it, scale it) just as you would select and transform any other object in Maya to be animated or just positioned. Furthermore, you can move a camera and rotate it using the Alt/Option key and mouse button combinations.

For example, click inside a new Maya scene perspective window to make it active. Select that view's camera by choosing **View → Select Camera**. The camera's attributes appear in the Channel Box. Try moving the view around using the Alt/Option key and mouse button combinations. Notice how the attributes change to reflect the new position and rotation of the camera. You can animate the camera—for example, zoom in or out or pan across the scene—by setting keyframes on any of these attributes.

Camera Types

You can create three types of cameras for your scene: Camera, Camera and Aim, and Camera, Aim, and Up (also known as single-node, two-node, and three-node cameras,

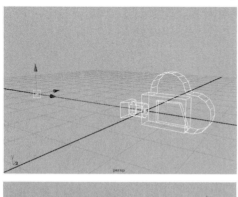

respectively). To create any of these cameras, choose **Create → Cameras**. You can also change the type of a camera at any time through the Attribute Editor.

The single-node camera (Camera) is the most common. This camera consists of a single camera node that you move and rotate as you would any other object for proper positioning. The *persp* panel's camera is a single-node camera.

The two-node camera (Camera and Aim) consists of the camera node and an aim node. You use the aim node to point the camera as opposed to rotating it to orient it properly. This is useful for animating a camera following an object. You animate the movement of the aim node to follow your object like a car around a racetrack. The camera pivots to follow its aim point and, hence, the object.

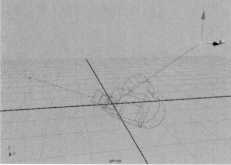

The three-node camera (Camera, Aim, and Up) has a camera node, an aim node, and an up node. The additional up node is to orient the camera's up direction. This gives you the ability to animate the side-to-side rotation of the camera as well as its aim direction.

Camera Attributes

As an example, load the `still_life_ render_v02.mb` scene from the Lighting project on the CD. You'll see a green box in the *persp* panel that displays the resolution (set to 640 × 480) and the name of the camera (camera1).

Special attributes control the function of camera nodes. To set these attributes, follow these steps:

1. With your camera1 camera selected, open the Attribute Editor (press Ctrl+A or choose **View → Camera Attribute Editor**).

2. At the top of the window, select the type of camera controls you want. The **Controls** attribute sets the type of camera from single- to two- to three-control nodes. Figure 11.12 shows the Attribute Editor for the camera.

Focal Length

The **Focal Length** attribute specifies the length of the lens. The lower the focal length (a.k.a. short lens), the wider the view. At very low numbers, however, the image will be distorted, as you can see in the comparison in Figure 11.13. The higher the focal length, the closer the subject seems to the camera.

Although adjusting the **Focal Length** attribute of a camera zooms in and out, it is not the same as moving the camera closer to your subject using the Alt+RMB procedure to zoom in view panels. Focal length zooming can create optical distortions; such as can be created with a fish-eye lens.

When you want to animate your camera getting closer to the subject of your shot, it's best to animate the camera and not the focal length. However, if you need to match some CG element in Maya to a photograph or video you've imported as an image plane, set your camera's focal length to match that of the real camera used for the background.

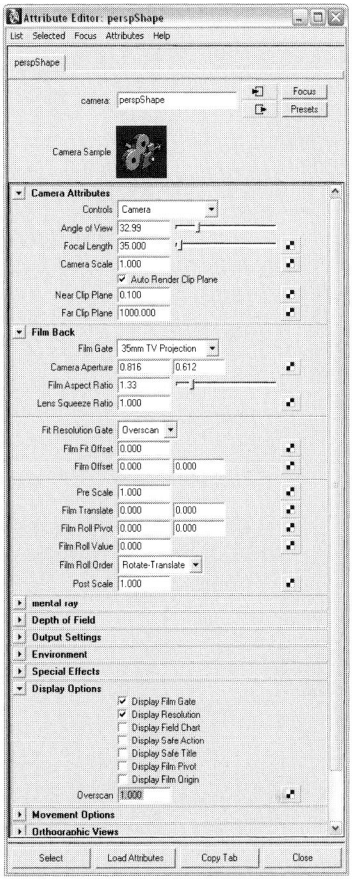

Figure 11.12

The Attribute Editor for the camera

Clipping Planes

All cameras in Maya have clipping planes that restrict the amount of information that can be seen through them. The clipping plane is defined by the **Near Clip Plane** and **Far Clip Plane** attributes. These set the minimum and maximum distance, respectively, of the clipping plane. Any object or portion of an object that passes beyond these distances will not show in the window and should not render.

If you notice objects disappearing as you move your camera and create a scene, it may be because of the clipping plane. Increase the **Far Clip Plane** attribute, and the objects should reappear in the view.

Figure 11.13

Different focal lengths

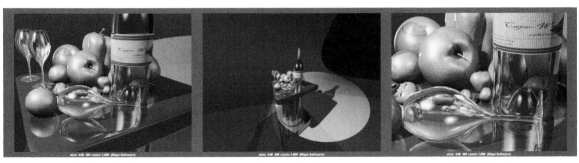

Focal Length = 35   Focal Length = 8   Focal Length = 60

Film Back

The Film Back attributes concern the type of output you'll be dealing with once your renders are finished and you're ready to put your animation on tape, DVD, film, or what have you.

Film Gate Defines the aspect ratio of your camera's view. Most images that are output to television have an aspect ratio of 1:1.33, exemplified by the 35mm TV Projection selection in the **Film Gate** drop-down list box, which is preferred for video. (For more on aspect ratios, see Chapter 1.)

Fit Resolution Gate Allows you to align footage you may have imported as an image plane to properly match up CG to live action.

Overscan

Found under the Display Options section, **Overscan** lets you resize the view without changing the film gate that will render. For example, the scene on the left is set up with an **Overscan** setting of 1.3, allowing you to see more than what will render, which is defined by the outline box. The scene on the right is set up with an **Overscan** setting of 2, which increases even more how much you see in the camera1 panel but does not change the view when rendered.

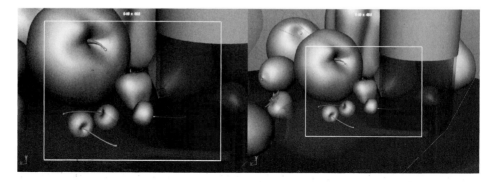

You can turn the green box in the panel on and off through the Attribute Editor for the camera. Also in the Display Options section are **Display Film Gate** and **Display Resolution** check boxes. Ideally, these two green boxes should align perfectly in the view pane. If the resolution box (the solid green line) does not line up with the film gate box (the dashed green line), change your film gate selection to match the resolution's aspect ratio in the Render Settings window. A resolution of 640 × 480, for example, has an aspect ratio of 1.33, the same as the 35mm TV Projection film gate currently selected for this scene.

Environment

In the Environment section you will find attributes to adjust the background color that renders and to create an image plane. As you saw in the axe-modeling project in Chapter 7, importing image planes can help improve your work flow.

In Chapter 7, you imported a drawing of an axe by choosing **View → Image Plane → Import Image** in the *persp* panel. You can also import an image plane by clicking the Create button in the Environment section of the Attribute Editor.

Click the color swatch next to Background Color to change the background color in your renders using the Color Chooser. The slider will allow you to control the value, or brightness, of the current color. Neither will change the background color of your view panels, however.

Motion Blur

Motion blur is an optical illusion that occurs when an object moves fast in front of a camera: it looks blurred as it crosses the frame. Maya renders out motion blur in two ways: 2D blur or 3D blur, though neither will render as reflections.

- In the 2D blur process, Maya calculates after the frame is rendered. Any objects moving in the frame are blurred with a 2D filter effect. The 2D blur is quite effective for most applications and faster than 3D blur.

- The 3D blur process is calculated while a frame of the sequence is rendering. Every motion-blur-enabled object is blurred with typically better results than 2D blur, but at a cost of a much longer render time.

To enable motion blur, open the Render Settings window, and in the Motion Blur section, click the Motion Blur check box. Then choose 2D or 3D blur.

Typically, you control the amount of blur rendered for 2D and 3D by setting the **Blur by Frame** attribute. The higher the number, the greater the blur. Using additional controls, however, you can increase or decrease the 2D blur effect in the render. The **Blur Length** attribute affects the streakiness of the blur to further increase or decrease the amount of motion blur set with the **Blur By Frame** attribute.

Use motion blur sparingly in most scenes. It takes a careful eye to choose the right blur amount for an object.

> Setting a camera's **Shutter Angle** attribute (in the camera's Attribute Editor in the Special Effects section) also affects the amount of blur rendered. The higher the number, the greater the blur.

Batch Rendering

You've used single-frame rendering numerous times to see a scene in the Render View window. But how do you start a render of an animation sequence? That is called *batch rendering* in Maya. To batch-render an entire scene, follow these steps:

1. Open the Render Settings window.

2. Choose Maya Software to render with, enter the start and end frames of your animation, and select your image format. Select your quality and resolution settings. Finally, set the camera you want to render in the **Renderable Camera** attribute.

Be sure to select name.#.ext in the **Frame/Animation Ext** drop-down list box to render out a sequence of files. Remember, if you leave the default setting, which is name.ext, only a single frame renders.

Figure 11.14

The Batch Render Frame dialog box

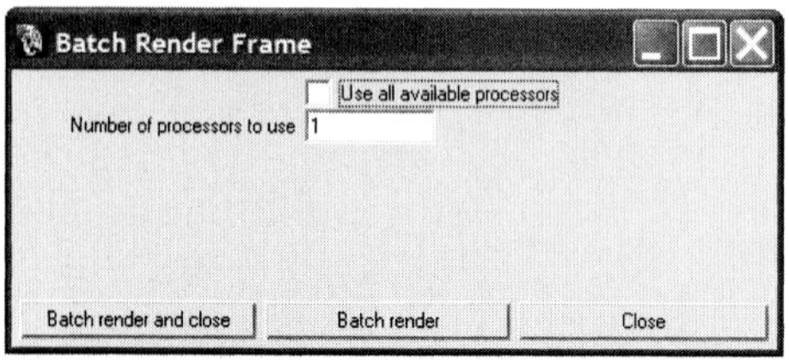

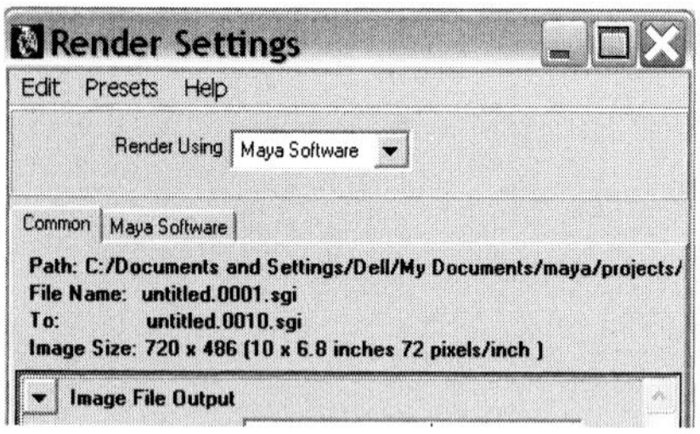

3. In the main Maya window under the Rendering menu set, choose **Render → Batch Render ❑** to open the Batch Render Frame dialog box, as shown in Figure 11.14.

4. If you have a multiprocessor, hyper-threading, or dual-core machine, select how many CPUs you would like to use to render your scene.

5. Click Batch Render to render the frame range you specified in the Render Settings window. The render occurs in the background, and you will see progress updates in the Command line at the bottom of your Maya screen and in the Script Editor window if you open it.

To see a frame as the batch render progresses, choose **Render → Show Batch Render**. To cancel a batch render, choose **Render → Cancel Batch Render**.

When you batch-render, your image files are written to the images folder of the current project. Make sure your project is properly set; otherwise, your files will end up in an unexpected folder. You can always see the render path and the image name at the top of the Render Settings window.

Rendering the Wine Bottle

In this section, you'll set up and render an animated camera to move over 25 frames of a wine bottle still life.

Load still_life_render_v01.mb from the Lighting project on the CD. You will adjust your render settings and some shader properties to make the wine bottle look more like glass.

Selecting Render Settings Options

Set your resolution and quality settings in the Render Settings window:

1. Open the Render Settings window, and select Maya Software. Click the Maya Software tab.

2. From the **Quality** drop-down list box, select Production Quality. This will preset the appropriate settings to produce a high-quality render.

3. Click the Common tab. Set **Frame/Animation Ext** to name.#.ext, set **Start Frame** to 1, set **End Frame** to 25, and set **Frame Padding** to 2.

4. From the **Image Format** drop-down list box, select Tiff.

5. Make sure that Camera is set to camera1. In the Image Size section, set Preset to 640 × 480.

Setting Up the Scene

Now set up some of the objects in the scene itself. The wine bottle has been imported into the still life scene, and three wine glasses have been added. All the lights are in place, as is the camera.

Start by setting this scene up to raytrace to get true reflections and refractions.

1. Turn on refractions for the glass shaders. In the Hypershade, select the Glasses material and open the Attribute Editor. In the Raytrace Options section, click the Refractions check box and set **Refractive Index** to 1.2. Set **Reflection Limit** to 2. Now select the Wine_Bottle material, and repeat the previous steps.

2. Since your lights' shadows are set to shadow maps, you need to change them to raytraced shadows. Remember that semitransparent objects cast solid shadows unless shadows are raytraced, so the glasses and wine bottle will cast shadows as if they were solid and not glass. In the Outliner, select spotLight1. In the Attribute Editor, in the Shadows section, enable Use Ray Trace Shadows. Notice that the shadow map options turn off. Repeat these steps for the remaining two shadow-casting lights: spotLight4 and spotLight3. Figure 11.15 shows the three shadow-casting lights in the scene.

> You cannot select all three lights at once to turn on raytraced shadows in the Attribute Editor. Any adjustments you make in the Attribute Editor affect only the most recently selected object, not multiple selections.

3. Open the Render Settings window, and turn on raytracing in the Raytracing Quality section. Set **Reflections** to 2.

Setting Up the Camera

Next you'll set up the camera to render the scene.

1. Open the camera's Attribute Editor through the camera1 panel (choose **View →** **Camera Attribute Editor**).

2. Select the Display Film Gate option in the Display Options section to turn on a dashed green box in the camera1 panel. Enable the Display Resolution option. Notice that the two boxes are not aligned.

3. Since the resolution is 640 × 480, you will use a 1.33 aspect ratio. Select 35mm TV Projection from the Film Gate drop-down list box. The two green boxes now align. Although it's not absolutely necessary to match the resolution with the film gate, it's definitely good practice to do so, especially if you will later insert CG in live-action videos.

4. As soon as you change the film gate, the framing of the scene changes. You'll have to move the camera out to frame the entire still life. If you try to use the Alt key and mouse button combinations to zoom out, you'll notice that you cannot move the camera in this scene. The movement attributes for the camera have been locked to prevent accidental movement that would disrupt the shot.

5. To unlock the camera, choose **View → Select Camera**. The camera's attributes appear in the Channel Box. Some are grayed out, signifying that they are locked and cannot be changed. Highlight the locked attributes and RMB choose Unlock Selected in the Channel Box.

Figure 11.15

Shadow lights

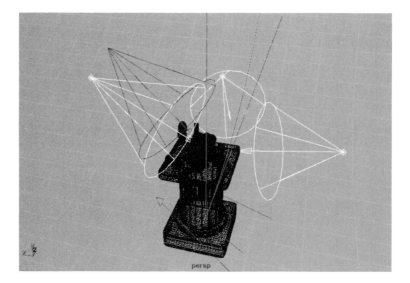

6. Create an animated camera move to slowly pull out and reveal the still life over 25 frames. Set your Range Slider to 1 to 25 frames. Go to frame 1. The camera1 view should be similar to that shown here. Select all three Translate and Rotate channels in the Channel Box, and RMB choose Key Selected to set keyframes for the first camera position.

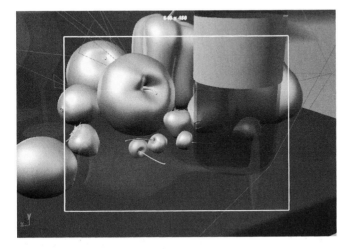

7. Zoom (actually truck) the camera out by pressing Alt+RMB to a wider framing to reveal the entire still life seen here. Highlight the Translate and Rotate channels again in the Channel Box, and set keyframes for them.

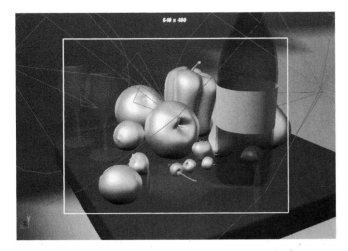

> You can choose to lock the camera to prevent accidentally moving the view once you set your keyframes, especially if Auto Keyframe is on. Select the **Translate** and **Rotate** attributes in the Channel Box and RMB choose Lock Selected.

Scrub your animation, and you'll see a pullout revealing the full scene.

Batch Rendering and Playing Back the Sequence

Now you're ready to render out the 25-frame sequence. Choose **Render → Batch Render**.

Since you are raytracing this scene at full resolution, this render should take anywhere from 20 minutes to an hour. To chart the progress of the render, open the Script Editor by clicking its icon on the Help line or by choosing **Window → General Editors → Script Editor**.

To see the frames playback, you will need a program that can load the images in sequence and play them back for you. You can also import the image sequence into a compositing or editing program such as Adobe After Effects or Premiere to playback as a clip and edit as you wish.

You can also use FCheck, a frame viewer that is included with Maya. This small and surprisingly powerful program plays back your images in real time so that you can judge your finished animation. To use FCheck, follow these steps:

1. In Windows, choose **Start → All Programs → Autodesk → Autodesk Maya 8.0 → FCheck** to open the FCheck window, shown in Figure 11.16.

Figure 11.16

FCheck, shown here with a sample image, plays back your rendered sequence.

2. Choose **File → Open Animation**.

3. In the file browser, find your images folder in your project and click the first frame of the sequence you want to playback. FCheck loads the images frame by frame into RAM and then plays them back in real time. Just set your playback speed and use the VCR controls to playback your sequence.

mental ray for Maya

You had some experience with mental ray rendering in the last chapter as you lighted with Global Illumination. In this part of the chapter, we will discuss mental ray options to begin to scratch the surface.

First, if you have not done so already, ensure that mental ray is loaded. Mental ray for Maya is considered a plug-in and may not load with Maya when you first start up. Choose **Window → Settings/Preferences → Plug-in Manager** to open the Plug-in Manager, shown in Figure 11.17. Make sure both the **Loaded** and **Auto Load** check boxes for Mayatomr.mll are checked to make sure it loads by default.

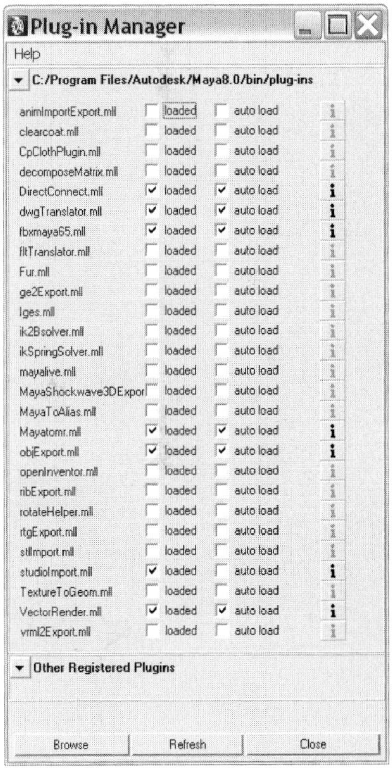

As with Maya's software renderer, the quality settings for mental ray center around anti-aliasing. mental ray for Maya, however, offers you finer control over how you set the quality levels through the Render Settings window. Under the Anti-aliasing Quality heading, you will find these attributes:

Number Of Samples These **Min** and **Max** values set the number of times mental ray will sample a pixel to determine how best to anti-alias the result. The higher the number, the finer the detail and the smoother your rendered lines will appear. These settings are *exponential*, so a small increase will yield a much greater quality and much longer render time. You typically will not need to set the **Max Sample Level** above 2 for most uses. Both **Max** and **Min Samples Level** can be set into the negative numbers for fast renders, though you will notice jagged edges. A good setting for most renders is 0 and 2 for **Min** and **Max** levels respectively.

What determines the exact sample level within the min and max range set by these attributes is dependant on the **Contrast Threshold,** which is explained later.

Figure 11.17

Use the Plug-in Manager to load mental ray for Maya.

Multi-pixel Filtering Filtering occurs on the results of the sampling of pixels to blend the pixels of a region together to form a coherent image. A high **Filter Width** and **Height** rate will tend to blur the image, whereas low filter values may look overly crisp. Box is the default filter as it is the fastest to render, while Gaussian (Gauss) gives the best result with the slowest render times. Usually, however, render times are not too terribly affected between different filter modes, so it's not like Gaussian will take four times the render time to render the same frame over box filter type.

Contrast Threshold **Contrast Threshold** determines *when* mental ray turns up the number of samples in a particular region of the frame. If the contrast level from one pixel to its neighbor is *below* the threshold value, mental ray will turn up the number of samples for that pixel to render a higher-quality result. Therefore, the *lower* the values set here, the *higher* the sample rate.

Contrast Threshold values can be set separately for each of the Red, Green, Blue, and Alpha values. Usually you would set them at all the same value, but you have the control to do otherwise to fully tweak and optimize your render to the *n*th degree.

Rather than setting high sample rates with **Max** and **Min Samples Level** attributes, lower the **Contrast Threshold** values to force mental ray to use closer to the Max sample rate only where it needs to. We'll see this in action in the next section.

Sample Options **Sample Lock** and **Jitter** attributes are turned on to reduce noise and artifacts in rendered sequences.

Render Settings in Action!

In this section, we will take a look at how **Contrast Threshold** and **Number Of Samples** work together to determine the quality of the render of the living room scene from Chapter 10. With Global Illumination still enabled, we left the render quality settings fairly low (**Min Sample Level** of –1 and **Max Sample Level** of 1). This gives us a render as seen in Figure 11.18. You can see jagged highlights on the furniture, especially the chair on the right side of the frame.

Figure 11.18

The living room with low anti-aliasing values. Notice the jagged highlights on the furniture.

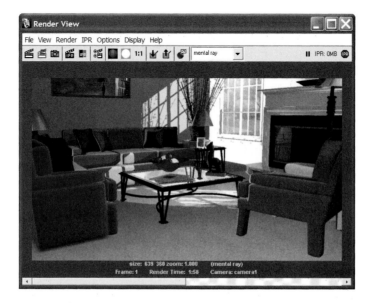

Figure 11.19

The living room with better anti-aliasing. Notice the fireplace looks better here.

Figure 11.20

The living room with still better anti-aliasing since Contrast Threshold was set lower

Now, if you increase the **Max Sample Level** to 2 and the **Min Sample Level** to 0, you will see an immediate increase in quality (especially in the lines of the fireplace) with a noticeable increase in render time (about 50 percent longer). But we can get a better image still, as seen in Figure 11.19.

But rather than crank up the sample levels to the heavens, lower the contrast thresholds to force mental ray to sample difficult areas closer to or at the max value of 2. Figure 11.20 shows the same frame with **Contrast Threshold** values set to 0.05 from the default 0.1. Also, the **Min Sample Level** was set to 1 but the **Max Sample Level** was left at 2. The render times did increase, but at a more acceptable margin than if the max sampling was increased beyond a value of 2, especially for a GI render of this detail. Notice how much finer the lines on the fireplace look with this render.

Finding the right levels to set are important to a quality render and an acceptable work flow. It's easy enough to crank the numbers to the sky, but render times will very quickly become unacceptable, especially when you have a supervisor or client breathing down your neck for the hundreds of frames you have to render by breakfast the next day.

Final Gather Rendering with mental ray for Maya

Final Gather (FG) is a type of rendering with mental ray that includes a single light bounce within the scene. Like Global Illumination (GI), it traces light as it reflects off surfaces to illuminate the scene for a nicely realistic render that takes into account color bleed of light from one surface to another. For example, a red wall will cast a red hue on the surface right next to it. This is achieved easily with FG. FG is an intricate dance of settings and numbers to get perfect renders, and it is tough to cover in an introductory text such as this. However, this section will give you a primer in how to start using FG.

The basic premise is that FG uses the illumination in the scene from lights as well as objects with color and incandescence set in their shaders to create a soft natural light. And its base settings will give you nice results right off the bat.

To render the still life fruit scene with FG, begin by creating a dome light, which is essentially light(s) that evenly illuminate a scene from a dome around the scene. The term *dome light* is a bit of a misnomer, however, as it is not actually a light. We will construct a simple NURBS sphere cut in half to create a dome and give it an incandescent shader to provide for the light in the scene. This type of quick FG setup is extremely useful for rendering out soft lighting and shadows to show off a model or a composition.

To light and render with FG, follow these steps:

1. Ensure that mental ray for Maya is loaded.

2. Load the still life scene file `still_life_mentalray_v01.mb` from the Lighting project from the CD. In the *persp* view, not the camera1 panel, create a NURBS sphere and scale it up to enclose the entire scene. In the Channel Box, click the makeNurb-Sphere1 heading to select that node and set the **End Sweep** attribute to 180 to cut the sphere in half. Rotate the dome to fit over the scene as shown in Figure 11.21.

3. Now you will add an incandescent shader to the sphere to give the scene some illumination through FG. In the Hypershade, create a new Lambert Shader. Turn up its incandescence to a light gray, though not quite white. Assign the new shader to the sphere.

4. There is a feature in Maya that automatically creates a general default light in a scene that has no lights when you try to render it. Using this feature, you can test-render your scene quickly. However, since this incandescent dome light should be our only

Figure 11.21

Create a sphere to act as the dome light.

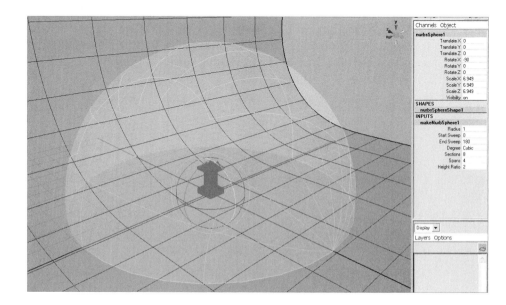

light source in the FG render, we will have to turn the default light feature off before we render. Open the Render Settings window, and in the Common tab's Render Options section, turn off the Enable Default Light check box.

Don't forget to turn Enable Default Light back on when you are done with this FG exercise.

5. At the top of the Render Settings window, switch the **Render Using** attribute to mental ray. You can keep the settings in the Common tab to render at 640 × 480. Choose the mental ray tab to access its settings. Set the **Quality Presets** to PreviewFinalGather to load the preset. This will give quick results. Notice raytracing is enabled under the Raytracing heading. Click the Final Gather heading to expand the attributes therein. You can leave the settings at their defaults for your first render. Figure 11.22 shows the Render Settings window.

6. Now we'll need to make sure the sphere we're using as a dome light does not render out in the scene. Select the sphere, and in the Attribute Editor under the Render Stats section, turn off **Primary Visibility**. Highlight the camera1 panel and render the frame. You will notice Maya will make two passes at the scene and show you something like in Figure 11.23.

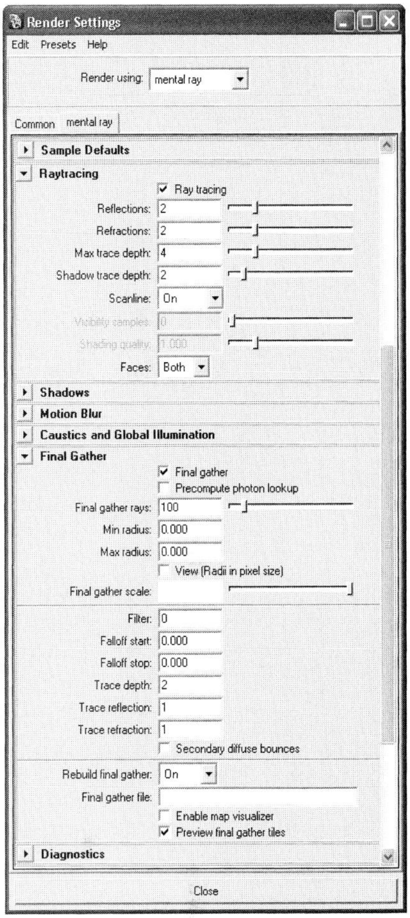

You can adjust the level of lighting by increasing or decreasing the amount of incandescence on the light dome's shader. The proximity of the sphere will also affect the light amount, so moving the sphere closer or farther away will change the lighting level of the still life as well. You can also insert lights into the scene as you see fit. This sort of setup with only a light dome, however, gives you a quick and evenly lit render that is great for showing off models.

You can improve the quality of the render by adjusting either of the following two settings in the mental ray tab of the Render Settings window:

Final Gather Rays Increase this number for a more accurate render. You do not want to greatly increase this number, as it will slow down your render. Figure 11.20 shows the still life rendered with Final Gather rays of 100, and Figure 11.24 uses 500. The soft shadows are noticeably smoother.

Final Gather Scale Use this setting to globally adjust the lighting level in the scene.

Min and **Max Radius** attributes along with the others optimize and further control the FG settings for optimum efficiency and results. Consider using the basic settings as shown in this chapter to get familiar with mental ray for Maya, and then use FG to crank out fast

Figure 11.22

The Final Gather default settings in the Render Settings window

Figure 11.23

The Final Gather render of the still life

Figure 11.24

Final Gather rays set at 500 increases the smoothness of the soft shadows.

and elegant renders to show off your models until you get more comfortable with mental ray. Also, consult the Maya documentation for more on the advanced settings when you get into complicated and intricate mental ray renders. For now, however, using FG with basic settings will get you going.

Render Layers

An important notion to keep in mind is that a CG image need not be created entirely in a single render. It is best most of the time to composite different elements together to form the final image. Professional CG work flow almost always requires multiple render passes that are composited together later for the maximum in efficiency and quality.

Maya does a great job of making rendering in layers much easier with Render Layers. As you saw earlier in this book, using Display Layers helps a great deal in keeping your scene organized. Render Layers operates in basically the same way, though it functions by separating different elements of the scene into separate renders.

The functionality behind Render Layers is very powerful. We will address the most basic and commonly utilized here: separating objects into different renders. You will select elements in a scene and assign them to different render layers. Once you batch-render the scene, Maya will render each of the layers separately and save out the files into *their own subfolders* in the images folder of your current project. You will then need to load all the different rendered layers into a compositing program such as Apple Shake or Adobe After Effects and composite the layers together.

Rendering the Still Life in Layers

In this example, we will separate a scene into different layers for rendering. In an exercise in the section "Ambient Occlusion" later in this chapter, we will explore a more advanced function of Render Layers.

To separate a scene into different layers, follow these steps:

1. Open the still life scene (still_life_v02.mb from the scenes folder of the Lighting project on the CD) to start there. This scene already has lights and a camera setup. Set your camera view to *camera1*.

2. To start, we will separate the scene into different renders. In the Layer Editor, click the **Render** button to switch to the Render Layers view. Select the foreground lemon and click the **Create New Layer And Assign Selected Objects** icon (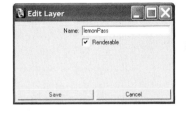). This will create a new render layer called *layer1* and will assign the lemon to it. (See Figure 11.25).

3. Click *layer1* and you will notice that everything else in the scene will disappear and only the lemon will remain (Figure 11.25). Double-click *layer1* and rename it *lemonPass* as shown.

Figure 11.25

The newly created render layer with the foreground lemon assigned

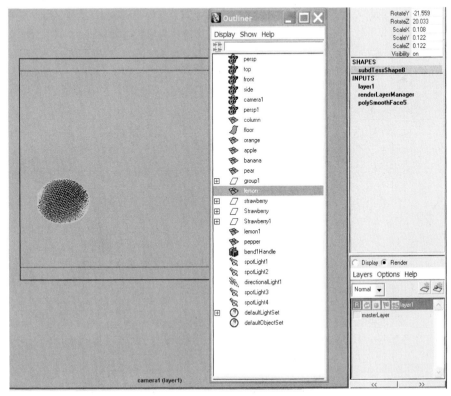

4. If you test-render a frame, the frame should turn out black. You will need to assign your lights to the render layer as well. Select all the lights in the scene using the Outliner as shown. RM click on the *lemonPass* layer in the Layer Editor and select **Add Selected Objects** from the shortcut menu. If you render a test frame now, the lemon will render as seen in Figure 11.26.

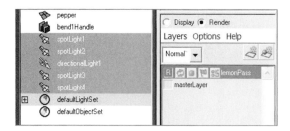

5. Now create a render layer for the column. Select the column, the floor, and all the lights in the scene, and as you did with the lemon, click the **Create New Layer And Assign Selected Objects** icon ( ) and then click on the new layer to select and display it. Double-click the layer name to rename the Render Layer *columnPass*. Figure 11.27.

6. Finally, select all the rest of the fruit as shown in figure 11.28, and create their own render layer called *fruitPass*. You should now have three render layers and the default *masterLayer*. The *masterLayer* is always created to house all the elements of the scene as soon as you create the first render layer in a scene. By default, it is not renderable.

Figure 11.26

The lemon rendered on its very own layer

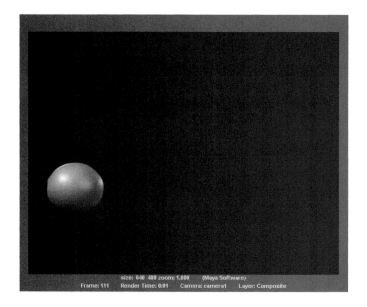

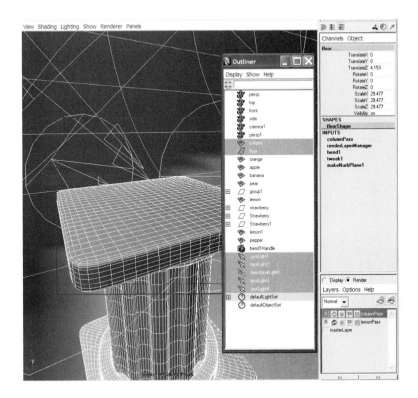

Figure 11.27

The background is assigned to its own render layer.

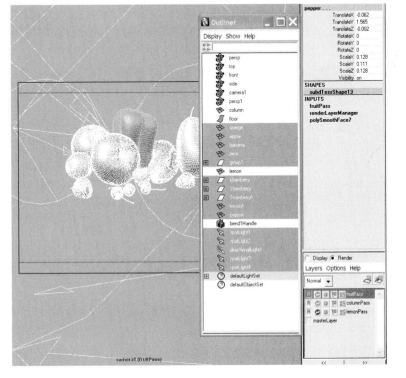

Figure 11.28

The newly created *fruitPass* **Render Layer**

7. Notice the *R* in the first icon on each of the Render Layer entries in the Layer Editor. This means those layers are renderable and will render out when you batch-render the scene. Make sure all your render layers are renderable and leave the *masterLayer* off. Since we have all the elements of the scene assigned to one render layer or another, the whole scene is covered.

8. Now, with the *fruitPass* render layer selected, test-render a frame as seen here. You should see just the fruit and not the background, column, pear, or banana.

Test-Rendering Everything Together

By default, Maya will render only the selected visible render layer. You can, however, tell Maya to test-render and show you all the layers composited together to give you a preview of what you will end up with once you composite all the layers together after batch-rendering the scene.

To test-render all the layers together, click the **Options** menu in the Layer Editor as shown in Figure 11.29, and toggle on **Render All Layers**.

Now if you test-render a frame, Maya will render each layer separately and then composite them together. Test-render a frame with Render All Layers enabled and you should notice that the foreground lemon is missing, as seen here (center left).

This is simply because the Render Layers in the Layer Editor need to be reordered so that the *columnPass* is on the bottom, the *fruitPass* is in the middle, and the *lemonPass* is on top. This is the layer ordering for the composite. You can reorder the Render Layers by MM clicking on a layer and dragging it up or down to its new location in the Layer Editor as shown here (right).

Now if you render the frame with Render All Layers enabled, you will see the scene properly placed as shown (bottom left).

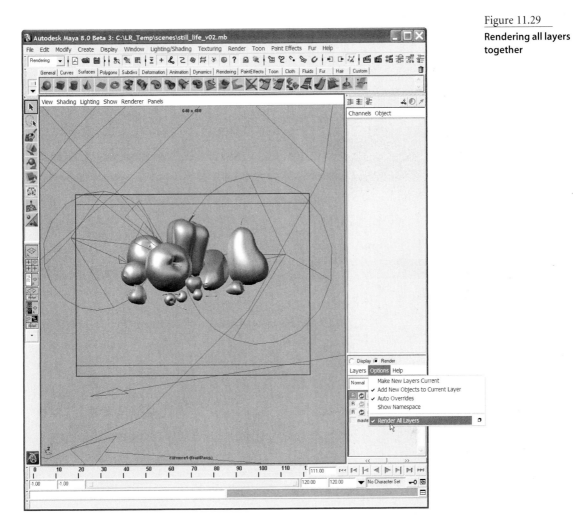

Figure 11.29

Rendering all layers together

Creating a Shadow Pass

But where are the shadows?!? If you recall from earlier in this chapter, this scene renders with shadows, and now some of the shadows, particularly the ones that fall on the column, are gone. This is simply because the shadow-casting objects are on different layers than the column. Shadows cannot be cast from one layer onto another. You will need to create a layer for shadows to composite on top of everything.

Rendering everything in layers requires a work flow where you are essentially assembling everything in composite after your CG work is done and rendered. Creating a whole render pass for shadows is just one step in this work flow. Just as we created different layers for the different objects in the scene, we will create a new render layer to handle a shadow pass. A *shadow pass* in Maya is a render of just the shadows in the scene.

To create a shadow pass, follow along with these steps:

1. Select all the objects in the scene and create a new render layer by clicking the **Create New Layer And Assign Selected Objects** icon (🖼). Rename the layer shadowPass, as seen in Figure 11.30.

2. Select the *shadowPass* and RM click on it in the Layer Editor. Choose **Presets → Shadow** to set up that render layer to render a shadow pass only. This *shadowPass* layer now has a *Render Override* applied to it. Now all the objects in the layer will obey certain render settings that in this case will force Maya to render only the shadows for those objects.

Figure 11.30

Rendering all layers together

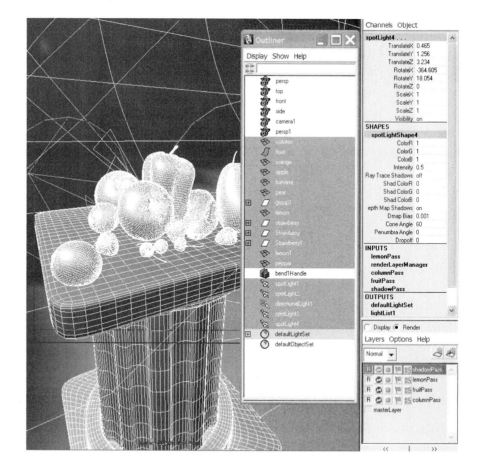

3. In the Layer Editor, choose **Options → Render All Layers** to toggle it off for now. We just want to see the *shadowPass* test render. With the *shadowPass* selected, test-render a frame. You should see nothing but black in the Render View window as shown. In such a pass, shadows will render *only in the Alpha channel* of the image (below right).

4. If you click the **Display Alpha Channel** icon (⬚) in the Render View window, it will show you the shadows in the alpha channel as seen here (below left).

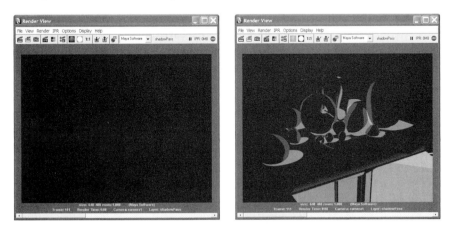

5. Now, re-enable **Options → Render All Layers** and render the scene to see how the still life now looks once Maya composites everything together for your test render, shown in Figure 11.31.

Figure 11.31

The still life rendered in layers and comped together in a test render with shadows

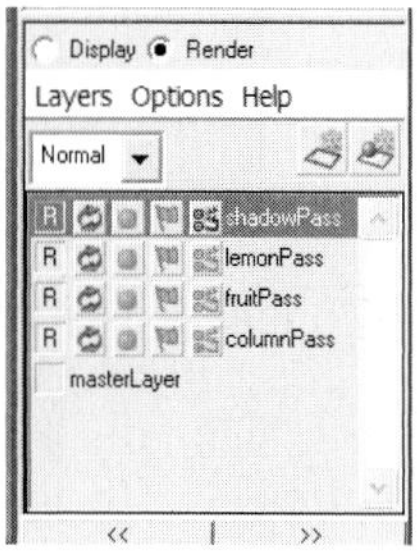

Batch Rendering with Render Layers

Yay! Now that we have everything separated out into render layers, let's talk about batch-rendering the scene out to composite later. Make the render layer you wish to render out renderable by clicking on the R icon next to each render layer as seen here.

First make sure in the Render Settings window that the **Renderable Camera** is set to *camera1* as shown here. Then, simply choose **Render** → **Batch Render** to render the scene. Now since Render Layers are enabled here, Maya will render the scene out into different subfolders under the images folder of your current project. Each render layer will get its own folder in the images folder, as seen in Figure 11.32.

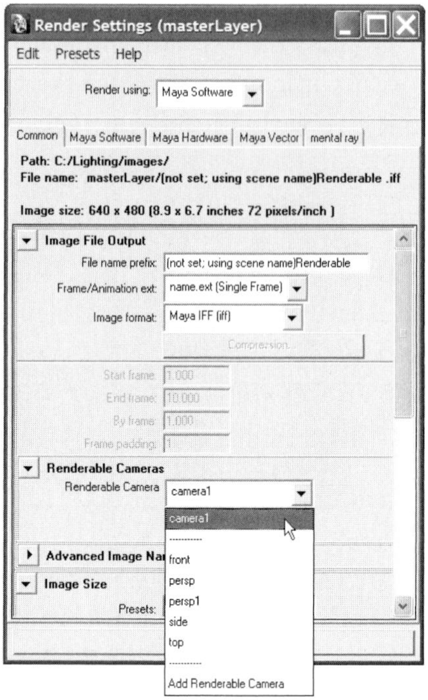

Render Layers is a very powerful addition to Maya's rendering work flow. We have only begun the scratch the surface here, and once you get the hang of rendering, and as your CG needs begin to grow, you will find a plethora of options when rendering with layers. This and the next section are only to familiarize you with the basic work flow of Render Layers. You can find a wealth of information on rendering in layers in Maya's online documentation under the Help menu.

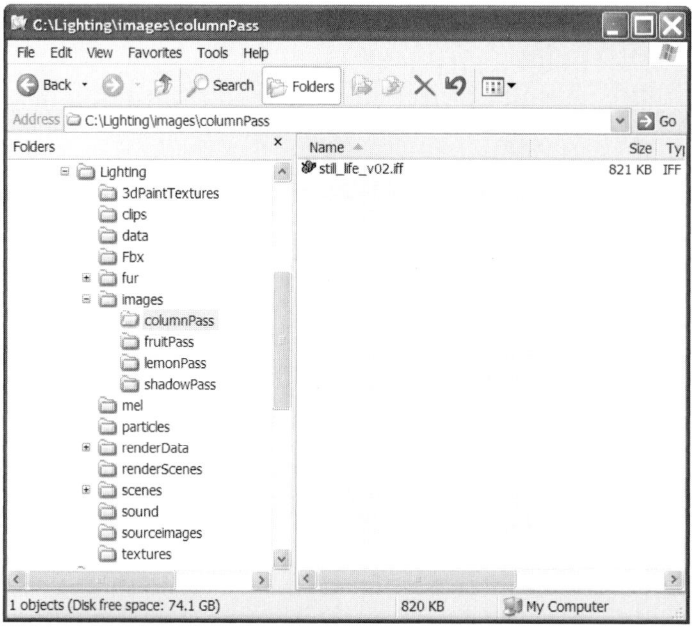

Figure 11.32

Render Layers will batch-render into subfolders under the images folder of your project.

Ambient Occlusion

Ambient Occlusion is a special render pass that helps add depth and reality to a render. Ambient Occlusion goes by the premise that when two objects or surfaces are close to each other, they reduce the amount of light at the intersection. Ambient Occlusion passes make for great contact shadows and bring out the definition in surface creases and corners very nicely. Figure 11.33 shows an Ambient Occlusion pass for the living room scene from the previous chapter.

Figure 11.33

The Ambient Occlusion Pass is black and white and is used to darken areas of the original color render.

How the composite works is very simple. Ambient Occlusion will give you a black-and-white pass of the same geometry you have already rendered. This pass is then *multiplied* over the color render. That means a brightness value of white (a value of 1) in the Ambient Occlusion pass will not change the color of the original render (when the original color of the render is multiplied by 1, it stays the same color). The black parts of the frame (with a brightness value of 0) will turn those parts of the original render black (when the original color of the render is multiplied by 0, it goes to black). And the gray points of the multiplying image will darken the original render. Sounds confusing, but once you see it, it makes much better sense.

The Living Room Redux

We will now take the living room render from the previous chapter and add an Ambient Occlusion pass using Render Layers. Set your current project to the Livingroom project you copied from the CD, and open the livingRoom_v2.mb file from the scenes folder to proceed with the following steps:

1. Make sure you have mental ray loaded, of course. As you did earlier, we will need to create a new render layer for the Ambient Occlusion. This layer will require all the objects in the scene *without* any lights, which in this scene is the single directional light. In the Outliner, select all the top nodes of the scene, but leave out the light as shown here (right).

2. Click the Render radial button in the Layer Editor to switch to Render Layers, and then click the **Create New Layer And Assign Selected Objects** icon. This will create a new layer (*layer1*) as well as a *masterLayer* as shown here (left).

3. Click the new layer (*layer1*) to activate it. Everything in the scene should display as it did before. Double click *layer1* to rename it *ambientOcclusion*.

Figure 11.34

**The Ambient Occlu-
sion Shader**

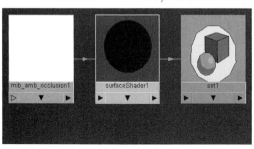

4. Now we're going to use a preset to create a *Material override*. This will take all the objects in the scene and assign a single material to them, in this case an Ambient Occlusion Shader to generate the Ambient Occlusion pass for the entire scene. RMB click the *ambientOcclusion* layer, and select **Presets → Occlusion** from the shortcut menu. If you are in shaded mode, everything should turn black. This is normal, as now everything has an Ambient Occlusion Shader assigned. If you click the *masterLayer*, everything will pop back into place and vice versa. Figure 11.34 shows the new Ambient Occlusion Shader that is now assigned throughout the scene.

5. While still in the *ambientOcclusion* layer, render a frame and you should see a something a little like Figure 11.35. You needn't worry about most of the Render Settings window settings; the layer preset takes care of it all. Well, almost all of it. It will not turn off the Global Illumination pass that we used for the original color render; that we need to turn off manually in the next step. Now if it could just make a good smoothie.

6. In the Render Settings window, you will need to turn off **Global Illumination**, but just for that layer. RMB click on the **Global Illumination** check box and choose **Create Layer Override**. The attribute lettering will turn orange to signify it is being overridden for that render layer. Uncheck the box. It will not turn off GI for the *masterLayer* pass. You just don't need to spend the time with rendering GI for this pass.

Figure 11.35

**The first Ambient
Occlusion layer pass
render does not look
so great. It's too
dark (well, that's an
understatement!).**

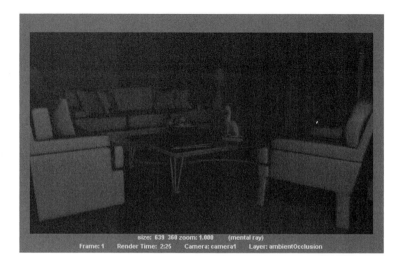

7. The render is mostly black, which will multiply the original color render to black pretty much everywhere. We need the Ambient Occlusion Shader to render mostly white with some darkening at the corners and where objects contact each other. We will adjust the Ambient Occlusion Shader to fix this. Click the Shader Override icon on the *ambient-Occlusion* layer in the Layer Editor (⬤) to open the Attribute Editor with the Ambient Occlusion Shader (*surface-Shader1*) automatically displayed.

8. Notice that the **Out Color** attribute has texture connection to it (signified by the ⬚ icon). Click this button to display the *mib_amb_occlusion1* texture node in the Attribute Editor as shown.

9. Set the **Max_Distance** attribute to 4.0 as shown and render the frame again. Your Ambient Occlusion layer should now look like Figure 11.36. It should have also taken less than half the time to render. Woo!

Figure 11.36

The Ambient Occlusion layer pass looks much better now, but we ain't done yet!

10. Notice that the glass in the window and the glass on the coffee table have shadow on them. Since glass is clear, they should not have any Ambient Occlusion applied to them; it would look odd in the final composite. So select those pieces of geometry (Figure 11.37 shows the Outliner view for those pieces).

11. With the glass geometry selected, select **Display → Hide → Hide Selection**. Now the glass will not render in the Ambient Occlusion pass. But since you hid the objects in this render layer, they will still appear in the *masterLayer*, so no worries; they will still render as glass in the color pass.

12. Render the frame and you should have something similar to Figure 11.38. Now this is the Ambient Occlusion pass we need to composite.

Rendering the Results

Now, you could save the image in the Render View window to use in the composite and then render the *masterLayer* for the color pass and save that frame as well. But let's batch-render the scene to show you how Maya handles rendering with layers enabled, shall we? To batch-render the scene, follow these steps:

1. Turn on the **Renderable** check box for the *masterLayer* and make sure it is on for the *ambientOcclusion* layer as well, as shown here.

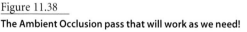

2. Click to activate the *masterLayer*. Now open the Render Settings window and in the Common tab, check all the settings to render a single frame (name.ext in the **Frame/Animation Ext** field) at 639 × 360 (which is half 720p HD resolution). Also, select *camera1* as the renderable camera.

Figure 11.37

The Outliner view of the glass geometry in the scene

Figure 11.38

The Ambient Occlusion pass that will work as we need!

3. Now if you batch-render (by choosing **Render → Batch Render**), Maya will render both render layers into the images folder of your project in separate folders, as shown here.

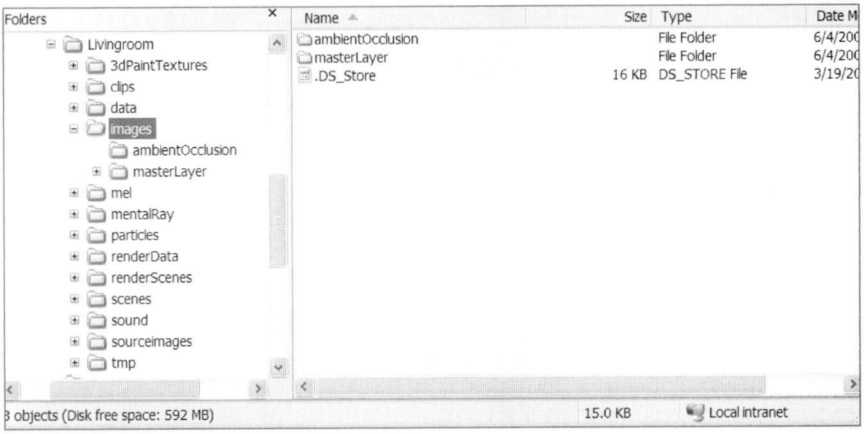

If for some reason your renders do not show up in the images folder of your project, open the Script Editor window and take a look at the batch render report. The render feedback will show you where the rendered images were saved, as shown.

```
// Result: Percentage of rendering done: 0 (Z:/Intro8/Intro8_Projects/Livingroom/ambientOcclusion/livingRoomRenderLayers_v10.sgi) //
// Result: Percentage of rendering done: 5 (Z:/Intro8/Intro8_Projects/Livingroom/ambientOcclusion/livingRoomRenderLayers_v10.sgi) //
// Result: Percentage of rendering done: 10 (Z:/Intro8/Intro8_Projects/Livingroom/ambientOcclusion/livingRoomRenderLayers_v10.sgi) //
// Result: Percentage of rendering done: 15 (Z:/Intro8/Intro8_Projects/Livingroom/ambientOcclusion/livingRoomRenderLayers_v10.sgi) //
// Result: Percentage of rendering done: 20 (Z:/Intro8/Intro8_Projects/Livingroom/ambientOcclusion/livingRoomRenderLayers_v10.sgi) //
// Result: Percentage of rendering done: 25 (Z:/Intro8/Intro8_Projects/Livingroom/ambientOcclusion/livingRoomRenderLayers_v10.sgi) //
// Result: Percentage of rendering done: 30 (Z:/Intro8/Intro8_Projects/Livingroom/ambientOcclusion/livingRoomRenderLayers_v10.sgi) //
// Result: Percentage of rendering done: 35 (Z:/Intro8/Intro8_Projects/Livingroom/ambientOcclusion/livingRoomRenderLayers_v10.sgi) //
// Result: Percentage of rendering done: 40 (Z:/Intro8/Intro8_Projects/Livingroom/ambientOcclusion/livingRoomRenderLayers_v10.sgi) //
// Result: Percentage of rendering done: 45 (Z:/Intro8/Intro8_Projects/Livingroom/ambientOcclusion/livingRoomRenderLayers_v10.sgi) //
// Result: Percentage of rendering done: 50 (Z:/Intro8/Intro8_Projects/Livingroom/ambientOcclusion/livingRoomRenderLayers_v10.sgi) //
// Result: Percentage of rendering done: 55 (Z:/Intro8/Intro8_Projects/Livingroom/ambientOcclusion/livingRoomRenderLayers_v10.sgi) //
// Result: Percentage of rendering done: 60 (Z:/Intro8/Intro8_Projects/Livingroom/ambientOcclusion/livingRoomRenderLayers_v10.sgi) //
// Result: Percentage of rendering done: 65 (Z:/Intro8/Intro8_Projects/Livingroom/ambientOcclusion/livingRoomRenderLayers_v10.sgi) //
// Result: Percentage of rendering done: 70 (Z:/Intro8/Intro8_Projects/Livingroom/ambientOcclusion/livingRoomRenderLayers_v10.sgi) //
// Result: Percentage of rendering done: 75 (Z:/Intro8/Intro8_Projects/Livingroom/ambientOcclusion/livingRoomRenderLayers_v10.sgi) //
// Result: Percentage of rendering done: 80 (Z:/Intro8/Intro8_Projects/Livingroom/ambientOcclusion/livingRoomRenderLayers_v10.sgi) //
// Result: Percentage of rendering done: 85 (Z:/Intro8/Intro8_Projects/Livingroom/ambientOcclusion/livingRoomRenderLayers_v10.sgi) //
// Result: Percentage of rendering done: 90 (Z:/Intro8/Intro8_Projects/Livingroom/ambientOcclusion/livingRoomRenderLayers_v10.sgi) //
// Result: Percentage of rendering done: 95 (Z:/Intro8/Intro8_Projects/Livingroom/ambientOcclusion/livingRoomRenderLayers_v10.sgi) //
// Result: Percentage of rendering done: 100 (Z:/Intro8/Intro8_Projects/Livingroom/ambientOcclusion/livingRoomRenderLayers_v10.sgi) //
// Result: Rendering Completed. See mayaRenderLog.txt for information. //
```

Compositing the Results

Now that you have the two layers rendered in their respective folders, load them into your favorite compositing package. You will then layer the Ambient Occlusion pass over the color render using a *multiply* transfer mode. For this exercise, we will be using Adobe After Effects 7.0 to demonstrate how the Ambient Occlusion pass is composited over the original color render.

Figure 11.39 shows After Effects with the *masterLayer* color pass loaded. Figure 11.40 shows the *ambientOcclusion* pass layered *on top* of the color layer. Finally, Figure 11.41 shows the ambientOcclusion pass changed to a *multiply* transfer mode (as it's called in After Effects). Notice how the dark areas of the Ambient Occlusion pass help give contact shadows and depth to the color pass. Voila!

This is a prime example of rendering different passes to achieve a more realistic goal. Remember, you need not get everything in on a single pass. Plan for different layers to put your final images together in composite. The more you work with CG, the more this will become easier to manage and plan for.

You can see the difference Ambient Occlusion made to the image in the color section of this book as well as on the CD.

Summary

In this chapter, you learned how to set up your scene for rendering. Starting with the Render Settings window and moving onto the different render engines available, you learned how to render your scene for a particular look. Then we covered how to preview your render and how to use IPR for fast scene feedback. We moved onto how to render reflections and refractions, how to create and use cameras, and how to render motion blur. You tested your wares on a wine bottle scene, and to batch-render it out into a sequence of images, you checked it in a program such as FCheck. Then we covered a mental ray for

Figure 11.39

The *masterLayer* render pass is loaded into After Effects.

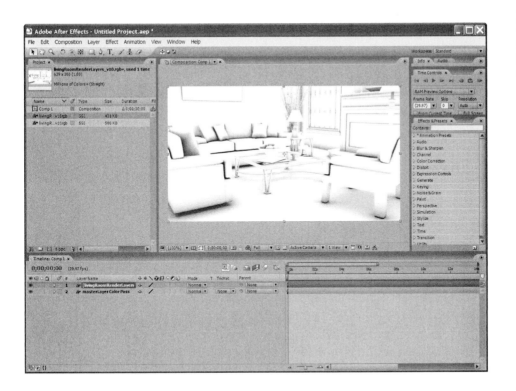

Figure 11.40
The *ambient Occlusion* render pass is loaded into After Effects.

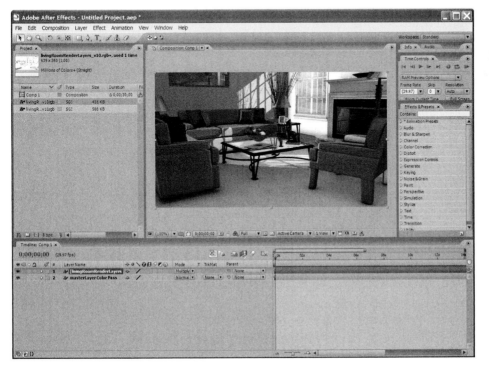

Figure 11.41

The *ambient Occlusion* pass is multiplied over the color pass and creates a more realistic image.

Maya rendering method called Final Gather before moving on to learning about Maya's Render Layers and rendering and using an Ambient Occlusion pass to increase reality in renders.

Getting to this point of a scene can take some work, but once you see the results playing back on your screen, the work all seems more than worth it. Nothing is more fulfilling than seeing your creation come to life, and that's what rendering is all about. But don't consider the rendering process a mere pushbutton solution when planning your animations. Always allow enough time to ensure that your animations render properly and at their best quality. Most beginners seriously underestimate the time needed to properly complete this step in CG production.

After you create numerous scenes and render them out, you'll begin to understand how to construct your next scenes so that they render better and faster. Just be sure to keep on top of your file management; rendering can produce a bevy of files all over the place!

CHAPTER 12

Maya Dynamics

Autodesk's Maya is renowned for creating special effects animation that simulates not only physical phenomena such as smoke and fire, but also natural movement of colliding bodies. Behind that latter type of animation is the Maya dynamics engine, sophisticated software that creates realistic-looking motion based on the principles of physics.

Another powerful Maya animation tool, Paint Effects, can create dynamic fields of grass and flowers, a head full of hair, and other such systems in a matter of minutes. Maya Unlimited also offers dynamic simulations for hair, fur, and cloth. Here we will cover the basics of dynamics in Maya and get you experienced with particles right away.

Topics include:

- **An Overview of Dynamics**
- **Rigid and Soft Dynamic Bodies**
- **Animating with Dynamics: The Pool Table**
- **Particle Dynamics**
- **Emitting Particles**
- **Animating a Particle Effect: Locomotive Steam**
- **Introduction to Paint Effects**

An Overview of Dynamics

Dynamics is the simulation of motion through the application of the principles of physics. Rather than assigning keyframes to objects to animate them, with Maya dynamics you assign physical characteristics that define how an object behaves in a simulated world. You create the objects as usual in Maya and then convert them to *dynamic bodies*. Dynamic bodies are now defined through dynamic attributes you've added to them, which affect how the objects behave in a dynamic simulation.

Dynamic bodies are affected by external forces called *fields*, which exert a force on them to create motion. Fields can range from wind forces to gravity and can have their own specific effects on dynamic bodies. You'll learn how to use fields later in this chapter.

In Maya, dynamic objects are categorized as bodies, particles, hair, and fluids. Dynamic bodies are created from geometric surfaces and are used for physical objects such as bouncing balls. *Particles* are merely points in space with renderable properties that behave dynamically. Particles are used for numerous effects such as fire and smoke, but they're also useful in tons of other situations and, as such, are a specialty all in their own for professional animators. Particle basics will be covered in the latter half of this chapter. *Hair* consists of curves that behave dynamically, such as strings. *Fluids*, available only in Maya Unlimited, are in essence volumetric particles that can exhibit surface properties. Fluid dynamics can be used for natural effects such as billowing clouds or plumes of smoke. Soft bodies, hair, and fluid dynamics are advanced topics and will not be covered in this book.

Rigid and Soft Dynamic Bodies

The two types of dynamic bodies are rigid and soft. *Rigid bodies* are solid objects such as a pair of dice or a baseball that moves and rotates according to the dynamics applied. Fields and collisions affect the entire object and move it accordingly. *Soft bodies* are malleable surfaces that deform dynamically, such as drapes in the wind or a bouncing rubber ball. In brief, this is accomplished by making the surface points (NURBS, CVs, or polygon vertices) of the soft body object dynamic instead of the whole object. The forces and collisions of the scene affect these surface points, making them move to deform their surface.

In this section, you'll learn about rigid body dynamics.

Creating Active and Passive Rigid Body Objects

Any surface geometry in Maya can be converted to a rigid body. Once converted, that surface can respond to the effects of fields and take part in collisions. When one Maya object hits another in a dynamic simulation, Maya calculates the animation of the colliding objects according to their velocity and other dynamic properties such as mass. Sounds like fun, eh?

The two types of rigid bodies are active and passive. An *active rigid body* is affected by collisions and fields. A *passive rigid body* is not affected by fields and remains still when it collides with another object. A passive rigid body is used solely to be a surface with which to collide active rigid bodies.

The best way to see how the two types of rigid bodies behave is to create some and animate them. In this section, you'll do that in the classic animation exercise of a bouncing ball.

To create a bouncing ball using Maya rigid bodies, switch into the Dynamics menu set and follow these steps:

1. Create a polygonal plane and scale it out to be a ground surface.

2. Create a poly sphere and position it above the ground a number of units, as shown in Figure 12.1.

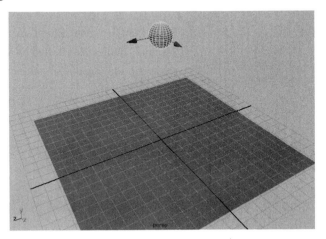

3. Switch to the Dynamics menu set (choose Dynamics from the main menu drop-down bar or press F5). Select the poly sphere, and choose **Soft/Rigid Bodies → Create Active Rigid Body**. The sphere's **Translate** and **Rotate** attributes turn yellow. There is now a dynamic input for those attributes, and as such, you cannot set keyframes on any of them. The dynamics engine drives the movement and rotation of the active rigid body sphere.

Figure 12.1

Place a poly sphere a few units above a poly plane ground surface.

4. Select the ground plane, and choose **Soft/Rigid Bodies → Create Passive Rigid Body**. This will set the poly plane as a passive rigid body to serve as the floor on which to bounce your active rigid ball. For this exercise stick with the default settings and ignore the various creation options and **Rigid Body** attributes; you'll explore the most important of those later in this chapter.

5. To put the ball into motion, you need to create a field to affect it. Select the sphere, and choose **Fields → Gravity**. By selecting the active rigid object(s) while you create the field, you connect that field to the objects automatically. Fields affect only the active rigid bodies to which they are connected. If you hadn't established this connection initially, you could still do so later, through the Dynamic Relationships Editor. You'll find more on this process later in this chapter.

If you try to scrub the Timeline, you will notice that the animation does not run properly. Since dynamics is a simulation of physics, no keyframes are set. You must play the scene from start to finish for the calculations to execute properly. You must also play the scene using the Play Every Frame option. Click the Animation Options button to the right of the Range Slider, or choose **Window → Settings/Preferences → Preferences**. In the Preferences window, choose **Timeline** under the Settings header. Choose Play Every Frame from the Playback Speed menu.

To playback the simulation, set your frame range from 1 to at least 500. Go to frame 1 and click Play. Make sure you have the proper Playback Speed settings in your Preferences window; otherwise, the simulation will not play properly.

When the simulation plays, you'll notice the sphere begins to fall after a few frames and collides with the ground plane, bouncing back up.

As an experiment, try turning the passive body plane into an active body using the following steps:

1. Select the plane and open the Attribute Editor.

2. In the rigidBody2 tab, click the Active check box to turn it on. This will switch the plane from a passive body to an active body.

3. Play the simulation and you'll see the ball fall to hit the plane and knock it away. Because the plane is now an active body, it will be moved by collisions. Since it was not connected to the gravity field, however, it does not fall with the ball.

To connect the now active body plane to the gravity field, open the Dynamic Relationships window, which is shown in Figure 12.2 (choose **Window → Relationship Editors → Dynamic Relationships**).

> You can also connect a dynamic object to a field by selecting the dynamic object or objects and then the desired field and choosing **Fields → Affect Selected Object(s)**. This method is more useful for connecting multiple dynamic objects to a field.

On the left is an Outliner list of the objects in your scene. On the right is a listing where you can choose which category of objects to list: Fields (default), Collisions, Emitters, or All. Simply select the geometry (pPlane1) on the left side, and then connect it to the gravity field by selecting the gravityField1 node on the right.

Once you connect the gravity field to the plane and run the simulation, you will see the plane fall away with the ball. Since the two fall at the same rate set by the single gravity field, they will not collide. To disconnect the plane from the gravity, deselect the gravity field in the right panel.

RELATIONSHIP EDITORS

The relationship editors, such as the Dynamic Relationships window, are a means to connect two nodes to create a special relationship. The Dynamic Relationships window specializes in connecting dynamic attributes so that fields, particles, and rigid bodies can interact in a simulation. Another example of a relationship editor is the Light Linking window, which allows you to connect lights to geometry so that only they light that specific object or objects. These are fairly advanced topics; however, as you learn more about Maya, their use will become integral in your work flow.

Turning the active body plane back to a passive floor is as simple as returning to frame 1, the beginning of the simulation, and clearing the **Active** attribute in the Attribute Editor. By turning the active body back to a passive body, you regain an immovable floor with which the ball can collide and bounce upon.

Moving a Rigid Body

Since Maya's dynamics engine controls the movement of any active rigid bodies, you cannot set keyframes on their translation or rotation. With a passive object, however, you can set keyframes on translation and rotation as you can with any other Maya object. Since the object is not active, the dynamics engine does not regulate its movement with fields or collisions. You can easily keyframe an object to be either active or passive, however, for the widest of options.

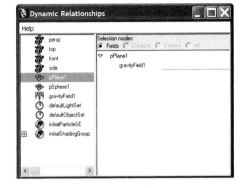

Now, any movement the passive body has through regular key-frame animation is translated into momentum that is passed on to any active rigid bodies with which the passive body collides. Think of a baseball bat that strikes a baseball. The baseball bat is a passive rigid body that you have keyframed to swing. The baseball is an active rigid body that is hit by (collides with) the bat as it swings. The momentum of the bat is transferred to the ball, and the ball is sent flying into the stadium stands.

You'll see an example of this in action in the next tutorial.

Rigid Body Attributes

What makes an object a rigid body is the addition of several attributes that help govern how it behaves in a dynamic simulation. Here is a rundown of the more important attributes for both passive and active rigid bodies as they pertain to collisions.

Figure 12.2

The Dynamic Relationships window

Mass Sets the relative mass of the rigid body. Set on active or passive rigid bodies, *mass* is a factor in how much momentum is transferred from one object to another. A more massive object will push a less massive one with less effort and will itself be less prone to movement when hit. Mass is relative, so if all rigid bodies have the same mass value, there is no difference in the simulation.

Static and Dynamic Friction Sliders Set how much friction the rigid body has while at rest (static) and while in motion (dynamic). *Friction* specifies how much the object resists moving or being moved. A friction of 0 makes the rigid body move freely, as if on ice.

Bounciness Specifies how resilient the body is upon collision. The higher the *bounciness* value, the more bounce the object will have upon collision.

Damping Creates a drag on the object in dynamic motion so that it will slow down over time. The higher the *damping*, the more the body's motion diminishes.

Animating with Dynamics: The Pool Table

This exercise will take you through the creation of a simple scene in which you will use dynamics to animate a cue ball striking two balls on a pool table.

Creating the Pool Table and the Balls

You will create a simple pool table as a collision surface for the pool balls. To create the table, follow these steps:

1. Create a polygonal plane for the surface of the table. Scale it to 10 along its height and length.

2. To create the pocket holes, you'll make two simple holes in opposite corners. The easiest way is to duplicate the tabletop plane and offset slightly in both directions, as shown here. This will create a pair of square holes in the corners for the ball to drop through. For this simple exercise, it will do perfectly well.

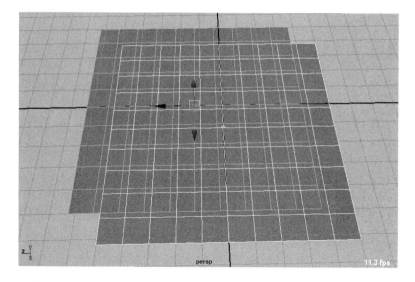

3. Create a polygonal cube, and scale it to fit one edge of the plane to create a rail. Duplicate the cube three times, and then move and rotate the pieces to create the rails around the table as shown in Figure 12.3.

4. Create three poly spheres, and then scale and place them as shown. It is important to place them slightly above the pool table surface. Although it's not imperative to have the same exact location as shown in Figure 12.4, it's a good idea to get rather close to the layout shown.

5. Shade your pool balls to make each one different. The figures in this exercise show a solid white ball, a striped yellow ball, and a black eight ball, as shown in Figure 12.5.

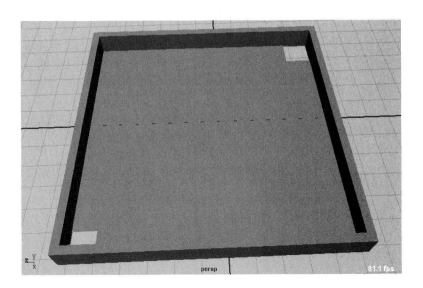

Figure 12.3
A simple pool table

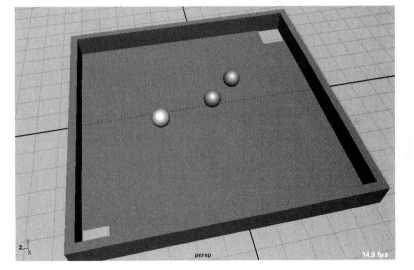

Figure 12.4
Scaling and placing the three spheres

The spheres are placed a bit over the table surface so that the geometries' surfaces are not accidentally crossing each other; also known as interpenetrating. When surfaces interpenetrate, the dynamics results will usually be as welcome as sand in your eye. Starting all colliding rigid bodies a little bit away from each other should guarantee that their surfaces do not interpenetrate. And using a simple pool table that we've set up will make the dynamics calculations quick and easy.

Figure 12.5

The pool balls in texture view

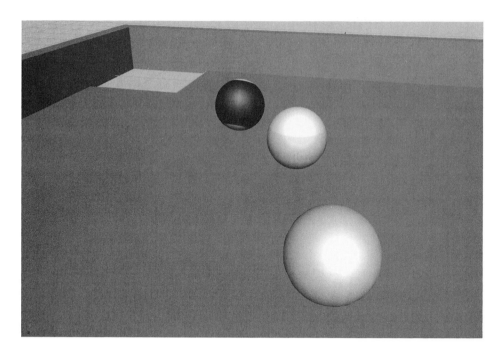

Figure 12.5

The pool balls in texture view

Use the file Table_v1.mb in the scenes folder of the Pool_Table project on the CD as a reference or to catch up to this point.

Creating Rigid Bodies

Define the pool table as a passive rigid body and define the pool balls as active rigid bodies. Follow these steps:

1. Select the two planes that make up the tabletop and the four cubes that are the side rails. Choose **Soft/Rigid Bodies** → **Create Passive Rigid Body**.

2. Select the three balls and choose **Soft/Rigid Bodies** → **Create Active Rigid Body** to make them active rigid bodies.

3. With all three pool balls selected, create a gravity field by choosing **Fields** → **Gravity**. The gravity field will automatically connect to all three balls.

4. Run the simulation and you'll see the balls fall slightly onto the tabletop; check to see that none of them interpenetrate the table surface. If any of them do, Maya will select the offending geometry and display an error message in the command feedback line, turning it red.

Animating Rigid Bodies

If you need to, enable Texture view in your view panel by pressing 6. The next step is to put the cue ball (the white sphere) into motion so that it hits the striped ball into the black eight ball to sink it into the corner pocket. The easiest way to do this is to keyframe the cue ball's translation from its starting point to hit into the striped ball. But since active rigid bodies cannot be keyframed, you have to turn the cue ball into a passive rigid body. To do that, follow these steps:

1. Select the cue ball (the white ball). Notice the **Active** attribute in the Channel Box. (You may have to scroll down; it's at the bottom.) It is set to On.

2. Rewind your animation to the first frame. Choose **Soft/Rigid Bodies** ➔ **Set Passive Key**. Notice that the **Active** attribute has turned a dark yellow. You have set a keyframe for the active state of the cue ball, and it now reads Off. You can toggle rigid bodies between passive and active. Maya has also set translation and rotation keyframes for the cue ball.

3. Go to frame 10. Move the cue ball with the Translate tool so that its outer surface slightly passes through the yellow-striped ball as shown. Choose **Soft/Rigid Bodies** ➔ **Set Passive Key**.

4. Go to frame 11, and choose **Soft/Rigid Bodies** ➔ **Set Active Key**. This will turn the cue ball back into an active rigid body in the frame after it strikes the striped ball.

By animating the ball as a passive rigid body, keyframing its translation, and then turning it back to active, you set the dynamic simulation in motion. The cue ball animates from its start position and hits the striped ball. Maya's dynamics engine calculates the collisions on that ball and sets it into motion; it then strikes the black eight ball, which should roll into the corner pocket. The dynamics engine, at frame 11, also calculates the movement of the cue ball after it strikes the striped ball, so you do not have to animate its ricochet.

Go to the start frame and playback the simulation. The cue ball knocks the striped ball into the eight ball. The eight ball rolls into the corner, and the striped ball bounces off to the right. If the eight ball is not hit into the corner, you will have to edit your cue ball's keyframes to hit the striped ball at the correct angle to hit the eight ball into the corner pocket.

At the current settings, however, the eight ball bounces out of the corner without falling through the hole. You need to control the bounciness of the collisions:

1. Go back to the first frame. Select all three balls. In the Channel Box, change the **Bounciness** attribute from 0.6 to 0.2. Once you set the attribute value in the Channel Box, Maya will set the value for all three spheres concurrently.

> Changing the **Bounciness** attribute through the Attribute Editor changes the value for only one sphere even when they're all selected. You will have to change the value for each sphere individually in the Attribute Editor. This is true for all values changed on multiple objects through the Attribute Editor.

2. Playback the animation and you'll see that the balls do not ricochet off each other and the sides of the pool table with as much spring. The eight ball should now fall through the hole. You may need to increase your frame range if your ball doesn't quite make it by frame 120. Try 200 frames instead.

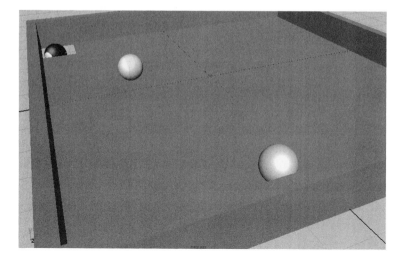

You can load the scene file Table_v2.mb from the Pool_Table project on the CD to compare your work.

Additional Rigid Body Attributes

In addition, using the pool table setup without any animation, try playing with the rigid body attributes to see how they affect the rigid body in question. Some of these attributes are defined here:

Initial Velocity Gives the rigid body an initial "push" to move it in the corresponding axis.

Initial Spin Gives the rigid body object an initial twist to start the rotation of the object in that axis.

Impulse Position Gives the object a constant push in that axis. The effect is cumulative; the object will accelerate if the impulse is not turned off.

Spin Impulse Rotates the object constantly in the desired axis. The spin will accelerate if the impulse is not turned off.

Center of Mass (0,0,0) Places the center of the object's mass at its pivot point, typically at its geometric center. This value offsets the center of mass, so the rigid body object behaves as if its center of balance is offset, like trick dice or a top-weighted ball.

Creating animation with rigid bodies is straightforward and can go a long way toward creating natural-looking motion for your scene. Integrating such animation into a final project can get fairly complicated, though, so it's prudent to become familiar with the workings of rigid body dynamics before relying on that sort of work flow for an animated project. You'll find most professionals use rigid body dynamics as a springboard to create realistic motion for their projects. The dynamics are often converted to keyframes and further tweaked by the animator to fit into a larger scene.

Here are a few suggestions for scenes using rigid body dynamics:

Bowling Lane The bowling ball is keyframed as a passive object until it hits the active rigid pins at the end of the lane. This scene is simple to create and manipulate.

Dice Active rigid dice are thrown into a passive rigid craps table. This exercise challenges your dynamics abilities as well as your modeling skills if you create an accurate craps table.

Game of Marbles This scene challenges your texturing and rendering abilities as well as your dynamics abilities.

Baking Out a Simulation

Frequently, a dynamic simulation is created to fit into another scene, to perhaps interact with other objects or such. In instances such as this, you want to exchange the dynamic properties of the dynamic body you have set up in a simulation for regular, good old-fashioned animation curves that you can edit along with the rest of the animated scene, if need be. You can easily take a simulation that you've created and bake it out to curves. As much fun as it is to think of cupcakes, *baking* is a somewhat catchall term used when you convert one type of action or procedure into another; in this case, we're baking dynamics into keyframes.

We will take the simulation we set up with the pool balls earlier and turn them into keyframes to give you a quick idea of how it can be done and the curves that you will get. Dynamics is a deep layer of Maya, and there is a lot to learn about it. Keep in mind you can use this introduction as a foundation for your own explorations.

To bake out the rigid body simulation of the pool balls, follow these steps:

1. Open the scene file `Table_v2.mb` from the Pool_Table project on the CD, or if you prefer, open your scene from the previous exercise. We will bake out the motion of all three pool balls on the table to see their keyframes.

2. Since the simulation is already set up and working to our liking, we can jump right to it. Select all three pool balls, and choose **Edit → Keys → Bake Simulation ⯁**. In the option box, as shown in Figure 12.6, set the Time Range to Time Slider (which should be set to 1 to 150). This, of course, sets the range you would like to bake into curves.

3. Set **Hierarchy** to Selected, and set **Channels** to From Channel Box. This ensures we have control over which keys are created. Make sure that **Keep Unbaked Keys** and **Disable Implicit Control** are checked and that **Sparse Curve Bake** is turned off. Before clicking the Bake or Apply button, in the Channel Box select the **Translate** and **Rotate** channels. Click Bake.

4. Maya will now run through the simulation. Scrub the Timeline back and forth. Notice how the pool balls are moving around normally as if the dynamic simulation was running, except now you can scrub in the Timeline, which you cannot do with a dynamics simulation. If you open the Graph Editor, you will see something similar to Figure 12.7.

Figure 12.6

The Bake Simulation Options window

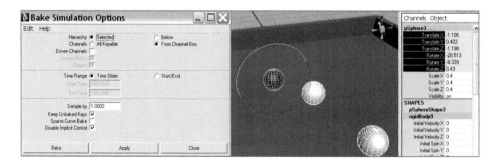

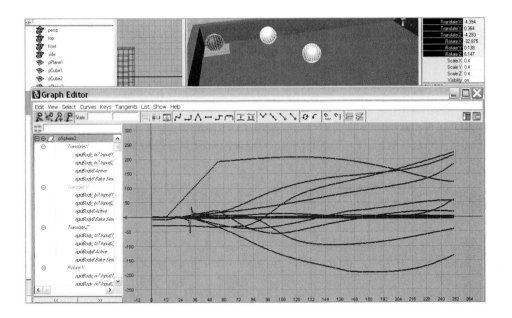

Figure 12.7
The pool balls now have animation curves.

5. The curves, however, are crowded; they have keyframes at every frame. A typical dynamics bake will give you results like this. We can, however, set the Bake command to sparse the curves for us; that is, it can take out keyframes at frames that have values within a certain tolerance, so that a minor change in the ball's position or rotation need not have a keyframe on the curve.

6. We will go back in time and try this again. Press Z for undo until you back up to right before we baked out the simulation to curves. You can also just close this scene and reopen it from the original project if need be. This time, select the balls and choose **Edit → Keys → Bake Simulation** ❑. In the option box, turn on the **Sparse Curve Bake** setting and set **Sample By** to 5. Select the channels in the Channel Box and click Bake. This time we are telling Maya to only look at every 5 frames of the simulation to set keyframes.

7. Maya will run through the simulation again and bake everything out to curves, this time making a more sparse animation curve for each channel since it is looking at 5-frame intervals, as seen in Figure 12.8. If you open the Graph Editor, you will notice that the curves are much friendlier to look at and edit.

Sampling by 5 may give you an easier curve to edit, but it can overly simplify the animation of your objects; so make sure to use the best **Sampling** setting for your simulation when you need to convert it to curves for editing.

Simplifying Animation Curves

Despite a higher **Sampling** setting when you bake out the simulation, you can still be left with a lot of keyframes to deal with, especially if you have to modify the animation extensively from here. One last trick we can use is to further simplify the curve through the Graph Editor itself. We will have to work with curves of the same relative size, so we will start with the rotation curves, since they have larger values. To keep things simple, let's just deal with one ball, the black eight ball. To simplify the curve in the Graph Editor, follow these steps:

1. Select the black eight ball and open the Graph Editor. In the left Outliner side of the Graph Editor, select **Rotate.X**, **Rotate.Y**, and **Rotate.Z** to display just them in the graph view. Figure 12.9 shows the curves.

Figure 12.8

Sampling by 5s makes a cleaner curve.

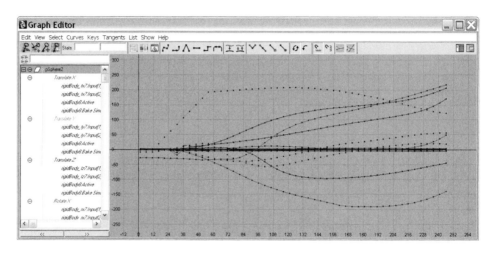

Figure 12.9

The Graph Editor displays the rotation curves of the eight ball.

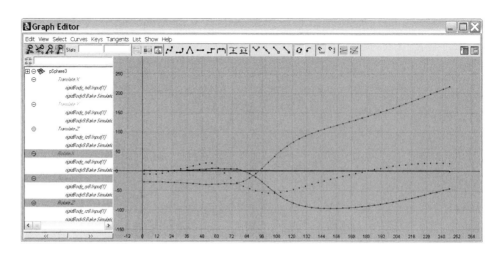

2. In the left panel of the Graph Editor, select the rigidBody_rx8.Input(1) nodes displayed right under the Rotate X, Y, and Z entries for all three curves as shown in the following illustration. In the Graph Editor menu, choose **Curves → Simplify Curve** ❑. In the option box, set **Time Range** to All, set **Simplify Method** to Dense Data, set **Time Tolerance** to 0.2, and set **Value Tolerance** to 0.5. These are fairly high values, but since we are dealing with rotation of the ball, the degree values are high enough. For more intricate values such as translation, you would use much lower tolerances when simplifying a curve.

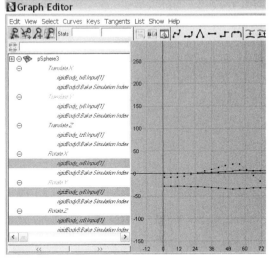

3. Click Simplify, and you will see that the curve retains its basic shape but loses some of the unneeded keyframes. Figure 12.10 shows the simplified curve, which differs little from the original curve with keys at every 5 frames.

Simplifying curves is a handy way to convert a dynamic simulation to curves. But you can also use this method to simplify other animation curves to make it easier to edit them as you animate the scene. Keep in mind, however, that you may lose fidelity to the original animation once you simplify a curve, so use it with care.

With this methodology, you could bake out the animation of any simulation, from dynamics as we just did to constraints and some scripts. The curve simplification works with good old-fashioned keyframed curves as well, so if you find yourself inheriting a scene from another animator and need to simplify the curves, have at it just as we did here.

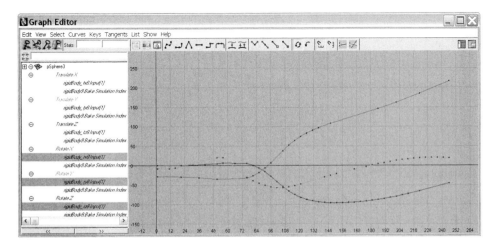

Figure 12.10

A simplified curve for the rotations of the eight ball

Particle Dynamics

Like rigid body objects, particles are moved dynamically using collisions and fields. In short, a *particle* is a point in space that is given renderable properties; that is, it can render out. When particles are used en masse, they can create effects such as smoke, a swarm of insects, fireworks, and so on. Although particles can be an advanced and involved aspect of Maya, it is important to have some exposure to them as you begin to learn Maya.

Figure 12.11

Creation options for a particle emitter

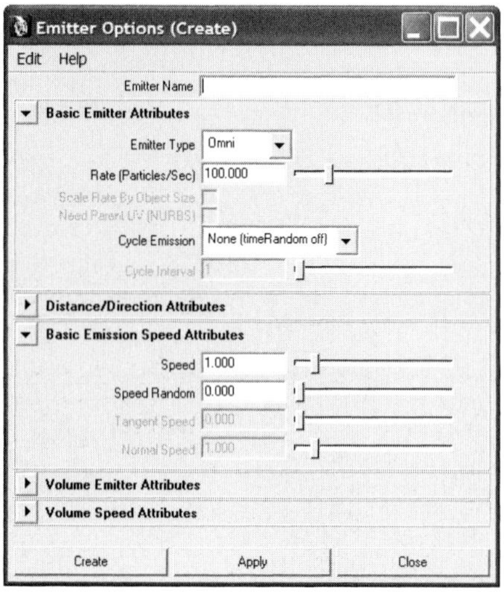

Much of what you learned about rigid body dynamics transfers to particles. However, it is important to think of particle animation as manipulating a larger system rather than as controlling every single particle in the simulation. You control fields and dynamic attributes to govern the motion of the system as a whole.

For example, with the pool table you control the motion of the cue ball and let Maya dynamics calculate the motion of the other balls after they collide. Each ball is a distinct part of the scene and renders out as a distinct object in the frame. Particles are most often used together in large numbers so that the entirety is rendered out to create an effect. To control a particle system, you'll create an emitter and define fields and attributes that control the particles' movement.

Emitting Particles

Typical work flow for creating a particle effect in Maya breaks into two parts: motion and rendering. First, you create and define the behavior of particles through *emission*. An *emitter* is a Maya object that creates the particles themselves. After creating fields and adjusting particle behavior within a dynamic simulation, much as you would do with rigid body motion, you give the particles renderable qualities to define how they look. This second aspect of the work flow defines how the particles "come together" to create the desired effect, such as steam. You will make a steaming locomotive pump later in this chapter.

To create a particle system, follow these steps:

1. Make sure you are in the Dynamics menu set, and then choose **Particles → Create Emitter** ❐. The option box gives you various creation options for the particles' emitter, as shown in Figure 12.11.

   The default settings will create an Omni emitter with a rate of 100 particles per second and a speed of 1.0. Click Create. A small round object (the emitter) will appear at the origin.

2. Click the Play button to play the scene. As with rigid body dynamics, you must also playback the scene using the Play Every Frame option. You cannot scrub or reverse play particles unless you create a cache file. You will learn how to create a particle disk cache later in this chapter. But for the most part, particles need to be played back to run properly.

You will notice a mass of small dots stream out of the emitter in all directions (see Figure 12.12). These are the particles themselves.

Emitter Attributes

You can control how particles are created and behave by changing the type of emitter and adjusting its attributes:

Omni Emits particles in all directions.

Directional Emits a spray of particles in a specific direction, as shown in Figure 12.13.

Volume Emits particles from within a specified volume, as in Figure 12.14. The volume can be a cube, a sphere, a cylinder, a cone, or a torus. By default, the particles can leave the perimeter of the volume.

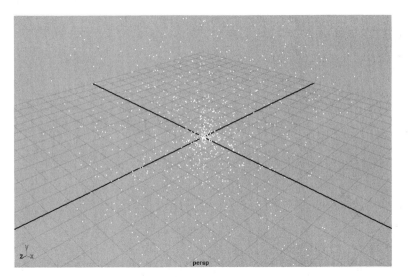

Figure 12.12

An Omni emitter emits a swarm of little particles in all directions.

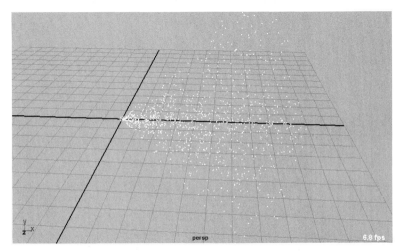

Figure 12.13

Particles sprayed in a specific direction

After you create an emitter, its attributes govern how the particles are released into the scene. Every emitter has the following attributes to control the emission:

Rate Governs how many particles are emitted per second.

Speed Specifies how fast the particles move out from the emitter.

Speed Random Randomizes the speed of the particles as they are emitted for a more natural look.

Min/Max Distance Emits particles within an offset distance from the emitter itself. You enter values for the **Min and Max Distance** setting. Figure 12.15 shows a directional emitter with a **Min and Max Distance** setting of 3.

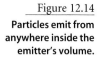
Figure 12.14

Particles emit from anywhere inside the emitter's volume.

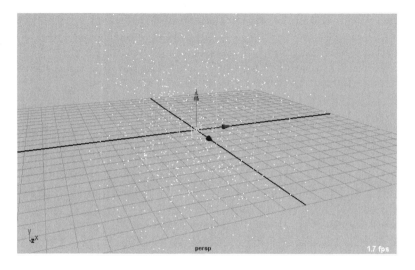

Figure 12.15

An emitter with a Min and Max Distance setting of 3 emits particles 3 units from itself.

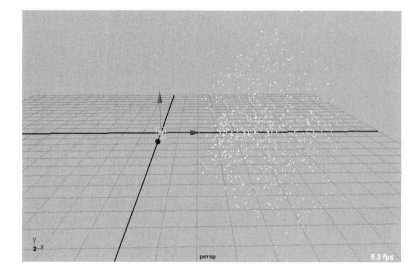

Particle Attributes

Once created (or born) and set into motion by an emitter, particles rely on their own attributes and any fields or collisions in the scene to govern their motion, just like rigid body objects.

In Figure 12.16, the Attribute Editor shows a number of tabs for the selected particle object. Particle1 is the particle object node. This has the familiar **Translate**, **Rotate**, and **Scale** attributes as most other object nodes. The shape node, however, particleShape1, is where all the important attributes are for a particle, and it is displayed by default when selecting a particle object. The third tab in the Attribute Editor is the emitter1 node that belongs to the particle's emitter. This makes it easier to toggle back and forth to adjust emitter and particle settings.

Figure 12.16

Particle attributes

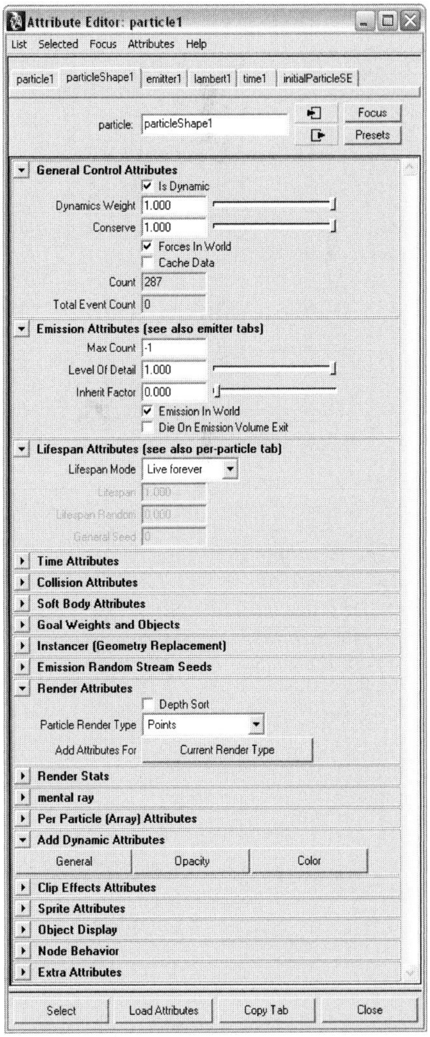

The Lifespan Attributes

When a particle is created, or born, you can give it a *lifespan*, which allows the particle to die when it reaches a certain point in time. Giving particles a lifespan is a good idea for a variety of reasons. As you'll see with the steaming locomotive later in the chapter, a particle that has a lifespan can change over its lifespan. For example, a particle might start out as white and fade away at the end of its life. A lifespan also helps keep the total number of particles in a scene to a minimum, which helps the scene run more efficiently.

You use the lifespan mode to select the type of lifespan for a particle:

Live Forever The particles in the scene can exist indefinitely.

Constant All particles die when their Lifespan value is reached. Lifespan is measured in seconds, so upon emission, a particle will exist for 30 frames in a scene set up at 30fps before it disappears.

Random Range This type sets a lifespan as in constant mode but assigns a range value via the **Lifespan Random** attribute to allow some particles to live longer than others for a more natural effect.

lifespanPP Only This mode is used in conjunction with expressions that are programmed into the particle with MEL. Expressions are an advanced Maya concept and are not used in this book.

The Render Attributes

The render attributes determine how your particles look and how they will render. Two types of particle rendering are used in Maya: software and hardware. *Hardware particles* are typically rendered out separately from anything else in the scene and are then composited

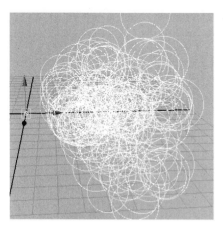

with the rest of the scene. Because of this compound work flow for hardware particles, this book will introduce you to a software particle called Cloud. Cloud, like other *software particles*, can be rendered with the rest of a scene through the software renderer.

With your particles selected, open the Attribute Editor. In the Render Attributes section, you will find the Particle Render Type drop-down menu, seen here.

The three render types listed with the (s/w) suffix are software-rendered particles. All the other types can be rendered only through the hardware renderer. Select your render type, and then click the Add Attributes for Current Render Type button to create and add the proper attributes for the render type you selected.

For example, if you select the Cloud (s/w) render type from the menu, your particles change from dots on the screen to large circles, seen here.

Click the Add Attributes For button to display several new attributes that will control the look of the particles. Each particle render type has its own set of render attributes. The cloud particle type attributes added will be **Radius**, **Surface Shading**, and **Threshold**.

In the *Per Particle (Array) Attributes* section of the Attribute Editor are attributes that affect individual particles, as opposed to affecting the entire particle object as one unit.

For example, the **Radius** attribute, which appeared when you clicked to create a Cloud render type, governs the radius, the size, of every particle in the system evenly. That is, with a **Radius** setting of 1.5, each particle in that particle system (particle object) will have a radius of 1.5.

By allowing you to control certain attributes at an individual particle scale, Maya gives you immense power to create realistic-looking effects. In the case of your Cloud particle's radius, you can create an attribute called **radiusPP** (for radius Per Particle) so that each particle can have a different radius.

Rather than manually enter radius values for every single particle, you control **Per Particle** attributes by connecting textures or expressions to them in the Per Particle (Array) Attributes section of the Attribute Editor. Notice that there is already a **lifespanPP** attribute that allows you to control the lifespan for particles on an individual basis.

Caching Particles

Would be nice to turn particles into cash, but I could show you how to turn your particles into a cache. You can cache the motion of your particles to memory or to disk to make playback and editing of your particle animation easier. To cache particles to your system's fast RAM memory, select the particle object you want to cache and choose **Solvers → Memory Caching → Enable**. Playback your scene and the particles will cache into your memory for faster playback. You can also scrub your Timeline to see your particle animation. If you make changes to your animation, the scene will not reflect the changes until you delete the cache from memory by selecting the particle object and choosing **Solvers → Memory Caching → Delete**. The amount of information the memory cache can hold depends on the system RAM of your machine. Although memory caching is much faster than disk caching, creating a disk cache lets you cache all the particles as they exist throughout their duration in your scene and ensures that the particles are rendered correctly, especially if you are rendering on multiple computers or across a network. You should create a particle disk cache before rendering.

> If you make changes to your particle simulation but you do not see the changes reflected when you playback the scene, make sure you have deleted any memory or disk cache from previous versions.

Creating a Particle Cache File

Once you have created a particle scene and you want to be able to scrub the Timeline back and forth to see your particle motion and how it acts in the scene, you can create a *particle disk cache*. This lets you playback the scene as you wish, without running the simulation from the start and by every frame.

To create a particle disk cache, switch to the Dynamics menu set and choose **Solvers → Create Particle Disk Cache**. Maya will run the simulation according to the Timeline and save the position of all the particle systems in the scene to cache files in your current project's particle folder. You can then play your animation back and forth and the particles will run properly.

If you make any dynamics changes to the particles, such as emission rate or speed, you will need to detach the cache file from the scene for the changes to take effect. Choose **Solvers → Edit Oversampling or Cache Settings**, and uncheck the **Use Particle Disk Cache** check box.

Now that you understand the basics of particle dynamics, it's time to see for yourself how they work.

Animating a Particle Effect: Locomotive Steam

You will create a spray of steam puffing out of the steam pump on the side of the locomotive that drives the wheels on the model you started creating in Chapters 4 and 5. We'll use the more detailed locomotive from Chapters 8 and 9.

Emitting the Particles

The first step is to create an emitter to spray from the steam pump and to set up the motion and behavior of the particles:

1. In the Dynamics menu set, choose **Particles → Create Emitter** ❑. Set **Emitter Type** to Directional and click Create. Place the emitter at the end of the pump as shown.

2. To set up the emission in the proper direction, adjust the attributes of the emitter. In the Distance/Direction Attributes section, set **Direction Y** to 0, **Direction X** to 0, and **Direction Z** to 1. This emits the particles straight out of the pump over that first large wheel and toward the back of the engine.

   The **Direction** attributes are relative. Entering a value of 1 for **Direction X** and a value of 2 for **Direction Y** will make the particles spray at twice the height (Y) of their lateral distance (X).

3. Playback your scene. You'll see particles emit in a straight line from the engine, as shown in Figure 12.17.

    You can load the file Locomotive_Steam_v1.ma from the Locomotive project on the CD to check your work.

4. To change the particle emission to more of a spray, adjust the **Spread** attribute for the emitter. Click the emitter1 tab in the particle's Attribute Editor (or select the emitter to focus the Attribute Editor on it instead), and change **Spread** from 0 to 0.25. Figure 12.18 shows the new spray.

Figure 12.17

Particles emit in a straight line from the pump.

Figure 12.18

The emitter's Spread attribute widens the spray of particles.

The **Spread** attribute sets the cone angle for a directional emission. A value of 0 results in a thin line of particles. A value of 1 emits particles in a 180-degree arc.

5. The emission is rather slow for hot steam being pumped out as the locomotive drives the wheels, so change the **Speed** setting for the emitter from 1 to 3, and change **Speed Random** from 0 to 1. This will create a random speed range between 1 and 3 for each particle. These two attributes are found in the emitter's Attribute Editor in the Basic Emission Speed Attributes section.

6. So that all the steam does not emit from the same exact point, keep the emitter's **Min Distance** at 0 but set its **Max Distance** to 0.3. This will create a range of offset between 0 and 0.3 units for the particle to emit from, as shown.

Setting Particle Attributes

It's always good to get the particles moving as closely to what you need as possible first before tending to their look. Now that you have the particles emitting properly from the steam pump, you'll adjust the particle attributes. Start by setting a lifespan for them and then add rendering attributes:

1. Select the particle object and open the Attribute Editor. For **Lifespan Mode**, select Random Range. Set **Lifespan** to 3 and **Lifespan Random** to 1. This will create a range of 2 to 4 for each particle's lifespan. (That's based on a lifespan of 3 plus or minus a random value from 0 to 1.)

2. Change **Particle Render Type** from Points to Clouds. The particles will be displayed as large circles that overlap each other. They are too large; however, it is often desirable for these particles to overlap so that the steam looks seamless.

3. You will control the radius of the particles individually, on a Per Particle basis, as opposed to changing the **Radius** attribute. In the particleShape1's Attribute Editor, in the Add Dynamic Attributes section, click the General button to open the Add Attribute:particleShape1 window. Click the Particle tab, select **radiusPP**, as shown in Figure 12.19, and click OK. This will add a **radiusPP** attribute to the Per Particle (Array) Attributes section of the Attribute Editor.

You just added an attribute to the particle object, just as you added a new attribute for the set driven keys for the hand in Chapter 9.

For this attribute, you will assign a texture to **radiusPP** to control the size of the particles. In Maya, a particle's attribute, such as radiusPP, can read the color values from a texture and use the texture to control the particle's behavior, in this case its radius, or size.

The texture you will create for **radiusPP** will be a ramp. Using a texture that has only one color will assign a static radius value to each particle. For example, if you use a white texture for **radiusPP**, each particle will have a radius of 1.0. White, in this case, is read to be a value of 1; black is a value of 0.

Using a gradient, such as a ramp texture, that grades from black to white will change the radius of the particle along its lifespan. The radius for each particle will begin at 0 (black) at its birth and increase along its lifespan to a value of 1 (white) at its death. This is one reason that assigning an active lifespan mode to your particles is a good idea.

To assign a ramp texture to the **radiusPP** attribute, follow these steps:

1. RMB click and hold in the gray text box of the **radiusPP** attribute. A marking menu will appear. Choose **Create Ramp** and release the mouse button. The **radiusPP** attribute will now read **arrayMapper1.outValuePP**. Simply put, this attribute is now assigned a ramp that will control the radius of your particles as they grow older.

2. To edit the ramp, RMB click **arrayMapper1.outValuePP** and choose
   arrayMapper1.outValuePP → Edit Ramp from the marking menu.
   The Attribute Editor will now display the ramp. For organization's sake,
   name the ramp radiusPP_ramp. The ramp also appears in the Hypershade and Multilister windows for editing.

3. Adjust the ramp settings so that the bottom is a dark gray and the top is
   a medium gray. Set the bottom gray to an HSV of 0,0,0.15 and the top
   color to an HSV of 0,0,0.5. This will make the steam particles small at
   birth (a radius of 0.15).

The ramp will make the particles grow to a maximum radius of 0.5
over their lifespan. The values are read from the bottom of the ramp at the
beginning of a particle's life to the top of the ramp as the particle ages and
dies. Playback the scene from the first frame, and you should have something
similar to Figure 12.20.

Load the file `locomotive_steam_v2.ma` from the Locomotive project on the CD to check
your work. Or, don't. It's your call, really.

Setting Rendering Attributes

After you define the particle movement to your liking, you can create the proper look for
them, and that means setting and adjusting rendering parameters for the particles. Since
Maya has several types of particles, particles are set up according to their type; this work
flow applies only to the Cloud particle type.

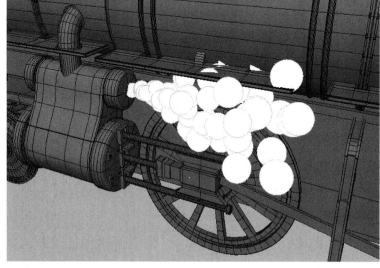

Figure 12.19
The Add Attribute window

Figure 12.20
The particles grow as they spray out from the pump.

Cloud particles render out when they are assigned a particle cloud shader. This shader is similar to the shaders you've used previously in this book. To create a steam shader for these particles, follow these steps:

1. Open the Hypershade window, and choose **Create ▸ Volumetric Materials ▸ Particle Cloud**. This will create a shader for use with Cloud particles. You will notice a particleCloud1 material already in the scene. Maya creates one by default in every new scene, but you will not use that one.

2. Double-click particleCloud2 to open the Attribute Editor. Rename the material to steam. Figure 12.21 shows the Attribute Editor for the steam shader material.

3. Change the color of the material from cyan to white. Now select the particles and assign the steam material to them by right-clicking the steam material in the Hypershade and choosing **Assign Material to Selection** from the marking menu.

4. In the Render Settings window, set the **Image Size** to 640 × 480, and in the Maya Software tab, set the Quality to Intermediate Quality. Run the animation and stop it when some steam has been emitted. Render a frame. It should look like Figure 12.22. The steam is too blotchy and travels too far down the length of the engine. Change the particle's **Lifespan** to 1.5 from 3.0, and change **Lifespan Random** to 0.5. When you playback the simulation, the steam ends sooner, traveling not as far as shown here. We could also use more particles, so select the emitter and change **Rate** to 350.

Render a 200-frame sequence of the scene at a lower resolution such as 320 × 240 to see how the particles look as they animate. (Check the frames with FCheck. Refer to Chapter 11 for more on FCheck.) First, the steam is too thick and too opaque. Also, in the animation you will notice that the particles "turn off" at the end of their lifespan.

Steam, however, dissipates. The particles here pop off when they die. You will need to make the particles gradually disappear as they grow older so that they are fully transparent at the end of their lifespan. This will make them fade instead of popping off. You will adjust the transparency of the steam material in the following steps:

Figure 12.21

The new steam shader material

1. Select the steam material in the Hypershade, and open the Attribute Editor. Instead of merely setting a higher value for the **Transparency** attribute (by making the gray color brighter), you will need to make a new ramp texture for the steam material's **Life Transparency**. As a ramp texture assigned to the radiusPP created growing particles, this new ramp will make the particles fade (become more transparent) as they get older and become fully transparent at their death. To create a ramp on **Life Transparency**, click the Texture button to the right of the text box in the Attribute Editor to open the Create Render Node window.

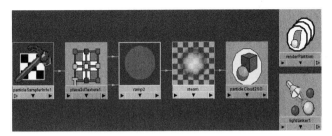

2. Click to create a ramp texture. Maya will create and display a particleSamplerInfo1 node in the Attribute Editor. You will not need to adjust this node, so select the new ramp node in the Hypershade to display its attributes in the Attribute Editor instead.

3. Rename the ramp from ramp2 to steam_transparency. Since the particles will read the ramp from bottom to top, set the bottom color to white. This will make the particles transparent at first. Set a medium gray color not too far above the black so that the particles fade in. Toward the top, set a white color. This will create a full transparency at the end of a particle's life. The ramp should look as shown to the right.

4. Render a frame to see the results. The steam will look more real and will animate better by just adding the transparency ramp to the lifespan of the particles. Compare the results (see Figure 12.23) to the previous render.

5. If you prefer not to have a gap between the pump and the steam, as this scene creates, try moving the emitter into the steam pump itself, or decrease the **Max Distance** attribute on the emitter. Also try angling it out to blow the steam away from the engine.

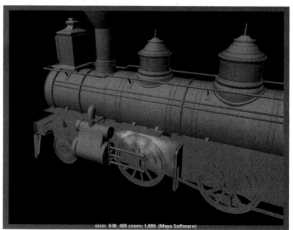

Figure 12.22

A single frame render of the steam

Figure 12.23

The steam dissipating more realistically

Load the file `locomotive_steam_v3.ma` from the Locomotive project on the CD to check your work.

Experiment with animating the **Rate** attribute of the emitter to make the steam pump out in time with the wheel arm. Also, try animating the Speed values and playing with different radiusPP sizes. The steam you'll get from this tutorial, while looking good, will not be as lifelike as it could be. You can do a lot more as you learn more about Maya, but those techniques are beyond the scope of this book. Particle animators are always learning new tricks and expanding on their skills, and that comes from always trying new things and retrying the same effects with different methods.

Once you feel comfortable with the steam exercise, try using the Cloud particle type to create steam for a mug of coffee. That steam moves much slower and is less defined than the blowing steam of the locomotive and should pose a new challenge. Also try your hand at creating a smoke trail for a rocket ship or a wafting stream of cigarette smoke, or even the billowing smoke coming from the engine's chimney.

Cloud particles are the perfect particle type to begin with. As you feel more comfortable animating with clouds, experiment with the other render types. The more you experiment with all particles, the easier they will be to harness. You'll quickly find Maya particles can create a wild array of realistic and stylized effects for your animations.

Introduction to Paint Effects

In Maya's effects arsenal is a tool called Paint Effects. Using Paint Effects, you can create a field of grass rippling in the wind, a head of hair or feathers, or even a colorful aurora in the sky. *Paint Effects* is a rendering effect found under the Rendering menu set. It has incredible dynamic properties that can make leaves rustle in the wind or trees sway in a storm. Though it does not use the same dynamics engine as particles or rigid bodies do, Paint Effects uses its own dynamics calculations to create natural motion. It is one of Maya's most powerful tools, with features that go far beyond the scope of this introductory book. Here you will learn how to create a Paint Effects scene and how to access all the preset brushes to create your own effects.

Paint Effects uses brushes to paint effects into your 3D scene. The brushes create strokes on a surface or in the Maya modeling views that produce tubes, which render out through Maya's software renderer. These Paint Effects tubes have dynamic properties, which means they can move according to their own forces. Thus, you can easily create a field of blowing grass.

Try This You will create a field of blowing grass and flowers, and it will take you all of five minutes.

1. Start with a new scene file. Maximize the perspective view. (Press the spacebar with the persp window active.)

2. Switch to the Rendering menu set. Choose **Paint Effects → Get Brush** to open the Visor window. The Visor window displays all the preset Paint Effects brushes that automatically create certain effects. Select the grasses folder in the Visor's left panel to display the grass brushes available (see Figure 12.24). You can navigate the Visor window as you would navigate any other Maya window using the Alt key and the mouse buttons.

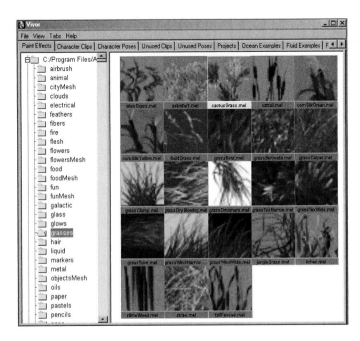

Figure 12.24

The preset grass brushes in the Visor window

3. Click the grassWindWide.mel brush to activate the Paint Effects tool and set it to this grass brush. Your cursor will change to a pencil icon.

4. In the persp window, click and drag two lines across the grid as shown here to create two Paint Effects strokes of blowing grass. If you can't see the grass in your view panel, increase the **Global Scale** in the Paint Effects Brush Settings to see them draw on.

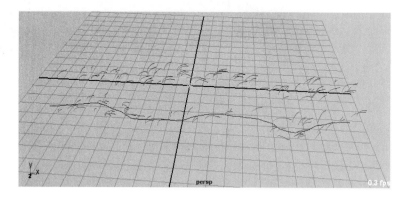

5. To change your brush to add some flowers in between the grass, choose **Paint Effects → Get Brush** and select the flowers folder. Select the dandelion_Yellow.mel brush. Your Paint Effects tool is now set to paint yellow flowers.

6. Click and drag a new stroke between the strokes of grass as shown.

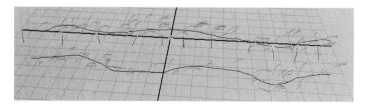

7. Position your camera and render a frame. Make sure to use a large enough resolution, such as 640 × 480, so that you can see the details. Render out a 120-frame sequence to see how the grass animates in the wind. Figure 12.25 shows a scene filled with grass strokes as well as a number of different flowers.

Once you create a Paint Effects stroke, you can edit the look and movement of the effect through the Attribute Editor. You'll notice, however, that there are a large number of attributes to edit with Paint Effects. The next section introduces the attributes that are most useful to the beginning Maya user.

Figure 12.25

Paint Effects can add realistic-looking flowers and grass to any scene.

Paint Effects Attributes

It is best to create a single stroke of Paint Effects in a blank scene and experiment with adjusting the various attributes to see how they affect the strokes. Select the stroke and open the Attribute Editor. Switch to the stroke's tab to access the attributes. For example, for an African Lily Paint Effects stroke, the Attribute Editor tab is called africanlily1.

Each Paint Effects stroke produces tubes that render to create the desired effect. Each tube (you can think of a tube as a stalk) can grow to have branches, twigs, leaves, flowers, and buds. Each section of a tube has its own controls to give you the greatest flexibility in creating your effect. As you experiment with Paint Effects, you will begin to understand how each attribute contributes to the final look of the effect.

Here is a summary of some Paint Effects attributes:

Brush Profile Gives you control over how the tubes are generated from the stroke, namely with the **Brush Width** attribute. This will make tubes emit from a wider breadth from the stroke to cover more of an area.

Shading and Tube Shading Gives you access to the color controls for the tubes on a stroke.

> **Color1 and Color2** From bottom to top, graduates from Color1 to Color 2 along the stalk only. The leaves and branches have their own color attributes, which you can display by choosing **Tubes → Growth**.
>
> **Incandescence1 and 2** Adds a gradient self-illumination to the tubes.
>
> **Transparency1 and 2** Adds a gradient transparency to each tube.
>
> **Hue/Sat/Value Rand** Add some randomness to the color of the tubes.

In the Tubes section, you will find all the attributes to control the growth of the Paint Effects effect. In the Creation subsection, you can access the following:

Tubes Per Step Controls the number of tubes along the stroke. For example, this setting will increase or decrease the number of flowers for the africanlily1 stroke.

Length Min/Max Controls how tall the tubes are grown to make taller flowers or grass (or other effects).

Tube Width1 and Width2 Controls the width of the tubes, that is, the stalks of the flowers.

In the Growth subsection, you can access controls for branches, twigs, leaves, flowers, and buds for the Paint Effects strokes. Each attribute in these sections controls the number, size, and shape of those elements. Although not all Paint Effects strokes create flowers, all strokes contain these headings; some may or may not be active. Each stroke has its own settings.

The Behavior subsection contains the controls for the dynamic forces affecting the tubes in a Paint Effects stroke. Adjust these attributes if you want your flowers to blow more in the wind.

Paint Effects are rendered as a *post process*, which means they will not render in reflections or refractions as is. They are indeed processed and rendered after every other object in the scene is rendered out. They will, however, playback in the work panels to give you feedback on your dynamic settings.

You can also convert Paint Effects to polygonal surfaces that will render in the scene along with any other objects so that they may indeed take part in reflections and refractions. To convert a Paint Effects stroke to polygons, select the stroke and choose **Modify → Convert → Paint Effects to Polygons**. The polygon Paint Effects tubes can still be edited by most of the Paint Effects attributes mentioned so far, though some, such as color, will not affect the poly tubes. Instead, the color information is converted into a shader that is assigned to the polygons. It's best to finalize your Paint Effects strokes before converting to polygons to avoid any confusion.

Paint Effects is a strong Maya tool, and you can use it to create complex effects such as a field of blowing flowers. With that complexity comes a large number of controls to create a variety of effects. Fortunately, Maya comes with a generous sampling of preset brushes. Experiment with a few brushes and their attributes to see what kinds of effects and strange plants you can create.

Summary

In this chapter you learned how to create dynamic objects and create simulations. Beginning with rigid body dynamics, you created a set of pool balls that you animated in the simulation to knock into each other. Then, you learned how to bake that simulation into animation curves for fine-tuning. Next, you learned about particle effects by creating a steam effect for the locomotive animation. Finally you learned a little bit about Maya's Paint Effects and how it can easily be used to create various effects such as grass and flowers.

To further your learning, try creating a scene on a grassy hillside with train tracks running through. Animate the locomotive, steam and all, driving through the scene and blowing the grass as it passes. You can also create a train whistle and a steam effect when the whistle blows, and you can create various other trails of smoke and steam as the locomotive drives through.

With power comes complexity of use. Maya dynamics has a rich feature set and compound controls. The best way to be exposed to Maya dynamics is to simply experiment once you're familiar with the general work flow in Maya. You will find that the work flow in dynamics is more iterative than other Maya work flows, as you are required to experiment frequently with different values to see how they affect the final simulation. With time, you will develop a strong sense of intuition, and you will accomplish more complex simulations faster and with greater effect.

Where Do You Go from Here?

It's so hard to say goodbye! But this is really a bit of a hello; a hello to learning more about animation and 3D.

Please explore other resources of information and tutorials to expand your working knowledge of Maya. Several websites contain numerous tips, tricks, and tutorials for all aspects of Maya, including the author's occasional tutorials and ramblings online at www.koosh3d.com. Of course, www.autodesk.com/maya has a wide range of learning tools. Check Chapter 1's bibliography for some suggested reading materials. You will surely find a wealth of information out there, and now that you have gained the all-important first exposure, you will be better equipped to forge ahead confidently.

The most important thing you should have learned from this book is that proficiency and competence with Maya come with practice, but even more so from your own artistic exploration. It is imperative to treat this text and your experience with its information as a formal introduction to a new language and way of working for yourself. The rest of it, the gorgeous still frames and eloquent animations, come with furthering your study of your own art, working diligently to achieve your vision, and truly having fun on the way. Enjoy and good luck.

Glossary

active rigid body A dynamic object that is affected by fields and collisions.

aim constraint Forces the rotations of an object to always point toward the position of another object or to the average of the positions of several objects.

alpha channel The channel of an image file that defines areas of transparency. The alpha channel is expressed in grayscale.

ambient lights Cast an even light throughout a scene.

animation curves Graphical representation of the animation of an object shown as a curve graph of an object's attribute value over time.

anti-aliasing Smoothing the edges of an object against the background in rendering. Low anti-alias levels create jagged edges where you can see pixelization.

anticipation An animation term referring to how an object or character behaves just before an action, such as an arm pulling back for throwing a ball.

area lights Flat, rectangular area of evenly emitted light.

attribute Value stored in a node that helps define a certain setting for the object.

auto keyframe Automatically adds a keyframe for an already keyframed attribute once that attribute changes in the scene.

back (or rim) light Light that is cast from behind an object to create a lighter edge to the object in the frame

baking Creating animation curves from dynamic simulation.

bevel surface Creates a surface to round a corner or the edge(s) of a model.

binding Attaching a mesh or geometry to a skeleton.

Blinn material A shader type that brings to the surface a highly accurate specular lighting model with increased control over the specular's appearance. This creates a shader that is good for use on shiny and metallic surfaces.

bounciness Rigid body attribute that governs how much the object bounces upon collision.

Boundary Surface Creates a surface within the boundaries of three or four surrounding curves.

caustics The scattering of light through semitransparent objects that cause a pattern of light with varying intensities, such as reflected light at the bottom of a pool.

center of balance The center of gravity of an object; a point upon which an object can perfectly balance.

control vertices (CVs) Points that define a curve using Bezier interpolation to create smoothness.

curve points Points that actually make up a curve; they physically reside on the curve itself.

dailies Progress on the scenes in production, usually reviewed in film on a daily basis.

damping Rigid body attribute that governs how fast a dynamic body loses motion. The higher the attribute, the more the body's motion diminishes.

deformers Functions that deform the shape of an object or surface, such as bending or twisting.

diffuse The color of an object as normal scattered (or diffuse) light strikes it.

directional lights Evenly emit light from one direction. Useful for sunlight

dynamic bodies Geometry that has dynamic attributes to allow it to react in a dynamic simulation

dynamics The simulation of motion through the application of the principles of physics.

edge The edge of a polygon or the place where two polygons meet.

edit points (EPs) Points that reside on a curve. Like CVs, they adjust the shape of the NURBS curve, maintaining a smooth curvature. *See also control vertices.*

emitter Object that creates particles by emitting them using any one of several methods.

extrude - To pull a face or an edge out to create a new surface on a polygon model.

Extruded Surface Creates a surface using a profile curve that sweeps along a path curve to form the surface.

face A flat surface made when three or more points on a polygonal model called vertices are connected.

fields Forces such as gravity, air, and drag that act on dynamic objects.

fill light Fills in darker areas of the frame and softens shadows usually cast by the key light.

flexors Deformers such as lattices that help smooth out parts of the geometry bound to a rigid bind skeleton.

fluids Modules that use volumetric particles that can exhibit surface properties. Motion is based on fluid dynamic mathematics that calculates the movement of properties of fluid-like density, temperature, and so on.

focus (F hot key) Positions the camera to display the selected object in the current view panel.

follow-through An animation term that refers to how an object behaves directly after an action, such as an arm swinging down after throwing a ball.

Forward Kinematics (FK) Skeletal animation based on directly rotating the joints.

freeze transformations Resetting the attributes of an object to their defaults (zero for rotation and translation, and 1 for scale) without actually moving or resizing the object.

friction Dynamic attribute that creates resistance to motion between sliding surfaces

ghosting Displaying the previous and subsequent positions of an animated object as well as it's current position to help an animator better edit their motion.

global illumination Rendering and lighting effect that bounces light within a scene for a more organic and natural lighting.

gross animation The establishment of an overall movement for a scene before getting to edit and refined timing and positions.

grouping Putting nodes together under a new empty (null) node.

hair Module that simulates the dynamic and rendering properties of hair; includes dynamic curves.

hardware particles Render out only through hardware rendering. These particles include sprites, points, streaks, multipoint, multistreak, spheres, and numerical.

history A buffer in which the construction steps of an object are stored to allow for later editing of earlier steps.

hull line Connects a row of CVs to be useful for selecting multiple rows of CVs at a time. See also *control vertices*.

image plane An image file or sequence of images that is loaded into a camera's view to allow you to line up models and animations.

incremental save Backs up your scene file every time you save your scene.

interpenetration Occurs when the surfaces of objects cross each other, which can cause problems with rigid body dynamic simulations when played back.

interpolation How the computer calculates the transition from one angle in a curve to another angle. Used commonly in animation curves in setting how they are shaped.

Inverse Kinematics (IK) Skeletal animation based on indirectly rotating the joints by using IK handles to pose the armature or character.

isoparms Mathematical curves that define the shape of a NURBS surface and are defined by CVs themselves.

joints The points at which skeleton bones meet and about which they pivot.

keyframing Setting keyframes to animate an object by recording the position, rotation, scale, or other such attribute at a particular frame.

key light The primary lighting of a subject to create a sense of light direction and primary shadows.

Lambert An evenly diffused shading type found in dull or matte surfaces such as a sheet of paper.

lattice A deformer that surrounds the geometry like a scaffold and gives you control to change the shape of the attached geometry.

layered shader Allows the stacking of multiple shaders to create complex shading effects—useful for creating objects composed of multiple materials.

lifespan The attribute that rules how long a particle is in the scene before it disappears.

light linking The method of attaching certain lights and objects together so that only those lights affect those objects and not others in the scene.

local axis The 3D axis as seen from the current view of an object.

lofting A method for creating a surface between multiple curves. The resulting surface can be NURBS or poly.

mapping Applying textures or images to a shader that is then assigned to an object in a scene.

mass The physical simulated weight of an object. Mass is a factor in how much momentum is transferred from one object to another.

material nodes Define the surface properties of a shader, such as color, opacity, shininess, and so on.

matte Also known as an alpha channel, a matte is an image channel or image that defines the opacity for an image. When the matte is white, that part of the image is seen; where nothing is shown in the image being matted, the matte is black. Grey tones define the transparency in between.

modeling Creating models in CG.

motion trail Display of an animated object's trajectory.

normalize Scale a large-scale value to fit between the values −1 and 1.

NURBS modeling Creating NURBS surfaces

orient constraint Forces the rotations of an object to always match the rotations of another object or the average of several objects' rotations.

Paint Effects A brush-based rendering effect in Maya that has built-in dynamics to create objects such as blowing grass, trees, and practically any other system that can be painted into the scene.

painting skin weights Painting the influence of joints on the geometry to which they are smooth bound to help make the geometry of the character (for example) behave properly when it's armature of skeleton is moved.

parametric modeling Adjusting only the parameters of an object to affect its shape.

parent node A node in a hierarchy that has nodes underneath it (child nodes). A parent node transfers all it's position, rotation, and scale information down to it's child nodes.

parenting Grouping nodes together by placing the first selected node under the second selected node to form a hierarchy; also known as grouping.

particle A single location in 3D space that is given rendering properties. When used in a system, physical effects such as smoke or fire can be simulated.

particle disk cache Writes the positions of particles to disk so you do not need to run a dynamic simulation to playback the particle motion. Useful for rendering out particle shots.

passive rigid body A dynamic object that does not react to forces or collisions, but can cause collisions with active rigid bodies.

patch modeling A NURBS modeling method that relies on creating patches of surfaces that are then stitched together to form a smooth model. Often used with character modeling.

patches Parts of NURBS surfaces that are stitched together to form smooth models such as faces.

path animation Animating an object based on its positions along a curve or a path.

per particle (array) attributes Attributes that affect every particle in a particle system.

pipeline The work flow for CG production and how it moves along from department to department or phase to phase.

pivot point The placement point for an object and the point around which the object rotates.

pivot point manipulator Adjusts the position of the pivot point for the selected object.

Phong A shading type that brings to a surface's rendering the notions of specular highlight and reflectivity. You'll find glossy objects such as plastics, glass, and most metals can be made well with a Phong material.

planar surface Makes a perfectly flat surface from an outline or outlines of curves.

point constraint Forces the position of an object to always be at the pivot point of another object or at the average of the positions of several objects

point light A single emission of light in all directions from that point.

polygon proxy A modeling mode in subD modeling that lets you make broad-stroke changes in creating your model, without having to reduce the complexity of your model's surface.

post process A rendering step in which an effect such as lens flare is composited onto the scene's rendered frame, whether in Maya or in composite.

practical lighting Lighting that must appear to be derived by a specific object, such as a lamp, in the scene

primitives Simple shapes (3D or 2D) created as NURBS, polys, or subDs from which models can be sculpted or formed.

project folder Contains the subfolders of your current project, including the folder for your scenes, rendered images, and so forth.

proxy A lesser-defined or lighter model that is used in place of the actual model to improve scene interactivity. Useful for animating large models in the scene first, and then importing the actual model to replace the proxy once the animation is complete.

raytraced shadows Calculated through raytracing, which creates sharp and accurate shadows.

raytracing Rendering method that traces rays of light from each light source to each object all the way to the camera lens. Makes true reflections and refractions possible.

refraction The bending of light as it travels from one surface density, such as air, into another, such as water.

revolved surface A method that requires only one curve that is turned about a point in space to create a surface, such as a woodworker shaping a table leg on a lathe.

rigging Creating a skeleton for a character (or an object), attaching or binding it, and creating animation controls to run the character.

Rigid Bind A method for attaching geometry to a skeleton. Maya groups the CVs of a NURBS or the vertices of a polygon into joint clusters that are then attached to the bones so that the character can deform with the skeleton.

rigid bodies Solid objects that move and rotate according to a dynamic simulation of physics-based motion.

root joint The topmost node of a joint chain that is the parent of all the other bones in that chain.

scale constraint Forces the size of an object to always match the scale of another object or the average of the scales of several objects.

scrub Move the scrub bar in the Timeline back and forth to playback your animation manually.

secondary motion Adding motion to secondary parts of a character or an object, such as a cape on a jumping character. Adds reality to the primary motion of the character or object.

sections The horizontal subdivisions of a NURBS surface as defined by location of its isoparms.

selection handle A small cross that usually displays at the pivot point of an object to allow you to easily select the object or node by choosing the handle as opposed to picking out the object itself in a heavy scene.

set driven key A relationship you set up in Maya to control an animation so that the keyframed attribute(s) of a driver object controls the behavior of a driven object.

shading Applying colors and textures, known as shaders.

shadow maps A method of calculating where shadows fall in a scene by writing out map files that correspond to the lighting of the scene. Shadow maps render out faster than raytraced shadows.

skeleton A chain or chains of joints that create an armature for creating animation for a model, such as the skeleton in a human body.

skinning Attaching a mesh or geometry to a skeleton. See also *binding*.

Smooth Bind A method of attaching geometry to a skeleton when more than one joint can influence more than one skin point on the model, allowing for areas of the model farther from the joint to bend when that joint rotates.

Smooth Tool Evenly subdivides a poly object or its selected faces to create a smoother look.

snaps Feature that allows you to perfectly fit the position of an object or a point onto another point or grid intersection.

soft bodies Malleable objects that deform according to dynamics, such as drapes or a rubber ball.

software particles Particles that can render out through software rendering methods. Software particles include cloud, tube, and blobbies.

source images A folder in the Maya project structure where you can store all the images you use for reference in your scene, especially for image planes for camera views.

spans The vertical subdivisions of a NURBS surface as defined by location of the surface's isoparms.

specular A highlight reflection hot spot on a surface, generally white; hints at the gloss of a material.

Split Polygon tool Creates a new edge to divide a polygon face between two selected points on the edges of that polygon face.

Spot light A conical emitter of light that begins from a point but casts light in a cone. Spotlights calculate quickly when rendering, especially for shadows

squash and stretch A cartoon animation term referring to how an object or a character can squeeze down or stretch out to give a feeling of weight during an action, such as a rubber ball squashing down when it bounces on the ground.

stitching Attaching NURBS patches together to present a smooth continuous surface for a model.

subdivide Create more faces on a polygon model or on individual faces.

subdivision surfaces A modeling method whereby you adjust varying levels of editing detail that allow you to adjust a surface from a global level. Large parts of the model are then

modified to a micro-level, where you have control over the densest surface points.

tangency The amount by which NURBS surfaces align so that their isoparms match to create a smoother transition from patch to patch.

tangency handles Handles in the Graph Editor that allow you to adjust the curvature of an animation curve at a keyframe point.

tangents Amount of curvature of an animation curve in the Graph Editor at a keyframe point.

texturing Applying a map, an image file, or other rendering node to a shader's attribute or attributes.

three-point lighting A method developed in film and television work that creates a primary key light, a fill light, and a back light to get good results quickly.

trimmed surface A surface that has been cut out of a larger surface to fit an outlined shape.

value A number that is set on an attribute to define it.

vertex A point on a polygon that helps define the shape of the polygon. Three vertices are needed to make a poly face.

volume lights Dissipates from the center of the volume out toward the edge.

volumetric lighting Adds atmosphere to a light to give the illusion of volume, such as a flashlight shining in fog.

walk cycle A repeatable cycle of an animated character walking.

weight An animation term that refers to how heavy an object looks in motion; sometimes defined with squash and stretch.

Index

Note to the Reader: Throughout this index **boldfaced** page numbers indicate primary discussions of a topic. *Italicized* page numbers indicate illustrations.

D

Wiley Publishing, Inc. End-User License Agreement

READ THIS. You should carefully read these terms and conditions before opening the software packet(s) included with this book "Book". This is a license agreement "Agreement" between you and Wiley Publishing, Inc. "WPI". By opening the accompanying software packet(s), you acknowledge that you have read and accept the following terms and conditions. If you do not agree and do not want to be bound by such terms and conditions, promptly return the Book and the unopened software packet(s) to the place you obtained them for a full refund.

1. License Grant. License Grant. WPI grants to you (either an individual or entity) a nonexclusive license to use one copy of the enclosed software program(s) (collectively, the "Software," solely for your own personal or business purposes on a single computer (whether a standard computer or a workstation component of a multi-user network). The Software is in use on a computer when it is loaded into temporary memory (RAM) or installed into permanent memory (hard disk, CD-ROM, or other storage device). WPI reserves all rights not expressly granted herein

2. Ownership. WPI is the owner of all right, title, and interest, including copyright, in and to the compilation of the Software recorded on the physical packet included with this Book "Software Media". Copyright to the individual programs recorded on the Software Media is owned by the author or other authorized copyright owner of each program. Ownership of the Software and all proprietary rights relating thereto remain with WPI and its licensers.

3. Restrictions On Use and Transfer. You may only (i) make one copy of the Software for backup or archival purposes, or (ii) transfer the Software to a single hard disk, provided that you keep the original for backup or archival purposes. You may not (i) rent or lease the Software, (ii) copy or reproduce the Software through a LAN or other network system or through any computer subscriber system or bulletin-board system, or (iii) modify, adapt, or create derivative works based on the Software. (b) You may not reverse engineer, decompile, or disassemble the Software. You may transfer the Software and user documentation on a permanent basis, provided that the transferee agrees to accept the terms and conditions of this Agreement and you retain no copies. If the Software is an update or has been updated, any transfer must include the most recent update and all prior versions.

4. Restrictions on Use of Individual Programs. You must follow the individual requirements and restrictions detailed for each individual program in the About the CD-ROM appendix of this Book or on the Software Media. These limitations are also contained in the individual license agreements recorded on the Software Media. These limitations may include a requirement that after using the program for a specified period of time, the user must pay a registration fee or discontinue use. By opening the Software packet(s), you will be agreeing to abide by the licenses and restrictions for these individual programs that are detailed in the About the CD-ROM appendix and/or on the Software Media. None of the material on this Software Media or listed in this Book may ever be redistributed, in original or modified form, for commercial purposes.

5. Limited Warranty. (a) WPI warrants that the Software and Software Media are free from defects in materials and workmanship under normal use for a period of sixty (60) days from the date of purchase of this Book. If WPI receives notification within the warranty period of defects in materials or workmanship, WPI will replace the defective Software Media. (b) WPI AND THE AUTHOR(S) OF THE BOOK DIS-CLAIM ALL OTHER WARRANTIES, EXPRESS OR IMPLIED, INCLUDING WITHOUT LIMITATION IMPLIED WARRANTIES OF MERCHANTABILITY AND FITNESS FOR A PARTICULAR PURPOSE, WITH RESPECT TO THE SOFTWARE, THE PROGRAMS, THE SOURCE CODE CONTAINED THEREIN, AND/OR THE TECHNIQUES DESCRIBED IN THIS BOOK. WPI DOES NOT WARRANT THAT THE FUNCTIONS CONTAINED IN THE SOFTWARE WILL MEET YOUR REQUIREMENTS OR THAT THE OPERATION OF THE SOFTWARE WILL BE ERROR FREE. (c) This limited warranty gives you specific legal rights, and you may have other rights that vary from jurisdiction to jurisdiction.

6. Remedies. (a) WPI's entire liability and your exclusive remedy for defects in materials and workmanship shall be limited to replacement of the Software Media, which may be returned to WPI with a copy of your receipt at the following address: Software Media Fulfillment Department, Attn.: *Introducing Maya 8: 3D for Beginners*, Wiley Publishing, Inc., 10475 Crosspoint Blvd., Indianapolis, IN 46256, or call 1-800-762-2974. Please allow four to six weeks for delivery. This Limited Warranty is void if failure of the Software Media has resulted from accident, abuse, or misapplication. Any replacement Software Media will be warranted for the remainder of the original warranty period or thirty (30) days, whichever is longer. (b) In no event shall WPI or the author be liable for any damages whatsoever (including without limitation damages for loss of business profits, business interruption, loss of business information, or any other pecuniary loss) arising from the use of or inability to use the Book or the Software, even if WPI has been advised of the possibility of such damages. (c) Because some jurisdictions do not allow the exclusion or limitation of liability for consequential or incidental damages, the above limitation or exclusion may not apply to you.

7. U.S. Government Restricted Rights. Use, duplication, or disclosure of the Software for or on behalf of the United States of America, its agencies and/or instrumentalities "U.S. Government" is subject to restrictions as stated in paragraph (c)(1)(ii) of the Rights in Technical Data and Computer Software clause of DFARS 252.227-7013, or subparagraphs (c) (1) and (2) of the Commercial Computer Software - Restricted Rights clause at FAR 52.227-19, and in similar clauses in the NASA FAR supplement, as applicable.

8. General. This Agreement constitutes the entire understanding of the parties and revokes and supersedes all prior agreements, oral or written, between them and may not be modified or amended except in a writing signed by both parties hereto that specifically refers to this Agreement. This Agreement shall take precedence over any other documents that may be in conflict herewith. If any one or more provisions contained in this Agreement are held by any court or tribunal to be invalid, illegal, or otherwise unenforceable, each and every other provision shall remain in full force and effect.